# DAILY LIFE OF
# THE EGYPTIAN GODS

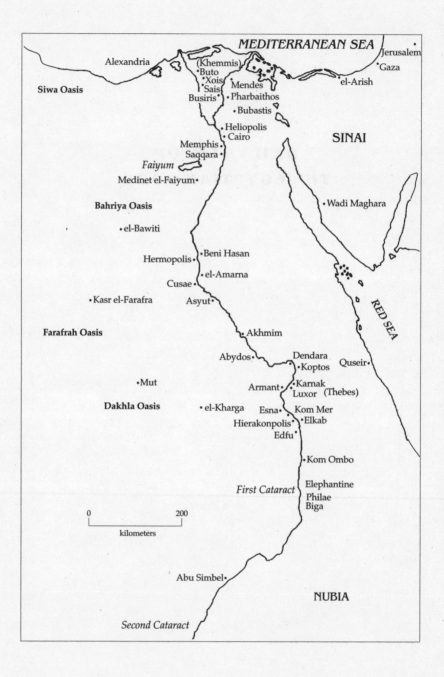

MEDITERRANEAN SEA

Alexandria

Siwa Oasis

(Khemmis)
•Buto
•Xois
•Sais
Busiris•

Mendes
•Pharbaithos
•Bubastis

•Heliopolis
•Cairo

Memphis•
Saqqara•

Faiyum

Medinet el-Faiyum•

Bahriya Oasis

•el-Bawiti

Hermopolis•

•Beni Hasan

•el-Amarna

Cusae•

•Kasr el-Farafra

Asyut•

Farafrah Oasis

•Akhmim

Abydos•

Dendara
•Koptos

Quseir•

•Mut

Armant•

•Karnak
Luxor  (Thebes)

Dakhla Oasis

•el-Kharga

Esna•

Kom Mer

Hierakonpolis•
Edfu•

•Elkab

•Kom Ombo

First Cataract

Elephantine
Philae
Biga

0          200

kilometers

Abu Simbel•

Second Cataract

Jerusalem
•Gaza

el-Arish

SINAI

•Wadi Maghara

RED SEA

NUBIA

DIMITRI MEEKS AND
CHRISTINE FAVARD-MEEKS

# DAILY LIFE

## OF THE

# EGYPTIAN
# GODS

*Translated from the French
by G. M. Goshgarian*

JOHN MURRAY

*Albemarle Street, London*

# Contents

Genealogy                                                    vii

Introduction                                                   1

## Part I | The Gods among Themselves
### DIMITRI MEEKS

1   Origins, Destinies, History                               13
2   Hierarchies, Prerogatives, Groups                         33
3   Divine Bodies                                             53
4   Spaces and Places                                         81
5   Intelligence and Knowledge                                94

## Part II | Mediating between the Gods and Humankind
### CHRISTINE FAVARD-MEEKS

6   The Machine of the Universe and the Universal God        111
7   The Gods on Earth                                        120
8   The Gods of the Hereafter, the Gods in the Hereafter     141
9   From the Dead to the Newborn God                         164
10  The Machine of the Universe Tottering on the Brink       187

Notes                                                        199
Glossary of Major Gods                                       235
Chronology                                                   242
Index                                                        243

## The Family of Heliopolis and Its Evolution

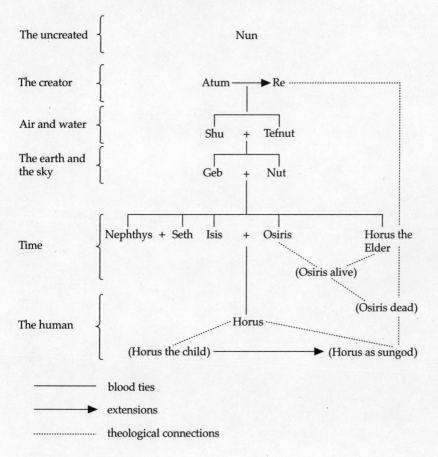

The uncreated {  Nun

The creator {  Atum ——▶ Re

Air and water {  Shu  +  Tefnut

The earth and the sky {  Geb  +  Nut

Time {  Nephthys + Seth   Isis  +  Osiris      Horus the Elder

(Osiris alive)

(Osiris dead)

The human {  Horus

(Horus the child) ——————————▶ (Horus as sungod)

——————— blood ties

——————▶ extensions

···················· theological connections

# DAILY LIFE OF
# THE EGYPTIAN GODS

# Introduction

**W**ell before Champollion deciphered the hieroglyphic writing system in 1822, ancient Egyptian religion had excited people's curiosity and astonishment. Although scholars in the seventeenth and eighteenth centuries could not read the texts themselves, they were familiar with certain striking features of this religion and its myths. Their perfect mastery of the authors of antiquity gave them access to the knowledge transmitted by the Greek and Roman classics, in which Egypt in general, and its religious beliefs in particular, held an important place. It is becoming ever clearer to contemporary researchers how faithful classical authors generally were to the letter of Egyptian beliefs and practices, but, at the same time, how often they betrayed their spirit. To European rationalism, whose origins our traditions locate in Greece, Egyptian religion could not but appear to be a hodgepodge lacking any precise significance—indeed, a mass of superstitions. Yet Egypt's venerable age made it a prototype of the immutable and an ultimate reference that never ceased to propound its riddle to Reason. A taste for well-ordered systems, along with the idea that a tradition as old as Egypt's had necessarily to be a source of great wisdom, led polytheism, especially Greek polytheism, to seek a new lease on life in Egyptian religion, which had in its turn been recast in the melting pot of Alexandria. This new religion, purged of its "barbaric" features, finds one of its most highly refined forms in Plutarch. "As J. Hani put it, system can be seen emerging which . . . includes the idea of a unique Deity, but also, subordinate to him, an evil principle, as well as secondary divinities or "Powers" who are ministers of the Supreme Being. . . . People had been searching for gods capable of mastering blind Fate, resolving the mystery of death, and satisfying their longing for an intimate relationship with the Divine. It was the cult of Isis which most closely matched these aspirations."[1] Around the triad Isis-Osiris-Horus— almost a Trinity—a religion grew up in which the strange, even shocking, images of ancient Egypt were reinterpreted as mere appearances masking a body of thought of a high level of spirituality. So regarded, they helped clear the way for the monotheistic faith that would soon sweep all before it.

Handed down through the centuries, this way of looking at Egyptian religion marked the beginnings of the nascent discipline of Egyptology. Vivant Denon was convinced that he had detected the presence of the Supreme Being in the ruins of the temple he had visited in Dendara during Bonaparte's Egyptian expedition (1799–1802): "I observed that the walls were covered with representations of their religious rites, farming methods, arts and crafts, and moral and religious precepts; and that the Supreme Being, the first principle, was everywhere represented by symbols of his various qualities."[2] Champollion's early death prevented him from producing a synthesis of his conception of Egyptian religion; although indications are that this conception, organized around the figure of Amun, was complex,[3] it did not break radically with previous notions of that religion as theistic. "Amun-Re, the primordial, Supreme Being, being his own father, is described as his mother's husband . . . his feminine side [is] included in his own essential being, which is both male and female . . . all the other Egyptian gods are merely forms of these two constitutive principles, considered successively from different points of view. They are nothing but elements abstracted from the great Being."[4] After Champollion's death, his brother, Champollion-Figeac, succinctly summed up the thinking of the founder of Egyptology as he understood it: "A few words will perhaps suffice to provide an accurate and complete picture of Egyptian religion. It was a true monotheism which took the outward form of a symbolic polytheism. That is, it possessed a unique God, all of whose qualities and attributes were personified by as many active agents or divinities obedient to his will."[5]

Only toward the end of the nineteenth century did the idea that Egyptian religion was monotheistic begin to be called into question and subjected to a critical reappraisal. The positivism of the day, exemplified by Adolf Erman, devoted itself above all to establishing and investigating facts. But Erman found himself vacillating between sheer consternation and facile solutions borrowed from the past. "One thing in particular makes it difficult to arrive at an accurate view of Egyptian religion: it is loaded down, at least in its official version, with all the absurd features of its early stages. It is not reasonable to expect anyone to take an interest in such barbarities. In our eyes, they loom large. In reality, however, they were secondary features that had no more significance in the actual religious life of the Egyptians of a more advanced age than traditional dogmas have in other religions."[6] Erman's followers preferred not to get involved in this debate; they contented themselves with doing purely descriptive work, which often yielded valuable results. Meanwhile, advocates and adversaries of the "monotheism" thesis continued to lock horns, without noticing to what extent they were all in agreement with the essential core of Erman's thinking. Egypt offered its students nothing more than a backdrop against which emerged the profound thinking of advanced Egyptians and, in perfect harmony with it, the personal beliefs of the individual who happened to be studying it. Polytheism, indeed, gradually ceased to be a real object of inquiry. Scholars spoke instead of pantheism or henotheism, terminologically conjuring away the essence of the problem.[7] As Erik Hornung suggests, Egyptology has still not succeeded in resolving the contradiction it has trapped itself in: convinced of the high cultural and ethical level of the civilization it studies, it is nevertheless haunted by the feeling that the Egyptians' conceptions of the divine fall short of this level.[8] To be sure, one strongly suspects that this contradiction never existed in reality, but rather stems from the fact that our conceptual tools are poorly adapted to the analysis of a culture they were not designed for. This conceptual inadequacy is in turn constantly exacerbated by the imperious, if unconscious, need to treat everything Egyptian as fundamentally assimilable, in its underlying structures, to one or another feature of the contemporary world. From the beginnings of Egyptology, the specialists have always been inclined to make qualitative judgments—this is a symptom of their often well-disguised concern to show us an Egypt that conforms, on the one hand, to notions of moral and aesthetic decorum palatable to a majority, and, on the other, to our mode of logical thinking.[9] Whether in the domain of beliefs, artistic expression, lifestyle, or writing, Egypt is glorified, in the scholarly works or the proliferating exhibitions devoted to it, only for those aspects of its civilization that command an approving consensus based on the most widely shared contemporary values. Egypt becomes acceptable only when fitted out with the identity we, applying our modes of thinking and being, foist upon it—at the cost of seeing what is alien to us in Egyptian culture as no more than a mask behind which a higher reality is concealed. Indeed, this reality is considered the "higher" the more it can be made to seem like the ultimate source of some aspect of *our* contemporary world. We are less interested in acquiring knowledge *of* Egypt than in recognizing ourselves *in* Egypt.

The debate between neomonotheists and neopositivists goes on even today. To be sure, both parties have left the naiveties of an older day far behind; now their arguments are based on meticulous textual analyses rooted in a thorough knowledge of the sources and a sure mastery of the language they are written in. Yet the true nature of the debate continues to shine through. Its stakes are ideology, not Egyptology: the most powerful research tools are used to ideological ends. Appeals to the latest philosophical theories and speculations, or to modern scientific research on multivalued logic and the founding principles of rationality, show to what extent all the questions asked have to do, first and foremost, with the researcher's own way of thinking. Nonetheless, as far as their results are concerned, these discussions have proven astonishingly productive. Our knowledge of the phenomenon of Egyptian religion has progressed considerably. Moreover, a number of different works have gone well beyond the monotheism/polytheism dichotomy, making it possible to refocus the debate. Philippe Derchain, using an anthropological approach to open up an independent line of thought,[10] and Erik Hornung, pursuing an analysis of Egyptian religion based on multivalued logic,[11] have both put us in a position to study Egypt, not to make it answer *our* questions, but rather to encourage it to give us *its* version of the facts. What would Egypt become if it were finally taken for what it was—neither morally acceptable nor morally shocking, and still less the mother of our own conceptions—what, if not something completely *other*? The time is ripe for posing the question. But how and on what basis should it be posed?

Ancient Egypt has left behind an impressive mass of material records. We are very far from having inventoried and published the whole of what is already known, to say nothing of the ongoing discoveries that periodically enrich our documentation. What Egyptology has accomplished in the little more than 170 years of its existence is at once derisory, given the quantity of material the Egyptians have left behind, and colossal, if one bears in mind how small has been the number of scholars able to devote themselves to studying this material. As far as religious texts are concerned, the discipline has had reliable editions at its disposal for less than twenty years; they do not yet include everything known to us, even if they do contain the most important texts. The work of establishing the basic facts, dear to the positivists, has in reality barely begun. The moment has come, then, to read or reread the texts, not to bring them into line with our own fantasies, as in the past, but to try to understand what they really mean. To *try*, it must be said, because, contrary to what might be supposed, we do not know the Egyptian language well enough to be perfectly sure of the exact meanings of words. In every religious text— indeed, in practically every line—uncertainty and doubts arise; we can dispel them only by cross-checking texts from all the various historical periods, using each clue we have gleaned to corroborate another. Obviously, these texts will continue to serve as the primary source for every investigation, despite the differences in their nature and the diversity of the periods in which they were composed. It should be recalled that the earliest religious texts, the Pyramid Texts (c. 2350 B.C.E.), do not appear until some seven centuries after the introduction of writing in Egypt. They are about the fate of royalty after death; initially, they concern only the Pharaoh, later widening their scope to include his immediate family. A few centuries further on, the Coffin Texts (c. 2000 B.C.E.), building on and considerably enlarging the existing corpus, extend the benefits of personal survival in the hereafter to one and all. The Middle Kingdom sees the appearance of the first mythological stories or tales, magic texts, and ritual texts. It is in this period that religious thought begins to express itself in ways more accessible to us. With the New Kingdom there appears the famous Book of the Dead, which reproduces some of the Coffin Texts, while adding new material. Original works were composed in this period. Initially inscribed on the walls of the royal tombs, each attempted, in its own way, to present a sort of physics of the world. Endlessly recopied and rearranged, these texts are a pot-pourri of information about the gods and their life, myths and rites, and the hopes human beings attached to the life after death. They even include learned works in which one or another author succeeds in reordering, as he sees fit, the mass of information handed down through the ages on a particular subject.[12] Plainly, this variety of content and approach raises, for minds accustomed to thinking of religious texts as "sacred books," the question of hierarchies of value and, at the same time, that of the degree of authenticity or dogmatic authority of the content of these texts. It bears emphasizing that, without being a civilization of the Book, Egypt was nonetheless a civilization of the written word. To be sure, it had no "revealed text" in the sense of the major contemporary religions: a definitive, immutable text serving as the object of human exegesis. Yet it remains true that, in Egypt, revelation was contained in writing as such. Every hieroglyphic sign was the trace of a being, a thing, or the world the gods wished to bring into existence. Thus writing was neither fixed once and for all, nor was there any limit to the number of signs it could include. The hieroglyphs were "divine words"—the literal meaning of the Egyptian expression. In and of themselves, they constituted a body of divine knowledge that had been handed down to men. Thus all writings were ultimately inspired by the gods. Their purpose, whatever it might be—entertainment, the pleasures of erudition, or the requirements of ritual and worship—had no impact on the profound coherence of the image of the gods they projected; the only thing that varied was the angle of approach. To write was both to recount and to explain the world; it was to undertake to reveal and, simultaneously as it were, to comment on it. All religious texts and mythical tales expressed the same truth. The variations from one version to another, the apparent contradictions between the formulas or expressions employed in them over the ages are not necessarily indications that a new mode of thought is struggling to define itself. Even less are these variations signs of a change in dogma. Rather, they reveal "a sort of creative euphoria on the part of certain very learned priests who had discovered new intellectual procedures and a new epistemology," "a way of speculating about texts" that constitutes "a mode of knowledge" and allows us to "define Egyptian theology as fascination with writing."[13] This writing, which is also, by its very nature, pictorial, necessarily broadens the conception of what a text is. "The unity of Egyptian art and writing is primordial; both arise from the same source, at the same moment, the beginning of the First Dynasty. . . . It is for this reason that one can say that the whole of Egyptian art is 'hieroglyphic,'"[14] declares Henry Fischer, who has devoted a superb study to demonstrating the point. Thus Egyptian iconography cannot really be considered in isolation from the texts. Images are also stories depicting the actions of the gods or describing various rites; thus they help explain religious thought.

Now that we have been forewarned of the temptation to use Egypt as a mirror, we may turn, armed with the information Egypt itself provides, to a consideration of the "daily life" of the Egyptian gods. That expression in itself contains a response to the very questions it poses to anyone who approaches it. The notion of "daily life" makes no sense in a religion that has only one god, inasmuch as this notion, implying a temporal framework within which a community lives out a collective existence, unambiguously suggests a polytheistic setting. Moreover, it almost automatically entails the absence of human beings, at least as actors of any importance. Is this way of looking at the gods artificial, and so unlikely to reveal much of anything about the subject, or can it bring out a basic dimension of Egyptian religious thought? In other words, do the daily life of the gods and the absence of human beings point to an essential mechanism, a reaction on Egypt's part to its own way of conceiving the world?

But do the gods *have* a daily life to begin with? The gods of Egypt, whose images have come down through the millennia unchanged, seem so little affected by the march of time that one might well doubt it. Yet these images are the work of men's hands. They played a sufficiently meaningful and important part in these men's daily routine to have outlived them. The gods existed for the Egyptians, and the trace they wished to leave of them still exists for us. Not the least of the Egyptians' merits is to have made us feel, even today, the full weight of their conviction. But the gods were not made to dwell solely among men. They were a community in and of themselves, in which human beings were regarded as only one consequence of the creator-god's desire to create the universe. What sort of life might they have led, whether amongst themselves or on earth—these gods whom one readily imagines to be as immobile as their statues or the relief in their temples? They were known to be active, even if they acted unseen: the results of their actions could only be perceived in the movements observable in nature, in the things the senses revealed or the body felt, whether as punishment or deliverance. But all this has to do with *our* daily life, not theirs. How can we possibly know what they are doing, if their activities are so far removed from our sphere? How can we know what feelings move them, if they have feelings; how are we to tell whether they change their behavior when they pass from their world to ours? Though the answers would appear to be beyond our ken, a considerable number of texts have come down to us that recount one of their adventures or allude to aspects of their daily routine. To be sure, one is never told in so many words how human beings acquired knowledge of these matters, how they managed to garner information about divine customs. However, let us recall that, in the Golden Age, people dwelt among the gods, so that human knowledge of them may have derived from a memory passed down from generation to generation. Certain human practices are presented as if they were mimetic prolongations of divine acts.[15] Moreover, under exceptional circumstances, one or another human could gain entry to the world of the dead and then return, doubtless bringing back precious information.[16] Again, it seems that there existed an oral tradition extending back to the dawn of time. Finally, the archives of the libraries contained treasures—the writings of Thoth himself, copied and recopied generation after generation. Indeed, this god left a considerable quantity of texts in secret hiding places on earth; with sufficient patience, wise men could ferret them out. Certain works the Egyptians often turned to, such as the Book of the Dead or the Book of the Opening of the Mouth, were specially composed by Thoth for their use.[17] A book placed under the side of the god Khnum came to the knowledge of mortals, no one knows how.[18] The gods themselves did not hesitate to pass some of their secrets on to people by letting a providential manuscript fall from the heavens.[19] Writing was, plainly, the instrument of revelation; it provided access to the world of the gods.

It is, above all, mythological and magical texts that tell us about the epoch of the gods. These texts recount the gods' deeds; more important, they also make known a large amount of incidental detail. Certain stories depict the life they led in their own sphere. Not many have been preserved, but indications are that they constituted a highly prized genre, in wide circulation from the earliest periods of Egyptian history.[20] What survives of Demotic literature shows that the genre must have been particularly prized in the late period of Egyptian civilization. Both mythological narratives and tales were intended for diffusion well beyond the narrow circles of the priesthood, not only among the educated classes, but also, in oral form, among the masses. In mythological tales or magical texts, the myths lost their otherworldly aura, taking on the semblances of everyday life. The special status of writing permitted an unproblematic transposition of the sacred into the secular, a procedure that could even become an intellectual game. Did one scribe not amuse himself by rewriting the scene of the weighing of the souls of the dead in secular terms, making it over into a purely technical operation in which the accent is put on weights, measures, and petty computations?[21] Unlike the mythological tales, other texts only rarely contain connected narratives; one is obliged to reconstruct the plot of a legend, usually bit by bit. What one learns from these various sources about the gods and their way of life basically has to do with the period preceding their separation from men, whose rebellion brought the Golden Age to an end. Thereafter, the life of the gods turns in a new direction, so that only magic could provide men direct access to their world. But these practices provided knowledge of the gods' best-kept secrets.

As to rituals, they show us the gods in their temples. The presence of priests, often in large numbers, might lead one to suppose that temples offered men a privileged place for communicating with their gods. But the reliefs which sought to portray the actual content of religious rites demonstrate that this is a mistaken assumption. Carved in stone, meant to last, they consistently represent the king acting alone on behalf of the gods or else making them offerings without assistance. Men—that is, priests—maintained only an ephemeral physical presence in the sacred buildings, leaving virtually no traces there. When they *are* represented, it is above all as bearers of liturgical objects, not as active participants in the rite. The texts explicitly state that they are simply delegated by the king, who, since he cannot be everywhere in person, maintains a constant presence throughout the land by way of the temple reliefs. As to the masses of the faithful, they were not admitted within the precincts of the temples. To get around this sort of exclusion, people set up, creatively, their own religious areas on the periphery of the temples, in their homes, and inside their tombs. But such areas lay entirely within the domain of the daily life of mortals. From our vantage point, priests and ordinary believers fall within the purview of a sociology of religion which has, for the most part, yet to be written; but that is not what this book is about.

For people's activities delimit the field of religious practice without really shedding light on the dogmas that justify and explain it. If one construes the texts and pictures literally, one ceases to see religion from an exclusively human point of view; one gains entry to the theological reality that forms its underlying structure. Thus giving priority to the letter of Egyptian religion makes it possible to identify the true actors of the ceremonies and rites. The gods and the king—as interpreted by the priests, to be sure—then take their rightful places in a perpetual face-to-face in which the king, son of the gods, reaffirms his role as mediator between the gods' world and that of men. In myth, every occurrence, every gesture, every word had the value of a founding act. The rites celebrated in the temple, an enclosed space which, though located on earth, was nevertheless divine, were reiterations of these founding acts, performed by or for the king. The daily activities of the gods which laid down the foundation of things never ceased to be repeated in the world. This recurrent process established cosmic equilibrium, but also revealed its weaknesses. Rites maintained the former and made up for the latter.

A system thus gradually comes into view in which concepts were translated into functions on the basis of mental schemes that, though different from ours, were no less rigorous. The gods figured less as "persons" than as illustrations of these functional concepts. At any given moment, each god filled a particular role; depending on the moment, each role could be filled by different gods. It was because the gods played a part in the establishment of the world that they could, and must, be "played" in rites. The rite was the sign that the divine was at work. Identity resided not in the deity, but in his or her function. Within this framework, syncretistic entities, such as Amun-Re or Ptah-Tatenen, represented an equation between two "different" deities exercising identical functions at a given point in time. These functions, which were, moreover, fairly limited in number, lent coherence to the profusion and proliferation of Egyptian polytheism. Incarnated in exemplary fashion by the divine family of Heliopolis, they are at the center of our attention; for it was these functions which wrote the drama of the world that the rites would later mime.

To recount the daily life of the gods, then—whether amongst themselves or face to face with the royal mediator—is to approach the essential structure of Egyptian myth not as an imaginary construct designed to justify the reality of ritual acts, but rather as a reality whose existence could not be maintained without rites. It is to confront the gods without intermediaries, as the extant documents suggest one should. The reader is accordingly invited to enter the strangeness of a perception of the world totally different from his own by walking right in, as it were, and taking things exactly as they come. Making his way through the pages that follow, he will perhaps begin to appreciate the inner logic of the gods' acts and come to believe, with the Egyptians, that the gods did indeed have a daily life.

# PART I

# THE GODS
# AMONG THEMSELVES

# CHAPTER ONE

# Origins, Destinies, History

The gods of Egypt did not always exist. On more than one occasion, Egyptian religious texts evoke the idea that they can be born and die and that time has a beginning and an end. If we have several different versions of the beginning of the world—often elliptical, sometimes fragmentary, and always rather dryly written—and if one chapter of the Book of the Dead refers explicitly to the end of time, there exists no real treatise describing the life of the gods in a sustained and detailed manner. We know only bits and pieces of the gods' origins and history, and our knowledge is often indirect. Yet the texts, our sole source of information on the subject, do raise the basic questions that each culture has, in its own way, sought to answer. These texts reveal that the gods existed in time and that they had a destiny.

## Origins and Ends

Let us examine the state of affairs that existed before the universe was created. The idea of nonbeing, total emptiness, absolute "nothingness" was foreign to Egypt, whose civilization had begun too early and was still too close to concrete reality to speculate about such abstractions. We are told that absolutely nothing existed. But the very difficulty of imagining this state required that things be made more precise, the more so as everyone knew that a boundless watery region had existed before the creation, its inert, unmoving waters swaddled in absolute darkness. This darkness was not that of night, for day and night had not yet been created.

To describe this very special state of affairs, the texts begin by proceeding negatively, drawing up lists of everything that did not yet exist. As any list is necessarily restrictive, and as the ones we have are as a rule quite short,[1] these lists enable us to see straight away, by antithesis, what the Egyptians considered to be the essential elements of the created world. Earth and sky did not yet exist, no more than gods or men; anger, noise, and fighting did not exist; the fear of what might befall the eye of Horus did not exist, nor did death.

If it is only logical to assume that the existence of the earth, sky, living creatures, and gods is the surest sign of the created world, the other items mentioned are rather surprising and cast a peculiar light on the state of creation at its very beginnings. The created world was characterized by "the sound and the fury," the presence of death, and the fear that something might befall the eye of Horus. The eye of Horus was not only the sun that bestowed life, but also, by a gradual logical progression, the whole of what had been created—Egypt itself, that is, the organized world. Death and the fear that the world would end were inherent in the act of creation; they proceeded from it.

But what were the origins of life? A passage from the Coffin Texts provides the beginnings of an answer. The creator-god there recounts what happened before the act of creation: "I was alone with the Primeval Ocean, in the inertness, and could find no place to stand . . . (the gods of the) first generation had not yet come into being, (but) they were with me." Addressing himself to the Primeval Ocean, he adds: "I was floating between two waters, totally inert . . . and it was my son, 'Life,' who roused my spirit, who made my heart live and gathered up my inert members." The Primeval Ocean replies to the creator-god: "Inhale your daughter Maat and raise her to your nostril so that your heart may live. May they not be far from you, your daughter Maat and your son Shu, whose name is Life."[2]

This beautiful text, in which one sees life emerging for the first time, describes three stages. In the beginning, the creator-god was meditating in solitude. The first gods, those who would begin to multiply after the act of creation, did not as yet exist, though they were, in a certain sense, contained in the creator. For no precise reason, life manifested itself spontaneously in him; we are told that it did so as Shu, the god of air. Immediately thereafter, the second stage, the creator began to speak; speech was the most obvious consequence of the fact that life had emerged within him. The Primeval Ocean himself had not yet become conscious at this point; properly speaking, he did not yet exist.[3] He was not aware that the creator-god was awakening and coming into being, for the process took place without his being able to perceive it.[4] This was how the creator-god detached or distinguished himself from the Primeval Ocean, which the Egyptians called Nun, a name that appears to mean "nonbeing." Thus the creator-god could address himself to the Primeval Ocean, providing the Ocean an account, as it were, of what was happening to him. His brief narrative elicited a response from the Primeval Ocean; this, the Ocean's awakening, constituted the third stage in the process of creation. Life gave rise to speech, speech engendered dialogue. Through a sort of maieutic, this dialogue revealed the forces that would both animate and also guarantee the creation to come: life, identified with Shu, god of the air, and Maat, whom the creator-god breathed and who was, as a result, essentially consubstantial with the air. Maat was nothing other than the Norm that would govern the regular occurrence of cosmic phenomena, but she also was the laws of society, together with the respect due them. The very rhythm of the creator's breathing ensured that air—life—would be exhaled, making the birth of the other creatures possible.[5]

At this point, the act of creation had not yet truly begun. The creator-god had not yet stirred; things were still in a preparatory phase. This phase brought developments that other texts permit us to study. Again, it is the creator who is speaking: "I brought my flesh into being by my own effectiveness; I am he who created himself; I fashioned myself as I pleased."[6] "I came into being as 'One who becomes'; I came into being and Becoming became. All beings came into being after I had come into being. Many are the becomings that came forth from my mouth. At a time when the sky did not exist, the earth did not exist, solid land had not been created, no more than the snakes which are in this place, I created some of them in the Primeval Ocean as Inert Ones, at a time when I had not yet found a place to stand."[7] Even before the act of creation had gotten under way, the creator fashioned his physical person, and then a few snakes, by means of the speech that was the first sign of life in him. The snakes assisted him with the rest of the work of creation, while the egg from which the sun would burst forth either appeared from the depths of the Ocean or, according to other traditions, fell from the sky.[8] These snakes were subterranean creatures who knew nothing but darkness, since the rhythm of day and night had not yet come about; their sole raison d'être was to be "in this place," on this mound of solid earth on which the creator-god would create light, and then, as the dry land expanded, the vast variety of beings. As subterranean creatures, the snakes served notice that the mound would emerge from the waters, and they were also its first inhabitants. They paved the way for the creation, but were not part of it. But neither were they pre-existing beings like the creator-god or the Primeval Ocean, both of whom had been present even before creation began. Thus these snakes were trapped in a hiatus. The creation confronted them with a barrier they could not cross; once the work of creation was finished, they would complete their time, as the texts put it, and would die. They were thus to become the first of the world's dead. But, we are also told, if their fate was sealed by the creator himself, "their earthly posterity has not come to an end."[9] This posterity was nothing other than the created world and the beings that would succeed one another in it. Because the inevitable death of these precursors had caused the creator a great deal of anguish, he decided to mummify them and place offerings on their tomb the same day every year. These offerings made "their throats breathe, in life, until the next occasion of his coming."[10] The first of the world's dead, and the first mummies, the snakes were also the first to receive a funerary cult—an ancestor cult. As we shall see, all the precursors of the creation would be treated in like manner.

After the world had been created, the gods and men took up their abode in it. The gods ruled on earth, one succeeding the next. This was the Golden Age. But the human race eventually rose up in rebellion, and the gods withdrew to the sky. Earthly kingship then devolved upon the Followers of Horus, who prefigured and paved the way for the family lines of human pharaohs. The Followers of Horus met the same fate as the precursors of creation, with whose cult theirs coalesced.[11] The period in which the gods reigned on earth, which we have here summed up in a few words, was an extremely eventful one; it provides the subject matter of the entire first part of this book. We shall see that, even among the gods, not everyone died a natural death. The violence and quarreling, whose future could be divined the moment the world was created, already contained the seeds of death. Here as elsewhere, one could kill innocence as well as punish whatever threatened the Norm.

Once humankind had fulfilled its destiny on earth, the end would come, and, with it, an end to "the noise and the tumult."[12] Yet, just as there had not been a void before the act of creation, so the end of the world would not be the end of all that existed. What had not been created could not be destroyed. The Primeval Ocean and the creator-god, who had both existed before the creation, would survive the end of the world and be reunited. For it was the act of creation that had separated them. The creator-god, the other gods, men, and, indeed, all creatures, lived in created space. The Primeval Ocean had been driven to the periphery of this space.[13] But the creation, the separation of the creator-god, and the death of the precursor snakes did not, contrary to what one might assume, leave the Primeval Ocean empty and inert. It was agitated by periodic movements, and various creatures inhabited it. The regular inundation of the Nile was one of the forms its resurgence took; it was beneficial only because the river receded, leaving the land free for cultivation. But the Egyptians were haunted by the possibility that the floods would be too strong or too weak. It was at the point of contact between the Ocean and the created world that the setting sun plunged into the regions where he would be regenerated. But it was there as well that a giant serpent lay in wait for him, attacking, every morning at sunrise, the bark in which he traveled. Every morning, the serpent was defeated.[14]

We are told that this serpent was the demon "who goes marauding, so that the seasons are no longer differentiated, and the contours of the shadows can no longer be discerned."[15] We find here a recurrence of the expressions used to describe the penumbra, the absence of day and night or of the seasons, those characteristic features of the uncreated state that also are the harbingers of the end of the world. Thus the Primeval Ocean, whose waters possessed regenerative power, also contained forces that threatened to disrupt the created world. The existence of such forces betrayed chaos's imperious need to win back the space wrested from it by the act of creation. A passage in a literary text vaunts the merits of the creator-god: "Men, god's cattle, are well provided for; he created heaven and earth for their sake; he checked the rapacity of the waters, he created air so that their nostril might live."[16] This rapacity or greed, the last vestiges of the Primeval Ocean's furor,[17] went down to defeat every morning in the person of the serpent who was held at bay on the edges of the world by the beneficent action of the sun. Only his daily return, a function of the Norm, made it possible to keep the serpent at a distance. Respect for the Norm, which imposed itself on all, was the best way of ensuring the preservation of the equilibrium that the Norm incarnated and that helped maintain the existing balance between the created and the uncreated.

But inasmuch as the Primeval Ocean never ceased threatening creation, whereas the creator-god was under no obligation to defend it, was the end of the world not inevitable? It had, at any rate, been predicted: "The Pelican will prophesy, the Shining One will come forth, the Great One will rise up and the Ennead will begin to cry out; the plain will be walled round, the two extremities will be reunited, the two riverbanks will be rejoined, the roads will become impassable for travellers, and the hillsides will be destroyed for those who would flee."[18] The pelican was a solar bird; his immense bill incarnated the door through which the sun entered and left our world. Living on the confines of the universe, he knew what would one day come to pass: the extremities of the creation would be reunited, or folded back one upon the other, until created space was abolished and no avenue of escape was left. Is this to say that chaos would win out in the end, or that the creator-god would eventually grow weary of his task? In a famous chapter of the Book of the Dead,[19] he complains to Thoth, god of wisdom: "O Thoth, what is to be done with the Children of Nut? They have fomented war, they have stirred up quarrels, they have caused disorder, they have fomented rebellion, they have committed massacres, they have imprisoned—in a word, they have debased what was great in all that I have created."

Who were the Children of Nut? They were Osiris and Isis, Seth and Nephthys, as well as the Elder Horus. As we shall see, their incessant quarrels culminated in bloodshed with the death of Osiris. They were the ones who set the bad example for the men who eventually rebelled against the supreme authority. The Children of Nut were thus all those who continually yielded to their evil instincts, perverting the world. Thoth, who was also the god of the reckoning of time, responded to the creator-god's lament by saying: "You should not tolerate error, you should not put up (with it)! Cut short their years, cut back their months, since they have done secret damage to all that you have created." The equilibrium that ensured the cohesion and continued existence of the creation would finally prove incapable of withstanding the gravest danger, because it came from within.

In the hereafter, a dead man who had overheard the conversation between Thoth and the creator began to worry. He had done nothing wrong, nor was he one of the Children of Nut: this was what justified his presence among the blessed. "And how long is my life to last?" he asked. What, indeed, was the exact nature of the eternity he had been promised? The creator responded: "You are destined (to live) for millions of millions of years. But I will destroy all that I have created; this land will return to its state of Primeval Ocean, to the watery state, like its first state. I am that which will remain with Osiris, when I have changed myself back into a serpent that men cannot know, that the gods cannot see." Thus the dead, like the gods themselves, had a limited life span;[20] their sole hope was one day to fuse with the one who represented them all. In a world that had returned to its initial state, the creator-god, after once again taking on the form of a serpent, would fall asleep in the Ocean. And although the mummies of expired gods were destined, we are told, to survive "for hundreds of thousands of years,"[21] they were nevertheless allotted a limited length of time and would therefore eventually have an end.

We have thus come back round to the serpent in whom all the others were subsumed. He was the true form of the uncreated creator-god, in whom both chaos and the forces of life were intimately intermingled. Two serpents merged in him: the one who encircled the world and threatened the sun, and the one who lay coiled at the bottom of the cavern out of which the Nile inundation, beneficial if it stayed within bounds and eventually receded, was thought to pour.[22] This inundation was the extension, in our world, of the Primeval Ocean.

This serpent, whose head rested on his tail, ensured the periodic, well-regulated rise and fall of the Nile; he also offered a means of escape from the end of the world. In *On Stilicho's Consulship*, the Latin poet Claudian, who was born in Alexandria and lived less than three-quarters of a century before Odoacer captured Rome (was that not the end of the world?), describes the creature and his den as follows: "Far away—all unknown, beyond the range of mortal minds, scarcely to be approached by the gods, is a cavern of immense age, hoary mother of the years, her vast breast at once the cradle and the tomb of time. A serpent surrounds this cave, engulfing everything with slow but all-devouring jaws; never ceases the glint of his green scales. His mouth devours the back-bending tail as with silent movement he traces his own beginning.[23]

Beyond the range of mortal minds, scarcely to be approached by the gods: these are almost exactly the same words the creator-god used to define the serpent, his own ultimate avatar, in the passage from the Book of the Dead we have already mentioned. The two texts describe essentially the same creature. But the serpent who bites his own tail—the Greeks' "Ouroboros"—was the very symbol of eternity and, above all, of the constant renewal of time, which, as Claudian says, "traces its own beginning."[24] There was, then, reason to hope that the creator-god would, after sinking into sleep in the Primeval Ocean, once again rise from his slumbers to create a new and, one would like to think, better world.

The Egyptians conceived eternity in a double form. It was, for them, both linear and cyclical: the period of linear time evoked the past, that of cyclical time, the future.[25] In this perspective, the creator was "He who comes into being after the end of the period of cyclical time, and does not disappear."[26] This cyclical time was human time; it was to last "until the return of the period of linear time,"[27] the time of the new Golden Age that would arise from a new creation. Thus the world would come to an end only to be reborn, in an eternal cycle, a rhythm resembling a vast cosmic breathing. For the creator, each of these immensely long cyclical periods would be no more than a passing day.[28]

## The Cosmic Enemies and Battles for Equilibrium

From the moment of its creation, the world was threatened by the forces of the uncreated, forces that the mere existence of a world drove back toward its periphery. There was no escaping these forces, even if they were pushed further and further back as the domain of the created expanded. Because they had not been brought into being by the act of creation, they could not be definitively destroyed. They could only be defeated periodically; their repeated onslaughts made it necessary to wage unending battle to maintain the integrity and equilibrium of creation. At the very moment when the creator-god was struggling to gain a foothold, for the first time, on the mound that had emerged from the primeval waters, he found himself face to face with a menacing serpent.[29] In hopes of conquering back the space that had been wrested from his control, this serpent, an incarnation of everything the created world rejected, launched his first assault on the creator-god. The two antagonists squared off in single combat; the victory went to the creator.

Certain sources say that this battle was fought out on the territory of Heliopolis itself, the capital of the sun-god; they present it as a struggle to take possession of the city. The serpent, called "He who is in his flame," led the revolt at the head of a band of twenty rebels.[30] Armed with a spear, the reptile attacked Re, who defended himself unassisted, at least at first. To foil the attackers, the sun-god threw up a barricade of masts; but his enemy leapt on to it, taking Re by surprise. Appearing from God knows where, a young woman with a braid in her hair diverted the demon's attention; she doubtless intended to act as a decoy. But this attractive lure might have been nothing more than an incarnation of one of the creator's hands, which he had used for solitary procreation.[31] We do not know the details of what occurred, but it seems that someone with a shaved head, possessed of great powers, stepped in to secure the victory for Re. This explains why the high priest of Heliopolis would later sport a shaved head and a braid.[32] The serpent who fought this battle, which would be fought again and again for all eternity, was often portrayed as an emanation of Apophis, or else as Apophis in person. Certain sources have it that Re benefited from Atum's help; others say that Atum took the monster on by himself, armed with a bow and arrow. As the monster was a serpent, the god opportunely took the form of a mongoose in order to fight him more effectively and defeat him.[33]

This event led to the first act of repression and punishment: in its wake, the gods created the slaughterhouse of the eastern horizon to torture and destroy their defeated enemies. The usefulness of this establishment had not made itself felt earlier, but, once it went into operation, it was never empty again; indeed, it was in constant use. Before being burned alive, the defeated enemies were, we are told, changed into human beings to make them all the more mortal. These were the "bestial men" whose descendants would once again rebel against the gods, bringing the Golden Age to an end; later, in the human world, they would fill the ranks of the criminals and misfits. As for the rebels' ringleader, he was changed to stone after having been consigned to the flames; this stone later served to cover the bodies of the massacred enemies. In the desert of Heliopolis not far from Cairo, the Red Mountain, composed of reddish or rust-colored quartzite, was believed to be a memento of the bloody massacre perpetrated in these parts, while the fragments of petrified wood in the rocks were thought to represent the remains of an immense, charred skeleton.

But the most frequent struggle, fought out again every time the sun came up, was the one between Re and the gigantic serpent Apophis, living summa of all the reptiles that threatened the cosmic order. Opinions diverged as to this monster's origins. According to some, he was descended of a bodily excretion of the creator-god's, a gob of spit the primeval gods had rejected and thus condemned to perpetual revolt.[34] Here again we find the notion of setting apart or exclusion that was at the root of cosmic antagonisms. The sun's daily combat was evoked in the many hymns addressed to him and also in the various books recounting his voyage.[35] Many other obscure episodes of these different solar battles are known to us. But, as a rule, we have only vague allusions that do not really enable us to grasp what was at stake or the exact roles of the antagonists. This holds for the story of the little group of four rebels who challenged Re's Heliopolis-based authority. They hailed from a little town north of Hermopolis, the home of Thoth.[36] Besides these geographical details, which show that enemies could crop up anywhere, we know that the insurgents were serpents and that they were burned or drowned after their defeat. Under different circumstances, Re had to square off with a troop of apparently quite vindictive wild donkeys.[37] These were, no doubt, the seventy-seven donkeys who fought the creator-god on the primeval mound.[38] The battle was hotly contested, and, although the enemies ended up with their throats cut, Re himself was wounded during the fighting. The wound was a deep one and bled profusely. The blood flooded the land around Re so heavily that the earth, terrified by what was happening to it, cried out for help. The warrior-goddess Anat, who had helped the god during the battle, hastily fetched seven silver and eight bronze bowls to collect the blood. Once they had been filled, the bleeding, to all appearances, stopped by itself, without anyone's having attended to Re's wounds. The bowls with their contents were thereupon offered to Re, who thus recovered the blood he had lost.

The cosmic enemy was not always visible, and did not necessarily carry out his attacks in the open. It is well to recall here that darkness was one of the basic elements of chaos. Night accordingly represented the quotidian return of the primeval shadows, bringing all the ambiguities attached to them in its wake. The egg from which the solar bird sprang on the first morning of the world was hatched in the dark;[39] acts recalling the gestation process of the first beings occurred at night. Osiris was buried at night;[40] Horus was brought into the world at night.[41] But the night harbored negative forces as well; in the dark, they were particularly unconstrained.[42] It was at night that scorpions lay in wait at crossroads for their victims. Horus was stung at night, like the wife of the Elder Horus.[43] The baneful events that jeopardized the order of things likewise took place at night: it was then that Horus and Seth fought.[44] Nocturnal events were all potentially negative, and darkness was likely to offer shelter to the cosmic enemy. Thus, when a god went out at night, he did so surrounded by light and accompanied by formidable protective forces.[45]

The world the creator-god willed into existence was fragile from the outset, both because he could not subject the uncreated to his will and because this will could only eject or push aside everything that failed to serve the needs of creation. Those forced into the margins by the birth of the cosmos were not hostile to the organized world out of mindless malice, but because it encroached on their territory. They therefore struggled to win back what they believed had been stolen from them. For their part, the creator sun-god and, in his shining wake, the whole of creation, struggled to preserve their gains—that is, their very existence. Equilibrium arose out of the incessant confrontation between these two counterposed wills. But, nolens volens, the creation forever bore the stamp of night.

## Divine Revolts and Divisive Battles

The creator had not intended to create evil as such. Describing his work to his entourage, he says, emphatically, "I created every man identical with his neighbor; I did not order them (men) to commit perversion; it is their hearts that violated what I said."[46] Men were, in fact, led to rebel against divine authority, as has already been noted. But we will see that, before such uprisings occurred, certain gods also challenged the supreme authority. Indeed, the age in which the gods dwelt on earth was not free of civil war, or, at any rate, of strife closely resembling civil war. Thus, in addition to his traditional cosmic enemies, the creator-god also had to confront adversaries among the gods.[47]

Some time after the universe was created, a group of divinities—of exactly what sort we are not told—set about plotting against the creator.[48] Despite the conspirators' circumspection, he got wind of their plot. When they went into hiding, he went out looking for them. But the aging creator was obliged to give due consideration to his own frailty; he was not capable of dealing head-on with the hostility of his enemies, his own children, and had to hide to avoid taking some very hard knocks. To arrive at a better estimate of the size of the forces arrayed against him, he decided, in a council, to send out a messenger who would also act as a spy. The messenger quickly tracked down the conspirators; he counted two hundred and fifty-seven conspirators and eight officers, backed up by a huge army. He drew close enough to hear the slanderous remarks they were showering down on the king of the gods. Apparently, he was spotted by the rebels, for they turned in his direction and stuck out their tongues. For Egyptian sensibilities, this gesture was not so much a sign of derision or defiance as a genuine and very serious threat, intended to intimidate the adversary and dissuade him from coming closer.[49] It is known that good spirits, for example, were accustomed to chasing away evil spirits by sticking out their tongues. The messenger managed to get away without suffering any further inconvenience; he went back to the supreme deity and reported on what he had seen. A discussion ensued between the creator-god and Thoth, his faithful counsellor. This time, there could be no question at all of the creator's going forth to take on the conspirators himself. Rather, he should, Thoth said, designate a hero to champion his cause in single combat. The Elder Horus, a warrior of proven valor, was entrusted with the mission and provided arms. Fully equipped, clad in armor, the warrior-god, no longer able to contain his fury, threw himself upon the enemies. They had neither the time nor the means to react. The result was a veritable slaughter; the vanquished enemies had no choice but to seek salvation in flight. To put themselves the more surely out of the mighty champion's reach, some changed themselves into birds and flew off into the air; others became fish and hid in the water. But, after each of these transformations, the champion too underwent the appropriate metamorphosis, exterminating the survivors wherever they had taken shelter. In the end, order was fully restored. As a reward, the Elder Horus was accorded the privilege of being considered greater or more important than the other gods. One thus learns, incidentally, that a god could be promoted to higher rank in the divine hierarchy for services rendered the creator.

A text known as the "Myth of Horus" reports the same events in the form of a continuous narrative.[50] But it considerably tones down those aspects of the story that are the most unfavorable to the gods. Thus the rebels are no longer the creator's "children," but henchmen of Seth, the eternal troublemaker. The supreme deity, in all his splendor, dominates the situation from start to finish. At no time does one have the sense that there is a serious threat; from the outset, it is clear that the insurgents' effort is futile, that they stand no chance of success. This version does not clutter itself up with a furtive spy. The enemies, spotted intuitively, almost accidentally, are relentlessly pursued. The warrior hero wastes no time on petty details; he massacres the miscreants. The enemies' numbers are not mentioned in this version until they have been captured and executed. The focus of the story is shifted toward the conspirators' ringleader, who, in the form of a hippopotamus, is taken prisoner and subjected to a ritual execution; a goodly portion of the text is given over to a minute description of this operation. Not without a certain satisfaction, the narrative dwells on the blows that come raining down on the defeated, trussed-up creature, and on the dismemberment of his body, pieces of which are later distributed to the jubilant assembly of the gods.

The sequel to these events, which eventually led to a second battle, can only be pieced together from scraps of information gleaned at random from various texts. Although untold allusions are made in all periods to what goes by the name of the revolt of the Children of Re or the Children of Nut, there exists no detailed account of this revolt and its suppression. Certain episodes can, however, be described with some accuracy.[51] After the various battles had run their course, the majority of the rebels were massacred. Yet it is explicitly stated that the ringleaders of the revolt were gods. We are told nothing of their ultimate fate. One detail does, however, take us some way toward solving the mystery. The Elder Horus, the hero who champions the creator-god's cause in various episodes of the story, is the personage whose eyes are nothing more nor less than the sun and the moon. When, on pitch-dark nights, these two heavenly bodies are invisible, Horus finds himself temporarily blinded, becoming "He who has no eyes." These periods of total blindness do not prevent him from engaging in combat, but, at such times, he can be dangerously wide of the mark. Thus, during a battle with the rebels, he flails away right, left, and center, lopping off, without realizing it, not only the heads of the enemies, but also those of a sizeable number of gods.[52] Various sources do in fact inform us that, during the tumultuous period just evoked, the gods lost their heads, which would not be reattached to their shoulders until after the troubles had subsided.[53] This general decapitation brought on a moment of extreme confusion. The gods took to their heels,[54] the solar bark came to a standstill, and the universe stood tottering on the verge of catastrophe because one of the four pillars holding up the sky had collapsed into the water lying beyond the borders of the world.[55] Re had even lost his sexual vitality, a sign that he no longer had the power to infuse creation with the energy required to maintain it in a state of equilibrium.[56] All these phenomena indicate that the beheading of the gods should be taken to mean, not that they had died, but rather that the kind of absence or invisibility that periodically affects the heavenly bodies had befallen the whole of the divine company.[57] A gestation process occurred in this period, leading to a renewal of the world and everything in it. It was then that the warrior-god recovered his sight, becoming "He who has eyes."[58] The climax of the whole process came when the gods reappeared with their heads firmly attached to their shoulders. By the end of the episode, the gods had acquired a new bodily status; the revitalization and renewal of their limbs announced the beginnings of the next cycle.

Another version of events, which conflates the vicissitudes of the first battle with those of the second, offers a more surprising and more poetic vision of the drama. We are told that Re one day summoned all the gods and goddesses to an assembly. As soon as they had come together, he took them into his belly by swallowing them. This was a form of punishment, as we know from other texts;[59] it was also a way of alluding to the gods' invisibility. In the cramped quarters of Re's stomach, it was not long before the quarrels and bickering began. They culminated in a free-for-all in which every last god was killed. After this mutual destruction, Re spat the gods all back out, thus creating, we are told, the birds and fish[60]—the very animals the enemies had changed into in the first episode to avoid being massacred, at least for a time. These events did not, however, put an end to the gods' existence; they continued to go about their daily business as if nothing had happened. In the course of this adventure, then, the gods in effect transmitted a portion of their divinity to the animal species brought into being in the course of it. But they also passed along something of their quarrelsome nature. This explains how certain fish and birds could be considered sacred, even while constituting the negative element in the gods' being, which they rid themselves of via this transformation. As this rejected negative element, the fish and birds acquired the nature of enemies, and could therefore be hunted down and sacrificed or presented as offerings.[61] All these practices accordingly appear as easy ways of suppressing the opponents of the established order without ill effect.

The second battle of the gods was interwoven with the revolt staged by men. The chronology of events here is rather vague. Obviously, the new revolt sparked a reaction from the creator-god; this had consequences which were compounded with those of the gods' rebellion. Here, too, despite the conspirators' prudence, the king of the gods was informed of the situation and convened a divine assembly. The gods then decided to dispatch the ferocious lioness-goddess Sakhmet, who was also the eye of the sun, to punish rebellious humanity. The objective, as the gods conceived it, was to reduce the number of human beings, not to wipe out humanity without a trace.[62] But the lioness, intoxicated by the smell of blood, got so completely out of control that the king of the gods had to fall back on a stratagem to avert the total destruction of humankind. He ordered a large quantity of beer made and had it colored with red ochre to make it look like blood. This beer was then poured over the ground not far from the place where the ferocious goddess was on her rampage. The lioness set to drinking the beer and was soon so drunk that she could no longer recognize human beings; this made her forget her destructive fury. But if the human race was saved, the goddess, once she had sobered up, felt that she had been hoodwinked and humiliated. She returned in a rage, sowing panic among the gods,[63] and then took flight, going into self-imposed exile in a remote region of Nubia. This flight of his eye deprived the creator sun-god of an essential attribute; its absence diminished his powers[64] and left the gods practically leaderless.[65] The land was plunged into consternation. The only way to re-establish order was to bring the solar eye back out of voluntary exile. This was obviously no small task; the fierce goddess was particularly irascible, and no one was willing to risk resorting to force. The mission was entrusted to Shu, who, for the occasion, took the name of Onuris, which means "He who brings back the distant one."[66] But it was in fact Thoth, in the guise of an impish little monkey, who induced Sakhmet to come back; employing flattery and subtle arguments, he succeeded in convincing the dangerous goddess to return to her native land, which she admitted feeling homesick for.[67] Now that she had calmed down, she gave up her fearsome lioness form to take on the more agreeable aspect of a cat, or, again, that of the goddess of love Hathor. Returning to Egypt, she was received at Elephantine, on the Nubian-Egyptian border, amid universal rejoicing; the joy was all the more intense because her return coincided with that of the beneficial Nile flood. Having recovered the very emblem of his power, the solar creator god, sick of quarrels and tired of humanity's ingratitude, asked Nut to change herself into the sky, place him on her back, and lift him up into the heavens.

The gods' battles, the revolt of the human race, and their innumerable consequences created divisions that served as the prelude to a new cycle. All these conflicts had negative effects on the state of the world and ended up diminishing the power of the gods. It was explicitly acknowledged that the period in which fighting had not yet broken out anywhere was the one in which "the Ennead was still in its first strength."[68] Now the world was founded anew. The gods parted company with men, leaving them the earthly domain. This moment of separation was a crucial one: indeed, it structured the new world.[69] Before ascending to the sky for good and all, the creator-god put the final touches on his creation. He created cyclical time to replace the linear time that had preceded it. A text succinctly sums up these developments as follows: "The rebels caused a disorder to come about on that day; the first day was then made on the first occasion."[70] In other words, measured time, the calendar with its first day, was not established until this moment.

## Personal Quarrels and Struggles for Legitimacy

Over and above the conflicts in which cosmic equilibrium and the cohesion of the divine company hung in the balance, the gods were agitated, as they went about their daily business, by rivalries and rows over their personal interests. Though the stakes here were more modest, the consequences were nevertheless still dramatic. These conflicts had their origins in various unfortunate incidents, a number of which will be evoked. For example, on one occasion when Horus interfered in human affairs, his mother Isis took a malign pleasure in thwarting his plans;[71] she doubtless meant to put him in mind of the violent treatment he had earlier subjected her to. Fortunately, the quarrel between mother and son eventually blew over.[72] An obscure quarrel likewise pitted Geb against Nut; before it was over, Nut's head had been split open. The text that mentions this episode, allusively, strongly advises the reader not to spread word of the affair, for fear, the suggestion seems to be, of provoking cosmic disorders.[73]

The most memorable of these conflicts between gods, and the one to which reference is most frequently made, opposed, first, Osiris and Seth, and then Seth and Horus. Osiris's assassination, Horus's upbringing in hiding, and the latter's triumph over his murderous uncle were the greatest of the gods' preoccupations. The struggles these events triggered off spawned all sorts of new developments, turning this quarrel into an interminable affair that was always capable of generating one more chapter. The only detailed narrative we have of this drama is Plutarch's Greek version. The Egyptian texts are for their part dispersed over several different periods and offer only a nebulous mass of disjointed facts. The chronology of events and the relationships between the major characters in the story (Seth appears now as Horus's brother, now as his uncle) are not, at first glance, particularly clear. But close analysis of the earliest texts, the Pyramid Texts, enables us to distinguish three essential stages in the plot.[74] In the first, the Elder Horus, the reigning king, was in conflict with his brother Seth. The quarrel was plainly over the exercise of royal power, which Seth sought to seize by force. In the decisive battle between Seth and Horus, the latter lost an eye and the former his testicles.[75] Each of the them kept the part he had torn from his adversary's body as a trophy. In the second stage, Seth slew the Elder Horus, who became, as a direct consequence of this murder, Osiris or "Horus who is in Osiris."[76] A new Horus was born of the posthumous union between Isis and Osiris: Horus the son of Isis. Once he had grown up, this Horus sought to avenge his father with the help of Isis, who provided him the weapons he needed.[77] The aim was to get back Horus's lost eye and undo the reciprocal mutilation caused by the first combat. Recovering the eye was also a means of recovering, symbolically, the royal power usurped by Seth and restoring it both to Horus, the living king, and also to Osiris, the dead king.

These duels and physical confrontations had their counterpart in endless legal battles, as a result of which each of the gods recovered his missing organ. Getting his testicles back obviously provided Seth satisfaction and relief.[78] Isis, for her part, was delighted to see Horus's missing eye back where it belonged, since this symbolized, as has already been said, the restoration of royal power to its legitimate possessor.[79] The fate reserved for Seth after these quarrels were over was as ambiguous as the mixed feelings animating the most eminent members of the divine company. As we will see, the creator-god had a soft spot for Seth, while Isis herself was torn between her love for her son and her ties to her brother. Her hesitation to espouse the just cause[80] was largely responsible for the bad blood that sometimes developed between her and her son. Finally, when not caught up in their power struggle, the Elder Horus and his brother Seth enjoyed moments of close companionship and provided one another brotherly mutual assistance.[81]

The settlement that put an end to this conflict took effect only gradually. The throne, initially shared between Horus and Seth, was finally unified under the sole authority of the former. This reunification put an end to a conflict-ridden dualism that nevertheless left a permanent mark on Egypt: right up to the end of the Roman presence in the country, Egypt was officially designated, in hieroglyphic texts, as the "Two Lands." In the daily life of both gods and men, this fracture was never really healed. Emotional and familial relations aside, Seth's brutal act put the question of legitimate royal succession before the gods; the trouble they had in finding a definitive solution to the problem shows how indecisive they were about how it should be resolved. But once it had been settled in favor of Horus and his party, the entire community eventually acknowledged his newly reconfirmed legitimacy. Seth, however, stubbornly maintained his position and committed one serious misdeed after the other, until he had exhausted the patience of his fellow gods and frittered away the last vestiges of whatever sympathy he had once enjoyed. His destructive activities ran the entire gamut of evil, from the profanation of all that his peers most revered to an attempt to alienate Horus the child from his mother by slandering him.[82] Eventually, all the misfortunes and accidents that occurred in the divine world would be charged to Seth's account.[83] A decision was made to banish him: he was expelled not only from the divine community but also from the land of Egypt, the center of civilization itself. This rejection of Seth, one surmises, effectively assimilated him to the original cosmic enemies, making him an ally in their perpetual struggle against the established order. In the end, Seth's own mother Nut repudiated him as well, joining the other gods in seeking his destruction.[84] It is sometimes even said that, instead of being banished, Seth was forced to commit suicide.[85]

## The Reign of the Gods on Earth

Before turning the world over to the human race, the gods reigned on earth in unbroken dynastic succession. The Royal Canon, an unfortunately very fragmentary document preserved in the Museum of Turin, provides, in its present state, a list of all reigning kings from the origins of the world to the beginnings of the eighteenth human dynasty, that is, roughly the fifteenth century B.C.E.[86] Although the very first part of this text has disappeared, one gathers that the gods who were supposed to have reigned on earth belonged essentially to what is known as the Ennead of Heliopolis, the family line of Atum, the creator-god, who lived in that city together with his solar pendant Re. The Royal Canon gives us the names of these gods and the length of their reigns, but only a few of the numbers are still legible. We know that Thoth reigned for 7,726 years, Horus for a mere 300. The existence of the divine lineage of Heliopolis is corroborated by other sources.[87] But the known traditions diverge—understandably, inasmuch as every god could be considered a potential sovereign. Thus certain sources say that Amun of Xois, for instance, reigned for 7,000 years.[88] However that may be, the fact that records of these family dynasties were handed down through the ages for so long that they were mentioned as late as the third century B.C.E. by Manetho, an Egyptian historian working in the service of the Ptolemies, suggests that the gods themselves carefully updated the annals of their reigns. Indeed, these annals are known to have been composed by Thoth himself, under the creator-god's supervision; they were inscribed on the leaves of a holy tree in Heliopolis.[89]

As the gods were immortal, it might seem logical that only one of their number should be king and exercise undivided power on a permanent basis. That the gods in fact succeeded one another on the throne thus raises a question: why each of them in turn gave up power, bringing his reign to what was by all indications a voluntary end, and what became of a former king after he had stepped down. Aside from the conflicts already described, the particular events of each reign are not known in detail. But a story that spins itself out over several divine reigns,[90] as well as certain more or less allusive indications scattered through the texts, permit us to suggest answers to these questions.

Each of the gods succeeded "his father" and devoted himself to defending and improving the existing laws.[91] Each received the regalia of office from his predecessor, along with a written document, a sort of transfer deed, that authorized him to rule alone in all legitimacy.[92] Succession from father to son was a rule that admitted of no exceptions other than the usurpation by Seth referred to above. Royal sovereignty extended to everything in the created world: gods, men, animals, the sky, the earth, the hereafter, water, air, mountains.[93] This was the period in which "the kingship over men and gods was one and the same matter."[94]

At the beginning of the world, the Primeval Ocean, Nun, also known as "the father of the gods," created "His Majesty," that is, the sovereign sun.[95] Located beyond the bounds of the universe, he did not rule; rather, the separation of the creator-god from Nun's waters identified the creator with the idea of organization as such, and so with kingship. Atum was the first to exercise this royal office, called, appropriately, "the office of Atum."[96] It was during his reign that the air cooled off and the land became dry. In certain traditions, dry land emerged through a kind of cooking process. The flame that flashed forth from the eye of the solar creator-god, who was none other than a form of Atum, literally solidified the elements that became the first dry land.[97]

Then the gods and humankind came together to form the god-king's entourage, marking a new stage in the organization of the world.[98] But the cosmic enemies made their presence felt by fomenting a rebellion. It was Shu, the son of Atum, who brought them to heel after inheriting the throne. It is not known how the transfer of power came about.[99]

After what seems to have been a peaceful reign, Shu, too, clashed with the hostile forces that resided permanently on the edge of creation. They attacked Egypt, scoring a provisional victory. After his divine palace on earth was sacked by the enemy forces, Shu and his entourage ascended to the sky, but not before finally defeating the invaders. Apparently, Shu left his wife Tefnut behind on earth as regent. Geb, however, sexually abused his mother and attempted to seize Shu's uraeus.[100] He only succeeded in getting himself severely burned and had to turn to Re for treatment. During a nine-day interregnum, the elements unleashed their fury upon the world. Order was then restored, after which Geb, the son of Shu, was crowned king in his father's stead.[101] These various incidents may well indicate that Geb was perhaps not entirely innocent, but had rather taken an active part in the revolts marking the close of the previous reign.

In any case, posterity regarded Geb's reign as emblematic. The royal throne and the authority emanating from it were happy to be known as the "throne of Geb"; kingship itself was often considered to be "a legacy of Geb's." According to a curious and poorly documented legend, the end of Geb's reign was marked by the rebellion of Geb's son Osiris against his father's authority.[102] Geb had to slay his own son in self-defense. But, horrified by the consequences of his act, he hastened to revive him. This return to life reintegrated Osiris into the ordinary world, whereas the murder of Osiris subsequently perpetrated by Seth confined him for all eternity to the world of death. Once revived, Osiris succeeded his father, becoming king in his turn.

Little is known of Osiris's earthly reign.[103] Plutarch, the only one who really discusses it, portrays it as a peaceful and happy interlude. The new sovereign, he tells us, taught humankind agriculture and showered the world with his beneficence. What happened next is well known. Seth, the king's brother, was as jealous as he was aggressive. Coveting power, he lured Osiris into a trap and killed him. He then cut his body up into pieces and threw them into the Nile. Isis, Osiris's wife, went out looking for them, found them, and put them back together, wrapping them in bandages. As a result of this last operation, the life returned to Osiris's body, so that he was able to couple with his wife and engender a son, Horus. In the Egyptian sources, the death of the god is what had symbolic significance: paradoxically, death took the place of life for Osiris, substituting itself for existence. Osiris's death *was* his real life: by a deliberate, significant antiphrasis, it made him into a "living god,"[104] but also a "God above the gods . . . more than the gods."[105] This is why the dead Osiris enjoyed a kind of constant preeminence in the eyes of his companions: they lavished more attention on his corpse "than on the body that had existed earlier."[106]

Osiris's murder represented a rupture in the ongoing line of divine kings. Seth had not succeeded in conquering the monarchy in its entirety; he reigned over the southern part of the country alone. Horus the child, who had taken refuge in a secret hiding place in the Delta marshes, continued to bear the title of king of the North.[107] Hence Seth's reign would be nothing more than a long search: he had to find the legitimate heir at all costs and do away with him in order to concentrate all royal authority in his person. But, his repeated searches and stratagems notwithstanding, one part of the kingdom forever eluded his grasp, incapable as he was of laying his hands on his rival. Horus managed to reach the age of adulthood, though not without difficulty, as we shall see. After he had grown up, he put an end to Seth's reign, for his own benefit. His rival's rule ended in both physical defeat and brutal destitution after a solemn trial and judgment.[108]

Just as Osiris's and Seth's existences were summed up by death in the one case and defeat in the other, so Horus's drew all its significance from his enthronement and coronation. All other events that had occurred on earth seemed to have been nothing more than preparation for this moment. Horus's life was a perpetual coronation. As a result, his reign did not lend itself to narration; nothing in it provided the stuff of anecdote. We know little more about it than that Isis counseled her son in the exercise of his authority.[109] Everything about Horus served to establish the institution of kingship as the end product of all the gods' quarrels, once these had at last been laid to rest. Now it was men's turn to bring about a rupture. Their rebellion took place "after Horus," as a text laconically puts it.[110] Whereas divine kingship henceforth pursued its orderly course in the celestial regions, the long line of earthly pharaohs was nothing other than a succession of endlessly repeated Horuses.

Thus each divine reign culminated in a confrontation in which a clash between father and son became one of the motifs in the theme of the transmission of power. Each of these conflicts was punctuated by the emergence of cosmic disorders and revealed the weakness of a sovereign forced to cede his place to a successor whose forces were still unimpaired. How power was transmitted is not known in detail. But we do know that the mode of royal succession, along with the title deed to the world, had long ago been written out in a special document by Geb, god of the earth.[111] Handed down from one sovereign to the next, this document ensured dynastic legitimacy and continuity. Earthly kingship would strangely resemble this model. Every political disorder recalled and reproduced the withdrawal of the gods from the world of men.[112] Every king was his predecessor's son, whatever the actual blood ties between them might have been. Every royal death was a disaster, and every new monarch a savior who restored cosmic order.[113] Last, this system not only authorized the transfer of power from father to son, but could also serve to legitimate any pretender. It ensured that the earthly throne would pass from Horus to Horus; the same god succeeded himself on the throne, in a single, perpetually renewed reign—down to the predicted end of the world, the end of Egyptian paganism.

FIGURE 1. Amulet representing the *udjat*-eye, also known as the "Eye of Horus" and the "Eye of Re." The right Eye of Horus, which could itself be a solar eye, was ripped out by Seth and eventually restored to Horus. The Eye of Re, the sun god, went off in a rage to Nubia and had to be brought back to him. A symbol rich in its associations, the solar eye was identified with the terrible goddess Sakhmet, the beneficent goddess Hathor, and the uraeus. It also symbolized that which was whole or restored, including the wholeness of the land of Egypt. The *udjat*-eye was pervasive in the religious art of Egypt, and it appears in other illustrations in this volume. Detroit Institute of Arts. T 1996.1. From a private collection. Photograph © 1996 The Detroit Institute of Arts, Founders Society Purchase, Mr. and Mrs. Allan Shelden III Fund, Ralph Harman Booth Bequest Fund, and Hill Memorial Fund. (See page 14.)

FIGURE 2. Book of the Dead vignette depicting the return of the solar eye. According to myth, the solar eye once became angry and exiled herself in Nubia. Thoth (himself a moon god and a trickster who was a thief of time) succeeded in coaxing her into returning. In Nubia, the solar eye was the raging goddess Sakhmet; returned to Egypt, she was the gentle Hathor. Here Thoth, in the form of a baboon, presents the *udjat*, or solar eye, to the sun god, who is depicted with the iconography of Re-Harakhty. Behind him, Neferrenpet, the owner of the papyrus, witnesses the scene. University of Pennsylvania Museum, Philadelphia (Object # E2775, neg. # S5-23173). (See page 26.)

FIGURE 3. The god Horus as a youth, a fact that is emphasized by his nude, chubby body and the "sidelock of youth" on the right side of his head. The head just above him is perhaps that of the protective god Bes. The text of this stela (the Metternich Stela) relates how Isis fled to the marshes of Buto to hide her son Horus from the evil Seth, and of a mishap that occurred when Horus, while still a young boy, was stung by a scorpion. Here, Horus holds scorpions and serpents in his hands, as well as a highly styled gazelle (or, perhaps, antelope) and lioness. He stands on a crocodile that might well symbolize the inimical Seth. Just above the shrine-like enclosure are two *udjat*-eyes, here provided with arms raised in a gesture of adoration. In Egyptian belief, there were two *udjat*-eyes, or Eyes of Horus: his right eye was the solar eye, and his left eye was the lunar eye. It is thus perhaps no coincidence that below the right eye (to the viewer's left), the divine figures wear sun disks on their heads or headdresses, while below the left eye, there appears the moon god Thoth, who is depicted as an ibis-headed man. The text of the stela informs us that Thoth intervened more than once to help Isis and Horus. On the extreme left is the vulture goddess Nekhbet, patroness of Upper Egypt; her counterpart on the right is the cobra goddess Wadjyt, patroness of Lower Egypt. The Metropolitan Museum of Art, Fletcher Fund, 1950. 50.85. (See page 60.)

FIGURE 4. Bronze depicting a worshiper kneeling before the jackal-headed god Anubis and two uraei. The uraeus on the left wears the red crown of Lower Egypt, while that on the right wears the white crown of Upper Egypt; they are thus evidently Wadjyt and Nekhbet, the patron goddesses of Lower and Upper Egypt, respectively. The Walters Art Gallery, Baltimore. 54.400. (See page 62.)

FIGURE 5. Statuette of the falcon god Horus. Like other Egyptian deities, Horus could be depicted in more than one form. He could be depicted in animal form, as a human with an animal's head (see figure 26), or in fully human form (see figure 9). The Walters Art Gallery, Baltimore. 22.409. (See page 62.)

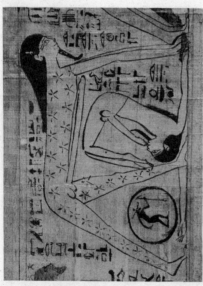

FIGURE 6. (left) Because of the permanent separation of the sky and the earth, the earth god Geb was reduced to pleasuring himself. Normally, the sky was depicted as the goddess Nut (see figure 11); its representation here as a very ithyphallic male is a highly unusual detail. Between the legs of the sky god is a sun disk; the ram-headed god depicted inside it indicates that the sun is the *ba*, or "manifestation," of the creator-god. Papyrus. Copyright British Museum. (See page 66.)

FIGURE 7. (below) Relief fragment depicting Osiris twice, enthroned and wearing the white crown of Upper Egypt. His sisters Isis (left) and Nephthys stand protectively behind him. Before each representation of Osiris is an altar heaped with offerings, while at the far left, a corpulent fecundity figure brings still more offerings. The Walters Art Gallery, Baltimore. 22.89. (See page 67.)

FIGURE 8. The conception of Horus. Coveting his brother's throne, Seth murdered Osiris. He then dismembered the body and scattered the pieces throughout Egypt. Osiris's consort, Isis, determined to produce a rightful heir to the divine kingship, recovered the body parts and bound them back together, creating the first mummy. Here, in the form of a falcon, Isis hovers above the revived penis of Osiris as she prepares to conceive a son. The falcons (or kites) whose wings are stretched protectively at Osiris's head and foot are Nephthys and yet another representation of Isis. Though he is not quite yet conceived, the falcon-headed god Horus presides over the scene at the left, while at the right, King Seti I looks on. Temple of Seti I at Abydos. Photo by Gaddis. (See page 77.)

FIGURE 9. Isis nursing Horus. After conceiving a son, Isis fled to Buto, where she kept Horus hidden in the papyrus marshes. Though misadventures occurred, her strategy succeeded, and Horus remained hidden from Seth until he was old enough to avenge his father. Here, Isis holds Horus on her lap as she prepares to offer him her breast. The Walters Art Gallery, Baltimore. 55.416. (See pages 85–86.)

FIGURE 10. Silver pendant depicting Amun, god of the city of Thebes, and later of other cities as well. In the New Kingdom, Amun of Thebes became the supreme god of the Egyptian pantheon. The Walters Art Gallery, Baltimore. 57.1416. (See page 91.)

FIGURE 11. Shu separating Geb and Nut. The god of the air holds the sky goddess in permanent suspension, while the earth god reclines wearily below. To the left and right of Shu are uraeus-headed goddesses who represent, respectively, the west and the east. These are repeated in fully human form outside the representation of Nut, raising their arms in adoration as they stand before tables heaped with offerings. On Nut's back is the barque of the sun god; the ram's head in the sun disk indicates that the sun is the *ba*, or "manifestation," of the creator-god. In the prow of the barque squats the moon god Thoth, in the form of a baboon, holding a lunar *udjat*-eye. Coffin of Khonsu-mes. Victoria Museum 228, Uppsala University, Sweden. (See pages 112–13.)

FIGURE 12. Divine birth legend of Ramses II. Having decided that he would personally sire the next king of Egypt, the supreme god Amun appeared one night in the queen's bedchamber in the guise of the king. The queen was awakened by the pungent aroma of the god. Quickly approaching her bed, Amun revealed his true form, and the union was consummated. Here, in the aftermath, the two are depicted sitting together tenderly on the bed, as the queen says to the god, "Oh, my lord, how great, indeed, is your power!" Originally from the funerary temple of Ramses II (the Ramesseum), this block was reused in the construction of the funerary temple of Ramses III (Medinet Habu), where it is still to be seen, positioned upside down in the wall. Photo by Lorelei Corcoran. (See pages 120–21.)

FIGURE 13. Presentation of Maat. Since the king of Egypt was divine, he was the mediator between the human and the divine realms. Thus, although the priesthoods of the temples carried out the daily cult ritual on his behalf, the hypothetical presence of the monarch is signaled by the fact that it is he who is regularly depicted as the sole officiant in the reliefs carved on temple walls. These reliefs depict selected scenes from the ritual, while a single papyrus preserves it to us virtually in its entirety. Here, in the forty-second episode of the ritual as preserved on the papyrus, the king presents a figurine of the goddess Maat, who represented truth and cosmic order. From the temple of Seti I at Abydos. Photo by Gaddis. (See pages 126–29.)

FIGURE 14. Presentation of unguent. The fifty-fourth through the fifty-seventh episodes of the daily cult ritual consisted in the presentation of various unguents. Here, the king has dipped the little finger of his right hand into a small vase and is about to anoint the goddess Isis. From the temple of Isis at Behbeit el-Hagar. Photo by Christine Favard-Meeks. (See pages 126–29.)

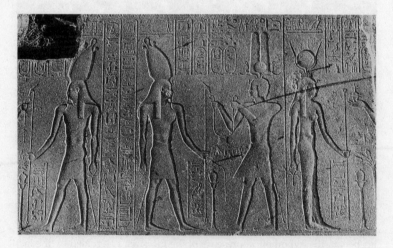

FIGURE 15. Presentation of a collar. Each day at dawn, the cult statues were purified by the burning of incense, dressed, anointed, and presented with food offerings. Here, in a scene not mentioned in the papyrus version of the ritual, a non-mummiform Osiris-Onnophris is presented with a collar that forms a part of his adornment. Temple of Isis at Behbeit el-Hagar. Photo by Christine Favard-Meeks. (See pages 126–29.)

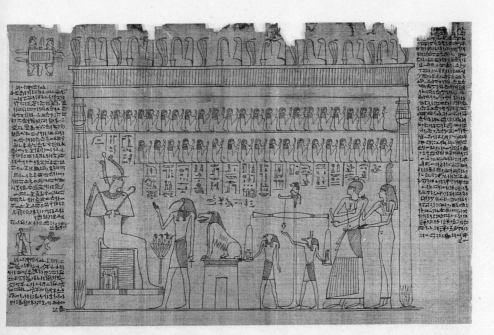

FIGURE 16. Weighing of the heart. After death and burial, each individual had to submit to a Judgment of the Dead presided over by Osiris, who after his death and resurrection by Isis became ruler of the netherworld. The deceased was obliged to make a "negative confession," assuring the court that he had not committed any of a long list of sins, and his heart, the seat of the mind and the conscience as well as of the emotions, was weighed against the feather that symbolized the goddess Maat. Maat and her symbols pervade this representation of the scene. Each member of the two rows of gods constituting the divine tribunal holds a Maat feather; there is a Maat feather in one pan of the scale; the deceased, Nes-Min, holds a Maat feather, and he wears a figurine of Maat as an amulet hanging from his neck; and at the far right, the goddess herself stands protectively behind him. Near the center of the scene, the falcon-headed god Horus and the jackal-headed god Anubis tend to the scale, atop which is perched a baboon representing Thoth. In front of the scale, the composite monster named Devourer sits on a shrine, ready to swallow the deceased if he fails this test. In ibis-headed form, Thoth, who is often shown recording the results of the proceedings, is here represented reporting them to the enthroned Osiris. Osiris is depicted mummiform, and sitting on the lotus in front of him are the four sons of Horus, the gods of the four canopic jars that held the entrails removed during the mummification process. Depicted at the upper left is the ultimate goal of the deceased, the home of Osiris, which was reputed to have a ceiling of fire, walls of live uraei, and a floor of water. At the lower left, the deceased and his *ba* are pictured. Detroit Institute of Arts. 1988.10.13. Photograph © 1996 The Detroit Institute of Arts, Founders Society Purchase, Mr. and Mrs. Allan Shelden III Fund, Ralph Harman Booth Bequest Fund, and Hill Memorial Fund. (See pages 146–48.)

FIGURE 17. The *ba* hovering over the deceased. Each Egyptian was believed to have a *ba*, a soul-like entity that accompanied him into the afterlife. Here, in a representation painted on the foot of a coffin, the *ba*, depicted as a human-headed bird, hovers over the anthropoid coffin containing the mummy as it is carried, strapped to the back of a bull, to the tomb. In the Egyptian writing system, the bowl of burning incense in front of the bull is employed in writings of the word *ba*. The tomb is depicted so elongated that it resembles an obelisk. The pyramidions placed on some tombs evidently replicated the pyramidions at the tops of obelisks, so the conflation of forms could be more than a result of relatively poor artistry. Obelisks and pyramidions were solar symbols, and one hope of the Egyptians was that after death, the *ba* would emerge from the tomb each day at sunrise to worship the rising sun. National Museum, Copenhagen, Department of Near Eastern and Classical Antiquities. 1038. (See page 148.)

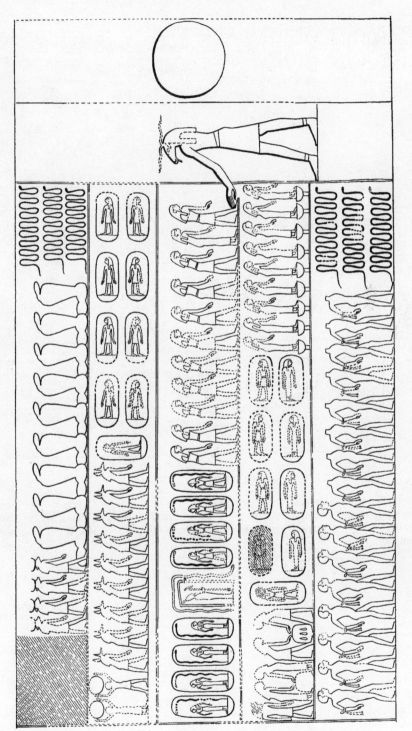

FIGURE 18. The first cavern of the netherworld from the Book of Caverns in the tomb of Ramses VI. (For a description, see pages 151–63.) After Alexandre Piankoff, *Le Livre des Quérerts* (Cairo: Institut Français d'Archéologie Orientale du Caire, 1946), plate 1. Reproduced by permission.

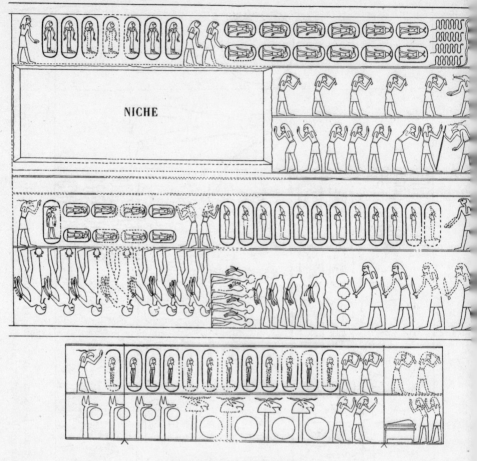

Representations in the niche

FIGURE 19. The second cavern of the netherworld from the Book of Caverns in the tomb of Ramses VI. (For a description, see pages 151–63.) After Alexandre Piankoff, *Le Livre des Quérerts* (Cairo: Institut Français d'Archéologie Orientale du Caire, 1946), plate 10. Reproduced by permission.

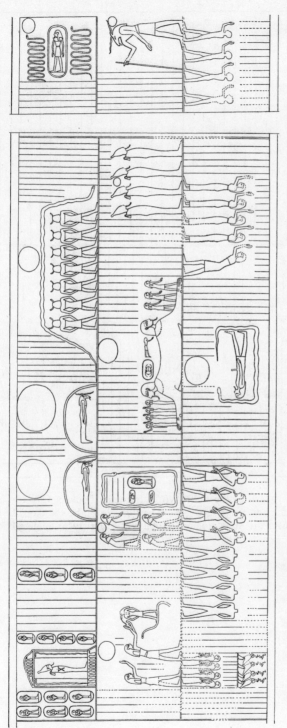

FIGURE 20. The third cavern of the netherworld from the Book of Caverns in the tomb of Ramses VI. (For a description, see pages 151–63.) After Alexandre Piankoff, *Le Livre des Quérerts* (Cairo: Institut Français d'Archéologie Orientale du Caire, 1946), plate 27. Reproduced by permission.

FIGURE 21. The fourth cavern of the netherworld from the Book of Caverns in the tomb of Ramses VI. (For a description, see pages 151–63.) After Alexândre Piankoff, *Le Livre des Quérerts* (Cairo: Institut Français d'Archéologie Orientale du Caire, 1946), plate 38. Reproduced by permission.

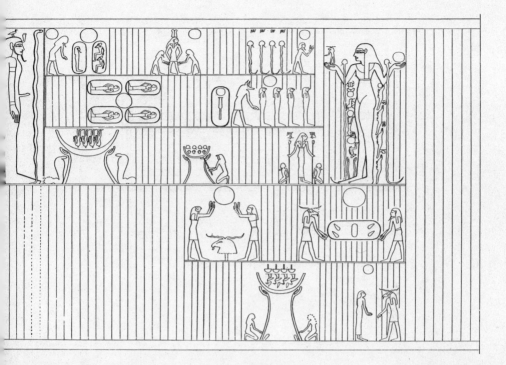

FIGURE 22. The fifth cavern of the netherworld from the Book of Caverns in the tomb of Ramses VI. (For a description, see pages 151–63.) After Alexandre Piankoff, *Le Livre des Quérerts* (Cairo: Institut Français d'Archéologie Orientale du Caire, 1946), plate 51. Reproduced by permission.

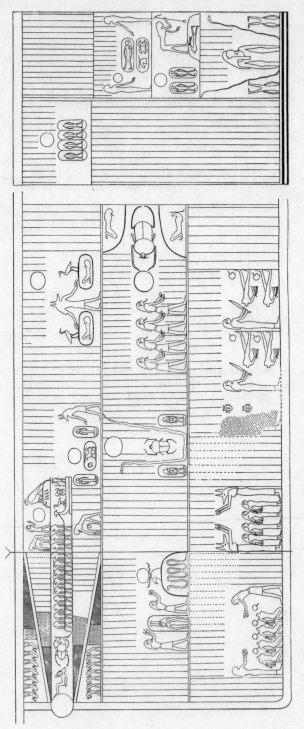

FIGURE 23. The sixth cavern of the netherworld from the Book of Caverns in the tomb of Ramses VI. (For a description, see pages 151–63.) After Alexandre Piankoff, *Le Livre des Quérerts* (Cairo: Institut Français d'Archéologie Orientale du Caire, 1946), plate 121. Reproduced by permission.

FIGURE 24. Hathor emerging from the western mountain. Hathor symbolized the western desert mountains of Thebes that served as the burial place of kings, their families, members of the royal administration, and priests, and she was pictured as a cow emerging from the mountainside to greet the deceased. In antiquity, a peak of the cliff overhanging the mortuary temple of Hatshepsut at Deir el-Bahri was modeled into the form of the goddess emerging from the mountain. The two shrine-like enclosures depicted here seem to imply that replicas of this image were worshiped in the Hathor shrines built by the monarchs Hatshepsut and Thutmosis III in that locale. The Osirid statues flanking the smaller shrine probably evoke statues of kings Montuhotep II and Amenophis I at the site. The scene is painted on a plastered linen wall hanging dedicated by an Egyptian family of relatively humble status, possibly that of one of the villagers of nearby Deir el-Medina, home to the workmen who excavated, decorated—and sometimes plundered—the royal tombs of Thebes. On the interpretation of the textile, see N. B. Millet, *Bulletin of the Egyptological Seminar* 10 (1989/1990): 95–98. Royal Ontario Museum 910.16.3. Drawing by Barbara Ibronyi. Reproduced by permission of the Royal Ontario Museum. (See page 164.)

FIGURE 25. Relief fragment depicting the jackal-headed god Wepwawet, who was believed to guide the deceased on the pathways of the netherworld, in the company of the earth god Geb. The Walters Art Gallery, Baltimore. 22.10. (See page 166.)

FIGURE 26. The "Baptism of Pharaoh." Officiating priests purified themselves in the waters of the sacred lakes of temples. Kings, too, had to be ritually purified, and in depictions carved on temple walls, this "baptism" is routinely projected onto the mythological plane. Here, in a relief from the temple of Kom Ombo, the falcon-headed Horus and the ibis-headed Thoth perform the ritual. The purification endows the king with "life" and "dominion," as shown by the fact that the streams of water are represented as chains of the hieroglyphic signs for these words. Photo by Lorelei Corcoran. (See pages 187–93.)

FIGURE 27. The three statues of the Mesen chapel and the rising sun. According to the texts carved on the walls of the temple of Horus at Edfu, the Uniting with the Sun Disk ritual was performed at New Year's and certain other festival occasions. The procession of cult statues to the roof of the temple, to be regenerated there by the rays of the sun, was led by the three statues in the Mesen chapel located directly behind the sanctuary of the temple. One of these was the crouching, ithyphallic *gemehesu*-falcon, the most potent cult image in the temple. The others were his consort, Hathor of Dendara, who was identified with Maat and imaged as the uraeus on the brow of the sun god, and the Falcon of Gold. Here, in a depiction of the ceremony from the Roman period mammisi (birth-house) at Dendara, these images are pictured along with an icon of the rising sun, which is identified as "Amun-Re, King of the Gods." It was believed that creation was initiated by an act of masturbation, and this icon identifies the sunrise of the festival day as an instance of *creatio continua*, that is, a continuation and renewal of the original creation of the cosmos. Like the ram's head in figure 11, the depiction of the rising sun as a human-headed bird identifies the sun as a *ba*, or "manifestation," of the creator-god. The image also makes a connection between the life-bestowing properties of semen and sunshine. After François Daumas, *Les Mammisis de Dendara* (Cairo: Institut Français d'Archéologie Orientale du Caire, 1959), plate 60 *bis*. Reproduced by permission. (See pages 193–98.)

# CHAPTER TWO

# Hierarchies, Prerogatives, Groups

It is not really known how many gods there were, and there is no reason to suppose that anyone or any rule could limit their number— even if one ritualist made the unusual boast that he could rattle off all their names by heart.[1] The creator-god was commonly called "the one become million."[2] He was said to sit in state before his millions of creatures,[3] "million" being, in Egyptian, the usual expression for what is infinite in number. Statements of this sort were intended, of course, to encompass the whole range of created beings, whether gods, animals, or men. The gods made up a smaller community at the center of this throng. The texts sometimes speak of the "tens of thousands and thousands of gods" who proceeded from the creator.[4] Like the other beings, the gods were what they were because he had willed them to be so. We saw in Chapter 1 to what extent the different categories of created beings were intermingled. The creator and the primordial gods aside, all were created almost at random, as circumstances dictated. The distinctions between the various categories of beings, like the ties uniting them, were not primarily based on the order in which they were created. According to certain traditions, humanity was created even before most of the gods were. The hierarchy of beings depended, then, on qualities intrinsic to each category. We are told that the nature of the gods is that they were created "greater than men."[5] But the different categories were not self-contained and sealed off from the others. As seen in Chapter 1, the rebellious gods were punished by being changed into human beings; indeed, they became "bestial humans," that is, nothing more nor less than animals destined for sacrifice. Conversely, people could become gods under certain circumstances, and certain animals could attain to divinity.[6] The demotion of the divine enemies implies the de facto existence of a scale of values in which each group of beings depended on that preceding it. This interdependence was willed by the creator: "Falcons live on (smaller) birds, jackals by thieving, pigs on the desert, hippopotamuses on the reeds of the marshes, men on grain, crocodiles on fish, fish on the water in the Nile, as Atum (the creator-god) has ordained."[7] In this chain, which made all creatures interdependent, the strongest bond was without a doubt that between the gods and men. The proper functioning of the world depended on the reciprocity that that bond implied, as will be seen in the second part of this book. Finally, as in the case of the animals in the text cited a moment ago, plainly visible structures and power relations developed *within* each category as well. The same held for the gods.

## The Society of the Gods and Its Hierarchies

The structures proper to the world of the gods were most obviously arranged in conformity with two independent but ultimately complementary hierarchies. The first, which might be described as natural, took into account each god's place in the creation—his "biological" rank. The second was based on the power relations every god was capable of establishing independently of the "biological" hierarchy. These power relations had their origin in each god's specific activity, the function that guaranteed his supremacy over all his fellow gods in a given domain. Each of the gods could be considered the most important in his turn, depending on the perspective one adopted. The emergence of these power relations counterbalanced the natural hierarchy in a way that allowed each god to affirm his specific nature. The interaction of these two realities made divine society a dynamic whole in which the emergence of conflicts and their resolution contributed to bringing about development and diversification.

The terminology used to describe the gods' hierarchical relations was quite simple. Divine society was divided into "great" and "lesser" gods; occasionally one comes across "intermediate" gods as well.[8] The "great" gods were set apart from the rank and file by the prerogatives they enjoyed; basically quite vague, these prerogatives came most clearly to the fore in the courtly etiquette in use among the entourage of the "king of the gods," whoever he happened to be. The existence of such rules of protocol, supervised by Thoth, is sometimes explicitly mentioned.[9] In the presence of a superior, the great gods remained standing as a token of respect, and the lesser ones had to prostrate themselves. A further distinction was made between "elder" and "younger" gods, that is, between the members of the different divine generations: those created when the world was, and the rest.[10] But age did not always imply superiority. Thus it is said that Thoth ordered gods "older than he was"[11] to deliver messengers. In his capacity as right arm, or, in modern terms, prime minister of the supreme deity, he was indispensable to the proper functioning of the world; this explains his special power to command his fellow gods, whatever their rank in other domains.[12] Over and above the hierarchy based on birth, established once and for all and, by definition, impossible to change, divine society gave every one of its members the chance to advance according to his individual merits and capacities. If every "great god" in the pantheon could legitimately proclaim himself "greater" than his fellows, without other justification than the obvious truth of his claim, certain gods acquired this status in the wake of a specific event. We have seen how the Elder Horus earned his stripes as a god "greater than the others." The expression reveals, moreover, the exceptional and, in a way, limited character of the epithet. The greatness it designated obtained only within the precise limits of one specific sphere of activity. Most of the time, it was the divinities endowed with uncommon physical strength or exceptional destructive capacities who encouraged their fellows to shower them with flattering epithets. Thus Montu, another intrepid warrior, struck fear, by his very nature, into the hearts of gods greater than himself, constraining them to obey his orders.[13] On the distaff side, the goddesses said to be "dangerous," Sakhmet and Bastet, constituted special cases. Their fits of rage were so terrifying that the king of the gods himself could not remain in their neighborhood without risk.[14] But fear was not the sole means of compelling respect. Thoth was respected for his competence; Osiris acquired, by his death, an importance and authority he had not enjoyed while alive.

To be sure, only a minority of gods was concerned with questions of hierarchy, which could not possibly occupy the whole of divine society. Every instant, every season, every month, every day, every hour possessed its duly accredited divinity;[15] so did every locality.[16] These gods, captives of a moment or a place, were likewise the prisoners of their humble, narrowly defined functions. Lesser gods, genies, or daemons were not quite the same as acolytes—petty, often anonymous servants of the "great"—but rather subalterns who had at all times to hold themselves in readiness to execute the decisions of their superiors.

The picture we have just painted shows us a community whose structuring elements barely made themselves felt, despite the existence of a hierarchy one might imagine as being heavily restrictive. The set of stories already mentioned goes to show that rank frequently took second place to individual passions or the group instincts of small bands.

Indeed, the whole of divine society found its only real point of anchorage in the person of the solar creator-god, generally incarnated by Re. As the uncreated one who first dispensed light to the world, he was the source of all life. Because he was the only one who could destroy the creation, he was the only unquestionable authority. He was the "lord of all he had created," "the Lord of the Universe."[17] Unlike his fellows, he could claim the title of king in an absolute, virtually atemporal sense. He was the First, the sovereign par excellence, the "god of gods," "the greatest of the great."[18] Yet we have seen how this rather categorical supremacy could be restricted, or even contested, by the combined operation of hierarchies and authorities. The very ambiguity of the royal function, which enabled gods other than the creator to gain at least temporary access to the dignity of this position, provoked frequent battles for supremacy. Moreover, these conflictual relations were not necessarily to be chalked up to the account of the most aggressive gods. Thus one finds the Lord of the Universe and Osiris engaging in a controversy, fought out in a long exchange of letters, over their respective prerogatives and powers.[19]

The creator and the reigning god each had a court, a suite of divine courtiers governed by the rules of etiquette already mentioned. Considered as groups, these courts did not possess sharp contours. Only the "corporation" of Heliopolis had a certain coherence. This family group of nine gods included the first three generations of the creator-god's descendants;[20] it was generally known as the *Ennead*. Although the creator-god belonged to it, he was not counted as one of its number: "unnumbered," he was simultaneously unique, as the first of the gods, and the tenth, that is, beyond the absolute totality represented by the number nine. As such, he embodied the guarantee that there would be a new cycle.[21] This familial organization provided a model that inevitably held a certain attraction for the divine community. The term *Ennead* eventually became a designation for groups of varying size, including more—sometimes many more—than nine gods; ultimately, it came to designate the whole community of the gods regarded as the organized entourage of the foremost god among them.[22] Lineage and the family unit thus become essential features in the life of the gods: they were the natural units of group life, on which vaster, more comprehensive structures often had a decidedly muted impact. As time wore on, the primacy of the nuclear family asserted itself. A god with his wife and son—a group constituting what is called a triad—became a virtually absolute model.[23] The triad formed by Osiris, Isis, and Horus was prototypical. Every Egyptian temple was organized around such a family group, in which the father-god had the main role and his son, a few exceptions aside, was a child. In this framework, the throng of other gods becomes a court, hierarchically organized in the temple according to the particular personality of its presiding divinity.

However, blood ties or relations of authority did not compel allegiance or respect in the secular sense alone. Even before men began to practice them, prayer and worship were required among the gods themselves to preserve the equilibrium of a creation which had been vulnerable from the very outset, as we have seen. Addressing prayers to the creator-god, for example,[24] was for the gods not simply a way of seeing their own wishes fulfilled, but also a means of participating, via their fulfilment, in re-establishing order in a world disturbed by their own actions. Thus even the creator-god had to establish a cult after the death and burial of the gods who had preceded creation. The assassination of Osiris extended this practice and gave it a new dimension. To the cult of these ancestors, whom Osiris joined, was added the complex process of mummification, which would make possible the regeneration of the god's dismembered body and, ultimately, his rebirth. The rites accompanying this metamorphosis of the body assured Osiris eternal life after death and associated all the gods with this renewal.[25] A simple cult intended to perpetuate the memory of an individual was thus elevated into a cult intended to perpetuate life as such.

Worship took place in the divine dwelling par excellence, the unique temple erected by the creator-god on the first land to appear after the defeat of the enemies of the cosmos. All of Egypt's temples were reflections of this first one. The practice of making offerings was instituted there as a necessary complement to the act of worship; this practice established a ritualization that gave rise to a new hierarchy, in which some gods could eventually become "more divine" than others.[26] That there should seem to be degrees of divinity is, however, partly an illusion due to the impossibility of finding modern equivalents capable of capturing the real semantic content of the words used by the ancients. The term we use to translate the Egyptian *netjer*, "god," obscures what the Egyptians perceived to be the true nature of the divine: netjer designated any entity which, because it transcended ordinary human reality, received a cult and became the object of a ritual.[27] Like the gods properly so called, the dead, as well as the king in his cultic functions, were netjer. A god was thus "more divine" than the others because he was more netjer, that is, because he was the object of a more elaborate or more important cult than others were. The sun-god, source of life, was a particularly good case in point, but so, finally, was every god in the temple in which he was master. For Osiris, this ritualization was, in the literal sense of the word, vital, because it was the life-giving rites performed by Isis that allowed him to become a "god" again,[28] to recover the divine status death seems to have robbed him of.

## Exercising Power

Except in the periods of crisis which called for his intervention and sometimes revealed his weaknesses, the supreme deity was generally quite inactive. It was Thoth, the god of wisdom, who, as a rule, exhorted the sovereign to take action or impelled him to make a decision by opportunely reminding him that he was master, that on such and such an occasion he had made a decision he must now enforce.[29] In cases of conflict, the opinion of the lord of the gods did not necessarily prevail; it might find itself in competion with that of other, more or less important personalities in the divine company.

One of the original features of the world of the Egyptian gods was that, in it, the exercise of supreme authority did not depend on the arbitrary will of a single individual. Though not subject to review, authority was nevertheless wielded with respect for certain norms. Although modern legal terminology is poorly adapted to the situation we are discussing here and must be used with extreme caution, we can say that there existed, if not "laws," then at least norms that governed the various facets of the life the gods lived together. One tradition claims that these rules were applied for the first time the day Seth was born,[30] because that was the day the first disorders broke out within the divine community. That fact by itself indicates that at least some of these rules existed before conflict had actually arisen and that they were established with a view to preserving the status quo. They were not necessarily dictated by individual cases or particular events: certain of them were products of the creator's inspiration or foresight.

The king of the gods was, theoretically, the unique source of this "law." He had every right to make decisions by himself; yet, as a rule, they came about only after debate and discussion. However, the creator could not promulgate and enforce decisions without Thoth's help. Thoth was the master cog in the machinery of divine administration. A veritable "prime minister" or "vizier," to employ the term in use among Egyptologists, he was constantly at his sovereign's side, giving him counsel, answering his questions, and suggesting solutions to problems the king submitted to him. This office of counselor was a prerogative that had been accorded him by the creator-god, who chose him over all others for the task.[31]

When he assumed office, Thoth apparently took an oath of allegiance, swearing to fulfil his obligations.[32]

The decisions made by the supreme deity had to be dictated to Thoth if they were to become operational: Thoth drew up copies of them and saw to it that these were made public.[33] So that no one would remain ignorant of a decision, the original text could be copied onto a stele and displayed for all to see.[34] Once a decision had been recorded in written form, Thoth personally saw to it that it was enforced, either by orally transmitting its contents to the party concerned, if what was involved was an individual case, or by informing the whole company of the gods in the same manner when the decision concerned a larger number. This meant that Thoth had to be constantly shuttling back and forth, which explains why he also served as the obligatory intermediary between the other gods (taken individually or collectively) and their sovereign, or why, again, he served as messenger: both these occupations flowed directly from his main function. The divine edicts bore on all aspects of the gods' daily life and on that of the people who lived among them as well. Indeed, every act performed by the creator-god was a creative act and thus constituted an edict. These "acts" were initially merely utterances. But they too were written down by Thoth and then repeated orally by him. By virtue of his capacity to write and transmit, Thoth directed and preserved the established order.[35] Basing himself on the creator's decisions, he laid down rules of conduct for the gods[36] and served as their spokesman when they wished to air grievances.[37]

Various other gods seem to have had the power to promulgate decrees the way the creator-god did, but such decrees were reiterations of the creator's, made necessary by the fact that these gods had their own spheres of responsibility and were charged with seeing to it that things ran smoothly in them.[38] Osiris was a special case. His dominion, the hereafter, was not subject to any authority based in the world of the living; the god of the dead did not hesitate to remind everyone of this from time to time. The discussions between the creator and Osiris concerning their respective prerogatives have already been alluded to. The netherworld came under a separate jurisdiction, as we would put it today. Hence one acquired the right to reside in the hereafter, to enter it, or to leave it, only if Osiris made a decision or issued a decree to that effect.[39] Osiris made all decisions required to ensure the well-being of those under his administration, and he did so with complete independence.[40]

The fact that the gods had a king assisted by a vizier did not mean that the community as a whole organized itself hierarchically on a pattern typical of the administration of a centralized state, in which each god would have had an office and an administrative title to go with it. Only one document, dating from the Roman period, claims that there existed a structure of this sort among the gods.[41] Administrative authority was, then, essentially limited to the two individuals already mentioned. This indicates, of course, that they could do the job by themselves; it also shows that the gods did not make up a diversified society requiring more elaborate communications networks to ensure the transmission of divine wishes. Individually or collectively, the gods were the first and last addressees of such wishes. Thoth's unique role as go-between drew all its import and significance from this state of affairs. Aside from the cases cited, then, the use of administrative titles was exceptional. Yet one is not surprised to find the Elder Horus occasionally sporting the title of "leader of the troops" of the sky-goddess, doubtless because of his capacity to lead the creator's armies in battle.[42]

## Assemblies and Law Courts

Among his major functions, Thoth was notably responsible for convoking the gods whenever this became necessary. When major upheavals occurred, the creator-god sought the advice of his fellow gods, whom he convened, as it were, in extraordinary session. There he presented the problem that had come up and heard the various opinions put forward by the others. Decisions were made in common, after a debate. They did not necessarily reflect the creator-god's first impulse. Such was the case during the litigation between Horus and Seth, as we shall see. Such was the case, again, when men rose up in revolt: on the advice of his fellow gods, the creator abandoned the idea of destroying the world, choosing to make it over instead.[43] One notes too that, before proceeding to massacre humankind, he sought the backing of the divine company.

If words of wisdom from Thoth sufficed to lay minor disputes to rest,[44] more serious conflicts between members of the divine community were settled at meetings or assemblies that acted as courts of law. In general, the creator-god presided over these assemblies, and Thoth served as judge.[45] But Maat, incarnation of cosmic order, could take Thoth's place.[46] A complaint or accusation directed against one or another member of the divine company would be brought before Re,[47] who decided whether or not to take action on the matter. Any god could find himself accused of wrongdoing, even those one might suppose to have been above suspicion, and all could incur a reprimand, Osiris or Maat not excepted.[48]

The best known case of this kind involved a complaint brought by Isis and Horus after the murder of Osiris.[49] As Seth, the murderer, had violently usurped Osiris's throne, the plaintiffs sought to recover what was rightfully theirs. Their claim was based, of course, on the law mandating that a father was normally to be succeeded by his son, with no interference from the brother of the deceased. The situation this drama created was a complex one. The kingdom, it will be recalled, had been divided in two: the South had been placed under Seth's authority, the North under Horus's. But this solution had taken into account neither the fundamental rights of the legitimate heir nor—inasmuch as it left the criminal unpunished—the fact that a crime had been committed. As to the duels that subsequently took place between the two antagonists, they did not resolve anything.

The Ennead was accordingly convened to sit in judgment on the matter. The Lord of the Universe presided over the assembly; Thoth directed the proceedings. Seated before the gods who were acting as judges, he read out the charges against Seth. This worthy then took the floor, opening his plea, of course, by denying the facts. More precisely, he accused Osiris of being the aggressor, claiming that he had only exercised his right to legitimate self-defense: "I did not do that . . . he is the one who grabbed me . . . he attacked *me*."[50] A number of gods pointed out that right should prevail over might and that Horus was plainly the legitimate heir to the throne. Thoth concurred; Isis, assuming that her son had carried the day, rejoiced. But she had failed to give due consideration to the sensibilities of the king of the gods, who, not without annoyance, saw that the issue was on the way to being settled before he had voiced an opinion. He let his displeasure be known: "What is the meaning of this, that you are making a decision all by yourselves?"[51] Seth took advantage of the creator's unexpected remarks to propose that he and Horus settle the question of the inheritance in single combat, with the throne to go to the stronger. He obviously thought that young Horus would not be able to stand up under the assaults of an experienced warrior like himself. Thoth, who was not duped by the stratagem, very wisely asked: "Are we not trying to determine who is in the wrong?" This remark threw the king of the gods into another fit of rage: unconcerned with the right and wrong of the matter, he wished to see Seth keep the power he had acquired by the murder, for he was counting on the assistance the murderer's proven strength and valor could provide him when it came to conducting the world's affairs. The company of the gods protested, whereupon it was agreed that it would be necessary to get an outside opinion. Ptah and the ram-god of Mendes were accordingly summoned to appear before the court. But these two gods, displaying a certain faintheartedness, pleaded their ignorance of the details of the affair and requested further information. Their attitude was astonishing, because the litigation had already been slogging on, as we learn along the way, for eighty years. What is more, the main lines of the case were well-known to all. Thus the two experts wormed their way out of the matter as best they could, doubtless so as not to have to take sides. Reluctantly, the divine tribunal then turned to Neith of Sais for advice. But as Neith was an important personage, there could be no question of issuing her a summons; rather, it was decided to send her a letter, which the creator-god proceeded to dictate to Thoth. The creator began with a plaint. While Sobek, he said, Neith's son, gave his mother no cause for concern, he, the king of the gods, had a son who had conceived the unhappy idea of getting himself killed, a circumstance that was causing him no end of trouble as far as the royal succession was concerned. He had decided to put the matter in the goddess's hands: "Tell us what we have to do." This time, the king received a response devoid of all ambiguity. What was right was right: Horus's father's legacy should be restored to him. At the same time, the goddess suggested, not without finesse, that Seth should be awarded compensation to prevent the conflict from dragging on forever; she had clearly sensed that he would feel aggrieved. When this letter was read out, the assembly of the gods was jubilant, believing that Neith had found a compromise solution acceptable to all. However, the creator-god flew into another rage when he saw that his desire to tip the scales in Seth's favor despite everything was about to be thwarted. He accused young Horus of being too weak and callow for the heavy responsibility he coveted. The confusion now reached its peak. The gods were furious; one of them, Babi, whom we will meet again, forgot himself to the point of gravely insulting the Lord of the Universe. Shocked and hurt, the creator-god, draping himself in his dignity, withdrew to his apartments in a sulk. With that, the assembly found itself adjourned sine die; it therefore dispersed, each of the gods returning to his usual occupations. The trial was now completely deadlocked, at least for as long as the king of the gods remained holed up in his quarters.

Hathor resolved to do something to prevent this situation from dragging on indefinitely. Going to see her father, she hiked up her skirts to put him in a better mood. The uplifting effects this gesture had on the gods' depressive states were well-known.[52] In this instance, it brought immediate results. The king of the gods went back to his post and the trial resumed. The respective positions of plaintiff and defendant had not changed. Seth continued to draw attention to his strength, knowing that the creator-god would be receptive to this argument. A majority of the gods continued to insist that the law should be respected, though a few preferred to butter up the master and his protégé. While the gods were trying to bring their stubborn sovereign to reason, Horus and Seth met in single combat outside the courtroom; this did not, however, result in a workable resolution of the conflict. Doubtless the affair would never have come to an end if Thoth had not proposed, in a last-ditch effort, to seek the mediation of Osiris, Horus's father. The Lord of the Universe granted Thoth's request; Osiris was accordingly consulted by letter, as Neith had been. The hereafter was hard to reach, and the letters traveled slowly. But a response from Osiris finally arrived. As might be expected, he warmly espoused his son's cause, expressing his astonishment at the fact that the child of a god as powerful as he was should be ill-treated. The creator-god thereupon conspicuously pulled rank on the god of the underworld, reminding Osiris that *he* had single-handedly created everything that existed. Nothing daunted, Osiris remarked, ironically: "Everything you have made is very beautiful indeed, O inventor of the Ennead! Yet justice has been permitted to be swallowed up in the netherworld." What had happened proved abundantly, he suggested, that justice had deserted the world of the gods. For good measure, he threatened the divine company with a visit from his irresistible emissaries of death, if they did not yield to the principle of justice. So terrible was this threat that it produced total agreement without further ado. It should be noted that the emissaries in question had absolute authority over anyone who wrought evil, regardless of who he might be. The upshot was a rather comic turnabout in the situation. The Lord of the Universe, rudely addressing Seth, whom he had been defending only a moment ago, asked: "Why do you resist being judged and then try to take for yourself the office that belongs to Horus?" Amid the general access of hypocrisy, Seth, not to be outdone, feigned astonishment: "Nothing of the sort, my good lord! Let Horus the son of Isis be summoned and let him be given the office of his father Osiris." The case was then heard and Horus was accorded the white crown he lacked, so that he could now reign over the two halves of the country, at last reunited.[53]

If, from the very beginning of the proceedings, the gods declared that Seth, guilty of his brother's murder, was in the wrong, right nevertheless won out only with difficulty: nothing but the most terrible of threats had induced the king of the gods to back down. He did not yield unconditionally: he demanded that the condemned party be put under his charge in the solar boat, to help him battle the cosmic enemies. As we have already seen, Seth's resentment was not assuaged for all that: his aggressive acts and dirty tricks were ultimately to result in his being banished from Egypt. From start to finish, this affair showed up the divine clan's hesitations and ulterior motives, which had had a powerful influence on the course of a trial in which personal interests involving each god's place in the hierarchy took precedence over elementary justice. The partiality of the king of the gods, obvious here, was not peculiar to his position; the gods' frequent lack of objectivity is mentioned elsewhere as well.[54] Such prejudice affected even the individual whose role was supposed to be that of neutral, even-handed arbiter—Thoth himself. The story of another trial will convince us of this.

Thoth and Babi were once involved in a dispute whose precise nature is not stated.[55] Babi did not enjoy a very good reputation among the gods. Violent, lewd, coarse—we have already seen him insult the Lord of the Universe—he held the post of executioner of the damned, hardly the sort of occupation to inspire confidence. To settle his controversy with Thoth, the Great and the Small Enneads (the Heliopolitan family and the other gods) were convened; their members were to act not only as judges, but also as witnesses for the prosecution. Thoth ushered them into the presence of the king of the gods, who demanded to hear their views on the matter. But, curiously, they preferred to remain silent. Babi thereupon decided to go on the offensive: he accused Thoth of pilfering offerings intended for Re. One of Thoth's responsibilities was to apportion offerings among the gods: the accusation was, consequently, a serious one, bearing as it did on a matter of vital importance. Furthermore, it implied that Thoth was not impartial and thus incapable of playing the role of arbiter. When they heard what Babi had to say, the gods of the two Enneads conveniently found their tongues again: they began bandying words like "scandal" and "lies," affirming at the same time, however, that they had seen nothing. This allowed Thoth to declare that Babi was in the wrong, despite the fact that the complaints of the two parties had not yet been examined, nor even so much as stated. Thoth thus avoided having to respond to the charge brought against him by the plaintiff. Only after he himself had pronounced sentence against his adversary did the king of the gods confirm it: "Thoth is right, and Babi is in the wrong." Obviously, the whole affair was rigged. Thoth was simultaneously judge and, in the fullest sense of the term, party to the action; Re, the supreme divinity, did not step in to influence the course of the proceedings, letting himself be swayed by the prevailing view of the matter. The two Enneads, after sizing up the opposing parties, betrayed their opportunism. Thoth, as we know, was an influential member of the divine company and the creator's right arm; Babi, notwithstanding his prerogatives, was held in small esteem. His case was therefore disposed of in a travesty of a trial. Of course, he continued to level accusations, "to speak ill of Thoth once again," as our text roundly declares. To silence him, Thoth did not hesitate to make use of his magic powers with a view to humiliating him and holding him up to public ridicule. The injustice involved here was the more flagrant in that the accusation Babi had brought against Thoth was perfectly well founded—we know this from other sources—and that the members of the two Enneads were aware of the truth of the matter.

The story is worth telling.[56] A clever, well-informed dead man wanted special protection from Thoth. To force the god to grant him this favor, he threatened to reveal a dirty secret if Thoth failed to comply with his request: "If you do not listen to what I say, I won't hesitate to reveal that you stole the offerings of the gods of the Ennead on the day of their festival, the night Thoth was completely hidden" (that is, the night of the new moon). Thoth, god of the moon, had in fact manipulated time so as to cut the lunar month back to less than the ideal thirty days. He was thus able to divert all unattributed offerings to his own use in the time that elapsed between the shortened and the thirty-day month. We learn, moreover, that the affair was more serious than it appears. Thoth was alleged to have served as Seth's accomplice in stealing certain parts of Osiris's dismembered body, doubtless with an eye to putting off the day when it would be reconstituted, thus disturbing, precisely, the flow of time. One sees, then, that Babi did not make anything up and also that the Ennead could not have been ignorant of Thoth's misdeed.

Whatever might have occurred in individual cases, the rules that governed the functioning of the divine tribunal are clear, at least in their broad outlines. The Ennead, which constituted the deliberative assembly, did not include all the gods. From a modern point of view, its members had extensive prerogatives: they were simultaneously judges, jurors, and witnesses for the prosecution or defense, depending on the case. The Lord of the Universe, who presided over the tribunal, and Thoth, who acted as court clerk and arbitrator, could assume one another's roles. It seems that, without them, court sessions could not legally take place. Whenever required, outside witnesses could be called. They were summoned to appear before the court or, alternatively, consulted by exchange of messengers. This distinction in the way witnesses were consulted doubtless depended as much on their rank in the hierarchy as on their geographical distance from the court. Plaintiffs and defendants pleaded their own cause, although, according to certain sources, both could seek the assistance of counsel.[57] Before a verdict could be handed down, it was apparently mandatory that the assembly, its president, and the arbitrator concur. In the absence of such unanimity, litigation could be pursued for a long time. Apparently no mechanism had been devised to resolve the difficulties such a situation inevitably entailed. Sentences were pronounced by Thoth with the approval of the creator-god.[58] They could be promulgated in a royal ordinance, which was drawn up in writing and, sometimes, inscribed on a stele for all to see. A text informs us that a counsel for the condemned party rose and covered his face with his hands when a sentence was pronounced.[59] It is not known whether this is just a picturesque touch or whether it reflects normal practice in such a situation. If one lends credence to the stories related above, the loser was, in general, left to the disposition of the winner. Thus Seth was condemned to carry the dead Osiris around on his back forever, or, in other versions of the story, to be put to death by Horus. The principle of abandoning the condemned party, and even close members of his family, to the person who had gotten the better of him is alluded to on other occasions as well.[60]

The texts mention a goodly number of divine law courts, but nothing indicates that different institutions were meant each time. These courts were identified by the name of the locality where they sat.[61] It is possible that what was involved was a single tribunal that traveled from place to place, depending on the cases it had to try. Thus the court of Heliopolis, which heard the case of Horus versus Seth, did not hesitate to travel about in order to conduct proceedings in a number of very different places; its proceedings could even took place in the open air.[62] If, on one occasion, this change of venue was justified by a need to find a calmer locality to ensure the serenity of the proceedings, the reason for this administrative nomadism is not known in any of the other instances.

Divine assemblies were not held for the sole purpose of rendering justice. Meetings also took place on the sovereign's initiative. Their objective might be, for example, to inform the gods about the state or progress of the universe. Apparently, those who had assisted the creator when he created the universe took part in these assemblies.[63] Among the various divine institutions, one merits particular attention: it was known as the Assembly Which Governs the Waters. In a country whose entire economy depended on the annual inundation of the Nile, the regulation of this phenomenon was seen to by a group of gods organized in a collegium.[64] These individuals lived on the confines of the world, the fringes of the sky, or in a small town south of Heliopolis. They were charged with attending to the regular return of the rise of the Nile, adjusting the water level, and ensuring an equitable distribution of the water over the whole land. One of them went as far as Nubia to find the floodwaters, fetch them back to Egypt, and conduct them all the way to the Delta. The most important task assigned these gods was to measure the rise of the waters with extreme precision, so as to bring them to the ideal level, neither too high nor too low, thus guaranteeing optimal irrigation of the land and the best possible harvests.

## Servants and Acolytes

The gods were assisted in their various tasks by aides, sometimes even by groups of servants, called "teams" or "troops."[65] Of course, there were domestics, almost always anonymous, whose function was to attend to the gods' small daily needs. One suspects that there was also a host of "little helpers," charged with humble tasks, whose presence can barely be made out behind the word "one": "one did" this or that for a god.[66] But the best structured groups were made up of lesser powers created to obey blindly; the gods used them to demonstrate their might or make their wishes known, both to other gods and to men. Usually armed with long knives as well as bows and arrows, they constituted a sort of personal guard charged with protecting their master from his foes. For example, Osiris, enfeebled by death, had a special need for strong, vigilant bodyguards.[67] The activities of these heavily armed creatures were not limited to defensive tasks alone. Osiris's guards, "of the pointed fingers and painful blades," were responsible for keeping the hereafter supplied with the damned.[68] We have seen that the mere threat of an intervention by these guards was sufficient to overcome the creator-god's pigheadedness during the litigation between Horus and Seth. The most famous of these teams of guards, but also the one it is hardest to identify precisely, was the group of messengers placed under the responsibility of the "dangerous" goddess, whatever form she might take (generally, Sakhmet). They were closely associated with the vengeful, punitive aspect of the solar eye, from which they were supposed to have issued.[69] Seven in number, they simultaneously personified the seven creative words pronounced at the beginning of the world and the seven arrows the dangerous goddess shot at the cosmic enemies; they were identical with the seven decans who accompanied the sun,[70] a circumstance that, for obvious reasons, ensured their periodic return. They were by nature ubiquitous. No miscreant could elude them, so swift were they and so sure of the mark were the darts they shot or spat.[71]

Of course, these emissaries could engage in more peaceful pursuits, serving, for example, as messengers or couriers. Osiris employed his to communicate news of the hereafter to the outside world.[72] Sometimes they had more surprising tasks. Thus Horus's messengers regularly retrieved the magic power that their master had permitted to stray far from his person.[73] As this power of his was quite simply the eye Seth had stolen from him,[74] it is easy to guess why a whole squadron of emissaries was required to get it back. We do not know whether this squadron was identical with the group of "confederates" who lent Horus a hand in his battles with Seth.[75] At any rate, in plotting and executing his crimes, Seth benefited from the aid of acolytes, often mentioned in the texts. Some of them, however, deserted him after his defeat, going over to Horus.[76]

This whole subgroup of the divine population led action-filled lives and carried out extremely varied tasks. The same cannot be said of all divine groups. Some were assigned very precise roles, or even a single, unique activity. This was true of the contingent posted to the divine estate (created when the world began) on which the ideal temple stood. These guards stood watch over this restricted area, which had to be preserved from impurity and protected at all times against hostile forces. Their role consisted, precisely, in not abandoning their post. They were organized in four companies, each of which defended one of the four cardinal points, forming an eternally impregnable, immutable rampart.[7] The crew of the boat the sun sailed in also belonged to this group of specialists. In principle, there was nothing warlike about their role, even if it seems likely that they took an active part in combating the monster Apophis. Without "ever knowing rest,"[78] they were supposed unfailingly to carry out their tasks of joyful rowers, eternally completing the daily circuit that made it possible for the sun to shine over every part of this world and the next in turn. In this respect, they differed from the crew of Osiris's bark, which on certain days devoted itself to hunting down Seth's confederates, given to hiding among the gods.[79]

The emissaries with multiple tasks could assume all manner of forms, human or animal. Thus Babi liked to travel in the company of seventy-seven dogs, who were identical with his acolytes.[80] These creatures had no personality of their own; their will was confounded with Babi's, so entirely were they emanations of their master. Their numbers could be multiplied indefinitely. Osiris's emissaries were born of his morbid discharges; Sakhmet's, as was already noted, had emerged from the solar eye, that is, from the goddess herself. It is possible that Seth's confederates were an exception to the general rule, that they were not mere clones of their master. Indeed, it seems that, on occasion, this group had opinions that diverged from his.[81]

Besides these groups or teams of servants, every nook and cranny of the world could harbor isolated genies. Their highly specialized tasks and narrowly circumscribed domains located them at the bottom of the scale of divine beings. It is known that some could be created by the gods virtually as the demand arose, and at any given moment. The genies known as *uryts*, who lived for the most part in water or moist environments, were all created for specific purposes. They were of such humble rank that human beings could occasionally keep one for personal use.[82]

## Defectors and Foreign Gods

Its compartmentalization and intensely local character notwithstanding, the organization of the divine realm was not entirely impenetrable for defectors come from elsewhere. Though they were associated with areas lying beyond Egypt's borders—and we shall see what kind of suspicion foreign countries could arouse—foreign gods ultimately accommodated themselves to the land of the pharaohs without undue difficulty. As early as the Old Kingdom, a god named Khay-tau, who apparently hailed from Byblos, found himself a niche in the Pyramid Texts as guardian of the celestial gates. He was later replaced by his colleague Reshep.[83] It is possible that the goddess Baalat makes a discreet appearance in the Coffin Texts, in which she seems to play the role of a demon hostile to the dead.[84] The New Kingdom period, richest in these borrowings, was the one in which the pharaohs carved out an empire in the Near East.[85] However, the Egyptians adopted only a small number of foreign divinities. One of the most interesting facts about these newcomers is that they came to Egypt with their original competencies and in their own mythic context.[86]

An unfortunately fragmentary narrative featuring the goddess Astarte reveals, in passing, how it was that she came to figure in the Egyptian pantheon.[87] The gods of Egypt found themselves, for reasons unknown to us, exposed to the depredations of Yamm, god of the sea. Yamm, who had an irascible temperament and imperialistic inclinations, made up his mind to demand tribute from them, much to their displeasure. He threatened to throw them all into prison if they failed to obey, and apparently had the means to make good his threat. Reluctant to brave this very powerful intruder, whom they were incapable, in any case, of confronting head-on, the gods decided to play for time by complying with his demand. Renenutet, goddess of harvests, was charged with taking him what he had demanded. But these gifts did not suffice. At a loss as to what they should do, the gods sent a messenger to Astarte; the messenger went to the land of the "Asiatics," if we understand the text correctly. Arriving at the goddess's house, he called to her through the window of her bedroom, where she was apparently sleeping. From this point on, the story refers to her as the "daughter of Ptah"; the latter plays the role of creator-god in this text. Astarte agreed to help the gods, whom we are next shown, without any transition, singing and laughing as they stroll along a beach. The voyage that brought them here must have been long and arduous: the text says that Astarte's sandals were full of holes and her clothes in tatters. But, despite this attire, which aroused Yamm's pity, the god, charmed, immediately fell in love. He promised he would drop his demands if the goddess were given to him in marriage. Meanwhile, Astarte was welcomed into the Ennead by the grateful gods, amid pomp worthy of the greatest figures in the pantheon. But there was a problem: the goddess had to be provided with a trousseau. This afforded Yamm, decidedly little averse to breaking his word, yet another opportunity to display his excessive fondness for gifts. Nut, goddess of the sky, had to surrender her pearl necklace; Geb, god of the earth, had to sacrifice his ring. All these objects were carefully weighed on a scale. The end of the story is mutilated, but two significant facts can be made out. Yamm continued to up the ante, threatening to flood the earth and mountains. It may be that he wanted nothing less than to become king of all the gods. In the end, Seth appeared on the scene—to do battle, we are told. He had already acquired considerable fame by calming the raging waters, and one is perhaps justified in assuming that he ultimately defeated the presumptuous sea-god, restoring peace to the divine company.

Another story, known from a few equally fragmentary sources, features the goddess Anat.[88] She is introduced to us as a woman "who acts like a warrior, who dresses like a man," a characteristic stemming from her non-Egyptian origins. Yet it was this special trait that enabled her to join the Egyptian pantheon as Seth's wife. Seth was well-known for his homosexual inclinations, so that a somewhat manly, or even quick-tempered and aggressive wife, was not ill-suited to his temperament. What is more, Seth was quite easily identified with Baal, who may have been Anat's brother or husband. It is not completely clear what role was assigned to Anat. After Seth had taken sexual advantage of a goddess named "Seed" or "Venom"—the two words are identical in Egyptian—the goddess threw herself at his face and bored her way into his forehead. Anat, astonishingly tractable and cooperative, even though Seth had been unfaithful to her, went to Re and asked him to deliver her husband from this seed that he was carrying around inside him and that was causing him great suffering. This is, then, a variation on the myth—we will have occasion to come back to it—in which Seth is tormented by Horus's semen.[89] Anat may be nothing more here than a surrogate for Nephthys, the childless woman who is Seth's Egyptian wife.

Other foreign divinities were more or less successfully absorbed into Egyptian mythology. Thus Kothar, known in Ugaritic religion as the architect who built Baal's palace, put his talents at the disposal of the Egyptian gods, constructing their chapels and becoming their servant.[90] It is even known that he had acolytes, executioners charged with putting condemned men to death.[91]

The criteria according to which newcomers were selected for admission into the pantheon are not always clear, the more so as foreign gods are not always included in mythical accounts, at least not in the sources currently available to us.[92] A comparison of Egyptian narratives with those in other Near Eastern religions that mention the same gods, reveals that the Egyptian religion did not content itself with borrowing individual figures and endowing them with a meaning adapted to its own needs; it also borrowed characters and types whose *functions* made them of interest. That is, the original mythical context of each of these gods was given due consideration. It was because this context contained elements analogous to those in one or another properly Egyptian myth that the exogenous divinity could take his place among the Egyptian gods. Yet the exogenous gods did not quite fit into spaces that had been left vacant, nor could they be perfectly superimposed onto existing figures. Rather, the Egyptian religion simply adopted one aspect or facet of a deity closely associated with foreign lands. The role of such a god was, as a result, rarely a prominent one; certain of these divinities even occupied a fairly subaltern rank in the hierarchy. The process of integration implied establishing a certain equivalence between the foreign culture involved and the Egyptian mode of thought. In this respect, the phenomenon was, despite appearances, different from the one that would appear in the Greco-Roman period, in which contact with an outside culture did not lead to the introduction of new personalities into the indigenous pantheon. In Greco-Roman times, the Egyptian gods, although remaining unchanged at home, underwent the effects of a double transposition. The first, which had to do with their names, permitted non-Egyptian thought to grasp the identity of a god who would otherwise have remained totally opaque and unintelligible: thus Thoth took the name of Hermes. The second involved the god's underlying personality and the way it was rendered in the iconography. In effect, a new god was created in whom one finds certain essential traits proper to both cultures in syncretistic combination. This result was a hybrid god whom the foreign culture could appropriate and who was also easier to export. Thereafter, he no longer quite belonged to Egyptian civilization properly so called.

From a strictly historical point of view, the elements borrowed from Near Eastern religions came to Egypt in the context of the close political and economic relations the country established with its neighbors, especially in the New Kingdom. Egyptian civil servants who had lived abroad, and, above all, foreign communities of slaves, artisans, and merchants established in Egypt, were the vehicles of this transfer. But the integration of foreign gods into Egyptian cults could not have taken place without royal consent or even support. This phenomenon falls within the purview of *human* history. Yet the integration of these foreign gods into mythical narrative was calculated to draw them into the daily lives of the Egyptian *gods*. In this setting, the new gods behaved as if they had always been present; they discovered family ties that, in a certain sense, negated their foreignness. For a long time, Seth and Hathor had been the only gods in the Egyptian pantheon to incarnate the foreign—with Seth personifying its masculine, Hathor its feminine aspects. The role that had thus devolved upon them was not free of a certain opacity. The ambivalent status of the outside world, which had both positive and negative aspects, was reproduced in these two gods, and at the very heart of the Egyptian pantheon; this ambivalence ruled out all possibility of a graduated transition between the organized Egyptian world and the chaos beyond it. The arrival of foreign gods tore a breach in this way of appropriating the outside, making it possible to define the attributes of both Hathor and Seth with greater precision. Hathor once again discovered her inclination for gentleness and love, and, without disappearing, her sexuality was more or less shorn of its excesses: to a certain extent, she passed on her sexual immoderation and warlike passions to sisters come from elsewhere. Seth was progressively confined to the role of exile and intruder, or even foreigner, whereas the new arrivals came to incarnate the positive values he himself had once embodied. The fact that foreign divinities could now lend a hand to the Egyptian gods in their struggle against Seth served to integrate them as agents who helped maintain the just order of the world.[93] These gods thus showed that order could be extended beyond the frontiers of the ideal creation that was Egypt and so suggested that the frontiers of chaos were perhaps farther off than had been thought. Henceforth there would be, between this ideal creation and chaos, a buffer zone; its dimensions, always ready to shrink, would vary with the vicissitudes of history. The foreign gods stood as evidence that human history had irrupted into the divine realm; the Egyptian gods no longer simply offered a model for history, but were themselves now subject to it. It has been observed that the Egyptians never brought images of foreign gods back to Egypt along with the rich plunder they amassed during their wars of conquest, whereas Egypt's conquerors never failed to carry off statues ripped from the temples of their vanquished foe.[94] This very captivity was the triumph of a certain vision of the world; it presaged the later dispersion of the Egyptian gods, voluntary this time, throughout the Mediterranean Basin. But their migration beyond the cradle of creation inevitably transformed them: subjecting them to rituals different from those they had known in Egypt, it served notice of their impending demise.[95]

# CHAPTER THREE

# Divine Bodies

The gods recognized one other, used one other's names, conversed. There was, then, something that differentiated one from the next; it ordinarily expressed itself in physical terms. The general assumption was that the gods had bodies and faces that endowed them with a perceptible identity and served as indispensable reference points in their communal life. A god's body had a certain materiality, inasmuch as it could be wounded or maimed, and its owner could die if it was destroyed. As with human beings, this body ensured the reproduction of the species; under certain circumstances, it could develop or undergo the changes brought on by the different stages of life. But these very familiar characteristics turn out to be no more than fleeting appearances as soon as one attempts to define the divine body as such. Its unity dissolves into a multitude of aspects; yet the sum of these parts does not represent the whole. The pain a divine body suffered did not affect it in its entirety. In everything one thinks one has succeeded in grasping about such a body, there always remains a certain indescribable remainder. Every god's body was shaped as much by the god's fate as by his free will.

## Inexpressible Bodies, Revealed Bodies

That it would be necessary to have a recognizable physical identity was evident to the gods from the very beginning. While still immersed in the Primeval Ocean, the creator-god took pains to differentiate the faces of the first beings.[1] Every god's characteristic features could be inherited as the son of a god might look like his father.[2] Generally speaking, it fell to Khnum, the potter-god, to conceive the forms of the gods as well as those of people or animals. He was believed to mold them all on his potter's wheel, relying only on the force of his breath; the nature of the clay he used was not known.[3] The special powers he possessed enabled him to destroy the body of the cosmic enemy Apophis, as well as those of his progeny.[4] A divine form created by Khnum constituted a totality that could not be apprehended in and of itself, for such a form coincided with the very being of the god it belonged to. It lay beyond what could be known or described and could only be grasped—imperfectly at that—through its projections. These projections constituted the *kheperu*, which corresponded to the series of ephemeral individual forms, indefinite in number, that a divinity was capable of assuming. None of them could encompass the totality of what a god was. Yet the passage from one to the other, although it showed that a god was caught up in a process of constant evolution, did not constitute a metamorphosis of his fundamental being. Each of these forms was a facet of the god in which he was fully implied. By adopting a kheperu, a god created for himself the possibility of signifying a state of his being or distinguishing one of his actions by individualizing it. To enter such a state or perform such an act was to inscribe the kheperu in visible reality. This projection, called the *iru*, was a perceptible, intelligible manifestation of the god, accentuated, as a rule, by various material attributes.[5] In the course of his journey through the sky, from sunrise to sunset, the sun passed through different stages making up so many kheperu: the most important of them bore the names Khepri, Re, and Atum. At various points in the story of Seth's and Horus's quarrels, which we have already referred to a number of times, the Lord of the Universe was called, indifferently, Re, Re-Harakhti, Atum, Re-Atum, or Khepri; yet the gods never made a mistake as to the unique identity of the individual in question.[6] The fact that major gods could, each in his turn, act as kheperu with respect to the others shows that the divine entity "sun-god" surpassed all the rest and could be apprehended only by approximation. To each of the different stages of the sun's journey there corresponded different iru, tangible, recognizable signs of the sun on his course: the scarab beetle, the falcon, the old man with a ram's head, and many more. Indeed, so difficult was it to dissociate the kheperu from the iru that the two terms could sometimes function as near synonyms in the texts. No one form was the exclusive property of a single divinity. Even the best-known identity of each god could be temporarily assumed by another, to various ends. Isis was transformed into Sakhmet the better to crush her husband's enemies; Seth took on the aspect of Anubis to hoodwink the guardians of Osiris's tomb.[7]

If it is clear that people recognized a god mainly in his iru and could come to perceive kheperu only by dint of religious and spiritual practices,[8] a question naturally arises as to the form in which the gods appeared before and recognized one another. It should be noted that the facial differences referred to earlier had essentially to do with iru.[9] However, each god could have secret kheperu or iru, unknown to the others.[10] This implies that both levels could be perceived in the divine world, but only if the god concerned wanted them to be. The very nature of these manifestations, like the game of hide-and-seek they could give rise to, makes it plain that the body of a god was inconceivable in the absence of a gaze directed at it. It is because they were made to be seen that the gods sometimes chose to hide. Failure to recognize a god when he appeared sometimes merely served to put off the moment when he *was* finally identified, thus creating an effect of surprise that, by focusing attention on him, constituted a kind of revelation. Thus, when a certain god arrived in grand pomp, and the others wondered, "Who is the god who is manifesting himself there?," the new-comer explained: "I cut off my umbilical cord and made myself a braided beard; and now I manifest myself as Hapy!"—that is, the god of the Nile flood.[11] This was apparently not obvious to the divine assembly. But we are told that Re "distinguished his form from the (other) gods."[12] If our understanding of the text is correct, we here witness the creation of a divine form in which the others would henceforth be able to recognize the god in question.[13] The same procedure came into play when Isis was beheaded by her son. Catching sight of the goddess after she had been changed into a headless statue, the creator-god asked Thoth, "Who is this new arrival who has no head?" Thoth replied, "My good lord, it is Isis . . . Horus, her child, has chopped off her head." Both anecdotes display the same pattern. A question is asked about a god who is regarded as a newcomer; the response makes it possible to establish his or her identity by describing the new attributes defining it. By way of such verbal exchange, which forges a link between the god's attributes and his name, the god enters the community's "field of knowledge."[14]

The gods involved in the cases just mentioned either wished to make themselves known or else had a need for recognition; this justified their resorting to the procedure we have just described, equivalent to the issuance of an identity card. Not submitting to this procedure sufficed to give a god an appearance even his fellow gods could not recognize. This might be a means of self-protection in case of threat; but it could also serve to fool others. Isis was particularly good at the latter sort of exercise. The other gods were not unaware of this and surrounded themselves with precautions to avoid being duped—frequently to no avail. Such was the case, for example, during the litigation between Horus and

Seth.[15] To spare Seth's sensibilities and prevent Isis from influencing an assembly already overly inclined to embrace her cause, it was decided that court would be held on an island to which Isis would be barred access. The assembly could maintain contact with the outside world only by ferryboat.[16] The ferryman, Nemty, received express orders not to ferry any woman resembling the goddess across the water: the accent was on the notion of resemblance and the goddess's ability to assume different outward forms. Isis thereupon showed up in the guise of a poor old woman. Nemty, of course, was suspicious, and pointed out that he had been forbidden to transport any woman whatsoever. One notes the shift in the way the prohibition was defined. Originally, it applied only to any-one who resembled Isis; but it ended up being applied to all women, as if the ferryman was not unaware that the goddess could appear in any feminine form she chose. Isis, however, was well acquainted with the ferryman's greed, and bribed him with a golden ring. Nemty should have been more cautious; everyone knew that the "old woman" was the form—the iru—that Isis assumed to manifest her status as a widow, as well as her magic powers.[17] Once she had reached the place where the deliberations were taking place, Isis abandoned this humble exterior, changing into a beautiful young girl. To the extent that all the gods were supposed to be young and beautiful, it was doubtless not her beauty that made her unrecognizable, but rather the fact that her new appearance was not one of the goddess's known manifestations. Catching sight of her from afar, Seth, an inveterate skirt-chaser, could not help but fall madly in love with her. She took advantage of this to make him look ridiculous in front of his peers, thus weakening his position in the litigation in prog-ress. The ferryman, Nemty, was severely punished for his disobedience. His toes were cut off and he was required to abjure the gold which had led him into temptation.[18] Such treatment would have been excessive if his error had consisted in failing to recognize someone who had made herself unrecognizable. Plainly, given that it was possible for him to iden-tify Isis, he was taken to task for yielding to bribery.

This episode is instructive in that it tends to show, if one takes what it says literally, that the gods' natural, everyday form was purely human.[19] On the other hand, it should be kept in mind that statements to the effect that a person or a king resembled a god or was the living image of a god referred to a function he performed, not to a physical resemblance. It is by no means obvious that, for the Egyptians, the beings the creator made were fashioned in his own image.[20] One should also note that Isis could only appear as a woman, and, furthermore, that the prohibition barring access to the gods' meeting-place applied exclusively to women. This shows that there was a barrier divine metamorphoses could not over-come: that of the sexes.

Aside from its formal aspect and the modes in which it could be recognized, the materiality of the divine body was ambivalent. At the very beginning of the world, the very substance of these bodies did not yet exist: it would not be created until after the first dry land had been taken possession of.[21] We will see further on that divine bodies could be mutilated and could bleed; this might lead one to suppose that they were made of flesh. Moreover, the word *flesh* was frequently used in speaking of the gods' bodies. But their ability to get over the worst sort of injuries plainly shows that divine flesh was not of the human sort. Only in the case of divine enemies under torture were the gods' bodies clearly depicted as fleshly [*charnel*]—one might even say meaty [*carné*]. But these enemies had undergone a transmutation, assimilated as they were to human beings or sacrificial animals at the moment of their execution. Such cases excepted, the bodies of gods were generally described as being made of precious minerals. Their flesh was gold, their bones silver, their hair lapis lazuli.[22] This lent them a radiance, an aura, that made a god a being "robed in brilliance and wrapped in turquoise."[23] The sun-god was so effulgent that he hid himself from the gaze of his own children.[24] On the Egyptian conception, stones never grew old; they lasted forever.[25] Thus divine bodies were thought to be impervious to change: that is why even Osiris's dead body could not really rot or decompose.[26] By their makeup or color, minerals constituted a set of signs that allow us to form some notion of what the complexion of the gods may have been like. As their flesh was of gold, it may reasonably be supposed that they had a coppery complexion, Egyptian gold being not yellow, but reddish.[27] Their hair, the color of lapis lazuli, must have been black with glints of blue: today we would describe them as "raven-haired."[28] Isis was, par excellence, "she of the black hair and coppery skin."[29] All this is a poetic transposition of the ordinary physical characteristics of an Egyptian, in ancient times as well as today. If a god did not conform to this standard, this was above all a way of signaling that he possessed a special power. For example, gods who had black or blue skin showed by this that they possessed powers of regeneration.[30] But it was above all eye color—whether or not it was compared to that of minerals—that most conspicuously betrayed certain attributes or character traits of a god. Horus's eyes were the color of lapis lazuli—that is, a very dark blue.[31] They continued to display their color, if indirectly, after having been gouged out and buried by Seth. In one version of this legend, they sprouted and brought forth lotuses[32] (light blue); in another, grapes (blue-black).[33] All these shades of blue are colors the sky can take on. The sun's eyes, when he was shining, were of electrum.[34] Seth's black eyes[35] indicated his connection with darkness, whereas Atum's green eyes[36] were reminders that he had originally been a serpent. Red eyes, eyes of coal glowing in the night, were characteristic of feline or predatory gods;[37] they underscored these gods' dangerous, aggressive character.

As it had a form and consisted of matter, a divine body manifested its presence in different ways, depending on whether it was to be seen by gods or people. For the latter, a divinity was omnipresent: he or she saw and heard all, everywhere. It was a commonplace to say that a god had seventy-seven eyes and seventy-seven ears.[38] Of course, this hyperbole was not intended as a description of real physical characteristics. The same holds for the expression that made the sun-god a man one million cubits tall. The creator-god's body was believed to encompass all creation as the creation had come forth from it.[39] When a god appeared directly to human eyes, he took the form that suited him, without, however, revealing his full physical nature, which was thought to be beyond human ken. Thus Imhotep appeared in the form of a scarab.[40] The god of an island a shipwrecked traveler once washed up on took the form of a snake.[41] Whenever direct contact was established between gods and people, the latter hid their faces so as not to be blinded.[42] If encounters of this sort could occur without causing harm, it was due solely to the goodwill of the gods.[43] If, on the other hand, a being gazed upon a god without the latter's permission, he caught fire and died, and his heart burned up.[44] Sometimes a divinity would take on completely human form, but, if so, it was in order to mix among people without being recognized.[45] Even in this case, an undefinable something could catch the attention of ordinary mortals, producing a certain feeling of uneasiness in them.[46]

Within their own community, the gods could choose to come forth in all their majesty, but there was no question of making themselves seem ubiquitous to the others. The fact that they needed messengers to communicate with one another is sufficient proof of this. A god's physical form had to adapt itself to that of his fellow gods. Thus the gods' size or stature was measureable in their own perception of it. Osiris the king was said to be eight cubits, six palms, and three fingers—fifteen feet, three inches—tall.[47] The extreme precision of this measurement, known from only one source, recalls a remark of Diodorus's according to which the archives the priests maintained included scrupulously kept records of the height of all the sovereigns who had ruled Egypt.[48] It is also known that the blissful dead who succeeded in reaching the world of the gods could come to measure as much as nine cubits—some fifteen feet, five inches— in height.[49] Finally, Horus the warrior is described as being eight cubits, or more than thirteen feet, tall.[50] There is a certain logic to these figures; it finds confirmation in the size attributed to the solar eye, said to measure seven cubits across, with an iris three cubits wide.[51] That the eye is of approximately the same size as the gods themselves clearly indicates that the solar eye was not perceived as a temporarily detached part of the body, but as an independent entity as big as an entire individual. One should not, however, be deceived by this concordance.[52] The texts that speak of Horus the warrior add that the god "takes the form of a human being eight cubits tall," whereas a passage in the Coffin Texts gives us a messenger charged with announcing "the number of cubits of Re in the form of Khepri."[53] This means that a god did not have a fixed height; his height varied with the aspects he was capable of assuming. Divine height had nothing to do with the realities of human perception: a god of seven cubits could, without undergoing any change in his nature, fit into a chapel only a cubit and a half high.[54]

The body of a god also had a distinctive "divine scent" we know little about.[55] This scent preceded the god, announcing his presence; by itself, then, it was a sign that permitted the other gods to recognize one of their own.[56] We know that a particularly soothing odor emanated from Hathor. Fragrant substances, such as olibanum or terebinth resin, were considered to be the equivalents, in the human world, of this particular aroma. When used in ritual fumigations, these resins conferred veritable divine status upon those who benefited from them.[57]

The great versatility of divine bodies, their capacity for slipping away at the very moment it seemed that they had at last been pinned down, explains why the physical characteristics peculiar to each god were never alluded to. The reliefs in the temples manifest this failure to describe the divinities' physical features in the most conspicuous manner imaginable. The gods represented in each temple all have identical faces; nothing distinguishes one from the other. Their dress, too, is completely unaffected by changes in fashion; it remains, throughout history, the same as it was in the earliest periods.[58] It was only mentioned in passing in the daily life of the gods and seems to have had no particular significance. The most we know is that goddesses wore red,[59] or, again, that the gods' clothing could wear out or be torn.[60] When clothes *are* referred to, it is clear that they serve as attributes identifying a form or a function—an iru. The loincloth given to Atum[61] served less to clothe him, in the strict sense of the word, than to permit him to manifest his royalty by means of a specific garment. This loincloth was content to be just a loincloth; it did not require description. Consequently, it was the regalia worn by the gods—crown, scepters, and other symbols of the authority and power they exercised in the context of a particular function—that were most frequently referred to. The scepter of papyrus that goddesses usually held, or the case the gods clutched in their fists, constituted allusions to papyrus as the material substrate of writing and also to the document that attested their hegemony over the land.[62] The case of Horus is especially instructive. Because he had taken possession of the heritage left him by his father Osiris, crowns, signs of his newfound power, spontaneously "sprouted" on his head.[63] Each god's insignia and attributes thus enabled him to express one of his aspects, quite as if they formed an integral part of his body. It was these insignia that iconography strove to render as faithfully as possible in the human sphere.

"Non-clothing," that is, nudity, could become a significant attribute in its turn. It was, first of all, the mark of childhood. Horus the child was naked. The many different variants of his image incarnated physical re-generation and eternally recurring rebirth. More generally, nudity was a sign of youth and immaturity.[64] Thus the primeval gods who helped the creator-god in the dark had, it is said, neither clothes nor hair.[65] Bare and hairless, they were immune to contamination because they had emanated from the Primeval Ocean. As such, they also personified the childhood of the world. Along the same lines, the nudity of the earth-god, Geb, evinced life-generating forces on the point of emergence.[66] As for females, nudity seemed to involve only sky goddesses, which would seem to jus-tify the conclusion that its purpose was not merely to emphasize their erotic character. Nut, the sky-goddess, her body sprinkled with stars, Hathor or Qadesh, the latter a goddess of Syrian origins—both of them "mistresses of the stars"—evoke, more particularly, a night sky pregnant with the sun that was about to rise.[67] In any case, nudity here evokes the promising period of gestation preceding a new birth.

## Animal Forms

What most surely broke the monotony of identical faces was the repre-sentations of the gods as animals or with animal heads. This iconography was a human invention, but it reflected a real feature of the divine world. Nevertheless, animals were hardly ever evoked for their own sake there. The only stories that afford some idea of their status all have more or less directly to do with the gods' conflicts and the revolt of men. Let us recall the episode in which the creator-god spat out, in the form of fish and birds, the gods whom he had previously swallowed. In the wake of this incident, the gods were supposed to have passed on a part of themselves to the animal species thus created, even as they continued to exist as gods. But what they passed on was a negative part of themselves, sloughed off at the end of a conflict. When the revolt of the human race was crushed, the most refractory rebels, we are told, fled into the desert, where they took the form of the animals who have inhabited these re-gions ever since. There was likewise no shortage of stories depicting gods taking animal form. Capable of embodying the negative forces the most hostile to the gods, but also the gods themselves, animal forms were neutral and completely open to whomever assumed them. By their very nature, they were more easily recognizable and so less anonymous than the other forms assumed by the gods. Every animal, by virtue of its natural behavior or habits, incarnated a particular faculty or power that generally exceeded human capacities. Through his animal form, a god served notice that he possessed and exercised this power. Hence the gods could incarnate themselves in a wide variety of animals, even if many of them had a special bond with one in particular. This bond made a specific aspect of the god's personality still more prominent. When we are told, for example, that Horus the child, developing in his mother's womb, is a falcon,[68] the aim is clearly to announce the singular destiny that has been promised him, supreme sovereignty. More generally, an animal form could serve to denote a situation or state that did not directly concern the god who took on that form. In the above-mentioned episode in which Isis tricked Seth by changing into a young girl, the goddess chose to take the form of a kite so that the crestfallen Seth would recognize her. The kite, emblematic of Isis, constituted an allusion to her role as mourner weeping over the dead Osiris. A subtle connection was thus forged between this well-known aspect of the goddess and the context—for the mortified Seth was about to burst into tears.

A god could of course assume many forms besides that of his specific animal, if only to make himself unrecognizable.[69] When disguise was the object, the motive was often to flee some danger,[70] in which case the animal form served as a screen, a veritable mask that made it possible to baffle the curiosity of another god. Herodotus recalls how Amun, pressed by his son Khonsu to reveal his true nature, manifested himself while yet hiding behind the head and fleece of a ram.[71] The ram here images the creative force of the sun and the prestige that derived from it;[72] Amun's artifice thus permitted him to comply only partially with his son's tactless request. Indeed, every animal lent its form to a divine state that the animal's most prominent characteristics somehow corresponded to. The crocodile and the pig, for example, usually embodied incorrigible voracity and gluttony. Because she daily devoured the stars, her own children, the sky-goddess Nut was identified with a sow.[73] When he made off with and then swallowed the eye of Horus, Seth took on the aspect of a black pig.[74] These forms of behavior were so thoroughly characteristic that specialists in Egyptian religion have not hesitated to speak of the crocodilesque or piggish aspect of the gods.[75] The passage from one animal form to another indicated a change of state. The sun, say the texts, was "the scarab-beetle become a falcon,"[76] meaning that he had passed from his nascent state (the scarab-beetle) in the bowels of the earth in order to shine, with all his force and brilliance, at the zenith (the falcon). The animal image becomes the common topos linking gods who share a certain trait. The "ape who is the name of the moon"[77] often lends his form to beings as yet unborn, who are, that is, still in a fetal state. This applies to the premature child Horus,[78] but also to the ape discovered by the desecrators of the reliquary-chapel in Heliopolis, where Osiris's body was supposed to lie. The ape they thought they saw[79] was none other than Osiris himself in the process of being reborn; his transformation was still incomplete. From this, one can see that an animal might well bear no relation to a god's usual aspect, for Osiris was rarely known to appear in anything other than human form. Indeed, a god could incarnate himself not only in the animal specially associated with him, but also in any other one he chose. For example, Anubis, the dog-god, could change himself at will into a snake or falcon.[80]

Thus animal forms had a special status. Certain texts define one of the relationships that could be established between a god and an animal by describing the latter as being "present to" this or that divinity,[81] which plainly implies that the animal was something independent of and exterior to the god who came to dwell within it. It must be emphasized that this possible presence involved the animals of both the divine and the human spheres and that it affected all members of a species. One cannot really speak of incarnation or hypostatization here, for it is quite obvious that such animals provided only temporary abodes for the gods. Thus such and such a species of snake, depending on how toxic its venom was and also on the season of the year, was or was not "present to" different gods.[82] Moreover, a single member of an animal species could harbor several different gods, simultaneously or in succession. This was true of a dog who played host to Osiris and Re at the same time,[83] without provoking any conflict. In contrast, another dog, because he had successively hosted Anubis and Seth, met a double fate: sacrificed and cut to pieces for having embodied Seth, he later found himself rehabilitated and elevated to a place of honor beside the god of the dead thanks to his affinity with Anubis.[84]

Attentive examination of the facts just mentioned brings out the subtle nuance distinguishing the iru-animal, one of the untold facets of the manifestation of a god, from the host animal, no more than a mortal, vulnerable body. This difference was plainly perceptible in the human world, where the distinction between image and real animal was easily made; the same holds for the distinction between the unique animal, which was the hypostatization of a god, and the other members of the same species.[85] In the world of the gods, on the other hand, the distinction was not at all sharp. There, the animals' bodies were so big that they could rival the other divine forms. The falcon of Horus could be one thousand,[86] or else just seven,[87] cubits tall. The mongoose in which Re manifested himself was forty-six, or else just seven, cubits long.[88] Indeed, the animal could tower so high that the god himself was incapable of taking it all in with a single glance.[89] Yet, its supernatural capacities notwithstanding, the animal body oscillated between inviolability and vulnerability. There is a story that reveals all the ambiguity of this situation. An ordinary mortal was, for reasons that are not stated, entrusted with a delicate mission by a god: killing the divine falcon and spiriting away its body.[90] The way the bird is identified makes it clear that what was in question was a unique individual, not just this or that member of its species. The falcon possessed special powers; one had to take certain precautions when approaching it to avoid being blinded. Moreover, it could be slain only with a special weapon fashioned on the instructions of the god who had commissioned the murder. The falcon was to be killed and buried without ceremony, but only after its head had been chopped off. In Egypt, this practice applied only to birds of evil omen; it took on its full import in this context. Although divine, the falcon does not intrinsically represent the god here. It came to what one can fairly call an ignominious end, one which, moreover, destroyed it to the very roots of its being.

## Eating

When one observes the representations, in the temple reliefs, of the mounds of food piled up as offerings to the gods, or when one peruses the lists and enumerations of the extremely varied foodstuffs intended for them, one tends to imagine that the gods reveled at lavish, sumptuous feasts liberally supplied with meat and drink. But this was not at all the case. The copious meals offered to the gods by men and ultimately eaten by the priests contrasted sharply with the eating habits that prevailed in the divine world. The gods avoided excess; as a rule, their meals were frugal. Throughout the lengthy litigation between Horus and Seth, during which the gods obviously needed to eat, one never sees them eating anything but bread.[91] The context itself is surprising. One would have thought that the divine assembly, lost in discussions of inheritance and basic legal rights, would have abstained from snacking during court sessions. A remark dropped by the Lord of the Universe, sick of the quarreling and the long-winded speeches, gives us to understand that eating and drinking constituted one of the gods' favorite occupations when they were fully at ease.[92] Bread and fresh water were the usual fare,[93] although other, more substantial nourishment could also be found on the divine menu. In response to a question of Re's,[94] a group of individuals who would seem to be gods expressed a preference for cooked meat, suitably carved,[95] with grain on the side; all of this could be eaten without salt. Eating meat in large quantities was not looked upon with particular favor and drew rebukes. During one of the conflicts that periodically agitated the world of the gods, Sobek, the crocodile, surprised a band of enemies and massacred them. A victim of his natural inclinations, he unhesitatingly devoured them all; but he carried their heads back home with him as proof of his exploit. The gods rushed toward him, shouting, "Prevent him from eating them (the heads), give him bread!"[96] One can imagine the expression on poor Sobek's face. This god was not particularly successful at keeping his predilection for meaty dishes under control and was sometimes overwhelmed by sudden cravings. When the dismembered Osiris was cast into the Nile, Sobek yielded to temptation and gulped down part of the body. He was subsequently punished for this lapse, due to his boundless voracity more than to a desire to do harm to the body of his fellow god: he had his tongue cut out. That, so the story goes, is why crocodiles have no tongues.[97] All the gods with carnivorous tendencies, whose daily fare consisted in the mortal remains of divine enemies, excited suspicion, if not dread. This was true of the warrior Montu, of whom it was said that "his bread is hearts, and his water blood,"[98] and also of the lionesses who "eat the raw and the cooked."[99] It seems, then, that raw meat did not make up part of the gods' normal diet. Excessive drinking was not approved of. This was Seth's specialty: when he made up his mind to drink, nothing could stop him.[100] Moreover, his name can be easily transformed into "*Setekh*," which means "the inebriated." Hathor, the goddess of love, was also known not to despise drink. Because a state of mild intoxication allowed her devotees to commune with her, they did not hesitate to add tiny quantities of narcotic substances to their beverages.[101] Inscriptions left behind by the members of expeditions to the Sinai quarries, which were under Hathor's patronage, show that the people there drank much less wine than they offered to the goddess.[102] Horus the warrior, for his part, preferred a drink made by squeezing the juice of grapes into water. It had the virtue of quenching one's thirst without going to one's head, gave one courage in combat, and killed pain.[103] Almost nothing is known about how the gods' meals were served, nor about the personnel to whom this task was entrusted. Only the individual charged with supervising the preparation of meals and laying out the tables had something of an identifiable profile. This "butler," as he was usually called, even if his functions more closely resembled those of a maître d'hôtel, apparently occupied a fairly high position in the hierarchy.[104] He was the trustworthy confidant of the great gods, to whom he was quite close, and was thus ideally placed to intercede with his master on behalf of the many favor seekers who sought his help. Occasionally, the carelessness of the minor kitchen personnel would reveal that the butler had been less than vigilant. Bastet-Sakhmet once complained that she had accidentally swallowed a sharp little bone that had found its way into a platter of grilled meat. The accident obviously caused her some discomfort and provoked no end of coughing.[105]

The gods digested their food the way people did, eliminating the waste products through natural channels. The texts have very little to say on this subject. The dead in the hereafter asserted that they were capable of defecating like Shu, god of the air, doubtless because he had a reputation for relieving himself with ease.[106] Isis's urine was known to have beneficial effects: it brought on rain and relieved the young Horus's aches and pains.[107] As might be expected, the gods rarely lacked food. They did, however, occasionally experience hunger and thirst,[108] often because of illness or pains which robbed them of their appetite, or else because they had strayed into remote, inhospitable places. Thus Horus, on a trek through the desert, had to chew the seeds of gourds to slake his thirst.[109] Once Isis's son, the child-god, was distraught by his mother's absence. He had not been nursed and was so weak with hunger that he could not so much as cry. When his mother came rushing back, he refused the bottle and demanded to be breastfed.[110]

A god could be repulsed by certain foods, but these were usually substances not normally eaten. Disgust of this sort found its explanation in mythological precedents or insurmountable antagonisms. Seth found the eye he had gouged out of Horus's head loathsome, and did not eat it.[111] Re was incapable of swallowing turtle-meat because turtles incarnated his worst enemy.[112] It was characteristic of a god not to eat what was fundamentally hostile to him. Malign creatures, in contrast, did not hesitate to feast on things the gods would have regarded as abominable. Thus the demonic serpent, enemy of the sun, gulped down mice and chomped away at the bones of rotting she-cats;[113] another monster ate only putrefied matter. It should, however, be recalled that ancient Egyptians did not consider everything just mentioned inedible or repugnant. People must occasionally have eaten river turtles, and we know that mice, too, though not ordinary fare, sometimes served as food. Finally, there was a difference between living gods and the gods of the hereafter. As a result of a sort of inversion of values between the two worlds, what was good or tasty for living gods was disagreeable to those beyond the tomb. For the former, honey was a sheer delight whose sweetness had affinities with the taste of Maat, or truth itself;[114] for the latter, it was only bitterness.[115] Similarly, the gods of the hereafter had a pronounced aversion to onions, like all other denizens of the netherworld,[116] and did not at all appreciate *djais*,[117] a plant whose nature is unknown to us. Indeed, specifically terrestrial food disgusted the inhabitants of the hereafter, who refused to eat it.[118]

The gods did not eat only human food. Their somewhat mineral nature enabled them to eat precious stones as well.[119] But their lives depended, above all, on the goddess Maat: they partook of her so as to be able to maintain the Norm, the cosmic order she represented.[120] Indeed, the proper food chain was part and parcel of the world order: to say, for example, that Hapy, the god of the Nile floods, was in heaven eating Maat, while Re was in the water eating fish, was to describe a world turned upside down.[121] Bodily secretions also had nutritional value: the gods could live on fragrant effluvia from the creator's body.[122] What is more, the vital energies lodged in a god sometimes found sustenance in the discharges that trickled from his eyes or the hair of his armpits.[123] One may therefore say that the gods also ate themselves.

## The Sexuality of the Gods

Manifestly, the gods were sexed beings, either male or female. Ambiguous cases were not at all common. Inasmuch as the creator-god engendered all other creatures, whichever their sex, he was considered androgynous by nature.[124] Yet his androgyny did not seem to affect his basic aspect: he remained masculine, both in his various manifestations and also in his relationships with the other gods.[125] The sexual habits of the gods were heavily influenced by the fact that they made up one big family, in which everyone was more or less connected with everyone else by close blood ties. Endogamy was standard practice. What is more, although the number of gods eventually grew very large, all were descended of a single ancestor, the creator-god, "the one who became many."[126] In his solitude, the creator-god had no choice but to masturbate in order to bring forth the first divine couple.[127] That sister–brother pair, in turn, had no choice but to mate in order to produce offspring. Owing to this special state of affairs, marriage between brothers and sisters was virtually the rule and was not regarded as incestuous. The physical separation imposed on Geb, the earth, and Nut, the sky, meant that they could not unite normally; this led the earth-god to fellate himself.[128]

The gods tended to form couples; a god normally had only one spouse. As their numbers grew, however, the restrictive conditions that initially prevailed became less rigid; the gods found themselves in increasingly varied situations, and temptations sprang up as a result. Instances of marriage to more than one woman began to appear. Besides Nephthys, his lawfully wedded wife, Seth had two other lady friends, Anat and Astarte. It is worth noting that these two goddesses were awarded to him officially, as compensation for the portion of Osiris' legacy he had once possessed but had had to turn back over to Horus.[129] Horus, for his part, had seven concubines in addition to Hathor. Obviously, a situation of this sort could give rise to jealousy and domestic scenes.[130] One of Horus's concubines once behaved in a particularly high-handed way with Hathor; sure of her charms, she felt confident that she could maintain her hold over Horus despite the great goddess's fury. The quarrel stirred up enough of a fuss to induce a third party, who remains nameless, to step into the affair; he advised the husband to put his domestic affairs in order.

It should be pointed out that, if the gods tended to accept a certain form of polygamy, not a single case of polyandry was to be found among them. Furthermore, legitimate sexual relationships were confined to the group comprised by one's wife and such secondary partners as one might have; any liaison outside this circle was regarded as adulterous. Yet the notion of adultery, or, for that matter, incest, did not always have the dramatic character one might expect. Thus the affair between Nephthys and Osiris,[131] though it may have made Isis sad or bitter, did not, in the end, affect the harmonious relationship between the two sisters: after a falling out, they were reconciled when Thoth intervened at the request of Osiris himself.[132] Rape was not unheard of, but it was usually to be imputed to Seth, the black sheep of the family. Geb's incestuous rape of his mother was treated as serious, but it is difficult to see what moral consequences it may have had in the inner circles of the divine company: the episode was only further evidence that Geb had violently usurped royal power.[133] It is also known that Horus did violence to his own mother.[134] In this case, however, Horus was simply an aspect of the ithyphallic god Min, whose liaison with his mother was well known—a liaison that was assigned an essential creative value, inasmuch as the sun was born of it.[135] Thus these relationships, which we would consider unnatural today, ranked as creative transgressions. They laid down certain basic features of the world: the examples mentioned above led, respectively, to the legitimation of royal power, the birth of the sun, and, ultimately, the adjustment of the calendar, a point we will come back to. A dream-book in use during the thirteenth century B.C.E. indicates that seeing oneself coupling with one's mother or sister in a dream is, in any case, an auspicious sign.[136] This general state of affairs explains how Hathor could decide to strip in front of her father just to lift his spirits.[137]

In addition to Seth's great fondness for women, homosexuality was a prominent feature of his character; it is evoked, though with significant variations, in the different versions of the legend of Horus and Seth. However, if Horus's bed was a particularly hospitable place,[138] his willingness to share it does not seem to have constituted, a priori, an incitement to engage in physical relations. When Seth suggested that Horus lie down with him in the same bed, Horus took up the invitation, doubtless because he didn't think it involved anything abnormal.[139] It is nevertheless clear that, in this particular case, Seth was not free of ulterior motives; they were to draw Horus into various misadventures. In the latest attested version of the story, Horus fell victim to a surprise attack. But an earlier variant, unfortunately fragmentary,[140] shows Seth using the subtle approach. He began by praising the beauty of Horus's loins. The compliment made Horus uncomfortable; he confided to Isis, his mother, that he suspected Seth of having special intentions. The goddess's reaction would be considered quite astonishing today. She advised her son to decline Seth's advances, on the grounds that Horus's body was too frail to withstand his assaults. (The sexual act could have painful consequences indeed, as Horus would learn to his cost.[141]) But, Isis told her son, if Seth carried out his intention, then he should collect Seth's semen in his hands. The text breaks off here, but, thanks to a later version, we know the rest of the story.[142] Apparently without Seth's knowledge, Horus managed to do what his mother had advised. Isis immediately chopped off her son's hands and threw them into the Nile, where they underwent adventures we will come back to. As to the sequel, the variants diverge. As the earliest versions have it, Horus ended up repaying Seth in kind, thus demonstrating his superiority.[143] According to the latest version, Isis masturbated her son, collecting his semen in a container. This procedure did not elicit any particular commentary; it was apparently not considered shocking. The semen Isis thus obtained was later poured over lettuce, Seth's usual fare, so that he would swallow it without noticing anything. Before the assembly of the gods, Seth, persuaded that he had gotten the better of Horus sexually, cited this point in support of his claim that he should be awarded the whole of Osiris's inheritance because he was stronger. The assembly approved the argument and jeered Horus. Horus protested, objecting that it was in fact he who had gotten the upper hand over Seth. To decide between them, Thoth ordered the semen of both gods to come forth, so that he could establish its whereabouts. As was only proper, Seth's semen responded from the bottom of the river it had been thrown into; Horus's showed up in Seth's body, to the latter's consternation. This semen then emerged from Seth's forehead in the form of a golden disk; it would henceforth serve as Thoth's headdress in his capacity as god of the moon.

Homosexual intercourse thus appears to have been, above all, a means of affirming one's supremacy over an inferior or subordinate; it was proof of a surplus of sexual power on the part of the active partner and a deficiency on the part of the one forced to submit.[144] But certain indications suggest that something more was involved. Sodomy practiced by a father upon his son and heir could wear the appearances of a beneficial act of initiation.[145] In question here was a rather crude version of what would become, in later texts, a deep affective bond, a spiritual union between father and son that brought about the rebirth or recreation of any god who was heir to another. According to the Kom Ombo legends, this is what occurred in Osiris's case: his rebirth resulted from the coupling of two male gods, Geb and Shu.[146] The first was the earth-god, Osiris's biological father, and the second, the god of the winds, was his grandfather. The process of resurrection was thus ensured by a fecundation of the earth by the air, the breath of life. Much the same thing occurred in the case of Khnum of Esna, born of the spiritual union between the sun-god Re and Shu.[147] In every such instance, the god thus brought into the world guaranteed the rebirth of nature.

It was normally the male who took the initiative in the sexual act, as Horus and Seth's argument about who dominated whom sexually shows. Goddesses who "played a man's part" were usually aggressive or warrior divinities. One thinks of Anat, a concubine of Seth's, who conducted herself like a man,[148] or else of the dangerous Sakhmet.[149] The case of Isis, who was also led to "play the part of a male,"[150] is a special one. It came about because of a major hitch, namely, the fact that the dead Osiris could not properly exercise his prerogatives: the marriage of Isis and Osiris was a very brief one, so brief, indeed, that they were not able to consummate their union while Osiris was alive. "Come to me, fair face who passed beyond without my having seen him," Isis says after the death of her husband,[151] leading one to suppose that he was murdered before their wedding night.

## Bodily Secretions and Creative Energies

The gods had the same bodily fluids as humans. Their blood, for example, was red,[152] whether they were major gods in the pantheon, minor gods, or fomenters of cosmic trouble. However, the gods' bodily fluids and secretions had special virtues. Generally speaking, anything that came from a divine body and touched the ground was productive.[153] The death of Osiris, together with the emotional shock it caused in divine society, makes it possible to understand the creative character of these divine secretions as well as their raison d'être. Under the impact of his emotion,

> Horus wept. The water flowed from his eye to the ground; it sprouted; thus dry olibanum was created. Geb was smitten by this (the violent death of Osiris); blood from his nose fell to the ground; it sprouted, and pine trees sprang up. Thus it was that resin was produced from his vital fluid. Shu and Tefnut wept copiously; the water of their eyes fell to the ground; it sprouted; thus it was that terebinth resin was produced. Re wept again. The water of his eye fell to the ground. It changed into a bee. As soon as the bee had been created, its activity commenced among the flowers of all the trees. Thus wax is produced, while honey comes from its water. Re was tired; the sweat of his body fell to the ground, and it sprouted and changed into flax; thus cloth was produced. . . . He spit, he vomited; thus bitumen was produced.[154]

The quotation could be extended. It shows that the divine humors, externalizations of an emotion or sentiment aroused by a striking event, gradually produced the substances that were more or less directly required for embalming and mummifying Osiris's body. But the process of creation described here was not limited to that end. The creator-god's discharges engendered plants in general.[155] Osiris's morbid secretions, in their turn, were the source of Nile floods and thus of cereals.[156] They filled the canals with healthful water and gave their names to the branches of the Nile.[157] The sperm Seth was in the habit of expending so thoughtlessly as to excite general reprobation sprouted and produced plants on the bare, arid plateau.[158] Even the traitors' blood gave rise to a lake of flames.[159]

Blood, sweat, tears, and spit never went to waste. Under various circumstances, not necessarily tragic, they served to prolong the creator-god's initial act, making it possible to improve and refine the creation by adapting it to the needs of the moment. These apparently ad hoc needs in fact prefigured realities destined to enjoy a lasting existence among the gods and, later, men. The founding act called up a supplement to the creation that, taking on permanence, was in some sense integrated into the definitive features of the world. The life of the gods—a turbulent one, all things considered—was not lacking in opportunities for weeping, perspiring, or bleeding. This mode of creation did not depend solely on the life-giving properties of everything that emanated from divine bodies; in many cases, it also involved plays on the words for what was emitted and what was created. Thus, according to a well-known legend, human beings (*romay*) were born of the creator's tears (*rimay*).[160] Divine discharges served not only to give material form to a new reality, but also to justify or explain its name. As we shall see, like those parts of a god's body which came to be detached from it for one reason or another, the spoken word, and even writings, were divine externalizations or emanations, and, as such, were imbued with creative power.

This life-giving prodigality, which made every god into a creative machine each time he spoke, moved, or was separated from a part of his body, however minute or undistinguished the part might be, finds its explanation in the fact that all the gods were invested with an energy called the *ka*.[161] The creator-god possessed this energy a millionfold. Thus, in addition to the initial act of creating the universe, he perpetually *re-*created it as he endlessly recommenced his daily journey across the sky.[162] The totality of creation accordingly constituted the sum of the creator-god's vital force.[163] This force behaved somewhat the same way divine forms did: it was simultaneously one and infinitely manifold. This explains why the gods could possess a variable number of ka, corresponding to the number of specific forms their creative power took. These ka could be grouped together on the basis of certain affinities to form veritable collegia of more or less independent entities; they constituted so many potential "gifts" the gods could bestow on people or the world.[164] The cohesion of the totality of all the energies in the universe was maintained by the snake Nehebkau, "he who keeps the energies together."[165] Being a reptile, Nehebkau was one of the primeval beings. He was by nature indestructible and invulnerable to acts of magic; in general, he was immune to all malevolent acts.[166] Conversely, the serpent who represented the uncreated forces threatening the world bore the epithet "He who destroys the energies."[167]

## Discomfort, Sickness, and Suffering

Though they were securely lodged deep inside their chapels, and were enveloped, or so one might suppose, in calm and silence, the gods did not always have all the peace and quiet they needed. Even here, they were subject to the hurly-burly of the world and to emotions such as fear or sadness.[168] For some of them, the moment of accession to the throne could be a delicate one: donning a crown was not always without danger for a god. We have already seen Geb struggling with the uraeus of his father Shu. Hardly had the casket in which it lay been opened than the snake-goddess, spitting fire, slew the god's entire entourage, severely burning the god himself.[169] The wig of no less a personage than Re was required to heal the wound. The snake-goddess's aggressiveness may have been due to the fact that Geb had overstepped his rights in this affair. But similar dangers lay in wait for all legitimate claimants to the throne. When Osiris put on the crown that was the mark of his power, it generated so much heat that he felt faint, while tumors appeared on his face—fortunately, only temporarily.[170] In this case, too, the lord of the gods had to intervene to relieve his pain and cure him by administering a bleeding.

More generally, the gods were subject to illness and spells of discomfort. They had stomachaches and headaches.[171] Re, the king of the gods, was not immune to such misfortunes, often due, it seems, to the malice of his fellows. Always, after a period of panic in which everyone got upset and shouted a great deal, order was restored. Let us note in passing that cries and shouting, very common in divine society, were always a sign that baleful events were in progress.[172] Dangerous animals like scorpions and snakes did not spare the gods either. Re himself once fell victim to a fainting spell when he trod on a scorpion by mistake.[173] Re's daughter, a she-cat who was ordinarily very careful, fell victim to a similar mishap. All her father's power was required to save her.[174]

Of all the parts of a god's body, the eyes were the most vulnerable. Whether they represented the sun or the moon, they suffered no end of injury, more or less serious. Blindings and mutilations of various sorts were somehow always followed by a recovery that restored the injured god to the state of bodily integrity essential, we are told, to the proper functioning of the world. It would be tedious to rehearse all these misadventures; a few examples will suffice. Horus's eye, even before it had recovered from the injuries Seth inflicted on it in the battles between the two gods, was subject to further tribulations because of a blunder of Re's. Re, who wanted to form some notion of the extent of the injuries the eye had sustained, ran an experiment whose pertinence is not immediately apparent. He asked Horus to cover his healthy eye and look at a black pig, which was, we know, the very image of Seth. At first, the animal Horus saw looked white, but, the next time he looked, he recognized the pig, and, with it, his eternal foe. This caused him such intense pain that he fainted and had to be carried off to his bed. Re, whom one might reasonably have expected to be a bit more tactful, noted without special emotion that "the pig is hateful to Horus."[175] Re, too, could be momentarily blinded and require a guide.[176] We have likewise had occasion to mention the Elder Horus's bouts of temporary blindness. Some sources say that he was born with a leukoma of the eye.[177] The effects of this disease were so disastrous that the priests did not hesitate to commission, for Horus's temple at Kom Ombo, a relief depicting a set of surgical and medical instruments; the eye doctor's occupied a prominent place among them.[178] The objective, without any doubt, was to be prepared for any eventuality, so as to forestall a recurrence of earlier misfortunes. Indeed, eye diseases seem to have been almost as common among the gods as among the ancient Egyptians themselves. At the odd moment in this or that text, it is not unusual to come upon one of them suffering from some kind of malformation or malady of the eye.[179] Some of these ailments were most curious indeed. Endless conjectures have been put forth to explain why worms should have been lodged in Atum's eye, the more so as what was in question was not an accident or a disease, but an ocular secretion produced at the god's own bidding.[180] As this infirm eye of Atum's was nothing other than the moon,[181] one wonders whether the spots visible on the lunar surface—the so-called seas—were not the work of worms that had eaten away at its surface in times long past.

Before developing into a vigorous young man who had, we are told, overcome his afflictions,[182] Horus the child was, of all divine beings, the one who suffered the most from the widest imaginable variety of troubles. There was no accident this prototype for all unhappy, frail, abandoned, sickly children was exempt from. Isis need only leave her son alone in his little shelter, and he would be stung by a scorpion. He was stricken with fever, he covered the ground with his tears and droolings, his body was enfeebled, his heart was exhausted, and the blood stopped pulsing through his veins.[183] His mother had to summon all her arts and the assistance of untold divine experts to save her child. Decidedly fragile and unlucky, he even had a case of hookworms.[184] Nothing was spared him; he once had the misfortune to swallow a demon while suckling at his mother's breast. Isis noticed nothing of what was going on.[185] Needless to say, certain mishaps were due to the innocence and inexperience of the child, who had the habit of sticking his little fingers into everything. Sauntering along the shore of a lake, he had the bright idea of catching and eating the fish sacred to Re. For an adult, this would have been sacrilege. But the child did not know what he was doing; he therefore quickly got over the stomachache that resulted from his unfortunate act.[186] In the face of so much adversity, the young child did not always confine himself to weeping and moaning. Overwhelmed by his sufferings, he took it upon himself to give his mother and his aunt Nephthys some advice; he urged them to go see whether Nut's nurses, who must have dealt with situations comparable to his own, might not happen to have a remedy for his afflictions.[187] To cover all the possibilities, he also asked his mother to go with him to see humankind, in hopes of getting some help from them.[188]

Childhood is the very picture of vulnerability; one is therefore not astonished to see the young Horus undergoing so many trials and tribulations, even if he was a god. The other gods, despite the ills that assailed them, do not appear to have been very fragile, except under certain rather specific circumstances. Coronations, which were moments of rupture in the divine hierarchy, animals, which were the physical embodiments of the enemies of the universe, and the changing phases of the sun and moon were essentially all they had to fear. Their maladies and moments of discomfort merely served to reveal the weak links in the universe.

## Mutilated Bodies, Broken Bodies

Divine bodies were apparently indestructible; not even the gods themselves could destroy them. Witness the case of Seth: endlessly tortured, put to death again and again, he nevertheless kept coming back, in full possession of his faculties, to commit new infamies.[189] We are told, for example, that he was mummified like a real corpse after his battles with Horus.[190] But, shortly thereafter, he turned up again, as if nothing had happened, to defy Horus anew. To be sure, he was again defeated and cut up into little pieces; but, nothing daunted, he returned to the attack. No sort of mutilation could finish off a god. The explanation for this malleability and invulnerability lies in the very nature of the divine body, whose profound essence remained inaccessible and inviolable no matter what the circumstances. Every god possessed, as has been noted, a number of different forms, manifestations, iru, and names; one could not claim to have completely annihilated the god[191] without destroying them all. Even then, success was not assured.

Mutilation, then, did not affect the bodies of the gods as such, but only part of their potential. The adventures of Horus's hands illustrate this. Sexually assaulted by Seth, Horus could save himself only by collecting the rapist's sperm in his hands. Isis came running to his side; seeing what had just happened, she chopped off both her son's hands to prevent the contagion from spreading, and threw them into the river. They sank out of sight.[192] To make sure she was rid of them for good, she called out to them, telling them that they were to remain separated from her son's body even if they should be found again. The situation was obviously an awkward one for Horus. Re sought the expert help of Sobek, the crocodile god, asking him to go down to the bottom of the river to look for the lost hands. The objective, as expressly stated by Re, was to put them back where they had originally been, Isis's wishes notwithstanding. But the hands had turned into incarnations of two of Horus's sons, and were now leading an independent existence; recovering them was thus quite a task. Sobek, however, was familiar with the watery element, and, using a fishing basket, did finally manage to catch them. Horus thereupon asked

Re to give him back what was his. To forestall new misadventures, Re decided to preserve the hands as relics in the city of Nekhen, and, at the same time, to restore them to their owner. This sort of double procedure, which was quite usual for gods, made it possible to comply with Isis's and Horus's apparently irreconcilable demands. According to another version of the story, Isis contented herself with providing her son substitute hands.[193] The way the story goes on shows that Horus was never entirely without hands; he was simply deprived of those which had been cut off. As soon as they were separated from the body they had originally belonged to, they became gods in the full sense of the word and ended up being honored as such.

The structure of this story and the relationships between its main characters recur, nearly point for point, in the episode of the multiple adventures of Horus's two eyes. We have already seen that they were gouged out and buried by Seth. But there exists a more detailed account of these events.[194] After Horus was mutilated, each of his eyes was, at first, carefully placed in a box, doubtless to protect them from renewed attack. From this moment on, the eyes were coveted by many different individuals. Seth started things off by stealing the boxes, hiding them up on one of the mountains bordering the Nile Valley. But Anubis discovered the hiding place; under cover of night, he cut out the bottom of the boxes, seized the eyes, and carried them off in two papyrus baskets. It is difficult to avoid drawing a parallel between Anubis's role here and that of Sobek in the story of the hands, nor can one fail to compare the fishing basket of the first story with the two baskets of the second. What happened next confirms the resemblance. The eyes took on an identity of their own, ceasing to belong entirely to their original owner. They gave rise to a vineyard, which Isis advised her son to acquire. The goddess then demanded that Re arrange for the eyes to be restored to Horus. The Lord of the Universe was only too happy to comply. Henceforth, the "vineyard-eyes," watered and looked after by Isis, flourished uninterruptedly; meanwhile, again by virtue of a sort of redoubling, Horus recovered the "seeing-eyes"—the regalia of his royal power.[195]

Thus we see that amputations carried out under emergency conditions or out of necessity were not the most common kind. As a rule, mutilation was a form of punishment or the result of a premeditated attack. The "children of their father," a way of referring obliquely to a group of gods the writer did not want to name directly, also had their hands cut off. In this case, mutilation was punishment for a sacrilegious act: by picking lotuses, flowers that spread open in the morning and so enable the sun to set out on his daily journey,[196] the gods had put the normal course of the world in jeopardy. It will be recalled that Nemty, the gods' boatman, had ferried Isis across the water after she had bribed him with a golden ring, although he had been forbidden to do so. Seth, the chief victim of this act of disobedience, demanded that Nemty be meted out an exemplary punishment. The ferryman had his toes cut off and had to abjure gold, the metal that had led him into temptation. Gold would later become an object of abomination in the ferryman's city.[197] Inasmuch as the flesh of the gods was made of it, Nemty did not, according to another tradition, lose only his toes: his skin and flesh were stripped away as well, leaving him only his bones, which were of silver.[198] Whatever the exact truth of the matter, the poor ferryman, maimed as he was, continued to live in the company of the gods.

On other occasions, anger or simple ill-will precipitated bloody dramas. Isis once inadvertently wounded Horus while trying to help him; in a fit of rage, he chopped off her head and took to his heels. His impulsive act of violence merited punishment, called for, moreover, by the king of the gods himself.[199] But Seth was a step ahead of everyone else: profiting from the fact that Horus had dozed off under a tree, he ripped out his eyes and buried them. This is plainly a variation on the story we mentioned earlier. In the end, everything returned to normal. A few drops of gazelle's milk, administered by Hathor, enabled Horus to recover his eyes and his eyesight. As to the petrified Isis, she patiently bided her time without a head. Thoth put an end to the situation by replacing Isis's head with a cow's.[200]

The gods' capacity for not suffering in any real sense from the most serious sort of injuries allowed them to do their part for the good cause by obligingly loaning out a piece of themselves. While Horus waited for his headaches to go away, one divinity or another offered to loan him his head.[201] Geb agreed to donate blood produced by his spinal marrow: it was effective medicine for the fits of fury Seth was subject to.[202] Furthermore, parts of the gods' bodies did a great deal of traveling—not always because their proprietors desired it. Such was the case with Horus's hands, discussed above, or the solar eye mentioned in Chapter 1. Of all bodily parts, this solar eye doubtless manifested its independent spirit with the greatest ease. It was often absent, out on a reconnaissance mission or punitive action. When Re convened the assembly of the gods to take counsel, the wandering eye would join them.[203] Indeed, a god did not need to separate himself from a part of his body in order to go where he wanted. Although Shu, god of the air, was busy holding up the sky, he could set out in search of the exiled eye. His nature was such as to permit him to be everywhere at once and to know where the goddess had taken refuge. Finally, a divine body could emit secondary bodies: sometimes identical to and sometimes different from his main body, they gravitated around it, serving as its assistants.[204] Mutilated, broken up, or multiplied, a divine body demonstrated its ubiquity in its own way, even while guarding the secret of its true nature.

## Birth, Life, Death

The birth of the gods was part of the general scheme of creation. Hence it was often referred to as an event that collectively brought all the gods into being. Nevertheless, on closer inspection, it appears that many gods had a specific place and date of birth,[205] and, as we have seen, a personal history. Whatever the circumstances, the birth of a god always had something unusual about it. Only after a sufficient number of gods had come into being was it possible for a female to bring a god into the world by a process of natural childbirth. The classic example is that of Horus the child, the son of Isis and Osiris. His birth was very much like a human birth; it was thus an exception to the rule. Isis suffered labor pains and even had to use threats to bring the divine company to provide her relief.[206] She gave birth after a pregnancy of ten months, a quite unusual length of time, but one necessary, or so it was thought, to produce a vigorous divine being. She nursed the baby for three years.[207] But Horus's conception did not conform to human laws. Osiris was dead, and Isis was obliged to use magic to bring him to life and so make possible their sexual congress. The event was extraordinary enough, even by divine standards, to awaken skepticism. When Isis told the Lord of the Universe how happy she was to be pregnant by Osiris, he treated her to a little lecture: "Restrain your heart, woman! How do you know that it's a god and heir of the Ennead (that you're carrying)?" Nothing daunted, the goddess proudly responded: "I am Isis, the most dynamic and the noblest of the gods. There is truly a god in my womb, and he is the seed of Osiris."[208] This straightforward declaration was enough to convince the others: no one questioned Isis's word. As a child, Horus had the growth problems associated with his age: for instance, he lost his baby teeth.[209] Like every upper-class adolescent, the young god was circumcised.[210] Hidden away beyond the reach of Seth, who was in pursuit of him, he would one day return to the bosom of his family, it was hoped, to avenge his father, "his members having grown strong, his power having matured."[211] In the meantime, the child assumed different aspects to make himself unrecognizable. One of them was unknown even to Isis, who had to go to see Thoth and utilize the method of identification described earlier—question, answer, the stating of a name, the definition of an attribute—before she could recognize this iru of her son's.[212] Subsequently, Horus's personality became increasingly fragmented. Horus the son of Isis was destined to grow up, attain a certain maturity, and avenge his father, whereas Horus the child, who would eventually be given the name Harpokrates, was to remain, in his basic role, forever a child, a point of reference and a prototype for all future children.

The Children of Nut—Osiris, the Elder Horus, Seth, Isis, and Nephthys—were born under special circumstances, our only account of which is given by Plutarch.[213] Though they were man and wife, Geb and Nut could not couple freely because of their separation; they thus had to have intercourse in secret. When Re found out about this, he cast a spell on the pregnant Nut to prevent her from giving birth to her babies at any time of the year whatsoever. To help Nut, Thoth played dice with the moon, winning part of the time that belonged to it. The time in question, five days, was added onto the regular year, enabling Nut to give birth to her five children. The Egyptian texts themselves barely mention this episode.[214] A veiled allusion suggesting that Nut's father, not her husband, as Plutarch says, was responsible for her pregnancy,[215] might have something to do with these events; if so, it would explain why Re did not want Nut to bring her children into the world. Other texts describe these matters a bit more forthrightly, though still discreetly; they speak of the moment "when the sky was big with gods, unbeknownst to men, while the great Ennead slept,"[216] indicating that the event took place within the interior horizon, that is, on the edge of the world, between light and darkness.[217] The list of miraculous or peculiar births could be extended. Suffice it to mention only a few of the births which involved neither copulation nor pregnancy. For example, Hathor was born of the liquid that oozed from the sun-god's eyes and fell onto the sands of the very first land to emerge from the Primeval Ocean.[218] As to Thoth's birth, the traditions vary. According to the most common, he came forth from the skull of Seth;[219] according to others, from the heart of the creator, in a moment of bitterness.[220]

Like the existence of the gods taken collectively, that of each of them taken individually was situated in time. They were allotted a lifespan that was measurable, even if it covered very long periods.[221] Yet this period of time or lifespan was not comparable with what men know of time. Born on the twelfth day of the first month of the year, Osiris was already an adolescent by the sixteenth day of the month and was murdered on the seventeenth.[222] The only surviving memory of his childhood was that of the baby-tooth he had lost.[223] Even if it is assumed that Osiris had barely reached adulthood when he died,[224] the length of his life was in no way comparable to a human lifespan. The same holds for all the gods. Horus had barely entered young manhood when he brought suit against Seth for the murder of his father, and the trial had been going on for eighty years at the moment when the story that relates its outcome commences.[225] Every human day was, at most, a passing moment.[226] Gods, indeed, traversed or "pierced" time without changing, to adopt the formulation used by an Egyptian text.[227]

Normally, the gods were not affected by old age. This was notably the case, we are told, with Thoth or Seth,[228] which perhaps implies that what was involved was not a general principle. Yet we have seen that the advanced age assumed by Isis was only an aspect, an iru; it showed both that she was a widow and that she had magic powers. The same apparently goes for her sister Nephthys,[229] and, again, for the old women from Cusae in Hathor's entourage;[230] rather like the Three Fates, these women foretold human destinies and had certain ties to the seven words that created the world. Those gods, who *are* described as being old, bore the marks of wisdom and respectability.[231] We have likewise had occasion to note that the primeval gods who assisted the creator-god died because they found themselves trapped in a gap between the creation and the uncreated. There apparently existed a category of minor gods who were specially created to help some more powerful god carry out a particular task and who died once it was completed. This was true of the gods who made preparations for Osiris's funeral.[232] The history of the divine world was strewn with collective deaths of this sort.[233] These deceased gods were not powerless, and one could call on them, even if they were "neither in the sky, nor on earth, and the light did not shine on them."[234] They were buried in coffins placed in special necropolises.[235]

Re's advanced age can only be explained by the fact that he possessed the nature of a primeval god. Though he was a creator, he had nevertheless come forth from the uncreated, and bore the mortal mark of this phase of the process of creation. He was already old when he was in the Primeval Ocean[236] and was considered to be immune to change.[237] He was the only old, or, at any rate, obviously old, god among the divine company. But the creator's old age had an impact on all of creation, which kept breaking down as a result of disorders and revolts. Re found himself obliged to surrender some of his powers, and, in order to come to terms with this new situation, had to reestablish the world on a new pattern in which men and gods would no longer live together, in which the solar cycle would ensure the daily regeneration of the divine world[238] and permit Re to pass continually through all the ages of man without ill effect.[239] Because what was involved here was a new creation, the gods were necessarily subject to the law that had prevailed during the first creation. They underwent a sort of redoubling. That part of them which had belonged to the old world died, and the rest, regenerated, led a new, independent life. It was for this reason that a god could easily visit his own venerated corpse in its tomb and weep over his own death, all the while pursuing his divine occupations.[240]

There remains Osiris, the only one of the gods to die altogether of his injuries and find himself permanently excluded from the world of the living. This exception seems all the stranger in that Osiris had already been slain a first time, accidentally, by his father, and then brought back to life in this world.[241] Thus only his second death, the one caused by Seth's attack, had the special character that prevented him from reactualizing himself in the present; it thrust him for good and all into the past represented by the world of the dead. To begin with, death affected Osiris in his most profound being, because his body had to be patiently reconstituted from little scraps. Although each of them retained a bit of vitality—for example, his head, which could still speak and thus reveal where the rest of the body was[242]—this reconstitution did not bring the corpse back to life. To accomplish that, all Thoth's knowledge and Isis's magic had to be brought into play.[243] But the divine being who was reborn as a result did not belong to the present; he was merely a simulacrum of what he had been in the past. Osiris, we are explicitly told, was "yesterday."[244] The present was Horus, born of Osiris's union with Isis. Like all dead gods, Osiris would receive a cult that Isis would faithfully practice.[245] Isolated in the hereafter, Osiris, like the gods regenerated by the second creation, also underwent a redoubling. He was thus simultaneously a corpse perpetually on the point of being reborn, and a living being who ruled the hereafter, going about his royal tasks. Each of these forms of Osiris led an independent existence. Osiris the king enjoyed freedom of movement within the limits of his kingdom, whereas his corpse stirred only sporadically, provoking earthquakes in our world whenever it did.[246]

# CHAPTER FOUR

# Spaces and Places

**O**ne tends to imagine that the gods lived in magnificent palaces located in luxurious natural environments bursting with color. Curiously, however, the spaces and places inhabited by the Egyptian gods inspired none of the descriptions, well-known in other civilizations, praising the ineffable beauty of their natural surroundings and the incomparable opulence of their dwellings. Without being quite absent, the environment as such is not described; it is present only insofar as its presence serves some practical purpose. In both the texts and the iconography, it remains nothing more than décor, barely sketched, as if its nature were so well-known to all that it required no superfluous description. Because of this descriptive restraint, one cannot always clearly discern the relations that might have existed between different sectors of the universe. Thus the links established between earth and heaven before their separation remain ambiguous. Although the gods and men mingled freely with one another, the heavens nonetheless also maintained an independent existence that permitted the sun to take his place in the sky and shine down on the whole of creation. We are told that the god's *ba*, his visible reflection, was to be found there.[1] If the sky was a natural abode for the gods of heavenly bodies—the sun or moon, for example—there are indications that it was not the permanent dwelling place of the gods in general. Precisely where the gods were situated in space depended on their functions. Re, the sun, naturally spent more time in the sky than the others; Geb, as his function required, dwelt on the earth.[2] Thus a distinction seems to have been established from the very beginning between "those above and below."[3] Although these categories were relatively imprecise, they were most frequently based on a natural system of classification. Thus, as soon as the world was created, those beings destined to dwell in the sky—the birds, the heavenly bodies—as well as those fated to live on earth—human beings and other living creatures—were assigned the places that would henceforth be theirs. The gods, naturally, were in the first category; the fact that they dwelt in the sky also implied their superior status in a hierarchical system of values. The heavens provided the setting for solemn events. Divine wishes descended from heaven to earth, where they were diffused orally or in writing.[4] The gods lived in the heavens but took their meals on earth;[5] thus they passed easily from the sky to earthly locales, even to bodies of water.[6] It must, however, be said that incidents and adventures that stirred the world of the gods usually took place in a terrestrial context. The heavenly domain was plainly calmer and less subject to disturbance; the earth had to be constantly watched over and kept in proper working order.[7] As a result, the worlds of heaven and earth maintained permanent relations with one another. The solar bark could make a halt in the heavens to supervise the course of an action from on high, resuming its journey once the action had been carried through to a successful conclusion. This is what happened when Isis called out to Re from the bottom of the Delta marshes to tell him that her young son was suffering and that she had not succeeded in relieving his pain. Hearing her plaint, the supreme deity dispatched Thoth to find out just what was going on and provide her assistance.[8] The artful Thoth was able to cure the child, after which the solar boat resumed its course. Nevertheless, the land of the gods and that of the living were separate spaces.[9] This should not be understood to mean distinct territories, but rather zones belonging to different levels of perception. The gods were situated at a level that living creatures could not possibly frequent, even when both were in the same "place." The gods were at once very close and infinitely remote. On his daily course, the sun was supposed to cover millions and hundreds of thousands of *shoinoi*[10] (a shoinos was equal to about seven miles).

The gods' earthly dominion was rather clearly arranged in concentric circles. Egypt, more precisely, the Nile Valley, occupied a central place in it. On the outskirts of the Delta, a vast papyrus marsh played a special role, one involving Horus's childhood. Encircling Egypt, the rest of the world was merely an outside, given over to the strange or foreign, if not the foreigner; depending on the circumstances, this outside touched on the disorder of the uncreated or even merged with it. Finally, the netherworld, the hereafter, constituted a place sui generis, which was not included within these subdivisions but was constantly on everyone's mind.

## An Egypt of the Gods

If one were to barge in on the gods' private life, one would find them going about their affairs in an essentially terrestrial habitat whose geography was patterned after that of the Nile Valley and the surrounding areas. There is nothing astonishing about the fact that the river and watercourses in general had an important place in the divine landscape. They could even be obstacles. During the litigation between Seth and Horus, Isis had to fall back on a ruse to induce the boatman to carry her over to the island where the proceedings were taking place.[11] Under very similar circumstances, the same boatman did not hesitate to take gold again in exchange for ferrying someone back across to the western bank, one way.[12] Isis bewailing the fact that she cannot find a ferry is a standard motif in the mythological tales,[13] even if, under exceptional circumstances, the goddess was able to walk on the water.[14] Boats figured as the most common means of transportation, because they were the most convenient kind of transport in a country whose desert sands and flooded arable land made the use of wheeled vehicles a risky business. Navigation was, moreover, nobler than other modes of travel. Horus traveled by boat, either for pleasure or else to do battle with his foes.[15] Re hardly ever used other means of transportation, even when he was simply going to see other gods.[16] But his bark was not always to be found sailing across the blue sky. It could drop anchor in solitary places: for example, in the middle of a muddy plain, devoid of vegetation and far from the beaten track, where Re stopped to help a humble herdsman working in his service.[17] Walking and especially running were more likely to occur in conflictual situations that involved catching a fugitive who had committed some misdeed.[18] Genies and other divine messengers were the only divinities for whom running was the normal way of getting about. Their speed, incidentally, inspired deep fear. The Egyptian gods also disdained horseback riding, for straddling the back of an animal was incompatible with their sense of dignity.[19] A god on horseback was a foreign god. It was possible to imagine a god astride a chariot only if he was manifesting himself in the pharaoh engaged in battle, or else in the context of the hunt, where a god on a galloping horse might shoot arrows at animals regarded as cosmic enemies. Yet even the god who engaged in this pursuit, Shed, showed signs of foreign influence.[20] In most cases, it is not stated how the gods betook themselves from one place to another.

The gods' activities shaped their earthly domain, gradually giving rise to its toponymy as well as the basic features of its geography—things men received as their heritage. This process of organizing physical space is well described in a narrative that recounts the reigns of the first gods on earth.[21] Besides the emergent land created by the creator-god, the administrative divisions, and the cities instituted by Shu,[22] the text inventories the construction and renovation work done by Geb. It represented, all told, "thousands of foundations and millions of places"; their names, together with a description, were preserved in the divine archives[23] from which humanity's archives ultimately derived. The land of the gods included cities whose names are clearly taken from the real world.[24] There was, indeed, a tradition among men that said that the cities of Egypt, founded when the world began, were initially inhabited by gods. Mythical events occurred within the context of a relatively precise toponomy, in which the names of well-known localities appeared side by side with more obscure place names (some of which were created to meet the needs of the plot) and functional toponyms. But this toponymy also included places that were topographical transpositions of concepts or objects that played a role in one or another mythological episode.[25] The action of the gods could also modify the physical landscape, sometimes only slightly, but always in such a way as to leave traces still visible in human times. Thus a heap of pebbles found in the vicinity of the city of Edfu had its origins in a hailstorm of gravel that Isis let loose in order to beat back a storm Seth had raised against Horus.[26] Places that had been marked by mythological events had a particular layout it was best not to tamper with, for fear of bringing on catastrophes. A hole which had appeared in Pharbaithos—no one knew how—and which had been subsequently filled in was not to be reopened for fear it would suck in the air around it.[27] Bit by bit, the gods installed all the elements of a landscape, but also those of an organized country of which the Egypt of men was but a reflection.

The lands of the gods are described as being inhabited by animals, but one soon realizes that the animals in question were almost always divine manifestations or their reflections. Certain bovids were the only beasts about whom it seems safe to say that their presence on the landscape had no further implications. For the gods owned cattle, which were, moreover, frequently threatened by wild beasts as they grazed peacefully in the fields. Horus turned to his sorceress of a mother to ask her to keep the dangerous animals "who feed on meat, who drink blood" far from his flock.[28] Usually, these flocks were watched over by a herdsman who was simply a god working for the others.[29] Though they were not always the main or the most active characters in the tales, herdsmen and shepherds show up sufficiently frequently in them to suggest that these stories had a pastoral background. Its role in and implications for divine society have, however, never been clearly explained.

The gods did not live together in one place. They were sometimes scattered so widely that one of their number might be thrown into disarray because he did not know where his fellows were.[30] Each of the gods had an affinity for his place of birth, to which he was particularly attached.[31] Up and down the earthly realm, the gods had houses that seem to have been different from the temples that they also lived in.[32] A brief remark shows us that these residences were made of precious materials, as one might expect.[33] Certain buildings were so huge that it was impossible to establish their dimensions; a number were so ancient that it was not known who had built them.[34] Each of the reigning gods had his residence, his palace, which he was at pains to enlarge and embellish from the first days of his reign.[35] The materials such palaces were made of, to the extent that anything is known of them, resembled those used for earthly temples.[36] The similarity or even identity between palace and temple is generally taken for granted in the texts. Yet not all the gods possessed a temple-palace from the very beginnings of creation. It is known that some of them acquired the right to live in shrines in exchange for their contribution to the proper functioning of the world.[37] The creator-god's palace was supposed to be located inside the great castle of Heliopolis.[38] From there he governed the world and issued his edicts.[39] Hence Heliopolis was generally considered to be the gods' seat of "government." It was in this city, as well, that one could find the mysterious chest that excited the attention and desires of one and all: the sarcophagus containing the body of Osiris, who was himself the sun in the process of rebirth.[40] Generally speaking, the buildings of the gods were supposed to have been constructed under the direction of the goddess Seshat, one of Thoth's assistants. Entrusted with the keeping of ground plans and charts, she was also an expert in the art of sighting the stars and planets, which made it possible to orient buildings properly. A late tradition has it that construction work was put in the hands of a group of genies descended of the potter-god Khnum. There is speculation that this is why certain minor divinities or genies had their abode in jars or vases.[41]

## A Protected Area: The Papyrus Thicket

The papyrus thicket in which Isis hid her young son while waiting for him to grow up had a special status. This swampy area constituted a region located on the periphery of the divine world. Because Osiris was dead, Isis's pregnancy had to be kept secret; she gave birth in a remote, well-concealed spot that the aged Atum had made inaccessible to Seth, the enemy of young Horus and his mother.[42] Although the thicket was "a city which had no ramparts,"[43] the child could live there unmolested—far from the company of the gods, to be sure, but out of reach of his enemy as well. He could hide there until he had grown big and strong enough to prevail in the struggle with Seth for the throne of his father Osiris.[44] Seth spent many long years stalking him, but did not find him until Horus had reached adulthood and could defend himself.[45] Yet the remoteness of the papyrus thicket had very unfortunate consequences. It forced Isis to leave the hideaway in order to attend to her affairs, or even to go begging in order to procure the necessities for herself and her son.[46] Whenever she had to absent herself from the thicket in which she had hidden her child, she took elaborate precautions so as not to be spotted. On the way back, she ordered her followers to keep their eyes trained on the road and not to dally along the way with anyone, so as not to leave traces that Seth might find.[47] These followers, seven scorpion-goddesses, were not always very amiable or obedient. They were supposed to protect the child, but would often sting him instead, though it is not known whether they did so more or less intentionally, under Seth's malignant influence, or simply because they were maladroit. The sole contact Isis had with the gods was through the sound of her voice, which carried all the way to the solar bark, enabling her to communicate with her father.[48]

The thicket had another distinctive feature: it was inhabited by human beings. Though people were not exactly absent from other divine regions, they played an active role there in the case of only one event, their revolt against the creator-god. At the heart of the thicket, men were genuinely involved in the events that occurred in the gods' world, as if this were the one place where they could exercise their free will while living together with the gods. They ceased to be an undifferentiated mass whose only raison d'être was that they had been created in anticipation of the moment they would revolt. Their behavior here was not monolithic: rather, one remarks the appearance within their community of, if not individual personalities, then at least types. When she set out in search of help for her son, Isis's route took her to the abode of a noble lady who spotted her from afar and slammed her door in Isis's face; a lowly inhabitant of the marsh, in contrast, generously opened her door to the goddess.[49] But this poor woman had no cure for her son. In her anguish, Isis then turned to the men dwelling in the marsh: "To whom among the men shall I call that their hearts may turn to me? I will, then call to the dwellers of the marsh region. They will turn to me immediately. The marsh inhabitants came to me from their homes. They jumped up for me at my voice. They all lamented, saying: 'How great is your sorrow!—but there was nobody who could conjure him with his spell."[50] These humble, compassionate people were unaware of who Isis really was. When Thoth stepped in to cure little Horus, Isis asked him not to reveal her true identity to the people who had crowded round. She also requested that he use his authority to convince them to watch over her son at all times and cover over any traces that might lead the forces of evil to the young child's hiding place. Thoth did as he was bidden, but, carried away by his fondness for making speeches, he expatiated (without revealing Isis's identity) on the child's royal destiny and his mother's magic powers.[51] The crowd that had gathered round did not utter a word, taking in this information as if there was nothing particularly surprising in it.

It seems, then, that men and gods did not mix easily, except when the gods needed to hide among men to conceal their identity. In all other circumstances, human beings lay outside the gods' concerns—until they revolted. This does not mean that people had no contact with the gods and knew nothing about what they did. During their rebellion, Re had to enjoin the gods he had summoned to keep their own counsel, so that humankind would not get wind of the gods' plans.[52]

## The Hereafter; or, How to Communicate

Opinions diverged as to how and why the hereafter came into being. Logically, it must have been created for Osiris and, subsequently, all the gods or men who were summoned to remain there. Yet we have seen that some were left by the wayside when the universe was created, dying because they had not experienced the crucial moment when the light first appeared. These unfortunate creatures had to be lodged somewhere. According to certain traditions, the hereafter was created by the solar creator god because he needed a place to rest at night.[53] The underworld empire of the dead is said to have been the result of a "finding," in other words, an invention,[54] supposedly hewed out, of necessity, by the creator himself.[55] Once cyclical time had been established, the sun only passed through this underground realm on the brief nocturnal voyage that "made the darkness acceptable" to those who dwelt there.[56] For the inhabitants of the hereafter could not bear light in its full intensity; on his own initiative, the sun therefore dimmed his brightness when he crossed their realm, so much so that he appeared to have been "darkened and clouded over."[57] The denizens of the next world had to give up their breath and the heat of their bodies upon arriving there, for these things were the marks of earthly life;[58] the sun warmed them up again when he passed by them, restoring them to life for the briefest of instants.[59] The other world was the place where "faces were reversed and things (were) mysterious."[60] Not even the gods themselves had a clear sense of the route Osiris had taken to get there;[61] they were afraid to go down roads that might lead them in that direction.[62] Nor did the souls of the dead reach the beyond with ease; they had to travel underground and overcome many obstacles.[63] In certain texts, the gods of the heavens and those of the hereafter are separated, as if they could not really meet.[64] This indicated just how difficult communication was between the hereafter and the other sectors of creation. It is true that, by pressing one's ear to the ground, one could sometimes make out cries coming from below the earth,[65] but the connection established in this way was a very fragile one. Yet there were days when the dead could walk the earth. On such days, it was best not to cross their path,[66] for they could cause all sorts of trouble. If they came back to disturb the living, it was, as a rule, because their dead men's desires had not been fully satisfied.[67] In this world, they assumed human form once again, for they had become gods in the hereafter and had therefore been, in some sense, transfigured.[68] The fact that they adopted the form they had once called theirs implies that they recovered the natural functions they had had when alive. These excursions back to the world of the living were subject to controls: one had to have authorization from Anubis in the form of a decree, backed up by a safe-conduct written out in Thoth's own hand.[69] Given their functions, these two gods were the ones who most frequently established the necessary connections with the other world. The most appropriate intermediary seems to have been Thoth, for he had the power to cross all barriers. Had the supreme deity decided that the hereafter would become Osiris's dominion? It was Thoth who was charged with transporting the royal insignia that would permit Osiris to be crowned a second time.[70] Had Horus the child contracted a life-threatening disease? Thoth was the one who was asked to visit the beyond to fetch the required medicine.[71] After helping bring Osiris back to life, Hathor too was in a position to play a role in maintaining a link with the hereafter.[72] She received the recently deceased on the boundary between the two worlds and helped them present their requests before the gods of the dead.[73] She could even, on occasion, sojourn in their domain; she would periodically go "back up," to earth, above all to receive her offerings.[74]

Finally, it was Osiris's servants who enjoyed the greatest freedom of movement and so could shuttle information back and forth between this world and the realm of the dead.[75] Hence Osiris valued them particularly highly, for the god of the dead was totally cut off from the rest of the world. Unable to leave his kingdom, he would have known next to nothing of what was happening elsewhere without their assistance. Fresh news of the outside was also brought by the new arrivals in his kingdom. The questions with which Osiris bombarded the recently deceased reveal the extent of his ignorance.[76] Were the temples flourishing? Were the required offerings being made, and, above all, were they plentiful? Were the living happy and well treated? It is easy to understand that relations between Osiris and his own wife Isis were practically nonexistent. Although she had managed to reach the beyond, the goddess found herself unable to communicate with her husband. "I arrived in the underworld and you did not speak to me, Wennefer (Onnophris), though I was before you. Did I (actually) reach you. . . . Have you abandoned the road to me?"[77] Forced to lead the life of a solitary widow, Isis never passed up an opportunity to remind others of her pain and grief. In contrast, we know nothing of the feelings or thoughts of Osiris, if, indeed, he had any. Nowhere in the texts does one find him concerned about much of anything other than his status as a sovereign who has triumphed over his adversaries. So that Isis's entreaties and lamentations might be given a hearing in the next world, the gods had to go so far as to promulgate a special decree proclaiming that they would not attempt to erect a supplementary barrier between her and her brother.[78] Nephthys, Isis's sister, tried to turn this situation to her own advantage. Living close to the shadowy zone also frequented by her legitimate spouse Seth, she was able to steal more easily into the realm of the dead. It is known that she let Osiris make love to her and that they had a son, Anubis.[79] Yet, her plaints notwithstanding, she was never to fulfil her wish of becoming coruler, with Osiris, of the hereafter.[80]

The world of the living, for its part, possessed only limited, imperfect means of communicating with the world of the dead. Letters exchanged between Osiris and the gods took days to get to their respective addressees.[81] When urgent matters were at stake, the slowness with which messages were transmitted was a serious problem that required the use of other methods better adapted to the situation. Once, when Re fell ill, it became clear that he could be cured only by one of the powers of the netherworld. The sun-god's entourage had no choice but to appeal to the authorities in Heliopolis to compose a letter. But, as the matter was urgent, Re's aides did not wait for the letter to reach its destination; they decided to read out their appeal near an opening in the earth, located in the west, that communicated with the beyond. Their hope was that help or advice would arrive more quickly that way.[82]

Horus could converse with his father because there existed, at Busiris, a passage to the hereafter that made it possible for Osiris's words to be heard by all those who went there. Yet matters were not as simple as they might seem, the more so as this passage was as a rule sealed off.[83] Arriving with an important piece of news, Horus had to ask the gods accompanying him to be quiet so that Osiris could hear what his son had to say to him.[84] This was not a very convenient procedure; it was preferable to use messengers who had access to the other world. The primordial spirits who belonged to the realm of the uncreated and were thus in a certain sense "dead" were charged with the task. Even then, these messengers had to be endowed with special powers if they were to fulfil their mission. One of them, charged precisely with prolonging the dialogue between Horus and Osiris, proclaimed: "Horus has invested me with his personality in order that I might transmit his concern to Osiris in the hereafter." But the Double Lion, guardian of the gates to the netherworld, did not see matters the same way. "How can you reach the confines of the sky? Though you have taken on Horus's appearance, you do not have his headdress!" The intermediary refused to be put off: "But I am indeed the one who transmits Horus's concerns to Osiris in the hereafter! (Moreover,) Horus has repeated to me what his father Osiris said to him in his coffin on the day of his burial." The Double Lion, suspicious, demanded proof. "Repeat to me, then, what Horus told you was the word of his father Osiris . . . and I will give you the headdress . . . (so that) you can come and go on the paths of the sky, and those on the furthest bounds of the horizon will see you."[85] Thus it was that Osiris was finally informed of the divine decisions that his son had implemented on earth in his father's absence: after triumphing over Seth in the name of Osiris, Horus had just reconquered the supreme throne.[86] The access routes to the world of the dead were, then, carefully controlled. For a messenger to succeed in reaching the god of the dead, he had not only to be qualified by his own nature to enter the hereafter, but also to have entirely assumed the personality of the god whose message he was carrying; that is, he had to have taken on his *iru*. He needed to know one of that god's innermost thoughts in order to prove that his metamorphosis was authentic: this thought served as a password, procuring him an attribute that he needed to circulate freely. This attribute made him recognizable and guaranteed him safe-conduct.[87]

## Exteriors and Limits

The land of Egypt did not encompass the whole of creation. Non-Egyptian or foreign countries existed, too, in accordance with the gods' express wishes. The contours and general shape of the world, as well as the natural frontiers that separated the different countries, had been established by Thoth himself, on the creator's orders.[88] Egypt was the place were the gods normally lived; the length and nature of their stays outside the country varied, depending on the regions involved.

The desert bordering the Nile Valley was not highly regarded by the gods. Only Seth was familiar with it; eventually he was sent into permanent exile there by his fellow gods.[89] This desert was already considered to be "far from Egypt";[90] certain gods ventured into it, but at their risk and peril. On several occasions, apparently, Horus found himself wandering in it—caught in a sandstorm, desperately thirsty, and without a messenger who could go to seek help. To make matters worse, he had forgotten to tie an amulet around his neck to protect himself against all the dangers that menaced travelers in these unsafe parts.[91] It is not known where he had meant to go on these occasions. Perhaps he had set out for the oases where he sometimes took refuge while a child, or, again, after beheading his mother.[92] The oases were, moreover, considered to be within the Egyptian sphere of influence. The gods had residences there, and a manual even describes what the statues in the temples established there looked like.[93]

The lands lying outside Egypt proper were hardly ever visited by the gods—not, at any rate, under normal circumstances. Living abroad without good reason, even if only briefly, was nothing to boast of. Amun was not very proud of the fact that he had sojourned in the depths of Nubia or that he had been born there. He stole back into Egypt unobtrusively, late at night, to avoid being seen.[94] Thanks to his origins, he knew the Nubian language, which had formidable magic powers; he utilized this knowledge against Horus.[95] Foreign countries were the enemies' province par excellence, the province of those who stubbornly sought to invade Egypt out of sheer delight in destruction.[96] As a rule, the gods could protect themselves quite well against such incursions, but, on occasion, they had trouble fending them off. We have seen how hostile forces sacked the residence of the god-king during Shu's reign. It was with a view to mowing down the enemies or preserving order in the face of grave threats that Re or Horus were forced to venture beyond Egypt's boundaries.[97] The sole exception to this rule was the country of Punt, located somewhere to the south-east. A land of aromatic spices, the place the phoenix came from, a region of light where the sun rose and the moon set,[98] Punt was more or less conflated with the "land of the gods"; that is, it was associated, rather vaguely, with the group of territories that produced the riches the gods found useful. The prevailing view of foreign climes was doubtless responsible for the notion that the sun traveled through foreign countries by night before appearing in the distant east, taking precautions to protect himself against the dangers that might beset him on his way.[99]

As time wore on, notions about foreign places changed; they came to represent less of a threat. The relations Egypt maintained with its neighbors ended up influencing the behavior of the gods.[100] Thus the gods did not hesitate to fly to the aid of Ramses II in the thick of the battle of Kadesh, on Syrian territory. One of Khonsu's emanations also accepted an invitation to journey to distant climes in order to extend the benefits of his powers to a foreign princess tormented by a demon.[101] Still later, Isis traveled from Syria to Egypt as if the former were merely an appendage of the latter.[102] In an Egyptian tale, which has, it is true, a Hellenistic tinge, the queen of the Amazons called on Isis and Osiris to help her win the unequal battle she was about to join with the Egyptian and Assyrian armies. All indications are that her wishes were fully satisfied.[103] For the Egyptian gods, the just cause had ceased to be an exclusively national one. The close connection between what was foreign and what was evil did not dissolve, but acquired a universality from which Egypt was not excluded. Henceforth it would be necessary to be on one's guard against disorders provoked "by the Bedouins, the Nubians, the Asians, the men of Egypt, or the foreigners from abroad"—that is, evil wherever it was to be found.[104]

The Universal Master was only master of what had been created; his power met its limits at the frontier where chaos began.[105] This realm of the uncreated, which we have already referred to a number of times and which we will have occasion to mention again, interested the gods only insofar as it represented a threat. The contacts the gods could have with so disquieting a region were necessarily limited. After the act of creation, the waters of the original chaos did not remain completely uninhabited. Immobile birds floated on their surface.[106] We are told that they had human heads and conversed in human language. Thus they looked very much like what the souls of the dead were said to look like. Without actually being souls, they were beings belonging to the realm beyond life. Periodically, under the impulsion of a prolonged fast, they shattered the immobility of chaos and flew off to the regions beyond it. The moment they crossed the border dividing the uncreated from the organized universe, they were struck by the sun's rays. They then transformed themselves into real birds in order to swoop down on Egypt. These were the migratory birds. Messengers of chaos, they were all the more naturally identified with the enemies of creation in that their flight path followed the route taken by earthly invaders. Their destiny was to be hunted down, caught in nets, and sacrificed in the best interests of everyone. Nun, though he was the Primeval Ocean as such, nevertheless had a place within the divine company because he represented the cradle of the world and was the "father of the gods." He resurfaced in this world in several different forms—the Nile floods, the ground water, and the seas that surrounded dry land. He himself lived in subterranean regions that the dead, whether divine or human, were likely to frequent; but one could approach him only after passing through a considerable number of gates.[107] Nun lived in a cavern of abysmal depth, in the proper sense of the word abysmal. It was there that the gods went to see him. This sometimes proved necessary at the end of the flood season, when the waters were on the point of receding. The gods came in grand pomp to ask Nun to maintain the waters a bit longer at a level propitious to good harvests; to persuade him to comply, they showed him a decree signed by Re. But this decree sought less to constrain the venerable Ocean to obey—he was not one to yield to such injunctions—than to flatter him by reminding him how deeply indebted the whole of creation was to him for his good services.[108] Thus, if Nun played a non-negligible role among the gods, he nevertheless rarely left his cavernous residence. He could be summoned along with the other members of the divine company to participate in the grand assemblies. His advice proved indispensable when the equilibrium of the universe was imperiled, as when the human race rose up in rebellion.[109]

# CHAPTER FIVE

# Intelligence and Knowledge

**K**nowledge, like everything else, was a divine creation. After the first gods had come into being, the creator-god created eyesight, hearing, language, the means of subsistence and, finally, the rules governing good and evil.[1] Included herein are the means of acquiring, structuring, and transmitting knowledge. The fact that certain gods could, in a story, suddenly set about thinking "very hard" has led one Egyptologist to remark that thinking was one of the Egyptian gods' most infrequent occupations.[2] According to all the witnesses that have come down to us, the gods acted and spoke with essentially pragmatic ends in mind. Divine acts and words, which were closely related, proceeded from a spontaneous kind of thought elaborated entirely a priori; at once omniscient and prescient, thinking of this sort allowed the gods to dispense with reflections about what had been done or was yet to do. The gods' secret thoughts, their "inner selves," were nothing other than the "intimate knowledge" lodged in their viscera, as we shall see;[3] this knowledge could not but express itself creatively. The totality of what could be conceived exactly coincided with the totality of what had been set in motion by the gods; this totality was reflected, at least to some extent, in the set of writings composed by Thoth. Nevertheless, what *could be* known never coincided perfectly with what *was* known. Between the one and the other, there remained a space open to the kind of knowledge that could be progressively elaborated and subjected to questioning. This type of knowledge was men's portion, and it set them on an endless quest. The books that had fallen from the sky, as well as those that had been discovered in mysterious chambers after being abandoned there by Thoth himself,[4] made advances in men's knowledge partly a matter of chance. It was not for them to invent anything, then, but rather to limit themselves to appropriating a part of what was already known, on condition that the gods gave their consent and provided the necessary means.[5]

## Omniscience and Knowledge

The gods' knowledge [*savoir*] oscillated between the two poles of omniscience and learning [*connaissance*], between inborn and acquired knowledge. Because they had appeared after the creator-god, the other gods could be ignorant of certain things: they were not capable of grasping matters they had not created or participated in. A priori, they were ignorant of the ends and modalities of creation.[6] Concealed within each of them was something that remained a mystery for the others; it ensured their individuality, for it contained the power that was specifically theirs. Thus the gods had certain things to learn about their peers—and they occasionally learned it at their peers' expense. This knowledge of others could be transmitted, because each god could reveal part of what he knew to another; but it could also be acquired by ruse or force. If the mechanisms and functioning of creation were unknown to the gods, they nonetheless had an osmotic relation to the matter it consisted of. They might occasionally not know where one or another of their companions was, but they remained sensitive to fluctuations in their environment; these fluctuations were often signs that an important event was under way. Isis's cries of distress easily reached the solar bark, where Re heard them.[7] Osiris was murdered and then thrown into the river in secret; but Re noticed the motion of the water, which, pitying Osiris, rolled back over the body; he rushed to the scene of the tragedy.[8] Hardly had Seth, in disguise, stolen Osiris's body than Anubis, the god of embalming, knew what he was about.[9] As soon as men set to conspiring against him, Re was aware of what was afoot, although no one had informed him of their plot.[10]

The special faculty that enabled the gods to perceive an event the instant it occurred, together with the reasons for its occurrence, was called *sia*. Sia embraced all the possible knowledge brought into existence by the act of creation.[11] Only the creator himself comprehended this knowledge in its totality. Sia resided in his brightly shining eye, which illuminated the world and saw everything that transpired there.[12] This capacity, which every god possessed in some measure, was a dormant kind of knowledge that became active in the presence of the event that brought it out; it enabled a god to grasp, in the fullest sense of the word, what was going on.[13] It made it possible for already existing knowledge, reactivated by a signal, to emerge at the conscious level. "Sign of recognition," that is the basic meaning of the word *sia* in Egyptian. Not to have sia of something (or someone) was thus not a matter of not knowing it, but rather of not being able, or of no longer being able, to recognize or identify it. Thus was established a rather clear-cut distinction between sia, or synthetic, knowledge, and knowledge as technique and praxis, called *rekh*. Sia operated like an absolute intuition irreducible to logical knowledge. Rekh implied a way of defining concepts that necessarily entailed the use of speech, and, later, writing; they endowed it with its specific character, that is, the capacity to be transmitted. Only if filtered through the spoken and written word could sia become accessible in the field of rekh.

The kind of knowledge and intelligence that could be articulated and could create resided in the heart, the seat of directing and organizing consciousness. Yet not all intellectual faculties were concentrated there. There was a profounder, more intimate place, the intestines; a special power lay concealed in them, one that drew all its force from the energy of life itself. This energy was called *heka*.[14] To swallow heka was to strengthen and develop this power; to swallow one's own heka was to refrain from putting it to use.[15] Heka was what resulted from giving form to all the energies (ka) one absorbed; it constituted an inward, personal sort of knowledge distinct from the universal or collective type of knowledge mentioned above. Heka was often directed against one's enemies and served essentially as a means of self-protection;[16] it was at once weapon and shield. A repository of knowledge bound up with an individual, such as knowledge about a god's real name (we shall see how important this was), heka was rarely transmitted to others, at least not voluntarily. When it *was* transmitted, it was transmitted, as the nature of the information passed on required, from the entrails of the one who possessed it to those of the one receiving it. Consequently, the malignant forces ranged against the gods preferred to attack their hearts and viscera in order to gain complete mastery over the powers their victims possessed.[17] To penetrate—as a fly might, for example—the belly of a god was an easy way to establish oneself in the most intimate part of his being and acquire a position of domination there.[18]

These different kinds of knowledge and their use bore no obvious relation to a god's intellectual level or to what his imagination might encompass. To be sure, such matters are rarely mentioned, and we know next to nothing about them. From our contemporary vantage point, Nemty, who was tricked into taking a bribe from Isis, might be regarded as foolish or naive. For the ancient Egyptians, foolishness and stupidity were the special province of only two divine beings: first, Horus the child, who had a tendency to act before thinking and whose quite temporary foolishness was simply the consequence of his innocence and tender age;[19] second, Seth, who was traditionally considered to be the least refined and least intelligent of all his fellows. Violent and impulsive, Seth was easily duped; he would himself propose stupid wagers that turned out badly for him. Thus he suggested to Horus that they each build a stone ship and engage in a boat race to see who was faster. Horus took him up, but then secretly built a wooden ship, plastering it over so that it would seem to be made of stone. Seth made a boat of real stone, which sank pathetically the minute it was launched.[20]

Finally, we should ask whether the gods could conceivably have had a place for works of the imagination [*un imaginaire*]. The world of the gods was a reality from which fictions were excluded. Lies—which, in any event, only Seth was in the habit of telling—cannot be treated as a genuine product of the intellect. Thoth, master of writing,[21] never produced poetry or fiction, although he had no trouble making measurements and recording the gods' adventures. There remains the question of dreams. The gods needed to sleep.[22] Only Re did not let himself sleep, because of the nature of his function.[23] But there would seem to exist only one text that describes a god—Horus—in the act of dreaming.[24] He is said to see "something far off, in his own city"; what he sees is a nightmare. We know that, in the world of men, bad dreams were sent by Seth and that nightmares were closely associated with the terrors of the night. But these terrors were merely projections of the dark, evil forces threatening the equilibrium of the world.[25] Should we conclude that Horus's nightmare is peopled by anguishing images presaging the end of the created world and the disappearance of all the gods?

## Knowing a Name; or, The Conquest of Power

Buried deep within the "inner self," whose role we noted above,[26] the real name of each god was kept secret from all the others. It was to be found alongside other intellectual powers whose function was to ensure the protection of the individual; it was, moreover, one of these protective powers. Closely bound up with the cosmic dimension of a god, his real name defined his basic role and, in a certain sense, his special status vis-à-vis the other gods.[27] To reveal one's name was to renounce this status as far as the god one confided it to was concerned and to put oneself completely in his power. Hence, to protect himself, a divinity tried to "strike terror into those who tried to learn his name."[28] For greater security, a god's full name was made up of a virtually infinite series of segments that were, in their turn, so many different names.[29] The name was thus practically impossible to remember, and it took a very long time to pronounce. Reciting the name of one of Horus's wives, Seperteres, took three years.[30] When secret names *were* "revealed," the result was often an evasive pirouette that projected a god's character onto the animal world, providing only partial insight into it.[31] In any case, a name that one had come into the possession of was only used as a piece of knowledge that supplemented knowledge one already had. There could be no question of pronouncing it lightly, for that could unleash events everyone had grounds to fear. "If one pronounces his name on the banks of a river, the river will run dry. If one pronounces his name on earth, it will go up in flames."[32]

At the beginning of the world, none of the gods knew the names of any of the others. Re, in particular, took special precautions to keep knowledge of his name from being used against him. Profiting from the fact that, like all the gods, he had a large number of names at his disposal, he changed names on a daily basis.[33] Isis, about whom we are told that "her heart was more rebellious than an infinite number of men, more smart than an infinite number of gods," and that she was "more clever than an infinite number of spirits," had a particular kind of personal knowledge, a heka she inherited, though it is uncertain from whom: perhaps from Geb,[34] god of the earth, or even from Re, her own father.[35] She was to use it to Re's cost, at a time when, the burden of his long reign weighing heavily on his shoulders, he had become old and somewhat senile. One morning, when he was taking his place amid his crew in the solar bark as it was about to set forth on its journey to illuminate the world, a drop of spittle dribbled from his mouth and fell to the ground. Unbeknownst to everyone, Isis mixed the saliva with the earth that clung to it, fashioning this mass into a snake to which she gave a particularly pointed shape. She left the snake on a path the supreme deity walked down every day. The inevitable occurred: Re went out to take the air, followed by his court, and the snake bit him. He was immediately assailed by unbearable pains. Because he traversed the world daily and had perfect knowledge of everything he had created, Re correctly surmised that he had not been bitten by one of his own creatures. Certain sources say that this incident brought on a cataclysm similar to the end of the world; the earth was plunged into darkness, shards of pottery began walking about, stones began to talk, and mountains took to wandering hither and thither.[36] Re appealed for relief to all the gods of his entourage known to possess special knowledge. They all came running. Isis, of course, was among them. She pretended to be astonished: "What is it, my divine father? What is the matter? . . . one of your children has raised his head against you?"[37] Re described the agony he was in. Without beating around the bush, Isis said, "Tell me your name, my divine father." The god launched into a long recital of his names and attributes, but Isis was no dupe: "Your (real) name was not among those you mentioned to me," she replied. Meanwhile, the poison redoubled its destructive effects on the god's body. Under the impact of this torture, Re finally gave in, but not without first stating a condition: Isis was not to reveal the secret he was about to tell her to anyone but her son, and not even *he* was to hear it until he had taken an oath not to divulge it to anyone else.[38] Once Isis had agreed to this condition, Re revealed his name to her; she immediately pronounced certain benign magic spells, delivering the god of his suffering. Among the various versions we have of this story, hardly a one dares spell out Re's real name. Even the one exception falls back on a ruse to keep it at least partially secret: it prefaces each of the different parts of the name (which is in fact interminable) with the Egyptian word meaning "name," but changes the order of the two letters comprising this word. The effect of a direct disclosure is thus defused, because what is revealed is not the name as such, but an inversion that alters its true nature.[39]

Of course, Isis passed along what she had learned to her son Horus, who became, in his turn, a well-known magician and medical practitioner.[40] Inspired by his mother's example, he did not wait long to avail himself of the same methods she had used to wrest valuable secrets from others. For example, he profited from his wedding night to force his wife or concubine, Ta-Bitjet, a fearsome scorpion-goddess, to tell him her name; he thus acquired the power to heal the bites of poisonous animals.[41] This episode shows that the name by which the gods were known and which they used to identify themselves was, in the last analysis, only a stand-in. It was entirely possible for a husband to be unaware of his wife's real name if he did not use ruses or force to discover it, as here. Nemty, the ferryman, was to be another of Horus's victims, for Horus learned the contents of his name as well.[42] The story is quite similar to that of Isis and Re, except that in this case Horus did not have to resort to trickery to get what he wanted. While he was crossing the river on Nemty's ferryboat, the ferryman was bitten by a snake and appealed to Horus to save him. Horus turned the occasion to advantage, refusing to help Nemty until the latter had told him what he wished to know. Nemty did not prove very skilful at handling the situation. He clumsily decked himself out with names that were very obviously not his; some were even known to be the names of gods more important than he was. In fact, he was simply showing off and stalling for time. Horus was hardly about to be taken in by so crude a maneuver. The boatman finally had to disclose his real name in exchange for being cured.

In all these episodes, acquiring knowledge, often violently, is also a matter of acquiring power at the expense of those who are forced to give in and reveal their names. Already an accomplished magician, Isis, once she had learned her precious secret, became the foremost practitioner of Re's art—that of relieving the gods' aches and pains.[43] In the course of these adventures, Re can plainly be seen to be losing his touch: the knowledge that enabled him to cure those of his peers suffering from poisoning was losing its force. If he succeeded in providing relief for one or another god, or even in helping the distraught Isis save her own son, he could also be seen fretting over one of his stricken friends and using make-do methods to keep the poor fellow's condition from worsening while waiting for Horus, now in a better position to treat the ailment than he was, to come and administer a definitive cure.[44]

However, this personal knowledge, or heka, was not absolutely fail-proof. While Seth and Horus were locked in merciless combat underwater, Isis tried to step in to help her son. She fashioned a harpoon that she threw at Seth. But the weapon missed its target and buried itself in Horus instead. Horus brought his mother's error to her attention by howling with pain. As one follows the twists and turns of the story, one gathers that the goddess's heart was wavering between two creatures equally near and dear to her, her brother Seth and her son Horus—a circumstance that clouded her judgment and prevented her from freely exercising her power.[45]

## What Thoth Knew

Thoth was charged with important responsibilities in the administration of the world.[46] He owed his privileged position at the creator's side to the fundamental role the latter had assigned him. As the creator's heart and tongue, Thoth was the instrument by means of which the creation took concrete shape.[47] His mastery of the written and spoken word permitted him to give active form to the creative thought of the creator-god. Without Thoth's involvement, the creation would have remained, properly speaking, a dead letter. Addressing himself to all the gods in the universe, he could proudly proclaim: "I am Thoth. I repeat to you what Re has declared, (for) someone has spoken to you before my words were heard. I am Thoth, master of the divine words (the hieroglyphs) which put things in their (proper) place. I give the offerings to the gods and to the blessed dead. I am Thoth who puts Maat in writing for the Ennead. Everything that comes out of my mouth takes on existence as (if I were) Re. I am he who cannot be driven from the sky or the earth because I know what is concealed in the sky, inaccessible on earth, and hidden in the Primeval Ocean. I am the creator of the sky, he who is at the origin of the mountains . . . I make the gods and men live."[48] It is through Thoth's offices, then, that the world is kept in good working order. If the solar bark is provided with a crew who make sure it moves along, it is Thoth who takes the helm to keep it on course.[49] Thoth, it is said, is the one who lifts the sun into the sky,[50] and it is likewise Thoth who "created the structure of Egypt and the organization of the provinces."[51]

Though he was not the creator, Thoth ensured the permanence of knowledge. He was the memory of the gods; he recorded their words and enabled the creator to be continuously informed of all that existed.[52] The creator knew the future; Thoth, for his part, acquired a vision of it that was, thanks to his archives, unerring.[53] There was thus a reciprocal relation between what Thoth and the creator knew;[54] it made Thoth the intermediary between omniscience and revealed or acquired knowledge. He was at once the Perceptive One (sia) and the one who knew everything (rekh).[55] The two kinds of knowledge were harmoniously combined in his person. His peculiarity was to receive the first one (sia) and to transmit the second one (rekh). Thoth was the one who comprehended (the ancient word was "swallowed") the Two Lands;[56] he had an intimate understanding of the creation. The recorder and preserver of knowledge, he also had the power to diffuse it, among the gods as well as men.[57] Writing was the medium used to transmit this knowledge, the vehicle of learning (rekh). Yet, according to a legend recounted by Plato (though its basic content may well have been inspired by Egypt), the diffusion of learning by means of writing did not arouse much enthusiasm among the gods.[58] Describing the advantages of the art of writing, Thoth advocated passing the practice of this art along to men. Atum, the creator (called Thamos by Plato) saw nothing but drawbacks in his plan. If men made use of writing, he said, they would come to distrust their memories, relying instead on material signs to recover memories that their minds would no longer preserve a trace of. This amounts to saying that the assiduous pursuit of rekh must necessarily lead to the progressive loss of sia, and, ultimately, to the abandonment of creative thought.

Two logics clash here. The affirmation that only sia is truly creative links rekh with repetition, condemning it merely to find what has already been created without contributing anything of its own. Thoth's capacity to handle rekh and sia with equal skill gave him a balanced, even-handed role that led others to compare him to the plummet of a scale and invested his intermediary function with its full significance. But it also threw the limits and dangers of his knowledge into relief. Doubtless, he was a sage among the gods, but his awareness of the fact made him pretentious and pedantic. His penchant for set speeches and his somewhat stilted solemnity could get on others' nerves when an urgent matter needed attending to. When Re dispatched him to go see Isis, who needed medical help for her sick child, Thoth got bogged down in convoluted speeches so entirely out of place that the irritated goddess was provoked to the point of exclaiming: "How wise is your heart, Thoth, but how slow are your decisions!"[59] In a world in which conflicts were settled by brute force or by the power of words, the god of wisdom did not always put his knowledge to good use. Nor was he devoid of duplicity or bad faith. In his hands, finally, writing—far from consistently contributing to the harmony of the world—served as a means of gaining the upper hand over his fellow gods through trickery and falsification. As the gods' ritualist, he worked in secret, as would his human disciples later on.[60] He also kept the list used to apportion offerings among his fellow gods[61]—their most vital concern. He used his position and his power over the heavenly bodies to manipulate the movements of the stars and disturb the course of time in order to steal, as we have seen, part of what was due the other gods.[62]

## From the Spoken Word to Writing

Speech or writing: which of the two ruled the world, and in what did their difference consist? Was the language of the gods, to begin with, the same as that of men? The fact that, under certain circumstances,[63] the gods addressed themselves to humankind orally by no means implies that the language they spoke among themselves was the one men used. Indeed, what was true of the divine forms and aspects held for language as well: discourse adapted itself to circumstances. The gods understood the language of animals—that of fish[64] or birds, for example. The latter often brought them messages and were given their responses.[65] Involved here was, plainly, a special privilege of the gods, for men did not normally have access to this type of communication. The hero of a tale who seized the mysterious scrolls Thoth had long ago left at the bottom of an underwater chest could, simply by reading the spells written there, understand everything all animals said, wherever they might be.[66] But this was purloined knowledge: the hero paid for his exploit with his life, and took the precious manuscript with him to the tomb. In certain Greco-Egyptian magic texts, a magician chooses to address a god in "bird-glyphic" in order to be better understood; he also resorts to dialects such as "falconian."[67] Birds, who often flew high in the sky, were naturally likely to communicate with the gods and act as intermediaries for men.

Generally speaking, animal languages could be perceived as expressions of the supernatural simply because they were non-natural and could not be learned by men. Travellers who heard a cow mooing at night might well conclude that what they actually heard was gods conversing.[68] Thus the animals who greeted the sunrise with cries of joy— baboons, for example—were thought to be speaking a mysterious language pleasing to the creator.[69] Moreover, "baboonian" held an honorable place among the many languages spoken by the magician mentioned a moment ago. Indeed, many languages in use in the world of the gods were foreign to men; among them were those spoken by the powers of the east,[70] or the language in use among the genies of the hereafter, which the dead who hoped to avoid falling into their traps had every reason to try and understand.[71] Not all these languages necessarily belonged to the animal world. Here, the animals merely lent their voices to others.

Speech, that is, articulated language, had been invented by Thoth;[72] it was likewise Thoth who had created the differences between the languages spoken by men.[73] The multiplicity of tongues, although it made for problems in the realm of the dead, where interpreters were sometimes needed,[74] did not necessarily represent an obstacle for the gods. Thanks to his origins, Amun was familiar with Nubian.[75] Yet it is only logical to suppose that Egyptian had special status, as it had been bequeathed to the inhabitants of the Nile Valley, where the gods preferred to dwell. Iamblichus, a fourth-century neo-Platonic philosopher well acquainted with Egyptian thought, notes that it would be absurd to believe that the gods spoke this language in particular, yet adds: "Since the Egyptians were the first to be accorded the privilege of communications from the gods, the gods preferred to be invoked according to the usages of this people."[76] But, in the hermetic treatises, Thoth is made to say a great deal more: "The special character of the sounds and the proper intonation of Egyptian words embody the energy of the things one says . . . we do not use mere words, but sounds full of power."[77] Not only was speech creative, but it also found its most adequate transposition in the Egyptian language. This is precisely the idea developed in the Egyptian texts themselves. The breath of life that emanated from the mouth of the creator, sustaining the life of other beings, was one and the same thing as the words he uttered.[78] The sound of the creative voice, called *hu*, was assimilated to the food needed to sustain life. It, too, resided in the god's entrails.[79] When the world, in the very first moments of its existence, was still afloat in the Primeval Ocean, the creator-god began by imagining the names of the beings and things in it.[80] Then, using hu and sia, he pronounced these names in order to endow them with definite existence.[81] According to a well-established tradition, the world was created by seven words pronounced one after the other by the creator.[82] These "words" first structured the world geographically.[83] They then became individual beings that, like all those who helped the creator at the beginning of the world, were fated to die. Apparently they were shut up in a chest.[84] Pronouncing the creative words again would have been dangerous; it could have brought on the end of the world.[85]

In the final analysis, everything the gods said was creative. One of their favorite modes of expression consisted in what we call "wordplay." A sentence or a turn of phrase that one or another god used in talking about a place or a living creature gave this place or being a name and thus endowed it with tangible reality.[86] This was one of the creative methods most often employed by the creator-god.[87] Indeed, no matter which divinity was involved, every verbal comment endowed its object with real existence. If Horus, in the form of Harendotes (the Greek version of the Egyptian name meaning "Horus avenger of his father"), succeeded in avenging his father, the reason was that Osiris had literally created this function by pronouncing this name when he was roused from the sleep of death, after the embalming rites had been performed.[88] In the Myth of Horus, every act provided the occasion for a spoken commentary, thus generating the places and participants in the cult of Horus, as well as its principal sacred objects.[89] Generally speaking, it was enough to announce an event for the event to take place.[90] Hence insults or threats contained a reality that wanted nothing more than to emerge in concrete form: the target of a threat or insult was subjected in actual fact to what had been verbally inflicted upon him.[91] Thus the spoken word was a weapon that had the power to subjugate or annihilate one's enemies. This was obviously true in Thoth's case,[92] but the same held for gods of a more physical bent, such as Seth. It was enough for him to tell an enemy of his strength for the latter to beat a retreat.[93] His voice, often identified with the rumbling of thunder, intimidated the most dangerous and the most intractable—for example, the raging sea.[94]

Hieroglyphic writing had only one name: "divine words." This established its status. Writing could not function independently of the spoken word, of which it was merely a transcription. It maintained an a posteriori existence and was essentially limited to a commemorative or archival function. Writing was merely a putting into form, an "in-formation" of the world. With its help, the gods constituted the archives of important events; everything touching on the conflict between Horus and Seth, for example, was carefully written down.[95] Given the role writing played in the world of the gods, there could be no works of fiction there. Written signs themselves were defined as "imprints" of everything contained in creation. Every living creature and every thing could be utilized as written signs. All divine writings without exception were considered "emanations of Re," or faithful representations of the will of the creator.[96] To draw up a catalogue of written signs was to draw up a catalogue of all that had been created. It is possible that Thoth kept an inventory of these "imprints" and could make a tally of them.[97] Here, too, he functioned as an intermediary, as the one who knew how to read, that is, "to turn script into words,"[98] and thus to turn it back toward its origins, to its originary force. Thoth reduced the opposition between writing as "rekh" and the spoken word as "sia," but he also ensured their transmission.

Although no limits were placed on the use of writing among the gods, the actual *practice* of writing was rather restricted. Few of the gods actually wielded the pen. Neith appears to have managed to conduct her own correspondence.[99] She had extensive power over the written word, for she could call back the book carried by her messengers, thus rendering the deceased a service by helping him avoid condemnation.[100] Osiris, isolated in his remote otherworldly realm, clearly had scribes of his own at his disposal.[101] Isis, who possessed, as we have seen, formidable knowledge, proved capable of writing a book to ensure her brother's well-being.[102] The same was true of her son Horus, who inherited many of his mother's secrets.[103] But reading and writing were not common divine occupations; these tasks fell almost exclusively to Thoth, for reasons that should be quite clear by now. Among all the means of communication and information used by the gods, writing had only an accessory role; sometimes it even turned out to be superfluous. Thus, during the litigation between Horus and Seth, the king of the gods sent a letter to the tribunal, pressing it to make a decision; he simultaneously intervened in the oral proceedings. Yet nothing suggested that he had left the place where he was supposed to have been.[104]

According to a little-known custom, the twentieth day of the first month of the year was set aside for the exchange of letters between gods.[105] The text that mentions this indicates that the exchange had to do with the give and take between life and death, as both were at work in the written texts. The place where these writings were composed was called the "House of Life"; it was there as well that a Horus specially charged with putting the cosmic enemies to death was supposed to live.[106] Here writing appears to be closely bound up with the cult of Osiris and the resurrection of the god. Osiris "who had achieved his cycle," that "yesterday,"[107] came back to life in writings, themselves only reactualizations of a past memory.

## Gods, Quite Simply

If it were not for the fact that they were forever quarrelling, the gods would appear quite inactive, and one might well ask what purpose they ultimately served. Our long sojourn amidst all this commotion has nevertheless enabled us to see that the quarrels, victories, and defeats of the divine beings indicate their most basic functions. Each of them possessed talents that were not, as a rule, negligible. These talents corresponded to specific kinds of savoir-faire and more or less accurately reflected the role each god played within the divine community. This role was portrayed as something as well hidden and difficult to know as the god's name.[108] Accordingly, each god's special skill [savoir-faire] corresponded to a lack of this skill [non-savoir] in the other gods, who were generally speaking not able to imitate a skill they themselves did not have.

The creator-god defended his creation, trying to settle conflicts as best he could. At his side, Thoth was the faithful assistant; he relayed decisions and mediated between different kinds of knowledge. The violent Seth both unloosed storms and tempests and brought them back under control. Khnum, the potter, formed all the beings in creation on his wheel. Certain aspects of the gods were endowed with special abilities. Rams, especially the Ram of Mendes, had prophetic powers; their declarations had the force of law for one and all.[109] Horus became a doctor in consequence of the many illnesses he had suffered as a child,[110] but also thanks to the knowledge his mother handed down to him. Thus it was that Horus the child became a "Savior"; this particular facet of his personality was created by Thoth.[111] Clearly, these various activities ensured the proper functioning of the world. Manual labor, properly speaking, was not normally performed by the gods themselves. Certain objects were in fact reflections of divine elements and did not have to be created.[112] Crafts were hardly practiced. Ptah, the god of artisans, supposedly took it upon himself to use his special skills to accomplish practical tasks,[113] but it is unlikely that he did any actual work himself. Petty chores usually fell to minor divinities, like the obscure daughter of Osiris who molded mud bricks, doubtless because they were needed for her father's tomb.[114] When such work was performed by more important gods, the labor itself was secondary and usually found its justification in a mythological episode in which the activity in question had been carried out for the first time. We have seen that Horus built himself a boat to take up a challenge of Seth's. Apparently he often built boats; he constantly needed vessels on short notice to set off in pursuit of his enemies.[115] Isis and Nephthys became weavers and spinners[116] when they had to mummify Osiris, but also, it seems, when Horus the child's various illnesses and accidents created a need for bandages.[117] This kind of work became a veritable métier for Isis, one she practiced regularly.[118] It occupied her attention so entirely that she failed to hear the cries of her son when he was stung by a scorpion. We likewise read that the goddesses were, in fact, forced to work by Seth,[119] and also that Thoth, to exonerate them of the obligation to perform this menial labor, had to negotiate with Neith until she agreed to let her own weavers take their place.[120]

Overall, one cannot say that the personalities of the Egyptian gods were defined in other than functional terms. One finds few character traits indicating distinctive, sharply etched personalities. Seth stands out as the sole exception. It must be said that he was the "excessive" god, and that this lent him a profile that his reputedly perfect fellows lacked. Violent, aggressive, given to drink, he was also brave, and a pitiful victim of his own passions. With other gods too, one discovers, if one examines the texts closely enough, certain personal particularities that are not always apparent at first glance. Thoth was wise but boring, or even a wee bit pompous; he was also something of a con artist. Re, the supreme divinity, was occasionally somewhat weak and indecisive, torn as he sometimes was between the different opinions aired by the gods of his entourage. His hand was forced now and again. At other times, in contrast, he could be stubborn and rather unscrupulous, willing to juggle the facts to impose a point of view he knew to be unjust. Isis, the mother and weeping widow, sometimes overplayed her role, profiting from her situation to monopolize the attention of her peers. In fact, she was rather cold and proud. She was not in the habit of letting her scruples get in the way of her objectives, but, in this, she was quite like her fellow gods. It was universally acknowledged that she was perfectly faithful to her deceased husband and wholeheartedly loved his child, even if her love was not devoid of tactical considerations. Osiris could seem colorless and excessively narcissistic, not to say egotistical. His precious self, power, and privileges were his chief preoccupations. His wife was absent from his thoughts, while his son existed for him only insofar as he would ensure his triumph in the hereafter while seeing to it that he also maintained his power everlastingly in this world. Nemty was greedy and perhaps a bit of a simpleton. Thus only a few rare personalities stand out from the pack; but they are less personalities, perhaps, than archetypes, as if what were involved were conventional roles in a universal tragi-comedy in which all the main actors were nothing more than shadow-figures.

These gods with virtually unlimited powers fought like adolescents still trying to find their direction in life. Their mistakes and failings left their mark on a creation that went sliding down the slope of a destiny the gods did not really control. Ultimately, they left it to men to assume co-responsibility for their share of the world. For that, they deserve our respect.

# PART II

# MEDIATING BETWEEN THE GODS AND HUMANKIND

# CHAPTER SIX

# The Machine of the Universe
# and the Universal God

**B**y means of a series of creative acts, the solar creator god set up a closed universe driven by a precise mechanism that was entirely at his service. A hymn—one of several—offers a theoretical description of his activity and power within this closed space:

> Hail to you, Re, at (your) rising, and to you, Atum, at (your) setting. You rise every day, you shine brightly every day, while you appear in glory, king of the gods. You are Lord of the sky and Lord of the earth, who has created the creatures above and those below. Sole god who came into being on the first occasion, who made the land and created human beings, who made the Nun and created the Nile, who created the waters and imparted life to what is in them, who raised up the mountains and bestowed existence upon men and herds . . . Divine youth, heir to eternity, who engendered himself and gave birth to himself, unique one with many forms.[1]

The solar character here assigned to Re is the distinguishing feature of all Egyptian creator-gods. The territorial organization of the country, divided up into provinces in which each major city had its own temple and principal god, made it possible to conceive the figure of the creator in various local forms. As regional traditions each had their own particular features, they offered many different variants on the creation story.[2] These variants are not all equally well-known, but all eventually bring a figure representing the sun into their account of the creation; he either anticipates the

creation, paving the way for it, or puts the crowning touch on it by causing the light to shine forth.

## A Woman's Body as the Sky

The sky, both the portion that men could see and the portion that remained hidden from them, was incarnated by the body of a woman who
took her place on high in the final stage of creation.[3] This body, that of the
goddess Nut, represented the limits of the domain Re traveled through
every day. It made it possible to put the entire mechanism of the universe
into place and established the framework of the organized world, of
which it was an integral, concrete part. But Nut's body and the area de-
limited by it did not constitute the whole of existing space. Beyond it
were regions the sun never reached. Unknown to the other gods or even
to the dead, this peripheral zone was shrouded in eternal darkness: the
sun never rose there. It would one day serve as the creator's ultimate
refuge: he would return to it when the world came to an end, as we saw
in Part I.[4] Confined to this universe, which was the limit of his movements, the sun engendered its constitutive elements by providing himself
with descendants. What the creation might originally have looked like
remains something of a mystery. The earth, Geb, and the sky, Nut, belonged to the third generation of gods; their parents were Shu and Tefnut,
son and daughter of the creator-god. Thus there must have been a transi-
tional moment when the ultimate structure of the universe was not yet
visible, when "the solar disk was not yet in the sky," although the head of
the sun-god "had reached the distant sky."[5] Moreover, certain texts state
that the creator-god conceived Shu in order to "see what he had created."[6]
Shu was thus a rather ill-defined airy zone that had existed before the
firmament was put in place in the final stage of creation. According to
certain traditions, once the universe had been created, the world enjoyed
a golden age.[7] "The world saw a period of abundance, bellies were full;
there were no famines. In the days of the primeval gods, walls did not
fall, nor did thorns prick. Perversion did not exist on earth, the crocodile
did not carry off his prey, the snake did not bite."[8] As this initial period
wore on, "while the Ennead was still in its prime and disorder had not
yet come about,"[9] the creator-god grew old. After a series of events that
have already been described, he decided to quit the company of men for
the distant sky. On his orders, Shu divided the earth from the sky and
became the air that held up his own daughter Nut. From then on, Shu
would occupy the space between earth and sky, permitting the sunlight
to spread through all of creation.[10] Shu's act brought the gradual creation
of the mechanisms of the universe to a close; the process had required the

participation of three generations of gods. By holding earth and sky permanently apart, Shu ensured that his father would have a well-defined sphere all his own. Though he distanced himself from men after their rebellion, Re did not withdraw his light from them. He shone by day; in the evening, when he had grown weaker, he disappeared, to regenerate himself and be reborn the following morning, as powerful as he had been the day before. By redefining the spatial roles of his children in a renewed creation, the sun-god established a cyclical form of time; it enabled him to avoid growing steadily older, and so assured him eternal existence.

This structuring of the universe laid down the rhythms of the day and year once and for all and established the diurnal and nocturnal movements of the sun. It set up a year divided into three seasons of four months each: twelve months made up of three ten-day periods—"decades"—or thirty-six decades of ten twenty-four-hour days. But this three-hundred-sixty-day year left five days outside the perfect equilibrium of the numbers. Like space, time too had an organized inside and a chaotic outside. Traditionally, the five days excluded from the real year were assumed to be those during which Nut's five children were born. Because the separation of the earth and the sky prevented Geb and Nut from procreating, Nut only managed to bring the children in her womb into the world with the help of a ruse of Thoth's, as we have seen.[11] Born outside the ideal model, these children were perceived as intruders and were often called "the children of disorder," a name amply justified by their incessant quarrels and the disturbances of time they provoked. On their father's side, they belonged to the earth; the lives they were assumed to lead were organized around Osiris, and followed the rhythms not only of the solar, but also of the lunar cycle.[12]

By day or by night, Nut offered a space for men to observe. Yet what they saw only hinted at all that was concealed from them. The heavenly bodies—no matter which ones were involved and no matter when one observed them—were but the luminous images of a vaster whole one could only guess at. The more intense the light—and the sun's is intense—the more it hid, and the more effectively it prevented people from looking at it. As we shall see, men received all manner of things from the day sky; from the night sky, they had all manner of things to learn. The sun had knowledge of all the space he traveled through; but he delegated the nocturnal space of knowledge to the god of the moon.

### The Diurnal Voyage of the Sun

Nut, the heavenly vault, stretched from west to east: her head lay to the west, her lap and legs to the east. To make her body include the four cardinal points, and thus provide a more coherent representation of the world as it was perceived, certain texts indicate, more precisely, that Nut's head lay to the northwest and her lap to the southeast.[13] Thus Re was born in the southeastern part of the sky. In the representations to be found in certain royal tombs, Nut's diurnal body is embellished with details that vary with the taste of the artist.[14] In the tomb of Ramses VI, for example, two rows of black stars frame twelve red disks laid out in a row;[15] these disks perhaps represent the twelve phases of the sun—the twelve hours of the day. Nut's disproportionately elongated body is meant to suggest the infinite length of the journey of Re's bark. To the east, Nut's toes, evoked by a simple yellow line, rest on the earth; the tips of her fingers touch the ground to the west. Between the sky and the earth stretches a long river, criss-crossed by several boats representing the hours of the day. Imbued with the idea that their natural surroundings reflected the will of the gods, the Egyptians naturally imagined their creator moving about in an aquatic environment similar to the one they were familiar with on earth. This river, which Nut ultimately swallows, has its source in a series of mysterious canals at the level of her pubis.[16] There the night boat and the day boat meet, so that the god can pass from one to the other. There were, to be sure, some variations in the course of the sun. Depending on the season, the sun's daytime and nighttime journeys would be longer or shorter.[17] They were of exactly equal length only during the third and ninth months of the Egyptian year, which was, of course, when the vernal and autumnal equinox occurred. Up and down the southern bank of the river, minor divinities or genies, often anonymous, form a line along the sun's route. Doubtless each of them had a specific task, but only in rare cases do we actually know what these gods' function was. In addition to the offering-bearers and gods armed with knives or spears, we see the oarsmen and boat haulers.[18]

One of the fullest textual and pictorial versions of the sun's voyage shows us seven boats in the daytime sky; their positions doubtless mark off the principal stages of the sun's course. "In order to sustain the life of men, and all the cattle, and all the worms, [everything] he has created," the god sets out on his course in the first hour of the day, showing himself to the horizon dwellers. If human beings can already perceive his first glimmerings, they cannot yet see him rising above the horizon. He is welcomed and worshiped by all those who dwell in the "land of the inhabitants of the horizon"[19]—chattering apes and mythical creatures. The first boat is towed by six divinities, ram-headed or anthropomorphic. Their efforts permit the boat slowly to leave its moorings. At its center stands the falcon-headed sun-god in his naos, whose doors are thrown open. On the poop deck, we see Sia, personification of omniscience; he gives his name to the two oars that serve as a rudder. Positioned behind the naos, Hu, personification of the sound of the creative voice, takes the form of the hieroglyph that stands both for the god's entourage and also for his power over life and death. In front of the naos stands Heka, incarnation of the god's personal knowledge. Sia, Hu, and Heka are the creator-god's usual companions; indeed, they are personifications of his vital creative powers.[20] Their presence serves as a reminder that every sunrise creates the world anew.[21] To the fore of the boat, Geb appears to be cast in the role of a helmsman busy sounding the waters in order to avoid the shallows. This may remind us that, as god of the earth, he is well acquainted with all its cracks and crevices, even those to be found underwater. Behind him, between two forms of Horus, is the "Lady of the Boat"; she wears a crown that shows that she is simply a manifestation of Hathor, the god's own daughter.

The same gods make up the crew of the second boat, although the outward appearance of some of them has changed. The boat haulers have disappeared. At the prow, one sees a new goddess, called "she who causes ascending";[22] one arm stretched out before her, she utters spells that now enable the boat to ascend to the sky. Before her are four uraei; they form a protective screen between the boat and the immediately following scene, which depicts the slaughter of the serpent Apophis. This monster, who has emerged from the waters of chaos, glides into the river and attempts to stop the sun on his course. Two genies spear Apophis, while a third tries furiously to hack him to pieces. The deceased pharaoh himself, Ramses VI, takes part in the action. With the third boat, we approach the sixth hour of the day, the zenith, during which the gods once again clash with the demon Apophis. Apophis has begun gulping down the waters of the heavenly river so that the boat will run aground on the sand bars.[23] The same individuals who attacked him earlier do so again, raining blows down upon him until he is forced to vomit up the water he has swallowed. The boat then tranquilly resumes its journey. With the sixth boat, the landscape changes. Re reaches the Fields of Reeds, a mysterious region of the western sky known for its miraculous crops.[24] Grain grew to enormous heights of from two to three yards there; the gigantic ears were at least a yard high.[25] Cities with walls of bronze are already coming into view; one of them is even called "the city of Re." All indications are that we are approaching the earth. The journey through this area takes place, or draws to a close, in the ninth hour. Here gods and goddesses await the sun-god. Among them we can recognize Osiris and the Great Bear, in the form of mummies.[26] The entrance to the netherworld is nearby. A multitude of creatures crowd round; they are the counterparts of those who acclaimed the sun at the beginning of his journey. This is also the place the blessed dead are admitted to, after many trials and tribulations, as we shall see.[27] After crossing it, the solar bark peacefully pursues its journey toward the west, or, rather, the northwest. In the eleventh and twelfth hours, it encounters the Spirits of the North. Endowed with the power to drive storms from the sky, these spirits raise winds that facilitate the boat's entry into port. Boarding it, they take charge of the delicate docking operations, manipulating the stays fore and aft. The river widens considerably at the level of Nut's mouth, which the solar disk now makes ready to enter. It is, at last, the twelfth hour, during which the god is said to "set in life" in the west horizon.

## The Sun's Night Journey

The sun vanishes, then, into Nut's mouth, from where he embarks on a journey inside her body, the space of night. From one end of his itinerary to the other, his boat is towed by circumpolar stars, called "the unwearying stars" because they shine all night long. We are apparently no longer on a river, but on a bed of sand, where the boat cannot advance unaided. This, region, too will be crossed in twelve hours; the distance covered each hour makes up one stage of the journey, marked by a door through which the boat has to pass. But the voyage inside Nut's body does not actually begin until the third hour of the night.[28] Hugging the goddess's body, the sun begins his nightly round by moving along her arms.[29] This is the moment when the last glimmers of twilight may be discerned. A late tradition establishes a precise correlation between the parts of Nut's body and the hours. For example, her lips correspond to the second hour, her teeth to the third. Her throat and bust are crossed during the fourth and fifth hours. In the tenth hour, the sun finally reaches her vagina and is reborn. The top of the goddess's thighs marks the eastern horizon.[30]

Contrary to what occurs during the day, on this journey there is no change in the number or nature of those who are either aboard the solar boat or else accompany it on its course. The naos, which is still positioned in the center of the boat, is now wrapped in the coils of a serpent, Mehen; closely related to Ouroboros, he is a symbol of the process of gestation the sun must go through to be reborn. The god maintains the same form throughout, that of a ram-headed man; this is the visible sign that his regeneration is under way.[31] In each of the twelve boats, Maat, face to face with Re, presents him with the hieroglyphic sign for life so that he can inhale life throughout the journey. Hu and Sia stand alone on deck with the sun-god, in front of and behind the naos. Sia directs the towline toward the haulers to make sure the boat does not wander off course. The procession advances cautiously. Torches are set blazing, both to light the way and also to ward off hostile forces. Genies wielding knives surround this whole group to guard against all eventualities. Guides are constantly on hand to keep the bark from going astray. It follows a linear course; only during the seventh hour does the sun-god make a detour, stopping before the door that opens on to Naref, one of Osiris's cemeteries. He does not, however, enter.[32] The sun appears here in all his fragility, constantly watched over and protected, ringed round by all the guardians of his vitality. Yet, during the voyage, his form remains strangely unchanged. The gestation process that he undergoes here is never directly portrayed or alluded to. It takes place unseen inside the goddess's body. The depiction of the journey is repetitious, or rather geometric; it conjures up the terrors of hell itself only briefly, representing them in deliberately undramatic fashion. The whole of this voyage clearly differs from the one—we will come back to it—that the sun makes through the netherworld. There, the god's body is identified with that of the dismembered Osiris, and we witness his recomposition amid scenes somewhat difficult to interpret.[33]

## Thoth's Heaven

While the sun pursued his course inside Nut's body, outside, the moon, the stars, and the planets appeared. With the exception of the moon, all of these heavenly bodies followed the path blazed by the sun during the day, rising when he set and setting when he rose. Their disappearance was ascribed to the voracious appetite of Nut, who was thought to swallow them the moment they faded at daybreak. After disappearing, the stars in their turn set out on a voyage within the goddess's body, to be reborn in the east in the evening.[34] The heavens were divided into thirty-six decans in accordance with the rhythm at which certain stars disappeared below the horizon and then reappeared; these stars formed a belt around the universe which the sun was thought to travel through in the space of a year. Each of the thirty-six sections of the sky Re passed through offered shelter for ten days to a god who was one of his aspects.

It was also in the course of this annual journey that the descendants of the Lord of the Universe arrived to animate, each in his own manner, the different sections of the sky, bringing on specific events that punctuated the daily life of both gods and men. Thus the Children of Geb and Nut, although they were children of the earth, also had their place in the firmament. They might appear as planets with their own particular movements in the sky, or else as fixed heavenly bodies, the stars or constellations. Always, they endowed the heavenly bodies they inhabited with specific functions. Different aspects of Horus were manifested in Mars, Jupiter, and Saturn. Venus was linked with Re or Osiris, depending on whether she was the morning star who heralded Osiris's rebirth as the rising sun, or the evening star bidding welcome to the aging sun about to turn into Osiris. The constellation Orion likewise incorporated the dead Osiris and was closely linked to Isis-Sirius,[35] who accompanied him. The latter star played a dominant role in the life of humankind, whose means of survival depended on the Nile flood. Its appearance announced that the Nile was rising and at the same time marked the beginning of the new year. "It is Sirius . . . who prepares (for you) your vegetables of the year, in his name of Year."[36] As for Seth, although he was identified with the planet Mercury,[37] he was above all associated with the constellation of the Great Bear, in which he was visible at all times. The Great Bear was tied for all time to the North Star, which the Egyptians imagined to be attached to a stake; thus this constellation was incapable of disappearing over the horizon. It symbolized the fact that Osiris's enemy could not go down to the netherworld to commit still further mischief and strike yet another blow against his brother. As for Nephthys, she seems to have maintained only a modest presence.[38] Yet she was, along with her brothers and sister and other, less familiar gods, one of the divinities of the epact, the eleven days intercalated to adjust the shorter lunar year to the civil year. Like the others, Nephthys covered an irregularity in time.[39] In the sky, traveling in the form of the heavenly bodies, the Children of Nut carried on their quarrels.

At night, the sun's absence left men in the dark. The light of the stars was too pale to dispel the shadows in which all manner of dangers might be lurking. The creator-god therefore arranged matters so that the moon would replace him in the night sky, leaving humankind with at least some light. As he had already done when attending to other earthly affairs, the creator delegated part of his powers to the moon god, Thoth, who became his substitute in the sky.[40] "You will be in my place, my substitute. You will be called 'Thoth, Re's substitute' . . . I will cause that you encompass the two heavens with your beauty and your brightness. Thus it was that this moon of Thoth came into existence."[41] The movements, and, above all, the different phases of the moon, provided men with a way of rapidly reading the heavens outside the blinding glare of the sun; the moon thus offered them a more immediate way of measuring time.[42] Lord of the stars, Thoth/the moon distinguished the seasons, months, and years; he was therefore "the reckoner of time for the gods and men,"[43] the one who taught them to learn about the heavens. For this reason, the lunar calendar, born of men's observations of the sky, was the one that served both to establish the rhythms of the events celebrated in Egypt's religious festivals and to structure the time of the liturgy. It was likewise Thoth who marked out the major seasons of one's earthly existence, that of the king as well as that of ordinary mortals. Thoth had the power to determine lifespans; again, with the help of Seshat, he recorded the major moments in the reigns of the kings. Every year, he cut a notch in a palm-frond to keep track of the passing years of each reign. At each of the jubilee celebrations, whose purpose was to restore all the king's vigor and power, Thoth traced the name of the sovereign on the leaves of the sacred tree of Heliopolis. One accordingly finds him acting as a veritable master of ceremonies during the celebrations of royal rites in the temples.

# CHAPTER SEVEN

# The Gods on Earth

The creation stories accounted simultaneously for the establishment of the cosmic and social orders. Presiding over these inextricably intertwined systems were the creator-god and the pharaoh. There was evil in creation. We have already discussed the sequence of events that . induced the creator-god to withdraw into the heavens, taking the other gods with him. But human beings preserved a memory of the divine presence they had been deprived of, and they would employ a variety of means to recapture it and keep it on earth. The departing gods themselves helped them do so by leaving a Horus, the king, on earth to serve as a mediator between themselves and men. What the king did on earth associated humankind, by way of cults and rites, with the preservation of cosmic order. Cults and rites were enacted in the temple, whose very foundation and conception were divine, and recalled the initial foundation of the world. Rituals were addressed to the images of the gods on earth—statues and sacred animals—which were in their turn linked with the king, though in different ways.

## The Divine Origins of the Royal Intercessor

The gods' interlocutor on earth owed his divinity to the fact that his royal function was identified with that of his divine lords. The king was Horus; he was the son of Isis and Osiris quite as much as he was the son of Re. Although the creator had withdrawn into the heavens, he intervened in earthly affairs in order to choose his heir and, if necessary, modify the course of history. There is a tale that helps us understand to what extent the sun-god was perceived as an absolute lord and the direct source of royal legitimacy.[1] Wishing to put an end to the line of pharaohs of the Fourth Dynasty, Re coupled with the wife of one of his priests. Three children, destined to found the Fifth Dynasty, were born of this union. Re lavished very special attentions on them. When their earthly mother Red-dedet went into labor, he delegated Isis, Nephthys, Meskhenet, Heket, the goddesses of maternity, along with the god Khnum, to assist her with what promised to be a difficult birth. They had precise orders: "Go and deliver Red-dedet of the three children who are in her womb and who will perform this good office throughout this land." To justify commandeering these illustrious divinities to perform so apparently humble a task, he added a word about the future kings: "They will build your temples, they will furnish your altars, they will make your libation-tables prosper, they will increase the size of your offerings." So that they might mingle among humankind without being recognized, the goddesses changed themselves into dancing musicians. As for Khnum, he simply carried their baggage; we do not much know what he was disguised as. The goddesses introduced themselves to Red-dedet's already completely flustered husband, declared that they were competent midwives, and offered to deliver her babies. With his approval, they went into the room where his wife was already in labor, shutting the door behind them so as not to be disturbed. Isis took up her place in front of Red-dedet, Nephthys stood behind her, and Heket proceeded to make the delivery. As each of the babies came into the world, Isis gave them names. Though they had been born of a mortal woman, their bodies bore the marks of their divine origins. Each of them was one cubit tall;[2] their bones were already solid and their members were inlaid with gold. All had hair of real lapis lazuli. After they had been washed by the goddesses, and their umbilical cords severed, "Meskhenet approached each of them and said, 'A king who will exercise a royal function throughout this whole land,' while Khnum bestowed health on their bodies."[3] Their destiny was thus irrevocably set.

Nearly a thousand years after the events just recounted, a series of scenes describing the royal conception and birth were engraved on the walls of certain temples; the various episodes coincide with the main events of our tale. The story of the royal theogamy was thus more or less directly transformed into ritual. The group of scenes engraved on the temple walls provided a pictorial version of the god's mystical marriage with the earthly queen, pharaoh's wife.[4] This time, the god was no longer Re, but Amun-Re; the divine personality had, however, undergone no fundamental change. The dynastic sun-god was still at the center of the action; he intervened, as before, to beget a descendant and representative on earth. In order to couple with the queen, he simply took on the appearance of the king himself. The queen awoke "at the scent of the god and smiled in the presence of His Majesty. He quickly approached her and, consumed with passion for her, gave her his heart, causing her to behold him in his divine form."[5] The baby was conceived with the discreet assistance of the divinities who presided over procreation and the breath of life. At his birth, he was given a name that prefigured the royal destiny that had been promised him, and was given the kind of care that his status as a newborn baby and future sovereign called for. As we shall see, all the pomp and even the account of the process of the conception and birth of this child would be taken over a thousand years later by the ritual of the birth of the divine child.[6] This direct borrowing would give the doctrine of the divine origins of kingship its most refined form.

### The Temple, the King, and the King-Gods

As the indispensable mediator between the gods and men, the king was also the gods' sole interlocutor. That his function as ritualist was delegated to the priests was a purely formal, administrative matter; it had no influence on the nature of his mediation or its theological significance.[7] This mediation maintained every element in creation in its proper place. To preserve that equilibrium, the king performed certain acts in the temple that, because it was a closed space and microcosm of the world, was intimately associated with the universe it represented. "For as long as the sky rests upon its four supports, for as long as the earth remains firm on its foundations, for as long as Re shines by day, and the moon shimmers at night, for as long as Orion is the visible manifestation of Osiris and Sirius is queen of the stars, for as long as the flood comes in its season and the arable land produces its plants, for as long as the north wind comes out in its (appropriate) time and fire consumes whatever exists, for as long as the decans perform their office and the stars remain in their places, the temple . . . will endure, firm like the sky . . . without end, like Re, eternally."[8]

As heir to the solar creator god, whose established order laid down binding norms for all times and all creatures, the pharaoh was, from a dogmatic point of view, the only one who could intercede with the gods. Men were fully included in this scheme of things; that is, indeed, the reason the creator-god created "kings from the very beginning" for them.[9]

Within the framework of this filial relationship, the task that devolved upon the king found direct expression in ritual acts. Central to ritual was the offering, which was established as a necessary complement to the cult service. Originally, the offering was essentially conceived of as nourishment; it was seen as a way of "returning energy" to the master of the temple. Later extended so as to benefit all the gods,[10] it developed into an exchange in which what was offered to the god embodied and made manifest what was being asked of him. Hence the offering par excellence, even if it took merely the form of a statuette of the goddess, was the offering of Maat, guarantor of the Norm and the equilibrium of the universe. Without ceasing to be food—we have already seen that the gods "live on" Maat—the offering became a vital act of barter that founded an economy of the world;[11] it enabled each of its participants to preserve and renew what the act of creation had set in motion. But the pharaoh was also the incarnation of Horus, son of Isis, the model of earthly kingship, and, as such, Osiris's heir as well. In fact, both these gods were embodied in his person. Alive, the king as Horus inherited the earthly realm from his father; dead, he gained access to the next world, becoming the ancestor par excellence. His funerary cult permitted him to be at one and the same time Osiris, sovereign of the kingdom of the dead, and the dead sun who would share the destiny of Re on his journeys.

These various relationships involved only the gods of the Heliopolitan family, those associated with the institution of kingship. The earthly cult manifestations of the two main gods of this group, Re and Osiris, seem to have differed appreciably from those of the other Egyptian gods. The solar cult must have required architectural structures that were at least in part open, whereas the necropolis was the essential setting for the cult of Osiris. The best known object in the cult of Re was the obelisk, whose gold-plated, pyramid-shaped tip was meant to catch and reflect the rays of the sun.[12] The cult of Osiris obeyed the logic imposed by his dismemberment. In the temples in which one of the parts of his body was preserved, the reliquary quite naturally became the object of the cult. Similarly, the need to reconstitute Osiris's body gave rise to a specific practice: every year, a mummiform statuette was produced to gave material form to the whole of the divine body, as we shall see.[13] The various solar and Osirian liturgies would be interwoven as the centuries wore on, eventually acquiring complementary roles in the framework of religious festival.[14]

Precisely by virtue of the uniqueness of their functions, Re and Osiris provided a model of universal kingship: the king would assume its solar or funerary aspects, to his profit. What is more, every royal dynasty could, through its connections with one or another regional metropolis, endow the main god of its city of origin with Re's universality, thus conferring upon that god a privileged place in the state religion.

## Building the Temple

Temple building was one of the gods' prerogatives. It was carried out in accordance with a precise foundation ritual, in which, from a dogmatic point of view, only the king and certain divinities took part.[15] For example, the operation that consisted in staking out the emplacement of the future foundations on the ground was overseen by Seshat: her task, carried out with the king's help, was to mark out the plan of the building by stretching a cord between two poles. This work was done at night. The texts inform us that the location of the four corners of the temple was determined by the position of the stars; the builders looked to the Great Bear for orientation.[16] To this end, we are told, the king possessed an instrument for sighting; he could use it as masterfully as could Thoth or Sia. For her part, Seshat, in her capacity as sovereign goddess of written texts and mistress of the library, made sure that the ground plan had been accurately laid out and provided the king assurances that the construction was stable. "As surely as your building is firm on its foundations, like the sky on its supports, so your edifice will endure together with its master, as the earth (endures) with the Ennead. Its years are (the years of) the horizon, its months are (the months of) the decans. Never will (it) know destruction on earth, eternally."[17] Time and space fuse to ensure that the edifice will endure.

It fell to the king to excavate the foundations to the depth of the water table, which was identified with the Primeval Ocean. Then, using moist silt mixed with straw, he molded bricks to be placed at the four corners of the temple. These bricks had the status of "cornerstones"; they symbolized the thousands of bricks needed to build the caissons. Once the caissons had been put in place, thus creating spaces within the foundations, the king had to fill them in with sand. This was a way of recreating the primordial virgin soil on which every sacred building had to be built. It should be emphasized that the gods were not directly involved in preparing the foundations and the virgin soil. Only the task of transporting the sand was placed under the responsibility of the god Ha, god of the western desert, for greater security. It follows that the manual labor called for here could be carried out only by the king, as picks, baskets, and brick molds are obviously tools hardly worthy of a god. Still, Horus, monitoring the progress of operations as a spectator, was nice enough to give the sovereign verbal encouragement: "I see your ardor and I rejoice at your activity."[18] Once the king had completed his labors, he placed foundation deposits consisting of pottery as well as objects made of gold, silver, copper, iron, stone, or fayence at the four corners of the temple. The deposits included little plaques bearing the king's name engraved in a cartouche, along with various small-scale models representing containers, tools, and offerings. By means of these objects, the king sought to leave his mark—safeguarded against possible acts of destruction—on this terrain he had consecrated to the god. It is interesting to note that the ritual did not take the construction work properly so called into account. The important thing was the foundations and markings that conferred on the building its initial form. The final act of the rite represented the king busy tamping down the flagging. Once the temple was completed, it was purified with natron and censed. Before being handed over to its presiding divinity, its statues and reliefs would be brought to life in a special rite.[19]

For the temple to function, the god it was meant for had actually to take up residence in it, together with his entourage. The divine community of the temple was incarnated in the statues located in various chapels and also in the bas-reliefs adorning the walls of the building. These were objects created by human hands out of inanimate matter. In their original form, then, they could not represent the divinity; they could do so only if the god definitively entered his various material supports. The ritual of the Opening of the Mouth, whose name indicates its function, came into play here. It was performed on all the representations of the gods in the temple. With the help of various instruments—essentially a carpenter's or sculptor's tools adapted to ritual use—the eyes, nose, and mouth of the images of the gods were "opened," so that essential vital functions could be imparted to them, permitting them to breathe, see, and so forth. The operation consisted in bringing the instrument into contact with the relevant parts of the body. The rite was enacted by priests impersonating particular divinities on behalf of the king. "Ptah takes his chisel to open the mouth and Sokar opens his eyes." Anubis's adze was then presented. Various animal sacrifices and presentations of offerings followed. This "opening" ritual was gone through again for the building as a whole, treated as a single unit. From then on, the temple, its statues, and its bas-reliefs were living, active beings. Thus the king had created a building that not only testified to the god's benefactions and power, but could also be used to enact rituals, now that the god's vital energy had been embodied in his images.

Not even these iconic surrogates of the god could be said to have a human origin. It was the creator-god who had "made the images that are on earth, by means of instruments he himself made."[20] "Thus the gods entered their bodies made of wood, minerals, clay and all the other things that grow and in which they took form."[21] This explains the participation of the patron gods of the crafts in the animation ritual. It was likewise because of the creator that the representations of the god came to life each time the sun appeared in the morning. "When your visible aspect (comes) to earth"—this was addressed to the creator—"what is carved becomes flesh."[22] These man-made representations were nevertheless not capable of revealing the whole of the being they embodied; they were, at best, approximations that a god agreed to inhabit as one of his aspects.[23] They continued to fulfil their function for as long as the temple stood. If, for one reason or another, it became necessary to rebuild or even to demolish it, the representations of the divinities had to be stripped of their senses, especially the sense of sight, through mutilation of the bodily parts that had been brought to life in the reliefs or statues.[24]

## The God-Object and His Daily Cult

The principal statue of a cult—the one that summed up all the others and provided the god with his basic image—was shut up in the temple's deepest recesses, in a shrine called the naos. A text describes its seclusion: "It is more inaccessible than what happens in the heavens, more veiled than the state of the other world, more revered than the inhabitants of the Primeval Ocean."[25] Although gods were by nature omnipresent, they apparently chose to absent themselves except when rites were in progress. The doors of the naos were sealed, not to shut the god as such in, but to protect this sacred space. Moreover, an elaborate ceremony was conducted every morning to invoke the god and capture his presence; for his presence was the end result of a complicated liturgical service in which other gods—or other aspects of the principal god—also enacted certain rites.

Before dawn, in the last hour of the night and the first of the day, the temple assistants were extremely busy. All sorts of preparations had to be made in the kitchen, abattoir, bakery, and brewery. Offerings were arranged on platters with great care—nothing was left to chance. The divine offering contained a precise message, a proposition that had to satisfy the one receiving it and solicit his benefaction in return. The fruits and vegetables, meat and birds, cakes and loaves of bread, and the jugs of beer, milk, and wine had to satisfy not only the god in his naos, but also all his other manifestations in the many chapels, and his entourage as well. While the offerings were being prepared, other temple assistants bustled about the well in the temple enclosure, for libations of water played a major role in the divine service. Everything that would come near the god had to be purified with this water originating in Nun, along with natron and burning incense.[26] Once the purification process was complete, a procession entered the temple bearing offerings. As these worshipers walked through the door, a text greeted them: "This beautiful door to the Grand Throne furnishes the offering-table of the Lord of the Gods with all the good things that come from the goddess of grain. Loaves of bread by the thousands and dishes by the hundreds of thousands come from the kitchen when the (divine) Face is unveiled."[27] "This is the gate by which one enters the temple, carrying everything that makes up the divine repast. . . . The vegetables are brought in in the hands of the bearers (as well as) all the flowers of the fields. . . . A priest is before you reading the book"[28] of the ritual. Once the offerings had been laid before the god, purified and ready to be consumed, the doors of the naos were opened, while a chorus bid the god to rouse himself. "Awake . . . in peace! May your awakening be peaceful!"[29] At this point, the king entered the shadowy sanctuary.[30] In its depths was the granite shrine, behind whose double-leaved door the cult statue stood. Lighting his way with a candle, the king broke the seal that protected the god's solitude, then drew the bolt,[31] assuring the god[32] that he was approaching in a state of purity and was not being pursued by enemies.[33] The god's face was unveiled[34] the instant the sun peeked over the horizon, so that the god would awaken in harmony with the rhythms of the universe. "Revelation of the Face. Adoration of the Face: rise over the earth, just as you emerge from Nun! May your rays illuminate the earth! Long live the gods who exhort his beauty: (they are) like (your) sons in the East."[35] Thus the ritual act the king performed at this point enabled the god to appear in material form. Pious acts of contemplation and adoration followed. The purpose of this face-to-face encounter was clearly stated: "He (the king) enters, pure, to replenish Horus's altar, to provision the table of the divine winged disk, to fill his house, to enrich his temple, to increase his daily service, to offer bread, to add to his food, to carry an offering to his *ka*, to worship his statue, to venerate his image, to acclaim His Majesty."[36] The meal served the god in his sanctuary was made up of items that had been taken from the offerings heaped up in the altar room. Presented to him on a platter and then placed on a pedestal table, the loaves of bread would remain before the naos until the next morning service. They would not actually be consumed in our sense of the word; the god in his naos satisfied himself without leaving visible traces of his appetite. To mark the end of the meal, incense was burned and a libation poured out.

Outside his chapel, however, like a king in his palace, the god, accompanied by his wife and son, could be venerated in his different manifestations along with all the gods of his divine court. They, too, had chapels or tabernacles; these surrounded the sanctuary. The principal god shared his regular temple service with them; its contents must have varied, depending on the recipient of the offering. For example, offerings of flowers and vegetables in the temple of Karnak were often presented to the ithyphallic form of Amun-Re. Offerings of wine tended to be made to the dangerous manifestations of certain goddesses, such as Hathor or certain uraeus divinities. In Edfu, but elsewhere as well, offerings of milk went to the child god, whereas female gods everywhere received offerings of sistra or *menat* necklaces. For his part, Onuris-Shu received the symbol of eternity in the course of the rite of the "lifting of the sky"; the rite reproduced the function the creator had conferred upon him when the world began.[37] Of course, certain offerings might mirror the production of a given region: this was the case with the papyrus offerings at Balamun, a city located in the Delta marshes. As to funerary offerings, they were always meant for the royal ancestors. At Karnak, for example, Ramses II honored the statue of his father Seti I with such offerings.[38] Varied menus, including beef, gazelle, birds, wild game, vegetables, and cakes,[39] were, as we shall see, reserved for feast days.

The god's toilet took place immediately after this meal. The clothes he had worn the day before were removed, and numerous purifications were carried out with water and incense, as the king walked around the statue. The god was then dressed again. Four different kinds of cloth were used—by turns, white, green, red, and blue. Certain versions of this ritual text expressly state that the white cloth safeguarded the god against his enemies, while the blue hid his face, the green ensured him bodily health, and the red protected him.[40] To bring the ritual to a close, the king dabbed his little finger with ointment and lightly touched the god's forehead. After it had been anointed with this fragrant oil, the revitalized statue, once again hidden from view behind the locked, sealed doors of the naos, was ready to bear the god's earthly presence. The king then left the sanctuary, effacing his own footprints with a broom.[41]

The two other regular temple services, which took place at midday and in the evening, were much shorter. The doors of the sanctuary were not reopened. Libations and the burning of incense were the only ritual acts performed. These services did not involve the principal god of the temple. As nothing was left to chance, each of the gods present in the temple in the form of a relief or statue was there to contribute something to the cult of the major god or the king. Often, these gods of the entourage were included more for the king's sake than for the major god's, since their mission was to prepare the sovereign for the face-to-face encounters that took place during royal ceremonies or religious festivals. The king benefited, for example, from certain rites enacted either by secondary divinities or by the presiding god himself. Thus Tefnut occasionally cleansed pharaoh of his impurities,[42] though Khnum was more frequently charged with this task.[43] The office that Khnum, god of the Cataract and guardian of the sources of the Nile, performed for the king recalled the one he performed for the whole land of Egypt. When he entered the temple and was presented to the god or goddess, the king was escorted by divinities who held his hand and served as his guides. Though the names and number of these gods could vary, he was often led in by a warrior falcon-god,[44] while Atum, with a human face, brought up the rear.[45]

The main god's entourage also joined in worshiping him. In Karnak, one finds the king associating the Great Ennead[46] with the homage he addresses to Amun-Re.[47] His motivations were not entirely selfless. Each of these gods, by performing the same gesture as pharaoh, took on the role of intercessor with Amun. After uttering words of praise, the gods of the corporation made, one after the other, a wish for the king. The leading gods in this divine corporation—Montu, a god of the Theban region, Atum, Shu, Tefnut, and Geb, the Heliopolitan gods we have so often mentioned—formulated wishes that specifically concerned the royal person, asking that Amun grant the monarch health, vigor, and strength. There followed wishes bearing on the royal office, formulated by Nut, Osiris, Isis, Nebyt, Nephthys, and Horus. Finally, Hathor, Sobek-Re, and Tanenet requested grants of food, including fish and fowl.

These impassive gods, who inspired all these attempts to capture their presence on earth, proceeded to reward their earthly interlocutor's efforts by granting him the throne or, depending on the case, commemorating his investiture. For example, when Amun wanted to bestow "an infinity of years" and "jubilees by the thousands" on his son, he abandoned his customary solemnity to extend the sign of life (the *ankh* sign) toward the king's countenance.

## Sacred Animals

A god could dwell in the body of an animal and so become a "living cult image."[48] But the connections between the animal and the god expressed themselves in a variety of ways. In most important temples, at least in the Late Period, the sacred animal that was the temple god's visible manifestation was kept within the temple enclosure. The falcon of the various Horuses, the ram of Amun, the ape and ibis of Hermopolitan Thoth, the crocodiles that were bred around Sobek, and many other animals as well, were, like the Apis bull, so many embodiments of the divine.[49] But these animals did not all have exactly the same status. Two different procedures determined the choice of a god's sacred animal. One required the material participation of a god and his priesthood: with a gesture, the god's statue would identify the individual animal that divine power had selected from among a sacred flock kept by the temple. This animal— different each year—became the image of Horus and, simultaneously, the king. As such, he was crowned with all the pomp of ritual, as we shall see.[50] But a god could also dwell in a particular animal from the day it was born to the day it died; this unique creature, whom specific markings set apart from all other members of his species, was sought out by the priests throughout the land, and then integrated into the life of the temple.[51] At his death, he became the object of a funerary cult, like the king. It may be that certain gods were satisfied to have a simple flock of their own without attempting to designate a particular sacred animal, whereas others singled out an individual member of the flock for life—but we have no definite indications that this was the case. Be that as it may, the falcon of Edfu and the Apis bull provide the textbook examples of the two best-known sorts of sacred animal. We will examine each in turn in an attempt to understand the functioning of what would gradually become an institution, and then an object of curiosity, derision, and even scandal for the tourists who visited Egypt in ancient times.

Within the temple precinct in Edfu, the living falcon[52] had a dwelling located within an enclosure reserved exclusively for him. This house consisted of a court and a small sanctuary with a balcony reserved for royal "appearances." The enclosure must also have included an aviary housing several exemplars of the same species; the god of the temple visited it once a year, as we have said, to select his sacred animal. The selection of the falcon of the year took place on the first day of the first month of the sowing season; the choice was made by the statue of the god Horus himself, brought forth from the temple by the priests. The latter, wearing falcon's-head or jackal's-head masks, represented the royal ancestors of Upper and Lower Egypt. The procession silently made its way toward the little temple of the living falcon. One by one, falcons the same color as Re were brought before the god. When the bird on whom Horus's choice would alight that year was presented to him, the divine statue moved toward it—spontaneously, it was believed. The falconer was then supposed to hold out a perch to the bird; it consisted of a light canopy surmounting a base decorated in imitation of the facade of the royal palace in primitive times. From this moment on, the falcon was the divine king; he was called "His Majesty." We are told nothing about the fate reserved for the bird of prey who had been king the previous year and was now stripped of his office. Once the choice had been made, the sacred falcon was conducted to the balcony of royal appearances, to be exhibited to the crowd of the faithful who had the privilege of attending these ceremonies. It was probably from this balcony, located above the entrance to the falcon's temple between the two towers of the pylon, that litanies were sung to Sakhmet and the Happy Year, an aspect of Hathor.[53] The object of these litanies was to obtain year-round protection for the new living falcon from the goddess Hathor-Sakhmet. Here, we see Hathor in two different manifestations. Wearing a vulture headdress, with a white crown atop it, and holding the palm-frond on which jubilees were inscribed, she represented Southern Egypt. Then, lion-headed and crowned with a sun disk, she became Sakhmet, who represented the northern part of the country. Wearing the crown of the North, the king enacted different rites in the presence of Hathor and the falcon. He was assisted by Thoth, who, in his capacity as master of ceremonies, carried the texts. The king next proceeded to perform two censings, describing what he was doing as he proceeded. "I cense Re, I adore the uraeus (Hathor). I call upon him, in all his names, to provide his protection." There followed a long invocation. Its purpose was to bring about the fusion of the king of Egypt, son of Re, with the living falcon, who was also a son of Re and a visible manifestation of the god. The litanies addressed to Hathor/the Happy Year were based on this fusion; they secured benefactions such as jubilation, power, abundance, happiness, duration, health (and many others) for the living falcon and, playing on the identification of their functions, the king as well. Indeed, each verse in the ritual text was devoted to an aspect of the year, which was identified with an epithet; it asked this aspect to grant it the good thing associated with it. "O Year, you who are healthy: grant that the bones of the living image, the living falcon, the living ibis, be healthy; preserve his flesh in health, strengthen his muscles, maintain all his members in good condition in plenitude, as you return regularly at each desired season!"[54] Prayers of supplication were then addressed to Hathor-Sakhmet, the dangerous aspect of the goddess; their object was to protect the living falcon and the reigning king from all possible danger during the year to come:[55] contagious diseases, plagues, massacres by the knife-wielding demons, and so forth. The list was a long one; Sakhmet was even called upon to protect the living image "from all of the year's noxious flies, that they might not 'stick' to him."[56] It was also requested that this protection be extended to "his retainers, his consort, and his little ones."[57] The litanies culminated in seven couplets that sought to safeguard the falcon-king against the "seven arrows of the year." These were symbols of all the dangers that might afflict Egypt and the sovereign: "O Sakhmet, you who love justice and abhor injustice, o mistress of men, come to King Ptolemy, the living image, the living falcon; save him, guard him, protect him from the sixth arrow of the year! O Sakhmet-Uraeus, you who 'open the circle,'[58] O mistress, come to King Ptolemy, the living image, the living falcon; save him, guard him, protect him from the seventh arrow of the year!" Finally, all the names of the divine falcon were recited to affirm his identity: "(He is) the king, Ptolemy, filled with life."[59] Then the sacred animal was taken down from the window of appearances and led into his temple. The priests escorted him: "Proceed to the Grand Throne in order to take the kingship from the hand of your father Horus of Edfu, great god of the sky."[60]

During the latter part of the ceremonies, the living falcon, and therefore the king as well, actually received the royal insignia from the hands of the god of the temple and his Ennead. "He arises, as king, on the throne of his father,"[61] was the cry. The ceremonies that ensued were in many respects comparable to the different stages of an actual royal coronation. To begin with, the living falcon was anointed. With the tip of his little finger, the celebrant placed ointment on the forehead of the bird, saying, "the oil is upon your forehead; may it gladden your countenance, o lord of the gods."[62] A hymn was sung to hallow the identification of Horus-Re with his animal manifestation. Then came the main offering, consisting of golden jewellery; it was meant for the living falcon and, probably, the statue of Horus. One of these jewels represented the symbol of eternity resting on the sign (hieroglyph) for "festival." A hymn was sung in the falcon's honor: "The river banks are your servants, because of the greatness of your power; they rejoice when they behold you. You have spread your wings as the divine falcon, and you subdue the hearts of your enemies."[63] Once fused with the god himself, the living falcon was capable of completely annihilating his enemies with the force of his wings, the fire thought to flash from his eyes, and the strength of his talons. At this point, he received a first bouquet of flowers: "Accept this bouquet from your venerable father, Horus of Edfu, the great god of the sky! He praises you, he loves you, he preserves you, he strikes down all your foes, dead or alive!"[64] The text then went on to recall the primeval form of the falcon-god, alluding to his resplendent emergence from the Nun. The floral bouquet was thus identified with the floating reed which, according to the Edfu cosmogony, had mysteriously appeared on the surface of the primeval waters at the beginning of the world, serving as a perch for the bird, who was also the creator-god. Next, Re, Amun, and Ptah, the dynastic gods, presented a second bouquet to the falcon. "Accept the bouquet of life of the Majesty of Re: it is (intended) for the countenance of the lord of humankind."[65] That is, this new offering symbolized earthly kingship and power over men. A third bouquet was placed between the living falcon and Hathor: "Accept this bouquet of your mother, the Mighty One,

Hathor the great, mistress of Dendara! She praises you, she loves you, she preserves you, she strikes down all your foes, dead or alive. . . . She rejuvenates your body once again. . . . She bestows the happiness of her brother Osiris upon you, she has taken possession of his throne for you, in triumph! She gives you the land of her son Horus."[66] This bouquet was linked with the funerary domain and the resurrection of Osiris. A last offering of flowers was placed at the falcon's feet, while a last hymn was sung to the setting sun: "Accept this bouquet of your visible manifestation, Atum. May joy enter your heart . . . O falcon of the East, you reach the mountain of the West, where the sun sets, (while) your bark remains steady in the sky!"[67] The whole of this ceremony summed up the life of the falcon and that of the sun-god to whom the falcon was assimilated. Both rose in the morning, just as if they were emerging from Nun; both ruled the world as they soared through the sky, and both served notice of their coming rebirth even before setting on the horizon.

At this point, Horus of Edfu and the living falcon made their way into the dim sanctuary, followed by Hathor. Two litters resembling Tutankhamun's funerary beds had been set up there. In this secluded spot, a sort of birth took place; the texts mention breastfeeding and the defenses erected around the fragile baby. The animal followed in the footsteps of the god it represented; the god drew it within his aura. Each stage of this process imparted additional powers to the animal, in the royal as well as divine sphere. Every succeeding phase of the ceremony, and, consequently, every advance in the acquisition of new powers, was identified with a process of gestation and a new birth. The objective was gradually to extend to the living god the benefits of all the sacerdotal knowledge the Egyptians possessed, so as to ensure him failsafe protection. A synthesis of all available divine powers was made in order to allow evil or bad luck no chance of success. Of course, Thoth and Seshat—and the king as well—enacted this cult drama. The rest of the liturgy associated the animal and the statue of the god ever more closely, while reiterating all the ceremonies that usually marked the coronation of pharaoh. This complex ritual, with all its manipulations of objects, also involved litanies and recitations. The king was supposed to perform the acts it prescribed and repeat the commentaries that accompanied them. But, in the course of the ritual, an irresolvable ambiguity gradually made itself felt. It became increasingly unclear whether the statue or the animal was the material object of the ritual gestures and speeches. A desire to merge the one with the other clearly seems to have been at work. If, in theory, the animal continued to be the object of the rite, the god was nevertheless present in filigree throughout. But, be that as it may, we shall now turn to the moment when the god was ceremonially arrayed in a headband, embroidered cloth, and a veil. The subject of the long litany naming the various amulets with which he was bedecked was the god himself as well as the animal; one might be permitted to wonder, in passing, just how graciously the latter submitted to the operation. Plainly, all this precious jewelry had a protective function. The form of the amulets, like the materials of which they were made, was never a matter of indifference. But placing the objects themselves on the body of the statue or the animal did not suffice to endow it with the power the ritual sought to give it. Pictures of the most important of these amulets, those representing protective divinities, were also traced in the sand under the litters, and a magic circle was drawn around the litters with a tamarisk stick. Apparently this stick gave the circle the power to drive off and destroy the god's adversaries. An eye with its red-ochre makeup (an *udjat*-eye) was likewise traced on the ground. Thus the litters found themselves at the center of a design that simultaneously symbolized the radiant eye of the sun and the unity of the land of Egypt; no image provided more powerful protection. These gestures and drawings were accompanied by further recitations that named the divine protectors, calling upon them to be active day and night and even to take up permanent residence in the temple. Thoth, of course, was not far off; his arms loaded down with books of spells, he was prepared to utter all the appropriate magic formulas.[68] Yet even this lengthy ceremony, which fell within the province of performative magic, was not sufficient to preserve the god from all possible danger. Little dishes on which figures of enemies had previously been drawn in red and black ink were therefore brought in and smashed on the ground. All the while, imprecations were uttered to ward off evil spells. It was also necessary to carry out a purification ceremony, which was repeated four times: it consisted in washing the god's face and spitting on the ground. Then it was time to make ready for nightfall. Protection against this dangerous moment also had to be secured, but in a special way. A knot was tied in the uppermost part of the god's garment; it would be undone at dawn. Apparently, it was supposed to entrap all the evil spirits likely to venture near him. When it was untied the following morning, all these hostile forces were of course liberated; dishes were therefore broken as the liberatory gesture was performed, so as to annihilate the hostile powers as they were freed.[69] The god was then given milk to drink. This drink, associated with birth, and therefore with the god's rebirth, had the further effect of definitively dispersing whatever demons of the night might still be lingering in the vicinity. Then the whole set of protective litanies was taken up again, to assist the rebirth of the sun. For good measure, the spells for "ward(ing) off the evil eye at the break of day" were recited one more time.[70] Thoth arrived to lend a hand. He addressed a supplication to

Re, asking him to protect the awakening god from all vengeful spirits, and to deliver him from all possible harm, wherever it might come from: "Men or gods, and souls of the dead, glorified or not, they will not carry out what their hearts contemplate (doing) to him! Living image, living falcon, sole god, brought into the world by the Radiant Lady, may the hands of the Powerful Lady protect his members! He is the falcon in his youth, in his nest at Khemmis!"[71] With this, a shift had occurred. The awakening falcon was now considered to be a fledgling, identified in turn with Horus the child, son of Isis, in his papyrus thicket. From this point forward, Isis, his mother, would ensure his protection. The young god was henceforth depicted in his new environment, capturing the enemies as if they were birds and gaining the victory over Seth and his threatening companions.

In the temple, the lengthy ceremony was at last nearing an end. But still more litanies and protective invocations were needed at this point. One of them identified each of the enthroned falcon's members with a particular god, thus turning the bird into a living compendium of the Egyptian pantheon; this was thought to provide it sure protection against any and all hostile acts. Care was taken not to leave out any of the divine forces peopling the universe, so as to make them all witnesses to the coronation, which was at last completed: "O gods who are in heaven, gods who are on earth, gods who are in the other world, who are in the waters, in the south, in the north, in the west, in the east! If we are enthroning the living Image, the living falcon, we are (also) enthroning you. . . . This is Horus, son of Isis: his eye is on his brow and his uraeus goes before him. The mistress of fear, the fearsome one, strikes human beings down upon their faces, strikes the spirits and the dead down upon their faces when, rising with her wings, she returns from God's Land." Thus Hathor assured the living god of her protection, so that her ties to the falcon could be summed up in these words: "Your being is his being (and) your life is in his members."[72] The ceremonies involved in selecting and enthroning the divine falcon, with all their convolutions, thus accomplished a task of crucial importance for Egypt, given the country's conception of the functioning and equilibrium of the universe. Having concentrated all possible forms of divine aid in his person, the living falcon would in his turn, during the year to come, guarantee the land the protection of both Re, the renewed sun, and the king.

Once the ceremonies had come to a close, the sacred animal was integrated into the daily life of the temple. The ceremonial procession accordingly left the main sanctuary in order to partake of the meal served by Shu, son of Re, who was impersonated by the king. Although this meal, the first of the day, was still part of the festival, it was also already part of the daily ritual we discussed earlier. A platter loaded with offerings was therefore presented to the living falcon and the statue. The dishes were obviously chosen with an eye to the sacred animal's natural preferences: the menu consisted of beef and wild game. This meat, as it was chopped up, also symbolized the captured and slain enemies. By a well-known process, the meal became an act of symbolic destruction of these enemies and a means of assimilating their strength and power.[73] What happened next confirms the idea that a gradual transition back toward the daily cult routine was already under way. Fumigations were performed; the odor of the incense was supposed to blend with the aroma of the meat dishes, so that the god "might seize his food in its fragrance."[74] Although the offering was made to the living animal in his temple, it is quite clear that he was treated exactly like the divine statue. The meat was still not accessible to his earthly appetite; only the olibanum transmitted its aroma to him. Of course, what was involved here was a purely ritual truth. On a more prosaic level, we know, thanks to a humble administrative delivery form, that the sacred falcon of a city (which may not have been Edfu) was fed donkey meat, that is, the meat of his traditional enemy Seth.[75] The falcon would live on for a year, as ignorant as we are of the fate that would be meted out to him when it was over. Having become, for a time, a material support of the divine, he would play his basic role of guaranteeing the king's regenerated powers and the universal order established by Re.

About the Apis bull, we have information of a very different sort; it comes from Memphis and Saqqara. We possess only scant information about the living animal himself. But the funerary cult devoted to him has left substantial, crucially important archaeological remains. The situation is thus just the opposite of the one involving the falcon of Edfu. Unlike the falcon, Apis belonged to that category of sacred animals whose special distinguishing marks had destined them to play a special role from the moment of their birth, and who continued to incarnate godhead to the end of their lives. Despite this difference, Apis too was closely associated with the king. His cult is attested in Memphis from the very dawn of Egyptian history. It is not known whether this animal was originally a completely independent divine entity, but he was, from the first, closely connected with the king's person, imparting his procreative power to him. He very soon became the living image of the dynastic god Ptah, his incarnation. Later he was associated with Re, from whom he seems to have borrowed the disk he wore between his horns. He was also linked with Osiris.

When an Apis died, it was the duty of the priests of Ptah's temple to comb all the pastures of Egypt, searching out the young calf who would succeed him. This calf was identified by various markings. He had to have a black coat, with distinctive white patches on his forehead, neck, and body. There were twenty-nine such markings, according to certain classical authors.[76] Once the animal had been found, a temporary residence was erected for him on the spot; it had to be big enough to hold his mother and nurses until he was weaned. Thereafter, he was transported to the big city of Memphis, after a forty-day stopover in Nilopolis, located just opposite Memphis. During this period, women were allowed to approach him, but only in order to lift up their skirts and show him their vulva; this was believed to guarantee fertility. Then, during the full moon, the animal arrived at his permanent residence, to the south of the temple of Ptah in Memphis. He was provided with a priesthood and a harem of cows—though the different traditions contradict one another on this last point. With one exception, no Apis had direct descendants.[77] This seems surprising if he was surrounded, as Diodorus claims, with a vast harem. Another tradition[78] offers a plausible explanation of the matter. It indicates that a cow was selected and presented to Apis once a year, and then put to death so that no offspring would come of the match.[79] For Apis's direct descendants might very well not display the divine markings, a situation that had of course to be avoided. The Egyptians preferred to believe that Apis, son of Ptah, was born of a mother impregnated by the god in the form of a fire from the sky.[80]

Next to nothing is known of the daily ritual devoted to this god, but we do know that certain ceremonies associated the king and the bull from earliest times.[81] For example, they engaged in a race, which was in fact a fertility rite that consisted in trampling a plot of cultivable land underfoot. Subsequently, this rite was incorporated into the series of jubilee festivals whose object was the regeneration of the king's powers.[82] Still later, Apis became the bull who transported the members of Osiris's recomposed body, which he was supposed to carry to its burial place. In any case, Apis was immensely popular. Like the Buchis bull, he was endowed with the power of prophecy, inasmuch as certain features of his behavior could be taken as signs; these gave rise to multiple interpretations. The hieroglyphic sources have yielded only the barest accounts of the oracles of Apis,[83] but classical authors describe certain famous consultations with great precision. Pliny, for example, indicates that the bull's behavior augured well for a person if the animal accepted food from him or her; it was an evil omen if he refused it. In an oft-cited instance, Apis foretold the death of Germanicus by refusing to take an offering from him. The prediction of Eudoxus's death took a different form: Apis delivered his message by licking Eudoxus's clothes. His ways of responding to questions were, then, varied. He was also capable of indicating what was good or bad for the country by choosing to enter this or that stall.[84]

Apis's mother received a cult at his side. An area in the temple of Ptah had to be reserved for her as long as she lived. At her death, she was, like Apis, buried at Saqqara; her funerary rites were supposed to be comparable to those of Apis himself.[85] Various sources suggest that Apis's mother could live elsewhere than in Memphis right up to the moment of her death, though she was certainly buried in that city's necropolis, in one of the burial chambers in the underground gallery of the mothers of Apis. Why did she sometimes quit her son's place of residence? One possible explanation is that, whenever an Apis died before his mother, she had to yield her place to his successor's mother, inasmuch as an Apis could not have two mothers at once.

The bull's funerary rites were of great importance. We are, moreover, in a position to draw a rather detailed picture of them, though it must be remembered that the established or presumed facts date from the Late Period; we do not know to what extent our information holds good for earlier periods. The oldest of Apis's tombs so far discovered dates to the New Kingdom. From then on, the ceremonies, which borrowed their essential character from human funeral rites, were caught up in a process of constant transformation. The practice of embalming the bull may, for example, have been adopted in the Twenty-Sixth Dynasty. It was, moreover, in this period that wooden coffins were abandoned in favor of the granite sarcophagi that can still be seen today in the galleries of the Serapeum. The lack of evidence for the existence of tombs in the earliest periods, coupled with the fact that the textual proof of a cult of the living Apis dates, as was noted, from a very early period, poses many questions. In an attempt to explain why no trace of the ancient tombs has come down to us, some have gone so far as to suppose that they never existed in a material sense: the bull, they say, was eaten by the king, who sought to assimilate his divine powers in this way. One of the arguments brought forward in favor of this hypothesis is based on a very old text, known as the Cannibal Hymn, preserved on the walls of pyramids. This hymn does in fact describe how pharaoh appropriated the power of the gods by eating certain parts of their bodies. The oldest burial vaults in the Serapeum—they go back to the period before embalming rites were performed—have yielded nothing but disorderly piles of bones. It has therefore been assumed that these were the remains of a banquet that reproduced in actual fact the mythic royal meal described by the early text.[86] If this vision of things is impossible to prove, it at least has the advantage of firing our imaginations.

When it comes to describing the process of mummification, we are on firmer ground. The moment he died, the bull was transported to the workplace where he was to be mummified. Today, one can visit the ruins of this workplace in Memphis, where an immense alabaster embalming table survives; the sides are decorated with a motif evoking a lion-headed funerary bed viewed in profile. The animal was placed on this table, and its blood was drained and collected as it flowed down a channel carved into one of the shorter sides of the table. As we have said, the embalming techniques were identical to those applied to human beings. The internal organs were removed and placed in special containers, the canopic jars. Then the body was packed in dry natron and left to desiccate for several weeks. Once it had been completely dehydrated, it was wrapped in bandages. The whole process was supposed to last around seventy days, the length of the period during which Sirius disappeared from the heavens.[87] The god's servants went into mourning from the moment his death was announced. They were supposed to take part in his wake and had to observe a total fast for four days, then a partial fast until preparations for the embalming had been completed.[88] A few additional bits of information about those who participated in these ceremonials may be gleaned from the steles that were set up in the underground vaults of the Serapeum on the authorization of the king or Ptah's priesthood. Anyone who had in one way or another helped bury Apis was granted, in return for his services, the right to a stele. The documents engraved on these steles shed some light on the bond between the god's mortal remains and his worshippers,[89] some of whom were even drawn from among the ranks of the royal family. When one Apis died, the future Psamtik III declared: "I am a true and favored servant of the great god. At his death, I went into mourning, I deprived myself of water and bread until the four days had passed. I was naked and I trembled on my seat. . . . No food went down to my stomach, except for bread, water, and vegetables, until the end of the seventy days, when the great god left the embalming-place and occupied his great tomb in the necropolis, in the western desert of Memphis."[90] Once Apis had been embalmed, a procession of weepers and mourners, preceded by a detachment of the army, conducted the god to the Tent of Purification, where he received funerary offerings. The mummy was then placed on a four-wheeled chariot surmounted by a dais and dragged from the valley up to the top of the cliffs where the necropolis was located.[91] An opening in the canopy of the dais allowed his head to appear. Once the funeral procession had reached the Serapeum, the ritual of Opening the Mouth was performed just as it was practiced on human mummies or, as we have seen, representations of the gods in the temples. It is difficult to determine whether the ceremonies just mentioned took place in the open sanctuary of Apis-Osiris that stands at the entrance to the catacombs. But we are certain that a sacred dance that was supposed to be performed by a dwarf took place at the entrance to the subterranean galleries.[92] This motivation for this rite is obscure. It is known that, for the Egyptians, dwarfs represented a fetal form of the developing sun on the point of being reborn.[93] One therefore presumes that this dance was related to the rites of rebirth every deceased person benefited from. These dancing dwarfs were professionals. One of them, the dwarf Theos, who participated in the funeral of an Apis, considered this moment of his life so important that he had an account of his performance engraved on his sarcophagus. Finally, the mummy was placed in a granite sarcophagus of impressive size: it was four yards long, almost two and a half yards wide, and more than three yards deep, and weighed up to seventy tons. This huge container, with the mummy in it, was hauled to the burial vault, which was then walled over. Thereafter, no one had access to the subterranean galleries of the Serapeum until they were reopened for the next Apis's funeral.

We know nothing about the Apis other than his funeral ceremonies, and nothing about Horus's falcon other than his coronation ceremonies. Both of them, each in his own temple, played a part in the cult of the local god. The king, to whom both had privileged theological ties, was nevertheless only formally and somewhat furtively present in Apis's case. Nonhuman creatures in the natural world, these sacred animals ensured, along with many other of their fellow beasts, that there would be a certain divine presence among men. This presence was not static and was more accessible to the masses than were the cult images in the temples; but, like them, and like the king, it helped guarantee the great equilibrium of creation.

# CHAPTER EIGHT

# The Gods of the Hereafter, the Gods in the Hereafter

**A** rather frequently expressed view has it that the hereafter was an idyllic domain ruled by a good-natured monarch. The dead who were satisfied with their lot were the "justified"; they had successfully passed the judgment of the divine tribunal. But, to reach this tribunal, the dead had to make a journey, and this allows us to form some idea of the places they passed through on the way. Once they had taken up residence in what is sometimes compared to a paradise, the dead enjoyed a state of well-being similar to that of earthly dignitaries. Yet, even in this state, they were not beyond the reach of certain vexations. Nor did this apparently peaceful abode leave them without ulterior motives and ambitions. Whatever the benefits of their situation, they hoped one day to secure Re's permission to climb aboard his boat. But, to fulfill that dream, they again had to surmount all sorts of obstacles. The dead were not the only ones to live in or travel through these regions beyond the grave. The sun too crossed this subterranean realm in order to recompose his being and renew his forces before rising again. These lightless regions may seem incompatible with Osiris's paradisiacal realm; the deep caverns visited by the dead sun may seem irreconcilable with heavenly spaces and destinies. But, as we will see, a certain logic welded these disparate elements into a whole that lent cohesion to a universe in which gods and men, after dying a real or seeming death, discovered the road to rebirth.

## Osiris's Kingdom

After Osiris had been murdered by Seth,[1] all Isis's magic power and the help of the other gods were required to revive him. It was then that Anubis created the first mummy. "Look: I have found you lying on your side, O completely inert one! My sister, said Isis to Nephthys, it is our brother, this. Come, that we may lift up his head! Come, that we may reassemble his bones! Come, that we may put the parts of his body in proper order! Come, that we may erect a protective barrier before him! Let this not remain inert in our hands! Flow, lymph that comes from this blessed one! Fill the canals, form the names of the watercourses! Osiris, live, Osiris! May the completely inert one who is on his side rise! I am Isis."[2] As is well known, this resurrection enabled Isis and Osiris to engender Horus, the son born after Osiris's death and recognized by the gods—after many an adventure—as his father's sole legitimate heir. Osiris's death cost him his earthly kingdom, but made him the monarch of a different world, neither earth nor heaven, but a middle region, a dark and silent beyond. We have seen how the perversion of men, along with that of the children of Geb and Nut, led to the reorganization of the original world in differentiated spaces in which the earth and the sky acquired their definitive functions. The hereafter, which may already have been in existence,[3] took its place within this new structure. Certain traditions say that it was established by Osiris to meet his own needs. "Osiris is the lord of the West; he has perfected the hidden world for his mummy. He is the chief who rules over the beings in the hereafter and commands the recumbent."[4] For the living, the Osirian underworld was concealed: "one does not know," it was said, the dwelling place of the "lords of eternity, with secret names, with mysterious sanctuaries."[5] But the underworld was not immediately or easily accessible for the dead either.[6]

A deceased person had to be ready to make a journey on which he would undergo many different trials and have many unpleasant encounters. But if his path was strewn with pitfalls, one reason was that all the human or divine miscreants capable of endangering the concrete basis for Osiris's resurrection, his mummy, had to be kept at a distance from the god's abode. Seth and his followers never gave up trying to make incursions on Osiris's domain. The fear of malevolent intruders was obviously not unfounded, and the various roads leading to the last, great hall in Osiris's palace, in which he sat in state, were well guarded.[7] Yet the just among the dead had written guides at their disposal; familiarity with such a guide sufficed to bring them to their goal without mishap: "Guide to the roads in Rostau, on water or land: these are the roads of Osiris; they are at the limits of the sky. He who knows this spell for going there is himself a god. Moreover, he can go to any heaven he wishes to go to. But he who does not know this spell for passing over these roads will be dragged from the offering-table (of the dead) which has been assigned to him who is without means, and his Maat will never exist."[8] Prior knowledge of these roads was, then, crucial. But it was not enough, for they were strewn with so many difficulties and dangers that one could not avoid them all simply by knowing the maps. To begin with, not all these routes necessarily led to a paradise: some culminated in fiery dead ends. Evil-minded demons lay in wait for the unfortunate dead who had set out "to serve Osiris,"[9] to contemplate him while living at his side. Fortunately, a few, often obscure spells, if they had been learned ahead of time, helped one get through a certain stage of the journey or arrive at one's goal while dodging certain unpleasant encounters. "Spell for passing close by the cities of the knife-wielding demons, those who cry out; this is its road (leading) downwards, do not take it!"[10] To make ready for all possible confrontations with sinister demons, a deceased person could utilize a mnemonic device that would help him identify troublemakers and suggest ways of dealing with them. "Head of furiously attacking hippopotamus is his name; this is his pond. Spell for avoiding them during the day; if someone knows (it), he reaches his pond and does not die (again)." "Head of dog rich in forms is his name. This which is before me is the spell for passing by him."[11]

Besides negotiating these obstacle courses, a deceased person had to pass through a certain number of gates.[12] If he intended to approach the gods, it was at these points in particular that he had to bring into play knowledge and skill similar to the gods' own. Thus there existed a "spell for entering Osiris's divine assembly, among the gods who rule the hereafter, those who guard their gates, those who announce (in) their gates, gatekeepers of the portals of the West."[13] According to the Middle Kingdom Coffin Texts, a deceased person would encounter three portals. The first was made of a blue flame so intense that it held all passers-by at a distance. "There are fifty cubits [eighty-five feet] of flames along its sides and the tip of its flame reaches up to this heaven. The gods have said of it, 'This is the blackness of coal . . . that has created itself and made prey of the gods.'" To escape the flames, the deceased called upon Atum, describing the guard's powers and asking Atum for assistance: "Save me from this god who lives on his victims, whose head is a dog's and whose skin is a man's, who guards this perimeter of the Lake of Fire, who swallows shadows, who tears out hearts, who casts the lasso without being seen!"[14] The guard at the second portal, called "the one with the tall horns," spit fire from his maw. Sitting atop this portal, an evil spirit known as "He who is in the great flame" spelled obvious trouble for the deceased, who had to protect himself against him. The deceased therefore turned to Osiris, who is not explicitly named, asking the god to save him from this obnoxious snatcher of souls, "who laps up putrefaction and decaying things, the shadow-dweller, the agent of the night, he who is feared by the shadow-dwellers."[15] As for the third portal, the deceased could not so much as approach it, because it was encircled by a ring of flames four shoinoi (about thirty miles) wide. The first shoinoi contained nothing but fire; the second, burning heat; the third was simply the fiery breath of Sakhmet's mouth; the fourth opened on to the boundless Nun. This was one of the most dangerous places of all, because it was apparently possible to cross it by mistake, and so find oneself trapped on the road that led to nowhere but damnation. Indeed, the dead who strayed into this region were automatically dispatched by Thoth to a tribunal that inevitably condemned them; there their doom was irrevocably sealed by none other than Shu and Tefnut. This was a terrible fate; the dead would beg the lord of the Ennead that it be spared them, crying: "Save me from these inflicters of wounds, whose fingers cause pain . . . who carry out massacres in hell, whose watchfulness it is impossible to elude! Their knives will not pierce me, I will not enter their hells. No, I will not enter your cauldrons!"[16]

Later, in the New Kingdom, according to one of the many existing versions of this journey, the dead had to pass through seven gates in order to reach Osiris's dominion.[17] The first was guarded by an individual explicitly identified as a spy. He was evidently assisted by a very indiscreet herald, called "He who growls with his voice." The deceased would, after introducing himself to the herald, state his titles with a certain aplomb. He would boast of being the "Great One, he who created his light." He would claim to be able to cure Osiris's ills and would even compare himself to the creator-god, declaring that he was "He who made all that exists." Obviously, the object was to impress the gatekeepers so profoundly that they would think the supreme deity in person was standing before them. At the second gate, the deceased would encounter the doorkeeper called "He who puffs out his chest," together with the guard and the inevitable herald. Here too, he would display a certain audacity, identifying himself with Thoth, "He who settles differences between the Two Companions" and who had, ages past, settled the dispute between Horus and Seth. The doorkeeper at the third gate engaged in rather disagreeable practices; this was "He who eats the excrement of (his) anus." This seems to have been an engrossing occupation, for this gate required the services of a particularly vigilant guard. The deceased would again deck himself out with Thoth's attributes, claiming to have power over the Nile inundation and Osiris's maladies. The doorkeeper at the fourth gate had a repulsive face, and was, moreover, given to barking. The guard and the herald were at their posts. Here, the deceased would vaunt his animal powers. He would claim to be a bull and the son of Osiris's kite, and would declare that he was bringing Osiris everlasting life. The individual guarding the fifth gate lived on worms. The herald here was someone we already know: "Head of furiously attacking hippopotamus." Given to wandering down remote side roads in the Coffin Texts, he pursued a more sedentary occupation here. The deceased, increasingly self-assured because he had succeeded in drawing steadily closer to his goal, would put himself forward as the greatest of the gods and claim to have had a hand in the rebirth of Osiris: "I performed Osiris's purification rites and assisted him at his justification; I assembled his bones and reunited his members." The deceased would then inform the sixth doorkeeper and his assistants that he had been created by Anubis and that the way must therefore be cleared for him. With this, he would have arrived at the last gate. Here he would recognize, among those in charge, one whose function was to reject the wicked. Of course, this personage was no obstacle for him. All through his journey, he had not hesitated to impersonate the greatest Egyptian gods—with seeming success.

The attitudes of the dead had changed considerably since the Coffin Texts were composed. The dead were no longer poor lost creatures making their way through hostile parts, unable to count on anything but their own knowledge or the help of protectors solicitous of their success. Rather, they declared that they were gods before presenting themselves to Osiris, managing to impress all those who had taken it upon themselves to bar their route. What was once a severe trial had become a formality. The knowledge transmitted by the funerary texts was itself responsible for this shift. These texts explained more clearly to the dead the information they needed to have, with the result that they were prepared for their ordeals well in advance. They were no longer in the position of people trying to learn everything they needed to know to bring their journey to a successful conclusion; they *knew*, for they had already learned the essentials. But access to this knowledge was restricted. Doubtless, the dead who knew how to read had no reason to fear the pitfalls of the next world, but the literate were never more than a tiny minority of society. All other dead people lacked this knowledge that their fate depended on, which they had not been taught and were incapable of acquiring. Thus their salvation hinged on the good will of those who, remaining behind on earth, could read out the appropriate magic spells for their benefit. But there was every chance that this good will would prove to be elitist. Indeed, the text of the seven gates culminates in an unsettling statement: "Every blessed one for whom this (text) is recited will be like a lord of eternity there, forming one being with Osiris. Not to be recited for the benefit of just anybody; beware!"

We have reached the great hall where Osiris sat in state. Welcoming the new arrivals was Anubis's responsibility.[18] The god saw them approaching when they were still a great way off and declared to a colleague standing beside him: "The voice of a man come from Egypt rings out. He knows our roads and our cities." From the outset, Anubis knew that the deceased had overcome all the obstacles and was familiar, in the fullest sense of the word, with the geography of the hereafter; he had thus already become, to some extent, part of it. Anubis assumed the role of intercessor between the new arrival and the assembly seated around Osiris; this was the ultimate tribunal. While the candidate for beatitude cooled his heels at the door, Anubis recited before all present the good deeds that the deceased had told him he had done; Anubis concluded by turning toward the deceased and saying, "May your weighing take place in our midst." Before entering the great hall, the deceased had to state, one more time, the name of the gate he wished to pass through, as well as that of its lintel and threshold, so that Anubis might then proclaim, "Enter, because you know." Now came the dread trial of the weighing of the heart, seat of the inmost thoughts of the deceased and storehouse of his good and evil deeds. Scales were set up before Osiris. The heart of the deceased was placed on one of the pans; it had to be at least as light as the feather of Maat placed on the other. Anubis proceeded to weigh it, while Thoth wrote down the result to eliminate all possible grounds for contesting the judgment. The assembly, presided over by Osiris, then listened patiently while the deceased recited two long lists of sins he declared he had never committed. There was no overlap between the contents of these two "declarations of innocence," as they are called; rather, they complemented one another.[19] The first was addressed directly to Osiris; the second, to the forty-two judges of the assembly. Observing the proprieties, the deceased began by saluting the god of the dead: "Hail to you, great god, lord of the two Maats! I have come to you, my lord, I have been brought that I might see your perfection. I know you and I know the names of the forty-two gods who are with you in this hall . . . who live by guarding sinners and lap up their blood the day characters are reckoned before Onnophris." The declaration properly so called followed: "I have done no evil. I have not begun a single day by taking a commission from people who were supposed to be working for me . . . I have not blasphemed against the divine. I have not robbed the orphan of his property . . . I have not killed. I have not given orders to kill." The sole object of the second declaration was to extend and amplify the first. But the deceased was not at the end of his trials after making it. There followed three examinations designed to test his knowledge of conditions in the hereafter; without such knowledge, he would prove incapable of living there as a permanent resident. The forty-two judges asked him to state his new identity as a divinized human being. He again had to describe and name the regions he had traveled through to reach the gods. Finally, he had to give an account of the actions he had performed during the journey, in order to demonstrate his knowledge of the mysterious relics of Osiris and the attentions they required. This satisfied the judges, but a new gate, the very last, the one that opened on to the abode of the blessed, now loomed up before the applicant. He had to respond to its questions and give the secret names of all its constituent parts. The gatekeeper, in his turn, was sure to ask what had brought him to these regions and whether he knew exactly to which god he should be announced. The deceased would of course know that he had come to see Thoth. If he stated this with firmness and assurance, the way would be opened before him. But Thoth had a set of questions of his own to ask. A dialogue between him and the deceased therefore began: "To whom, then, shall I announce you?" "Announce me to Him whose abode has a ceiling of fire, walls of living uraei, and a floor of water." "Who is that?" "It is Osiris." "Go! You have been announced." Only then was the deceased ushered into Osiris's presence by the latter's son, Horus, who confirmed that he had successfully undergone his various trials. Osiris and his assembly at last permitted the new arrival to be arrayed in new attire and partake of the funerary meals that were then served them. The deceased was henceforth integrated into the world of the blessed; offerings would ensure his survival.

Throughout this lengthy procedure, a hybrid monster with the head of a crocodile, the hindquarters of a hippopotamus, and the mane of a lion had been waiting, her huge maw agape. This female animal, who sat next to the scales, was known as "the Eater"; in the present case, she had waited in vain for the deceased to be turned over to her. But this was not always so. If a new arrival showed, by failing even one of his tests, that he was not worthy to be received among the ranks of the just, the Eater was immediately charged with eliminating him. Not all the damned, however, were turned over to her. Some of the wicked were destined for the fearful execution chamber, ruled over by "the Squatters, the agents of death of the secret slaughter chamber."[20] For there were different classes of genies charged with punishing or devouring the damned in the underworld. These auxiliary agents used whatever means they saw fit to neutralize evildoers. Not all were lethal: they included imprisonment, enchainment, and mutilation.[21] These auxiliaries' fierce determination and their small concern for details and fine points made them dangerous even for the blessed, who protested that they could never be delivered up "to those who are in the slaughter-chamber among those who do the carving";[22] it was well-known that these creatures lived on raw flesh.[23] Even after successfully undergoing all these trials, the dead continued to proclaim: "a sacrifice will never be made of me by the guardians of Osiris's chambers, those who make massacres."[24] It must be emphasized that Osiris could, under normal circumstances, display great cruelty, or else a certain callousness, for he would occasionally let all the genies in his service torture one of the deceased.[25] The names of these genies reflected their functions, and were, moreover, most expressive—torturer, murderer, miscreant, aggressor, and so on. There were also "those who eat their fathers" and "those who eat their mothers." Osiris, then, had not struck cannibalism from his list of defensive methods. Indeed, certain of the judges on his tribunal had names indicating that they engaged in this practice: breaker of bones, he who lives on blood, swallower of entrails.[26] It even seems that these killers made the "lord of life" offerings of children's flesh.[27]

This world of the dead might finally seem decidedly imperfect, even sinister. Osiris was a master who displayed a certain passivity and even a touch of despotism. He made many demands, though he also conceded some freedom of the will to everyone. The dead could either serve him, or else try, with the help of their souls, to gain access to the day, the celestial domain. This last stage of their journey, like all the others, was never completed without incident. As might be imagined, the divine servants in the hereafter were not much inclined to let an overly large number of Osiris's subjects slip from their grasp[28] by turning into gods.[29] This indicates that the dead wished to leave this world that they had had so much trouble reaching. Yet if their bodies—their corpses—remained forever confined there, their bird-souls, or *ba*, enabled them to circulate much more freely. However, Osiris's bodyguards, who protected the god against Seth and his rebel band and were invested with all sorts of powers, were also charged with guarding the ba-souls of all the dead, male or female.[30] They accordingly strove to prevent them from flying off. Liberation for the ba meant escaping the uncertainties of the kingdom of the dead, which was in the final analysis only an extension of the world of the living, with all its frightening features, obligations, and vexations. Hence the prayer of supplication Osiris's subjects offered up in an attempt to protect themselves against everything that might restrict the movement of their ba-souls: "You have not been seized, you have not been held captive by the guards of the sky and the earth; keep your distance from your body, which is in the earth, so as not to be among the wielders of pitchforks, among the guards assigned to the members, (for) you are a god who has the use of his legs, the son of a god who has the use of his legs. Keep your distance from your body, which is in the earth."[31] The allusion to the "wielders of pitchforks" served as a reminder of the corvée-labor that could be imposed on the dead. The hereafter finally only mirrored the land of pharaoh.[32] Doubtless Osiris did not forbid his blessed subjects to taste earthly pleasures again: "Behold me paddling this boat in the canals of Hotep. . . . Here I flourish and am strong, here I eat and drink . . . here I make love; here my magic incantations are powerful."[33] But forced labor was never very far off: "here I work and I harvest" figures prominently in the same text. It was also known that a dead person was "this pure one who cooks for Osiris in the course of the day. (His) fields are in the Field of Felicities among those who are competent, among those who prepare bread (for) Osiris."[34] The notion of corvée-labor is not always in evidence, but the living surely suspected that the monarch of the hereafter would, like pharaoh on earth, expect them to do their part to ensure the smooth functioning of his empire. From the orders the dead received, it is easy to imagine the kinds of tasks they were required to perform: "Take your picks, your hoes, your poles, and your baskets in your hands, as every man does for his master!"[35] Later, the same spell unambiguously describes the work to be done. Fields had to be cultivated, riverbanks irrigated, and sand transported from the East to the West.[36] It was doubtless to assist with this labor that the donkey could dwell in the hereafter, even if it was an emblem of Seth.[37]

The souls of the inhabitants of the Osirian kingdom, then, eagerly awaited the daily passage of the sun, but also lived in the hope of once again seeing the light of day and spending eternity in Re's company: "Behold me, men, gods, blessed ones, dead! I go forth by day. My eyes are open, my ears are open . . . I have gone forth by day; I eat with my mouth, I defecate with my bottom, I have gone forth by day."[38] The desire of the dead was to board the solar bark and ascend to the sky: "The deceased person here is encircled by Orion, Sirius, and the Morning Star. They place you in the arms of your mother Nut . . . you will not go down towards the slaughter of the beginning of the decade [ten-day week] among the guilty ones of the West."[39] One could not ascend to heaven to escape the dangers and abuses of the Osirian kingdom if one lacked the means to do so. Here, too, journeying up to the sky meant encountering untold obstacles—for example, the four winds.[40] Climbing aboard the solar bark was one of the readiest ways of gaining access to heaven. But it was also possible to set up a ladder[41] or change oneself into a bird. Once a deceased person had settled in the firmament, he could at last voice his triumph: "I appear like a god . . . I cross the space between earth and heaven, I occupy Shu's place."[42]

What held for the passage to the next world also held for the ascent to the sky: one had to know the right road. "Knowing the paths (up to the heavens): the paths in the heavens have been opened for me, the light of the sun descends the river northwards, passing through the South."[43] Words were the vehicle of this knowledge. "He who knows this divine word, he will be in heaven with Re, among the gods who are in the sky."[44] To know the right spell was thus to be Re in the heavens and, simultaneously, Osiris in the hereafter.[45] Spending eternity with the sun—a privilege reserved, in the beginnings of Egyptian history, for the king alone—had become the common aspiration of all the dead. Throughout the funerary texts, as we have seen, one finds ample testimony to the ambiguity of man's lot beyond the tomb. The dead vacillated between resigning themselves to the gloom and the constraints of the netherworld and nursing an almost desperate hope of being united forever with the light in its plenitude. The thoroughly theological solution to this dilemma was both clever and convenient: one abandoned one's cumbersome mortal remains in the depths so that one's winged soul might dwell unfettered in the celestial heights. This solution neatly reconciled approaches that were in reality sharply divergent. In the face of the choices the funerary texts held out to him, the Egyptian displayed considerable lucidity; in his heart of hearts, he harbored few illusions about what awaited him in the future life. Osiris's kingdom did not really have a good reputation, and the deceased did not fail to point this out: "How does it happen that I must travel to a desert, which has no water, which has no air, which is very deep, very dark, and altogether without limit?"[46] This vision was shared by the living themselves. When they accompanied a dead person to his final resting place, they could not help bewailing his fate. "The house of those of the West is deep and dark. There there is neither door, nor window, nor light to make things bright, nor north wind to refresh the heart. The sun does not come up there. They (the dead) will sleep every day because of the darkness, even in the middle of the day."[47] Finally, the rejuvenation the dead so hoped for in the next world was by no means certain. If it was true that the dead, "though they have grown old, do not die,"[48] it was also true that they stayed at the same age they were when they died; they did not become any younger.[49] This is a far cry from the promise of renewal so often affirmed elsewhere. Hence the interest of gaining access to the sun's domain: this ensured one an increase in spirituality and also union with the only true source of life and youth.

## The Sun's Voyage through the Netherworld

The Egyptians believed that the sun traveled through the body of his daughter Nut on both his day and night journeys. Yet they had not failed to observe that the setting sun plunged into the western horizon and then seemed to cross the netherworld in order to come up in the eastern sky in the morning. These two conceptions of the sun's apparent movements are contradictory, and it seems impossible, on first glance, to reconcile them. By depicting two Nuts—the day and the night Nut—back to back in certain royal tombs, the Egyptians sought to make a close association between the sun's two voyages, while, in a certain sense, physically separating them. In any case, there exists an abundant literature that does not portray the netherworld, with its various regions and its inhabitants, as an essentially Osirian realm, but rather describes it in terms of the different trajectories the sun follows through it. Several books, among them the Book of What Is in the Hereafter and the Book of Gates, attempt to describe as precisely as possible a remarkable universe in which the dead do not have the essential role, even if they are present. These texts are found, as a rule, on the walls of the royal tombs. They are, moreover, found in the vicinity of the figure of Nut, the female sky; yet this juxtaposition of two different approaches was not regarded as problematic. The Book of Caverns is undoubtedly one of the strangest and most complex of these compositions, but it may also be the one with the most to teach us about the fate reserved for the sun in the netherworld.[50] In this book, Re travels through six regions that it is quite difficult to match up with the hours of the night. Nothing suggests that each region corresponds to two full hours. Furthermore, it is not clearly stated how many caverns there actually are. These caverns, to use the Egyptian term, are home to different kinds of creatures and objects. The book is, first and foremost, a pictorial version of a mysterious transformation; the accompanying texts are simply glosses on the pictures. The meaning of the texts is often obscure, and one constantly needs to turn from them to the images to glean some notion of what the ancient editors meant to say. The style is dry; only a few words, awash in exaggeratedly repetitive phraseology, make it possible to identify the situations and the mythical functions that give the book as a whole its meaning. As to the vignettes themselves, they offer, at first glance, a static, frozen portrait of the hereafter; it is hard to see what kind of hope this place could inspire in its inhabitants. Generally enclosed within oval figures representing either a sarcophagus or an earthen container, the denizens of the other world are brought back to life for only a brief moment during the sun's passage through their region. "These gods behold the rays of the disk . . . and after he has passed by them, the darkness envelops them"; this sentence, together with a few variants, is monotonously repeated as the sun proceeds on his way. Yet, despite its difficulties, the Book of Caverns has proven to be one of the most interesting documents we have when it comes to understanding the way the Egyptians envisioned the regeneration of the gods who had been enfeebled by death, like Osiris, or by night, like Re. It offers a veritable theological physics of the recomposition and resurrection of divine bodies in the netherworld.

As a rule, each of the six regions of the world of the caverns is divided into three superposed registers for the purpose of laying it out on the walls of the tombs. The lowest register constitutes the "basement" of the netherworld; it is almost exclusively inhabited by the damned and those charged with torturing them. Let us enter the first region. At dusk, Re sets foot in an area that also seems to have belonged to the first hour of the night. He announces himself to the gatekeepers and gods of the place: "I am Re who is in the heavens, I enter the twilight shadows, I open the gate of the sky in the West. Welcome me with your arms (outstretched) towards me! Behold, I know your place in the hereafter. Behold, I know your names, your caverns, your secrets."[51] Re comes before gatekeepers and gods in the double form of an anthropomorphic, ram-headed god, followed by his disk; he will appear in one or both of these aspects throughout his journey. These are, it will be recalled, essentially the same forms he took during his voyage inside his daughter Nut's body. The world the first picture shows us is not exclusively reserved for the deceased. One sees gods and demons, some in animal forms, some not. Hybrid forms, part animal, part human, are also included in this population. Snakes, specifically subterranean powers, are present in large numbers. The damned are to be seen here, with their heads or arms cut off; but one also sees the blessed in their coffins, and, of course, recumbent divinities. Overall, the groups inhabiting the various caverns all display much the same features, a few variations aside. The only notable absence here is that of vegetation. Re first addresses himself to one of the snakes: "O Biter in your Cavern, Terrifying One, the greatest of the netherworld, bow down, draw back your arm. Behold me; I am entering the land of the beautiful West to attend to Osiris, to greet those who are with him."[52] Similar invocations are addressed to the other beings. Thus Re asks the forces protecting this basement register for permission to enter, requesting that they clear the way for him by "drawing back" their arms, to cite the expression employed. The god then turns toward nine figures confined in what are apparently coffins. They are considered "pacified," as much, doubtless, because they lie still, as because they have obeyed Re and earned their rest. They too draw back their arms to let him pass by. Behind these recumbent figures are a series of gods who act as watchdogs; recognizing the Lord of the Universe, they make no sound as he passes. Although they are "masters of provisions," they thrust out their muzzles "like dogs who dig around in garbage and lap up corruption and filth."[53] This less than inviting description is rendered in a more subdued manner in the accompanying picture: there we see a row of anthropomorphic genies with dog's heads, their torsos bent slightly forward. These creatures' task was to guard the souls who dwelt in this region; they were silent so as to allow their charges to rest in peace. Osiris is present in several different forms at once, as will often be the case in subsequent phases of the journey. His dismemberment, decomposition, and rebirth are summarized here by a round object containing a relic of his body, a god personifying his rotting corpse, and his own standing figure encircled by a serpent.[54] Re makes himself known to the god of the dead and asks him to guide him on the subterranean voyage he is setting out on. He reminds him of his life-giving omnipotence; this is a way of pointing out that it is in Osiris's best interests to help him. Next, other figures present on the scene, described as "great gods," lead Re to the mysterious chasms so that he can diffuse his light there. The snakes who guard the damned in the bottom register cannot, we are told, leave the cavern. The rebels they guard are none other than the enemies of Osiris who carry evil throughout the netherworld. The snakes have to watch them vigilantly to prevent them from escaping. The theme of the confinement of the guards and the damned often recurs in the following scenes. Re curses both those among the damned whose heads have already been cut off and those about to undergo this form of torture. "O you who ought to be annihilated, O you who ought to be decapitated, enemies of Osiris whose heads have been cut off, who no longer have your necks, who no longer have your souls, whose corpses have been annihilated, behold me: I pass above you, I abandon you to your woes, I regard you as no longer existing! You are those who are overwhelmed with woes in the place of annihilation."[55]

After greeting the gods at the entrance to the netherworld, obtaining permission to enter, and securing the services of a guide, Re leaves this area, plunging it into darkness, and passes into the second region of the netherworld, where he is welcomed by the snakes guarding the entrance to it. The sun-god gave a somewhat surprising piece of advice to the leader of their band, a god named Black Head: "Hide from me while I pass by and show yourself after I have passed by." Even the gatekeepers are asked not to expose themselves to view before Re leaves this cavern, in which everything must remain elusive, hidden, barely present or visible.[56] Those who can be glimpsed here are plunged in the semi-darkness;

certain parts of their bodies cannot be made out. Others lie in oval-shaped containers. It seems plain that these are the dead whom we have already met; having triumphed before Osiris's tribunal, they live out their blessed existences in sleep. The sad fate of these recumbent souls, brought back to life for only a brief instant by the passing sun, confirms the pessimistic visions we mentioned earlier. This cavern is, then, a bizarre place where all the departed are crammed together pell-mell, whatever the fate that awaits them. Though they share the area, their individual destinies differ. Some are condemned to remain here; the ba-souls of others will eventually enable them to escape: "Behold, I shine upon you, while your faces are turned toward me, and my face is turned towards you. . . . May your souls come forth, may your souls be powerful, may your souls rest upon your bodies in your containers. Your souls, I call them, they accompany me and they guide me."[57] Plainly, the privileged souls are those in a position to benefit from the shining light, those who were invited to come forth to serve as guides. We next meet, for the first time, blessed females in their coffins. Though they are cadaverous creatures, their flesh is incorruptible. Indeed, they are themselves containers in which lie beings in gestation. Thus they prefigure the process of rebirth visibly under way in the entrails of all the dead creatures in the caverns. Although they have a body, it has been separated from the ba-soul that should accompany it. So that he can set forth his journey and win over the forces stirring in these souls, Re makes them a promise: "(If) you lead my soul towards my body, I will guide your souls towards the containers that contain your corpses. I will shine upon you, I will dispel your shadows."[58] Thus we learn, in passing, the object of the sun's voyage: the regions he passes through contain various inanimate bodies belonging to the god; his ba-soul, here the solar disk on its journey, will bring these bodies to life for a moment or two, just as it does all the other inhabitants of these caverns. But let us observe his encounter with the wailers, whom we can recognize by their dishevelled hair hanging down in long strands over their faces. Shaken by sobs, they weep, sniffle, speak, and shriek all at once. Their tears do not go to waste. The wailers carefully collect them in their hands, for they seem to have protective and nutritive virtues. Notwithstanding all the racket the wailers make, they remain forever frozen in this one position. Behind them are the gods of the divine tribunal, of whom there are twelve in the Book of Caverns, one for each hour of the night; they lie in coffins. This group of gods is led by Horus who has no eyes, a form of the Elder Horus, whose adventures and misadventures we traced in Part 1. This Horus has the head of a shrew, a blind rat that fears the broad daylight.[59] His presence here is significant. As the sun, in his senescent form, passes before those who acclaim him, some turn toward him and others turn away to face a casket. In it lies the rotting body of a god who is at one and the same time Osiris, the sun, and even the deceased king. The casket is surrounded by heads and necks belonging to Re. The whole of this scene unfolds in front of and inside a niche cut into the face of the wall; the niche symbolizes the casket itself as well as the cavern it lies in. This group evokes the divine heads lost in the periods when the heavenly bodies disappear.[60] It is doubtless when the sun is in this very spot that his last glimmers fade from men's sight. This is also the point at which he commences his rebirth, in all his forms taken together, for this is the place of his "first" birth, as the text expressly says.[61] The rest of the cavern is taken up by twelve Osirises, major aspects of the god, multiplied so as to correspond to the twelve hours of the night. Behind them are still other members of the divine tribunal, lying, this time, in their coffins. Finally, the enemies may also be seen here, as in all the other caverns; they are either headless or about to be beheaded. With them are the demons charged with torturing them. A new group has joined them, that of the damned who walk upside down; their hearts have been torn out, and, as they go, they eat excrement that comes back up when they swallow it. A mysterious, complex place, this second cavern is where the initial stages of the solar and Osirian resurrections unfold. A place of shadows and secrets, it skilfully brings together the symbols of what has been lost (visibility, life), the decomposition due to death, and the beginnings of recomposition and rebirth.

To judge by the themes developed in it, the third region centers on Osiris; here he undergoes transformations whose details are, however, barely limned in.[62] The uppermost register of this region is not very explicit. Seven divinities with smooth faces topped by two antennalike members represent various aquatic spirits. Their names are related to those of fish or animals who prefer moist environments. They are protected by the serpent Nehebkau, the creature who was also believed to bind all the divine energies together in a cohesive whole. His presence indicates that this union of all the energies is about to be achieved. This group looks ahead to two scenes. The first shows the solar disk being united with his corpse; the second represents Osiris standing upright in a chapel, surrounded by gods who have, at Anubis's request, taken part in his mummification. We are informed that they have been buried in a standing position, and "that they cannot lie down, in accordance with vows they have made to themselves."[63] To go through the following stages, Re has stood up again, although he has retained the form of a ram-headed god. The disk that is usually shown accompanying him has been placed on the back of his neck under the horns; it serves as a reminder of the reunification that has just taken place. At the center of the middle register, dominating it, is the earth-spirit Aker, whose body consists of the foreparts of two sphinxes, attached to one another. He lies on his belly, so as to protect one of the bodies of Osiris that has been placed beneath him in the third register; we will return to this picture later on. The sun, we are told, clings to his back, doubtless in order to communicate his energy both to the Double Sphinx itself and to the body it shields. Other powers join the sun to help him with his revitalizing mission, the earth-god Geb and the scarab, both on the back of the Double Sphinx. Various representations of Osiris ranged on either side of the Double Sphinx confirm that we are witnessing an essential moment of Osiris's ascension toward life. Snakes are once again present, encircling Osiris or located beneath his feet; they underscore the role that the earth, considered as matter, plays in this metamorphosis. To the rear of the sphinx, between his paws, are four goddesses who have been confined to this restricted space for all time; they salute an Osiris who has been placed in a hollow, a cavern within the cavern, in which he stands face to face with the head and eye of the sun. Another Osiris follows this one. He seems to have a crocodile head and stands atop a snake; a spirit is tugging on the god's beard. Apparently this is a way of alluding to something we mentioned a moment ago, the ascension that gradually draws the dead god out of his lethargic state. The text spells out that these two registers are unknown to the ordinary dead, whom none of the figures represented here evokes, directly or indirectly. This is a clear sign that an especially mysterious event is in progress, one that must remain hidden from all but divine eyes. The bottom register is plainly identified as the basement of the cavern. As we have already seen, this area is always reserved for the enemies and the damned. They are, indeed, on hand, but are ranged on either side of an Osiris lying on his back and looking upward, in contrast to the damned. The god is not mummiform. He is, moreover, ithyphallic, a circumstance that signals the return of his sexual capacities. In a departure from custom, the sun goes to pay him a visit. He sweeps across the ground, taking advantage of the opening that the snake encircling Osiris has left above the god's head, where the ring he forms is not quite closed. The warmth of the sun's rays penetrates the earth, causing life to germinate there. The accompanying text explains that this is the corpse of Osiris, "ruler of the West, whose decay(ing flesh) is mysterious, whose decomposition is hidden, whom the dead may not approach, although those who dwell in the West live on the odor of his decay."[64] In front of Osiris, damned souls, segregated by sex, cry out to the sun for help, but he ignores them: "You are the enemies of Osiris, those enemies who have no soul. You are plunged in the shadows, (you) whose souls have been wrested from your bodies. In truth, you will be deprived of breath, in truth, you will be in the place of annihilation, while one among you, he who destroys the souls of evil-doers . . . will be your guard . . . you will not see my rays and you will be powerless against my rays."[65] In addition to those under torture and the beheaded figures represented behind the reviving Osiris, then, the Egyptian hell makes room for a special category of the damned, whose punishment is less severe than the others'. They are physically intact and can direct appeals to the sun, who has, however, turned away from them forever. Their suffering consists in a form of torture somewhat like that Tantalus is subjected to: they know that the sun is nearby, but cannot profit from his favor so as to be reunited with their souls and join the ranks of the blessed, who are bathed in light. In abandoning them, Re, although his infinite goodness is often extolled, "does evil after he has passed by them." The guard who accompanies them suffers an additional punishment, because he is also condemned to destroy the souls of those who have done evil. Not all the executioners in the Egyptian hereafter are, then, divine emanations. Some are ordinary human beings, whose torture consists in having to torture the others. At the far end of the scene, one sees "dead souls"; they have lost their bodies forever and are condemned to stand motionless, waiting for an impossible reunion. The closing text stresses the fact that two different hereafters come together in the region we have just traveled through. It is the only region to include a connecting passage between the two: this passage permits the sun to descend below the earth, by way of the Double Sphinx, in order to warm and rouse Osiris.

The fourth region is entirely given over to the simultaneous rebirth of Osiris and Re, on its way to completion here.[66] A long text that is in fact a hymn to Re refers to his departure from the preceding region and acclaims his nascent brightness and beauty. This text speaks of the air and the life it brings with it. The first scene shows Osiris alive, as he will soon be, lifted up on Isis's and Nephthys's arms along with the solar disk. This is a transposition of a well-known motif that portrays the two goddesses as guarantors that the sun will come up at the break of day. Osiris's body is elongated, and its ends are bent so sharply upward that it forms the arc of a circle, evoking the curvature of the mountains of the horizon. Somewhat further off, Osiris, flanked by Horus and Anubis, watches as his members are collected and his body is definitively reassembled. Horus performs the god's morning toilet. At this point, we discreetly rejoin the daily temple rites briefly described earlier. Behind this group, a bull-headed god, the "Bull of the West," incarnates an Osiris who has regained his vital powers. He leans toward two figures in containers; they too herald the sun's rebirth. One of them represents an ichneumon, another of the animals emblematic of the Elder Horus; it serves as a pendant to the shrew we met a moment ago and indicates that the god has recovered his eyes and his eyesight. The period of total invisibility is ending, and the first flickers of dawn are beginning to come into men's view. The other figure represents a heart, flanked to either side by a solar disk with its rays projecting downward. The text explains that this is Re talking to his heart. As we saw in Part 1, that was how the creator-god initiated the act of creation. Obviously, we are meant to understand that the reappearance of the sunlight that we witness here represents nothing less than a new genesis. In the middle register, Re, still portrayed with a ram's head, greets the guards of the region, announcing what we had already surmised: that he will cleave the primeval darkness enveloping the world with his light. He is now on the "great sand," doubtless the sandy riverbed representing the outer limits of the netherworld. The water is therefore near, and, with it, the bark in which Re will once again take his place. A bit further off, Harendotes, or Horus the protector of his father, leans toward his father's two mummies; this Horus, who ensures that Osiris's body will be put back together, is a prototype of the heir to the throne. At the far end of the middle register, Anubis bows respectfully before the living Osiris, who has now rejoined his ba-soul. This group of scenes indicates that the simultaneous recomposition and rebirth of Osiris, Re, and the deceased king have been brought about at last. The fragmentation and multiplicity of the images merely underscore the basic unity of this process. Whereas, in the preceding region, only deceased human beings were not allowed to witness the process of divine gestation, here all the gods, spirits, and dead are forbidden to draw near. The only gods on hand are the major deities who always took part in the process of divine resurrection. The bottom register, that of the damned, offers further confirmation of the uniqueness of the moment depicted here. A cat-god, a well-known emblem of the nascent sun, is waging victorious battle with the enemies who, every day, try to prevent the sun from rising. In the center of the picture, two destructive goddesses disable the guard of the damned. This guard, whom we have already met, is thus set apart from the other torture victims, who meet a different fate. Those who have been unambiguously damned are confined to the netherworld for good and all; they will never be able to leave it. Presumably it is here that the final destruction of some of them occurs. As for the guard, he seems to benefit from a sort of act of grace—in a relative sense, to be sure. In exchange for services rendered, he is authorized to quit the netherworld, but in no case will he be entitled to undergo bodily regeneration. He will remain forever in his present state of decay; he cannot shake free of the putrefaction that clings to him, for it is a sign of his degeneration, proof that he belongs irrevocably to the world of the dead.

In the fifth region, the sun prepares to leave the caverns for the outside world.[67] Two gigantic gods standing face to face to either side of this region enclose all three of its registers as if in brackets. At the entrance, Nut, the sky-goddess, stands looking at an ithyphallic god adorned with the regalia of kingship; a bird perches on his head. This god is at once Osiris, the resurrected king, and Geb, the earth-god. The whole scene takes place between the earth and the sky, or, more exactly, in the place where the earth and the sky meet on the horizon. The sun, we are told, has taken the right route. He sails along through the cavern, although there is as yet no water in it. One glimpses hills prefiguring the mountains of the east, where the sun will soon become visible to men's eyes. All along Nut's body, one finds representations of the sun in all the various stages of his gestation. Behind Nut are four crocodiles who embody primeval forces of the underworld; they point their snouts toward four different forms of the sun, representing his senescence, his coming back into being in death, and his recomposition. Balanced on Nut's right hand, in the foreground of the picture, is a small ram-headed god. On her left hand is the solar disk. These are representations of the two extremes in the life of the sun, his old age and his rebirth. Just in front of the goddess, four other forms lead the sun disk from his recomposition to his rebirth; a picture of a child being taken up by two outstretched arms symbolizes this process. The arms are those of the earth, opening to let the sun come out. They reach up from the goddess's right foot, in line with her celestial anatomy, which places the outer reaches of the east at this part of her body.[68] The child is called "He who has his umbilical cord." Although his gestation process is complete, he is still attached to his mother, and has not yet left her womb.[69] Nut is further framed by two erect serpents. They are, we are told, like a flame the gods cannot approach; they represent Nepay, one of Re's enemies.[70] Nepay is "He who is like a length of intestine"; this is simply a contemptuous name for the demon Apophis, with whom the rising sun wages a victorious battle, thus preserving the equilibrium essential to the world. The uppermost register of this region draws out the parallel between the birth of the sun and the creation of the world set up in the previous region. Four snakes with human heads loom up on the sun's path; their aim is to keep him from emerging from the "waters" in which he is still immersed. But their resistance is quickly overcome. Now Tatenen, "the earth which rises," incarnation of the primeval mound, stands erect before Re; he is maintained firmly in place by Atum, the creator-god, and Khepri, the sun as he comes into being. Although both Atum and Khepri are called corpses, they possess the "living word" and are thus capable of making use of the creative word that engenders the world.[71] Re speaks to them, encouraging them to perform the creative act. Behind these figures, two containers stand opposite one another under the protection of a guardian who bends toward them. There are two children in the first; one doubtless represents the sun in the fetal state, the other the newborn sun. In the second is a mummy that has "taken on the appearance" of Osiris.[72] The fact that they here face one another confirms that Osiris and Re, now reunited, are in the process of being reborn. At this point, the sun may be seen sailing toward the exit from the netherworld; he will soon meet and incorporate images that personify the elements of his manifestation in the world. Involved here are both the four phases of his evolution in the heavens as Horus and the scepter that is the sign of his authority.[73] A series of scenes placed at some distance from the others narrates the sun's farewell to his own body: in the process of being reborn, the god leaves his dead body behind in the other world. This is the body of both Osiris and Re. Though reassembled and revivified, it cannot reside anywhere but in the netherworld. The god examines the fragments of this dismembered body, gathered together in a container; he verifies that they are all there and in good condition and then entrusts them to two of his own manifestations, the Hidden One and the Traveler, for safekeeping. "O you two great, holy gods who guard my decay. Behold me; I have counted my secret things, my members remain upon me. My members are in peace, my flesh is intact, I have reunited it with myself. Hail to you, my members who are in me, my flesh, my bodies, I illuminate you with my rays, I dispel your shadows."[74] He then addresses Tayet, goddess of bandages and woven cloth, who will ensure the cohesion of his members by restoring his body intact. He also abandons the ram's head that symbolizes the fact that he is invisible at night. In the basement register of this region, the décor changes. To this point, the only creatures seen in this bottom register were the damned who were doomed to live on in eternal darkness, without air, immersed in putrefaction or destined to suffer bloody tortures. Now we witness their complete destruction. To begin with, torture posts are set up at the feet of the goddess of the sky. The rebels who have been condemned to death are bound to them. Next, three kettles are put in place; under them burns an inextinguishable fire that has been lit by the cobra-headed deities of flame and burning heat. The heads and hearts of the condemned are put in the first kettle; their life and spirit are thus destroyed and reduced to ashes. Their decapitated bodies are thrown into the second kettle, where they undergo the same treatment. After this, the enemies no longer exist in the physical sense. In the third kettle, finally, their souls and shades, which also make up part of their identity, meet the same fate, disappearing forever. Re passes them by without so much as a glance, and approaches the great king Osiris, who stands facing the goddess of the sky. He stops for a moment and politely asks Osiris how he has been.[75] The ruler of the hereafter has recovered his bodily integrity and his sexual powers and once again reigns as lord and master of his domain. Although he has reached the culminating point of his return to life, he must nevertheless remain in the netherworld, for he has been forbidden to set foot in the world of the living. Only the bird he bears on his head is authorized to follow Re outside. This bird is probably the phoenix that can be seen in the sky in the form of Venus, the morning star that heralds the appearance of the sun.

In the sixth region, all is at last ready for the final appearance of the sun himself.[76] The first scenes complete the depiction, begun in the previous region, of the sun's farewell to his body. Two mummified bodies, in fetal positions, lie in containers surmounted by their bird-souls. These bodies are under the protection of Anubis, who has, then, finished the work that leads to bodily resurrection. Various scenes once again pass the stages of dismemberment and recomposition in review, recalling the nature of the fragments of the god's body, their functions, and the creative will manifested in the word that enabled them to be reborn spontaneously, without outside assistance. All these scenes take place under the protection of various divinities who watch over the restored and reunited bodies of Osiris and Re. "The form has taken form . . . we guard your hidden things (while you) illuminate the Two Lands with your great disk, lord of forms, he who perfects the births of those who have come into existence, in order to create living beings."[77] As the living bodies are in good hands, the sun can shine serenely on the world. The middle register portrays the emergence of the sun in his divine reality, which human beings are not capable of perceiving. Rising out of the earth, a scarab beetle whose hind parts have not yet come into view pushes the solar disk before him like a ball. The sun is in a sort of antechamber of the world of the living, shedding his light on the inhabitants of the border region between the two worlds. Re now speaks, announcing his birth. "Behold, gods, I am coming into being, I am born, I am master of my disk."[78] The scarab beetle then confronts the serpent demon with whom he must do battle every morning. The snake wraps his coils around him, but the gods of the edge of the horizon know magic spells powerful enough to immobilize and disable him. The gods confirm that this operation has been a success: "Behold, we have enchanted the serpent Nik. We have cut off the soul of him who coils round you."[79] The area between the place where the sun emerges from the caverns and the edge of the horizon is where the domain of the blessed dead, known as the Duat, lies. The inhabitants of this region bid the sun welcome: "Hail to you who come out of the interior of the earth[80] and enter the Duat. . . . O Re, you shine upon us! For our part, we pay you homage and salute you."[81] Not far off, Osiris, who has taken the form of the star Orion and is now stand-ing atop a mound, tramples a beheaded enemy underfoot to show that he has definitively triumphed over death.[82] In the basement register, some of the damned who seem to have escaped the earlier massacres are being put to death; the two blood-soaked goddesses who carry out this opera-tion are painted in red. It appears quite likely that these are enemies of the sunrise; after being duly punished, they will not be able to leave the netherworld to interfere with the passage of the sun. This time, Re will come into view above the horizon. The scene, a double of the one in which the scarab beetle figures, is the more classic of the two; it corre-sponds more closely to the way human beings are likely to imagine the sunrise. The solar bark, represented here for the first time, is ready for its daytime voyage. The sun takes his place on it together with a scarab, symbol of his coming into being and also, it would appear, of Shu, the air that enables the boat to rise up into the sky. To the fore, one sees the phoenix or morning star. Three companies of haulers drag the boat over the sand all the way to the mountain of the East, where it will find the water it needs to sail properly. To either side of the boat, two figures grasp an object called a *mound,* although it exactly resembles—it consists of a stone with a hole bored in its upper half—the mooring stones that were used to anchor boats by the riverbanks.[83] One of these two figures, called "He who presides over the secrets of what is dry,"[84] directs the operation. Now the boat can navigate freely. Some distance ahead of it, the scarab of the netherworld is gradually transformed into a child and then into a reddish disk shown straddling the horizon. On all sides, wor-shipers hail these figures. We are informed that Re's head is firmly at-tached to his shoulders; this signifies that, from this point on, human beings can see him. Indeed, the god takes in, with a single glance, both humanity and all the creatures living on earth. Day breaks.

This complex composition contains the essence of the priestly lore about the transformation and rebirth of the bodies and divine beings most essential to the world of men. By reappearing at dawn, Re ensured that the world would be born anew every day; the resurrection of Osiris in the netherworld ensured the survival of the dead. To imagine both of these gods disappearing forever would have been tantamount to imagin-ing the end of the world. Yet one of them disappeared at night, while the other remained eternally invisible. There had, then, to exist a process that permitted them to assume their functions over and over again by perpet-ually renewing the totality of their power and their lives. From here, it was but a short step to imagining that this process, which could unfold only in the same invisible world, was identical for both gods. We have seen that they furnished men a schema that organized the ideology of the monarchy on earth, past and present. This physics of regeneration not only made possible the rebirth of the dead Osiris and the dead sun, whose remains merged, and with both of whom every dead king was also fully identified; it also reassured men about their fate in this world and the next.

Yet this voyage differed from the sun's nocturnal round inside Nut's female body. It took place in a region unlike the one the goddess offered the sun and also unlike that in which Osiris reigned as lord. All three logics nevertheless converged and complemented one another. In Nut's body as well as in the Double Sphinx's cavern, the sun made a detour to pay Osiris a visit in his own dominion. Nut is present in the Book of Caverns; her imposing presence marks its final zones. Moreover, the sun, just before emerging from the caverns, passed close by Nut as he traveled through the Duat, the abode of the blessed dead. The mere presence of Nut here is evidence of the ambiguity associated with the nocturnal body of the sky-goddess. Simultaneously the celestial vault and a nether-worldly space, Nut could be both the sky above and the sky below. The authors of the Book of Caverns had a clear sense of the bonds between these two regions. At the moment when Re emerges, says the text, he enters "into Nut's body."[85] What is meant is, of course, Nut's *daytime* body—her belly, under which Re is shown making his way, as we have seen. The logics of the two journeys are thus explicitly linked. The com-plementary character of Nut's diurnal body, her nocturnal body, and the Osirian netherworld is, then, evident. It offered those Egyptian thinkers who reflected on the matter the sense of unity necessary to a conception of the universe as something both well structured and well understood.

# CHAPTER NINE

# From the Dead to
# the Newborn God

The western cliffs were a point of intersection between the Osirian world and the world of the sun. We have seen that the entrance to the caverns was to be found in the western cliffs and that the exit from them opened on to the eastern cliffs. The mountainous region in the West was usually symbolized by Hathor the cow. Her head, emerging from the mountainside, seemed to bid a friendly welcome to the dead who appeared before her and to facilitate their entry into the next world. The way the goddess came jutting out of the side of the mountain was conceived as a veritable tectonic movement. "The mountain splits open, the stone is broken open, the caverns are broken open for Hathor."[1] In Thebes, one of the peaks of the cliff that overlooked the mortuary temple of Hatshepsut was refashioned in antiquity to make it look like this goddess projecting from the mountain, so that it would dominate the cliff-bound inlet of Deir el-Bahari.[2] Yet this lady who welcomed the dead did not belong to Osiris's underworld itself.[3] She offered the deceased, and in particular the dead king, a place of regeneration and rebirth that was also a place of transition and passage. On a daily basis, she played the same role vis-à-vis the deceased as did Nut vis-à-vis the sun. She was a container, a space, a dwelling place within which other gods could be seen, whether they were passive, like Osiris, or active, like all those who bustled about him.

Historically speaking, Osiris did not become the supreme god of the dead until he had gradually displaced the gods who had played this role before him in the great necropolises. Thus Andjeti in Busiris, Sokar in

Memphis, and Khenty-imentiu in Abydos were taken over and absorbed by Osiris, enriching his personality and expanding his sphere of influence. We have seen that the gods were not spared old age and death. We know, too, that the history of Osiris did not really begin until he died.[4] It could not have been otherwise. Osiris, let us recall, was the dead king, whereas Horus, his son, was the living king. For this reason, the murder of Osiris took on a very special character. It was a founding act. It explained and justified the royal mortuary cult that ensured the Horus kings their share of eternity. Osiris's was not simply one death among others. With it, injustice and violence had interrupted the normal course of a life and forced a childless widow to undertake the extraordinary. Seth killed Osiris to seize power from his brother for his own benefit. Isis was obviously motivated by the opposite desire, a desire to give the dead god the legitimate heir he had not been able to beget while alive. Isis was, first of all, a widow and a mother. Apparently her cult bore no trace of a wedding ceremony, in contrast, for example, to Hathor's.[5]

In the Old Kingdom, when the royal funerary texts began to appear on the walls of the pyramids, no details whatsoever were provided when the death of Osiris was referred to. A phrase such as "Seth having felled him to the earth in Nedyt"[6] sufficed to communicate the idea that he had been killed. A considerable portion of the funerary rituals, in contrast, was devoted to the consequences of this death. In the Pyramid Texts, again, a few sentences here and there soberly evoke the events that followed it; they also bring on stage not only Osiris's widow but also his two sisters, united in their common misfortune and common affliction: "Isis comes and Nephthys comes, one comes from the west, the other from the east, one comes in the guise of a female falcon, the other in that of a kite. They have found Osiris."[7] Or again: "The female falcon comes, the kite comes, that is, Isis and Nephthys; they come to look for their brother Osiris. . . . Weep for your brother, O Isis, weep for your brother, O Nephthys."[8] In these, the earliest texts, the accent lies on the two sisters' search for the body of the dead god and their role as weepers,[9] incarnated in this case in the form of two birds. Originally, the theme of the reconstitution of the body seems to have had little connection with Isis. Only on one occasion does an anonymous goddess, most likely Isis, claim that she has put her brother back together, that she has reunited his members.[10] Most often it was Nut and Horus who were charged with this task, in a formulation very similar to the one attributed, in the case just mentioned, to the anonymous goddess.[11] Over the centuries, over the millennia, this ancient tradition was to be enriched by numerous variants. The quest for Osiris's body unfolded in two stages. According to Plutarch, the body of the god was enclosed in a chest and thrown into the river. Eventually it reached the sea and then washed ashore in Byblos. The goddess, who had gone off to look for it, brought it back to Egypt, where the incorrigible Seth again seized and dismembered it, scattering the fragments across the land of Egypt. Isis thereupon set out on another quest to recover the fourteen fragments of her husband's body. Here, too, there are several divergent traditions. Every time she found part of the corpse, Isis buried an imitation of it to fool Seth. Thus there were as many tombs consecrated to this god in Egypt as there were bodily parts. Isis was intensely active in her role as widow. Practically minded, despite her grief, she succeeded in piecing her husband's body back together. Once this had been done, Horus, Geb, Anubis, Isis, and Nephthys set about organizing Osiris's afterlife. Together they performed the first mummification on him, as we have seen.[12] Then Isis, with Nephthys's help, reanimated her husband's dead corpse.

At a very early date, Abydos and Busiris became Osiris's chief cult centers. In Busiris, nothing remains of the sanctuaries dedicated to Osiris and Isis; hence it is difficult to form an idea of the cults and rites that were enacted there. We are more familiar with the Abydos cults. Moreover, the cemeteries in this city allow us to trace the outlines of a popular cult; one of its salient features was that it permitted the faithful to draw near the great god by constructing votive shrines. An inscription found on one of them proclaims, "I made this ex voto on the terrace of the great god, master of life, first of the Westerners, to receive the offerings and incense (coming) from the altar of the lord of the gods."[13] It was on this terrace, closely linked with Osiris, that ordinary people first acquired the right, in the Middle Kingdom, to depict themselves on funerary steles face to face with a god. The god in question was, in this period, not yet Osiris, but Min, guarantor of sexual power as well as resurrection, or else Wepwawet, who served as a guide to the roads in the hereafter. Nevertheless, the place people chose to erect these ex votos associated them with the god of the dead himself, who was constantly invoked in the texts carved on them. To ensure his survival in the hereafter, the deceased sought to avoid depending solely on the living; he found refuge with his god. The effectiveness of the traditional filial cult, through which the deceased received the offerings required for his survival from his son, was thus enhanced by the power of written formulas and the added force contributed by new visual representations.

## Temple and Tomb, Statues and Relics

Of the temple of Osiris in Abydos, only ruins remain; it is not known where the god's tomb was located.[14] In the Archaic necropolis of this city lay the tomb of one of the very first pharaohs in history, Djer, who ruled 3000 years before our era; during the Eighteenth Dynasty, at least, the Egyptians themselves believed that Djer's tomb was that of Osiris.[15] It is not certain that this was the case throughout the history of the necropolis. Yet the cenotaphs of the kings and the many statues and steles discovered in the Abydos tomb complexes cast some light on the cult of Osiris, whose popularity grew uninterruptedly from the Middle Kingdom onward. A number of texts even provide a glimpse into the nature of certain of the statues, and other material supports of his cult: it should be borne in mind that Osiris was the object of both a divine cult and a funerary cult.

Thus a Middle Kingdom stele provides information about what are conventionally called the Osirian "Mysteries"; we shall see how significant these plays would eventually become. This Middle Kingdom text attests to the preoccupations of the king, who saw to it that the ceremonies were properly carried out and took it upon himself to provide the funds needed to pay for the lavish festivities that accompanied them. The king, in this case Sesostris III, entrusted a high official named Ikhernofret with the task of organizing the annual festivities during which the statue of Osiris made its way from the god's temple to his tomb.[16] The sending of a letter of instruction by the king was an important event, and Ikhernofret arranged for the contents of this document to be reproduced on his stele. Thus we learn that the pharaoh ordered him to sail upriver to Abydos to attend to preparatory work on behalf of Osiris Khenty-imentiu. The main task was to adorn "his secret image with fine gold which he (the god) permitted My Majesty to bring back from Nubia, in victory and in triumph. You will certainly accomplish this in the best manner for the benefit of my father Osiris."[17] The king took certain precautions, for fear that his trusted aide might not do the work properly. He reminded him of the repeated benefactions he had favored him with since his childhood and said that he was, as a result, counting on Ikhernofret to accomplish the mission that had been confided to him. Ikhernofret seized on this detail to make it clear that he was one of the king's favorites. After citing the contents of the king's letter, he listed everything he had done for Osiris on his sovereign's orders: "I furnished his great bark (?). . . . I made a portable naos for him . . . of gold, silver, lapis lazuli, bronze, wood . . . and cedar. The gods . . . were fashioned and their naoses were refurbished. I saw to it that the hour-priests were at their posts; I caused that they knew the daily ritual and (that) of the festivals of the beginning of the seasons. I directed the work on the sacred bark, I fashioned the cabin. I decorated the breast of the lord of Abydos with lapis lazuli and turquoise, with fine gold and (semi)precious stones, which are the (usual) ornaments of a god's body. I arrayed the god with his insignia in my capacity as Master of the Secrets."[18] Ikhernofret proceeds to describe certain episodes of the festival proper, which began when the preparations had been completed. Unfortunately, his description is rather too elliptical: "I conducted the Great Procession, following in the god's footsteps. I made the god's boat sail, with Thoth directing the maneuver. I equipped the bark with a cabin." After putting the statue's insignia on it, Ikhernofret prepared the path the god would take to his tomb. He also alludes, in a few sentences, to the mythical settings of the Osirian drama and the ritual act he performed to neutralize its harmful effects: "I protected Onnophris on the day of the great battle. I overthrew all his enemies on the riverbank of Nedyt."[19] Then, after returning to Abydos, he followed "the god all the way to his house."[20]

This text is important, for it is the earliest known account of the Mysteries of Osiris. It tells us of a whole series of episodes that, increasingly elaborated on in later texts, recur right up to the end of pharaonic civilization.

It is known that Abydos possessed the holiest relic of the god, his head. But it is unclear whether the sole purpose of the tombs that are so often referred to was to preserve the local relic. What was the status of Osiris's reconstituted body from a cultural and ritual point of view? Was that body believed to exist, or did it rather have to be refashioned—and, if so, how? The architectural remains at Abydos provide no answers to these questions. But, basing ourselves on late texts, we can hypothesize that the statue of Osiris on which Ikhernofret lavished so much care, the one that made its way toward the tomb of the god it incarnated, was precisely the statue that symbolized the reconstitution and resurrection of Osiris's dismembered body. The official himself might well be alluding to this when he speaks of "gods . . . who have been fashioned."

## The Annually Produced Statuettes of Osiris and Sokar

The mythical content of the Osirian cult gave rise to a ritual practice rooted in a procedure that was the opposite of the one followed in the divine temples. By its very nature, the cult statue laid claim to being eternal; but there also existed statues of Osiris that were made *not* to last. The latter were produced every year during the Mysteries of Osiris, which took place from the twelfth to the last day of the month of Khoiak (the fourth month of the year), when, after the waters of the Nile had receded and sowing had been completed, the crops began to sprout. Two Osirian bodies, belonging to Osiris Khenty-imentiu and Sokar, were now fashioned, following procedures we will discuss in a moment. These statuettes replaced the ones that had been made the previous year and that were now solemnly buried.[21] As we have just seen, the first indications of the existence of the Osirian mysteries appear in the Middle Kingdom, but it is not said what form they took. There is archaeological evidence that gives one reason to believe that figurines of Osiris were already in use in the XIth Dynasty.[22] Only late writings, however, describe the various material supports of this particular cult of the god. The statuettes made every year to sum up the life, death, and resurrection of Osiris have ultimately survived in the ritual texts that tell how they were made rather than in concrete material form. The mummies of Osiris discovered in certain small cemeteries set aside for their burial are not very attractive. The nature of the relationship they most probably had with the Mysteries of Khoiak has yet to be studied.[23] In any case, the fabrication of the statues was the object of rites enacted by the gods, especially Isis. It was all the more natural to make gods and goddesses the sole participants in this liturgy as the liturgy was considered to be a mystery whose contents participants were not to divulge under any circumstances. Here one inevitably thinks of Herodotus, who, although he had been initiated into the Mysteries of Osiris, chose to give us a truncated version of the historical facts[24] rather than violate his promise not to reveal the secrets he had been made privy to. The nature of the practices and rites supposed to reconstitute Osiris's body is, however, described in detail in texts inscribed in the temple of Dendara.

The first step consisted in making two statues simultaneously, following exactly the same ritual. One represented a vegetal Osiris, and the other was a substitute for the local Osirian relic. On the first day of the ceremonies,[25] at dawn, Shentayit, an aspect of the widowed Isis who was believed to reside in Abydos, was taken to a place called the "Place of the Festival of Turning Over the Soil." A heap of barley seeds was deposited in front of her on a bed in which she stood naked. The goddess herself placed these seeds on a piece of material stretched out before her. There follows a list of mixtures that had to be skilfully compounded and that only Shentayit could prepare: "Take a bushel-basket, take a quart of seeds[26] from these seeds, half a quart (being the equivalent of) a pound. Divide it up into four parts, which makes half a pint for each part. Soak (the seeds divided into four parts) in five pints of water from the sacred lake in four golden cups until the sixth hour arrives."[27] Next, half a pint of sand was sifted to eliminate impurities, soaked in water, and blended with the barley. The four mixtures this yielded were divided into two sets: two were put aside for the statuette, and the other two were meant for the relic. A golden mould was used to cast the figurine of Osiris Khenty-imentiu. It was made of two parts connected by a joint: one was used to cast the front, the other the back of the statue. The end result was a mummy with a human face, its arms crossed over its breast: it held the crook and flail, and wore the wig of the gods and the uraeus on its forehead. The form of the two moulds used to produce the relic, which was made of silver, is not known. After the mold used to make the figurine had been lined with fine cloth, all four molds were filled. They were then placed in a vat between two layers of rushes.[28] Isis had to pour water over them at regular intervals, day and night, until the 21st of the month of Khoiak, so that the seeds contained in the mixtures would sprout. The water she used in this operation was conscientiously collected, for it represented the god's morbid secretions. It was also necessary to change the rushes every day and to bury the old ones in the necropolis, for they had been in contact with the god's discharges. The vat was covered with a wooden cover; its protection was ensured by an entourage including a large number of gods. Besides two forms of Shentayit, goddess of Busiris and goddess of Abydos, it included Horus, Thoth, Isis, Nephthys, the Two Kites, the Two Weepers, the Children of Horus, the gods of the mortuary workshop, the divine standards, the statues of the kings of Upper and Lower Egypt, and others. On the 21st of the month, the god was removed from the mold. Incense was placed on his two constitutive parts, which were then joined: "Place one side upon the other. Tie them together with four papyrus cords, to wit: one at his throat, the other at (his) legs, one at his chest, the other at the knob of his white crown, so that he takes on the form of a mummy with a man's face crowned with the white crown. . . . Expose him to the sun all day."[29] The same was done with the relic. The following day, around noon, there was a nautical procession of thirty-four boats on the sacred lake. This flotilla of small papyrus barks bore, along with certain minor divinities, the statues of Horus, Thoth, Anubis, Isis, Nephthys, and the Children of Horus, illuminated by three hundred and sixty-five lamps.[30] Why such lighting was required in broad daylight is not stated. The next day, the 23rd, came the bandaging of the figurine of Khenty-imentiu; the god was also bedecked with the fourteen amulets intended to protect him in the tomb.

Yet another figurine, of Sokar this time, was fashioned during the festival. The mold for it was made of gold, like the mold used to produce the statuette of Khenty-imentiu, and it was of the same length, but Sokar's headdress was different, varying with different traditions.[31] The initial preparations did not begin until the early morning hours of the 14th of the month of Khoiak—that is, two days after work had began on the vegetal figurine. In this case, too, it was Shentayit of Busiris who prepared the formula for the manufacture of the statuette. Measuring the ingredients out with great precision, she mixed date paste with clay soil, soaking this preparation with water from the Andjeti canal and the sacred lake of the temple. This initial mixture was wrapped in "sycamore branches so that it would stay soft," that is, to preserve the moistness of the dough.[32] Then Shentayit prepared the incense, terebinth resin wrapped in date-tree fibrils. She blended in a large number of "sweet-smelling" spices,[33] after crushing and sifting them. To the resulting mixture, she added twenty-four precious materials:[34] gold, silver, different varieties of quartz, lapis lazuli, turquoise, red jasper, garnets, green feldspar, galena, carnelian, etc. She crushed these as well, put them in a cup, and mixed them together. All told, the ingredients—clay soil, dates, myrrh, terebinth resin, spices, and precious materials[35]—came to seventeen and one-twelfth measures. The mixture was well kneaded and formed into an egg-shaped mass that was covered with sycamore branches to keep it moist and placed in a silver vase until the 16th of the month. Sokar's statue seems to have had a different function than Khenty-imentiu's. Its ingredients were measured out with containers whose fourteen different forms were replicas of the fourteen divine relics of Osiris, that is, his head, feet, arm, heart, chest, thigh, eye, fist, finger, phallus, backbone, two ears, neck, and two shin bones.[36] Thus, in Busiris, Isis-Shentayit effectively reconstituted Osiris's dismembered body using the mineral figurine; in Abydos, she prepared his rebirth with the help of a vegetal effigy. Starting on the 15th, the decorations for the coffin of the "Lord of life" were made ready; the statue of Sokar would be placed in this coffin. Preparations also began for the making of the sacred unguent. We know how this black unguent was made from another source. The ingredients included ground-up asphalt and pitch. They were placed in a kettle, to which was added the choicest variety of essence of lotus and olibanum, fine oil, wax, terebinth resin, and various spices. The resulting mixture was moistened with wine and oil, after which all manner of precious stones were ground into a fine powder and added to it; the whole was then mixed with honey and olibanum.[37] In Dendara, the baking of this preparation began on the 18th. By the 23rd, it was ready.

Very early on the morning of the 16th, the "Great genetrix of the gods," that is, Nut coalesced with Isis, was displayed. Horus, son of Osiris, sat opposite her on a stool.[38] "I am Horus who comes to you, Mighty One, I bring you this from my father." A silver vase containing the mixture was then placed on the goddess's knees; it was used to fill Sokar's mold, which was then closed and placed on a bed set up in a special room. This "Chamber of the Bed," as it was called, was "made of ebony and covered with gold."[39] Sokar's statue, in gestation, was well protected. Hu and Sia[40] were stationed outside; inside, guardian gods watched over the statue. The chamber itself, a kind of portable shrine, was placed in a pavilion made of fir. The pavilion had fourteen columns with bases and capitals of bronze. It was faced with matting; the interior walls were covered with different cloths. Three days later, on the 19th, the statue of Sokar was removed from its mold and exposed to the sun on a pedestal of gold. It was anointed with olibanum and sprinkled with water until the 23rd, when it was transferred to a pedestal of feldspar and painted: the face was painted with yellow ochre, the jaws the color of turquoise; the eye was drawn so as to resemble inlaid eyes, a wig of real lapis lazuli was set on its head, and the crook and flail were painted the colors of the whole gamut of precious gems. Then the statue was once again exposed to the sun for two hours. Sometime during the night of the 24th, it was shut up in a chest and placed in a chapel of the temple that would serve as its tomb for the coming year. There it joined the statue of Khenty-imentiu, which had already been placed there the 22nd, the day of the nautical procession.

Evidently, the old and the new statues could not live together; the representations of the gods made the previous year had to be removed. The old statue of Sokar was taken from its chest, its bandages were changed, and it was wrapped in netting made with stones, as prescribed by the embalming rites. The four Sons of Horus took charge of removing the body, which was deposed in another chapel—the funerary workshop— before being taken to the necropolis of the gods for final burial. The same day, more or less the same rites were performed on the statue of Khenty-imentiu and the divine relic of the previous year.[41] Isis, Mut, and Nephthys[42] removed them from the chapel were they had been kept for a year and again anointed and bandaged them, still following the "embalming rituals."[43] Each was then placed in a portable sycamore shrine, in which they would, in their turn, receive final burial. The three effigies' funeral rites took place on the 30th of the same month. Thus Sokar waited a total of seven days to be buried. This interval was prescribed by the ritual: "As to each of the seven days this god passes, after the festival of the embalming, while still unburied, from the 24th of Khoiak to the last day, while this god reposes on sycamore branches at the Upper Busiris gate—this is for the seven days[44] he remained in the womb of his mother Nut, when he was conceived in it: a day is for a month; the sycamore branches (stand) for Nut."[45]

Throughout these various ceremonies, as the moment or the circumstances required, the celebrant recited or chanted the holy texts. The lamentations of Isis and Nephthys seem to have been the most important of these recitations. All indications are that these lamentations were chanted repeatedly from the 22nd to the 26th of Khoiak, that is, in the critical period when the new statues were in the process of being "born," and the old ones in the process of "dying." The lamentations both expressed the grief of the two goddesses and contained a powerful appeal for the awakening of new life.

The burial of the previous year's divine effigies took place on the 30th of Khoiak, in the middle of the night, in a tomb that was considered to be Osiris's. As the location of this tomb was, theoretically, a well-guarded secret, the participants pretended to go looking for it and affected to have forgotten where it was from one year to the next. "It (the figurine) goes down into the crypt which is under the Persea trees. Enter by the western door; leave by the eastern door. Look for this crypt as if ignorant of it and do not know (anything about) it until the appointed moment arrives."[46] In Busiris, these funeral services were accompanied by another important ceremony, the erecting of the divine column, or Djed, that signaled the god's resurrection. "It is the day of Osiris's burial . . . in the tomb which is under the Persea trees, because it was on this day that Osiris's divine relics were brought here, after the shrouding of Osiris: erecting the divine Djed."[47] The death of the god and the production of effigies in each of the provinces possessing one of his relics caused quite a stir, requiring the gods who enacted the ritual to see to innumerable chores.

The texts we have just examined deal with only one particular aspect of the fabrication of the effigies and their ultimate purpose. The figurine made in the "House of Life" also merits our attention. Located within or else in the immediate vicinity of the temple precinct, the buildings that housed this institution seem to have been set aside for two different kinds of activity. To begin with, liturgical texts, ritual books, and manuals of theology and astronomy were composed, copied, and kept there, as were magical and funerary books. All of these sacred texts were collectively known as "the manifestations of Re," and the personnel who worked in the House of Life were considered to be "the personnel of Re." Second, the House of Life was conceived as a microcosm of the world, where Shu and Tefnut fashioned—at least in the case we will examine here[48]—a statuette that represented the body of Osiris and bore the name Life.

It was produced somewhat differently from the statuette that figured in the Mysteries of Osiris. Even if it was called Khenty-imentiu and was made of materials somewhat similar to those used for the figurine of Sokar of Khoiak, it contained essentially only aromatics, sand, and clay. Thus it was distinguished from Khenty-imentiu by the absence of cereal grains, and from Sokar by the absence of minerals. The mummy was fashioned in the House of Life and then coated with two unguents—"with the littlest of your fingers," the ritualist was told. The little coffin in which it would be placed was likewise coated with black unguent. The rite of Opening the Mouth was performed on the statuette by a god whose name we do not know. As the ritual proceeded, Shu and Tefnut labored over the body of Osiris, "He who existed before"; it may have been the previous year's mummy that was involved here, but nothing else is said on this score.[49] The mummy was placed in a wooden coffin. Once it had been closed, the coffin was wrapped in the skin of a ram and then in a mass of papyrus stalks and leaves. The whole was put in a golden vase, which was in turn placed inside a fir tabernacle that rested on a bed. Here one can see certain analogies with the ritual of Khoiak.

From the texts, we know how the House of Life was laid out, at least in theory. "It is in Abydos, and is composed of four main sections (of a building) and an interior section (made) of covered reeds (like a tent)." A sign of life could be found at the center of the building, namely, Osiris. The four corners were identified with Isis, Nephthys, Horus, and Thoth. The floor was Geb, and Nut was the ceiling. Superimposed on the material building was an invisible one; it coincided with the created universe. This House of Life had to remain secret and mysterious. Only the solar disk could penetrate its mystery.[50] Large numbers of gods were active in it; this time, Isis seems not to have played the leading role. Shu and Tefnut took particular care to prevent bandits and rebels from jeopardizing the work carried out on the premises. The goddess hid in a hole that had been dug in front of the god's tent: "She is a flame against the rebels in the earth's interior." But she also brought the freshness of the breath of life: "She is the north wind for the nose of her son Osiris."[51] Shu, "like the wing of a bird of prey,"[52] helped her in her task, cooling the god by fanning the air. Indeed, both Shu and Tefnut "personally saw to protecting this god, defending the king in his palace and putting down those who rebelled against him."[53] The other gods shrouded themselves in mystery. "Nut is hidden in her hiding-place, Geb is hidden in his form." Apparently, the earth and sky sought not only to make themselves invisible but also to gain the protection of Isis and Nephthys. Enemies were on the prowl, but were kept in check by the Horus known as the Slaughterer: it was this Horus who executed the rebels who rose up against his father Osiris. Meanwhile, Thoth could perform the ritual itself with perfect peace of mind, "without being seen or heard."[54]

It seems, then, that the figurine was made and brought to life at a moment of critical importance for the universe; this called for special precautions. The ritual took place on the occasion of Osiris's death, a moment of cosmic rupture.[55] It is significant that it unfolded in the House of Life, the place of writing par excellence. Writing harbored a power that assigned the ritual text its true raison d'être: it was that secret book "which breaks spells, which binds conjurations, which arrests conjurations, which intimidates the entire universe. It contains life, it contains death."[56] By way of all the rituals they put at men's disposal, written texts, "emanations of Re," made it possible to maintain the equilibrium of the universe. They also permitted the statuette, a support of life, to escape destruction. "You will be protected from sudden death, you will be protected from fire, you will be protected from the sky, it will not fall and the earth will not founder and Re will not make ashes with the gods and goddesses."[57] An expression of the syncretistic union of Osiris and Re, the figurine had to "fulfil the important role of acting as support for the life of the world."[58] Indeed, it was simultaneously Re and Osiris;[59] it was also, as Osiris was told, "the image of your heart." This heart, seat of the creative thought that first conceived the world, made the effigy of Osiris-Re a support and guarantor of the "Life" that it itself was and that was preserved by this human ritual, this text read aloud.

The Osirian being, reconstituted and alive, took its place in a tradition in which the priests and the artisans of the goldsmith's shops in the temples fashioned the statues of the gods and endowed them with life. The rules of this art, which made inanimate matter animate if it was knowledgeably selected and then measured out in the right proportions, were preserved in rituals whose performance ensured the living presence of the gods in the temples. The actual substance used, both for the statues of the gods and also for the complex mixtures that went into Osirian figurines, was only an outward appearance masking another reality that the ritual texts, whose circulation was of necessity restricted, strove to define.[60]

This living matter was not subject to the constraints that so sharply separated the world of the living from that of the dead, as an action-filled tale shows. A devoted official agreed to die in lieu of his pharaoh in exchange for a promise that the members of his family would be treated with dignity after he had passed away. As soon as he had reached the hereafter, he was assailed by doubts; he therefore made a "man of mud" who could come and go between the two worlds, keep him informed, and act in his stead among the living.[61] Endowed with supernatural powers, the man of mud gave orders to pharaoh, who carried them out. Created in the hereafter but acting with sovereign authority in our world, the man of mud was not far from possessing the magic powers attributed to the Osirian effigies. With his help, the enemies of the hero of the tale were destroyed, and the hero was able, it seems, to return to the world of the living. It is consequently tempting to establish a link between the mysterious practices that brought the statuettes, composed of a complex mix of ingredients, to life, and the procedures ancient alchemists used to produce artificial men.[62] The existence of a bronze figurine of Osiris with alchemical signs on the different parts of its body might perhaps be taken to demonstrate a connection between Greco-Roman alchemy and the ritual practices of Khoiak.[63] It is not certain when the figurine was made, but several of the signs on it were unquestionably in common use among ancient alchemists. The way they are distributed over the figurine's body associates the various parts of it with the elements of the universe and resembles the support for the life of the world fabricated in the House of Life. The unguent of the divine mineral, which is frequently mentioned in the rites of Khoiak and was used to endow statues and coffins with the color of black tar, reminds one of the fact that alchemists had identified their "perfect black" with Isis.[64] Isis was the very symbol of Egypt, the Black Land; during the Khoiak ceremonies, she played the crucial role of preparing the mysterious concoctions used in modeling the statuettes of the god, representations of his perpetually renewed life.

## From Osiris's Temple to His Tomb: Isis's Travels

After Osiris had been buried, and Horus had vanquished his foe and avenged his father, Isis, a tearful widow, protected her husband's various tombs by lavishing constant attention on them. She was assisted by her son. Between her own temples, Osiris's, the House of Life, and Osiris's tombs, the goddess was constantly on the move. She was frequently accompanied by Horus. Having been recognized as Osiris's legitimate heir on earth, Horus was duty-bound, like every son and heir in Egypt, to ensure the upkeep of his father's tomb and the permanence of its offering cult, for the benefit of both his father and his other ancestors. Individually or in tandem, Horus and Isis performed many different rites in Osiris's honor. Some of them were even integrated into the routine of temples consecrated to gods other than those in Osiris's entourage, where Osiris might have chapels of his own. In such cases, his cult was indistinguishable, a few nuances aside, from the general cult normally celebrated in those temples. Osiris was, however, a dead god, and all his rites would always be profoundly marked by funerary rites. The "Lamentations of Isis and Nephthys," which served as an appeal and a summons in the Khoiak festivities, as we noted, quite accurately define the relationship Osiris had with the deities related to him. These lamentations show just what the vigil for Osiris involved, at the emotional as well as the material level; they also explain the importance of the longed-for encounter between the dead god, his family, and the other gods on the site of his earthly tomb: "Come to your house, come to your house, perfect sovereign, come to your house that you may see your son Horus as king of the gods and men. . . . Your entourage of gods and men is at (your service) in the two sanctuaries, performing your rites; your two sisters are at your side, making libations to your ka, while your son Horus utters an invocation offering of bread, beer, cattle, and fowl. Thoth recites your hymns and invokes you with his glorifications. The Children of Horus are the protectors of your body, glorifying your ba every day. Your son Horus, the protector of your name and your sanctuary, deposits offerings for your ka, while the gods bear vases in their arms to make a libation to your ka."[65] The son was living proof of the fact that the royal line would be continued. This in turn guaranteed the unity between the world of the gods and that of men, closely associated with one another in the task of maintaining the equilibrium of the universe. This equilibrium ensured that the constantly deposited offerings required for the survival of Osiris's body, soul, and life force would be rendered effective by the rite that accompanied the offerings. Because he had taken responsibility for protecting his father's tombs, Horus the king enacted the rites associated with them. Thus it was Horus who regularly had to perform the rite known as "bringing the calves to trample the tomb and ward off the enemies from the necropolis":[66] "I bring the calves for you, that is, the black one, the white one, the speckled one, the red one, and the auburn one, so that all of your great, sacred land will be freed of all evil, your mysterious place concealed from all enemies." The objective here, realized in an essentially agrarian context, was to protect Osiris's body and his tomb. By trampling the soil, the calves performed, on the physical level, the act of threshing grain on the threshing floor; on the ritual level, they forced the worms incarnating the corpse's morbid discharges to come out of the ground, so that the process of resurrection might begin.[67]

As for Isis, our most detailed information about the journeys she made to look after her brother's tomb comes to us from the texts in her temple on the island of Philae. The tomb in question was located on the nearby island of Biga. Because of this setting, and the supposed proximity of the caverns the Nile floods came pouring out of, Isis's wanderings, and the associated rites took on a special meaning in which water and navigation played a major part. Every day, the goddess went to the tomb to perform a simple libation.[68] On the holiday that closed the ten-day week, which was, throughout Egypt, the day of the dead and the ancestors, Isis visited the tomb to make a more complete funerary offering and to carry out certain special rites. Taking up her eternal role as mourner once again, she soothed the god's heart with her songs of lamentation. To rejuvenate the body of her dead husband, she also brought him an offering of milk. She was "the Lady of Philae who crossed over to the Pure Island every ten days to offer Osiris a libation of milk, without making libations of any other liquid."[69] The close, constant attention Osiris's widow and son paid him led them to give him part of the offerings they received from the king in their respective temples. Thus, when the king made certain of these offerings, such as the "fumigation and libation of water," for example, Isis took his place as celebrant, carrying the pitcher herself so as to make the libation to her brother."[70] As for his son Harendotes, he daily shared with his father the wine offered him in the temple of his birth in Philae.[71] Of course, other gods also had duties toward their ancestors. Hathor's appeared under very special circumstances, for she took advantage of her visit to Edfu on the occasion of her marriage to Horus to associate her deceased ancestors, called the Children of Re, with her wedding ceremony.

## The Sacred Marriage of Hathor and Horus

The gods' multiple activities, then, required them to do some traveling. But visiting the tombs of their ancestors was not their sole reason for making voyages. A goddess might go to her husband's temple for the celebration of their divine marriage. As we will see, these two kinds of trips were not mutually exclusive. The best known of these journeys made by goddesses was the one Hathor, the goddess of love, undertook every year. Leaving her home in Dendara for nearly three weeks, she made her way to Edfu, some ninety-five miles upriver, to go see Horus the Behdetite. The nature of the festivities is quickly summed up. Their object was to make "the Mistress of Dendara go upstream, in her season of the year, for the happy reunion with her Horus."[72]

To join her eternal betrothed, Hathor of Dendara sailed up the river in a bark, accompanied by large numbers of pilgrims. Members of her priesthood carried her from her temple to the landing in her processional bark. Priests and scribes flocked round her, while people carrying censers cleared the way, burning resin and olibanum as they went. On the riverbank, she was hoisted aboard her bark, taking her place in a kiosk erected in the middle of it. From one end of her itinerary to the other, the bark was towed by a boat with eight oarsmen. The pilgrims took their places on a host of small boats that would accompany Hathor all the way to Edfu. Along the way, people who were not making the journey converged on the riverbanks to acclaim the nautical procession. The flotilla was gradually swelled by the constant arrival of new pilgrims. The name of Hathor's boat, "Great of Love," revealed the purpose of her voyage. The goddess profited from her trip, which lasted nearly four days, to visit other goddesses: Mut in Karnak, Anukis in Kom Mer. The object of her last stopoff was to see Horus of Hierakonopolis, who also joined the procession in his own boat. Meanwhile, Horus of Edfu had left his temple in his sacred bark to go meet his betrothed. Their reunion took place outside the main temple, in a chapel on the bank of the Nile to the north of the city. It occurred at a precise moment, which was certainly not chosen at random: the eighth hour of the day of the new moon in the eleventh month of the year. This festival bore the well-chosen name "She (Hathor) is led back." Receptions in honor of the goddess were held here.[73] Beginning on this, the first day of the festival, the inhabitants of Edfu embarked on a period of incomparable revelry. Then the procession sailed upstream to the city of Edfu. Somewhere along the way, Horus and Hathor left the Nile, making their way up a canal toward the landing of the main temple. They were accompanied by all the notables of the region. The goddess was joyfully received by people singing the praises of her beauty and universality: "She is the Golden One, the Mistress of the goddesses, she who comes in peace to her seat (the temple of Edfu). What a feast it is to behold her! How sweet it is to look at her! How happy is he who bows down (before her) because he loves her! Gods and men acclaim her, goddesses and women play the sistrum for her. . . . Tatenen adorns her body. She is the Mistress, the Lady of Inebriety, she of the music, she of the dance."[74] Her admirers described how dazzling she was in her rich attire: she filled the country with her beauty. Her creative capacities, that is, her attributes as mother goddess, were exalted. It was she who had brought the gods into the world, she who had formed the animals, shaping them as she saw fit; it was she who had fashioned men, created every offering, and brought greenery into existence. Radiant, she repelled the shadows and illuminated all creatures with her light. The inundation came at her command, the winds drew near on her orders. Once these praises had been pronounced, the procession made its way into the sacred precincts of the temple, leaving the pilgrims behind. Horus's and Hathor's barks were then installed in the sanctuary, where they would pass the night. Re, whose presence in this temple was unmistakable, also expressed his joy at Hathor's return.[75] The goddess had made this trip, indeed, not only to rejoin her husband but also to see her father: she was his flaming eye, his uraeus. Thus she would both couple with Horus in the course of these festivities and return to the place she had left on her father's forehead. "His (Horus's) heart takes pleasure . . . when the Mistress of Dendara comes . . . to see her father . . . to join the god of Edfu in the temple, to be united with Khepri's forehead . . . There she finds her father Re rejoicing at seeing her, (for) she is his Eye after it has come back?"[76] Hathor, "She who is led back," became the protectress of her father Re from the moment of her arrival in the temple. She also went to meet the ancestors. They made an appeal to her life force—

which, as we have seen, had created living beings and food—asking that she personally ensure the funerary offerings necessary for their survival.[77] The marriage ceremony drew to a close; Hathor and Horus spent their wedding night in the sanctuary. This union, brought off without delay, was in fact the prelude to long commemorative ceremonies in honor of the divine ancestors.

The next day, that is, the second day of the lunar month, the actual festival of Edfu began. The ceremonies resumed at dawn; they would go on for the fourteen days of the crescent moon. In the sanctuary, prayers were first addressed to all the divine souls inhabiting the place. After this service had ended, a procession made its way "up," that is, toward a necropolis that was probably located in the cliffs on the edge of the desert. This was the abode of "the dead gods of Edfu," whom Horus and Hathor would honor. The procession was a big one. The divine couple was accompanied by all the gods who had been following them from the beginning of the festivities. Their standards were also included in the procession. All the priests in the temple joined in, as did the choristers, musicians, and dancers, the local notables, and a crowd of people from the city. Horus and Hathor proceeded to make sacrifices to the recumbent gods. These were nine mummiform gods, primeval ancestors who had come forth from the creator sun-god and died after the creation had been completed. They were called

> the living gods come forth from Re, the Ennead of the children of Atum, hidden in their necropolis . . . to the southwest of Edfu after the creator sealed their fate, their posterity on earth not having come to an end. Their souls have flown up to heaven where they dwell among the stars. The heart of Re was overcome by sorrow when he saw what had happened to his children. His Majesty ordered that their bodies be mummified on the very spot on which they had been active. They were bandaged in Edfu and it was there that their bodies were made inaccessible. Calves trample the ground to hide (?) their tomb. The sacred orchard conceals their coffins in the same way as the one located in Heliopolis. The great sacred necropolis of Edfu gives shelter to the bodies of the gods of the caverns. Re goes there, the Majesty of his uraeus alongside him, to take care of his children, the great, venerable divine bodies which repose forever in Edfu. They (Re and his uraeus) deposit offerings. . . . They honor them and listen to their prayers until the moment comes for them to return.[78]

"Their tomb will not be destroyed, their mummies will not be harmed, the sand which is upon their sanctuaries will not be removed, offerings will be deposited for their ka every day, forever and ever."[79] In reality, of course, the gods left it to men to carry out all the tasks just mentioned. The ceremonies ended on a less gloomy note; after attending to the tomb, the priests enjoyed "a good day in this place."[80] The rites enacted here had made it possible for the mortal remains of the gods and their celestial souls to be reunited and come back to life. Although intended for the dead gods, these funerary rites were identical with the ones people reserved for their own dead.

The procession now made for the second holy place, where there was a sanctuary. Prophets chanted hymns that were then repeated in chorus by the entire cortège until it had reached the enclosure of this other temple. After it had arrived, a red ox[81] was sacrificed; its right foreleg was cut off and thrown to the crowd. This rite provided a vivid visual rendition of the defeat of Seth, who was the reddish ox. Accordingly, an actor in the role of Horus battling his foe seized the foreleg and set it on the neck of the sacrificial animal. This rite was so important that the sacrifice was carried out in accordance with precise rules. The animal was apparently eaten shortly after the ceremony, for the ritual texts prescribed removing its internal organs and filling the empty space with aromatics. Once Seth had been defeated and hacked to pieces, four geese, representing the four Sons of Horus, were dispatched toward the four cardinal points to announce that a triumphant Horus the Behdetite had donned the double crown. A volley of arrows shot toward the four points of the compass was supposed to destroy all the gods' enemies, wherever they might be. To mark the definitive destruction of Seth in all his forms, waxen effigies of a hippopotamus and two crocodiles were thrown into a fire and destroyed; the names of the enemies of Egypt had been engraved on them. Rounding out this "ceremony of all the king's enemies" was the curious rite of "trampling the fish." Here, too, what was involved were images of enemies who had to be destroyed. Certain sources state that there were four of these fish, to respect the logic of the four cardinal points. While trampling them underfoot, the celebrant would also strike them with a flint knife. The rite consisted not only in killing the enemies, but also in throwing them together pell-mell and furnishing them with weapons they could use to kill one another.[82]

The procession did not return to the main temple in the evening. The pilgrims, officiants, divine effigies, and the throng spent the night where they were. The next day, the participants performed exactly the same rites a second time. Then the procession set out in the direction of the necropolis of the gods. After a pause, it retraced its steps to carry out the sacrifice of the red ox. In the evening, Hathor and Horus went back to the main temple. On the third day, the same ceremony was reenacted, but the participants spent the evening where they were, returning to the temple only on the following day. For ten more days, "the whole ceremony was performed in like manner"; Hathor and Horus went back to their sanctuary every evening.

On the morning of the fourteenth day, Hathor set out for home. The procession formed again; the priests, arrayed in ceremonial attire—Horus's priest, for example, wore a panther skin—walked alongside the gods' barks. Dignitaries brandishing Horus's standards cleared the way before his bark, and the priest who had been assigned to Hathor's service during her stay in Edfu walked on ahead of hers, holding his sacred staff at chest level. In this way, Horus and Hathor proceeded to the temple landing, where the goddess was offered two jugs of beer. She was invited to drink them in her capacity as Lady of Inebriety. The procession directed its steps toward the river; when it reached the riverbank, the two deities boarded their boats. At this point, the river and the aquatic animals fell silent before the radiant power of Re, who was also on hand for the spectacle.[83] The farewells went on at great length, as if the divine couple was loath to be parted for a year. They began sailing downstream, stopping off at a place known as the Seat of Re to visit a chapel, where sacrifices were made in their honor. Another copious meal began: "The dishes are on the fire and the incense on the flame; the things to eat are without number."[84] Singers and women playing tambourines or sistra contributed to the joy of this final ceremony. Elaborate bouquets were placed before Horus, and he was given an ovation in accordance with a royal rite reaching back to the dawn of time. The moment when the couple would have to separate was approaching. "This is the departure of Horus of Edfu . . . seated on his great seat of gold. The scribe of the divine book lifts (him) into his bark. The five ensigns precede him until he reaches his temple. . . . Then Hathor (of Dendara) is lifted into her bark. She sails downriver to Dendara; she stops there on her great seat of gold. (May this be so) forever and ever!"[85] The extreme sobriety of this account of the return is noteworthy. The festival is over, and everyone is on the way home.

These events had two remarkable features: their length and also the fact that the wedding began and ended on the very first day. The sacred union of Hathor and Horus, like all sacred marriages, involved, above all, fertility rites and annual renewal. Without this fertile marriage, none of the other ceremonies could have taken place. Indeed, it gave them the meaning they had and was the condition for the visit that gave new life to the deceased gods. It conferred on the kingship of Horus the fullness of its power, confirming it through a series of rites marking his victory over his enemies.

## The Divine Birth

The marriage rites in Edfu, then, would seem to have redounded principally to the benefit of the husband. In Dendara itself, they went unmentioned. But Hathor's son, Harsomtus, occupied an important position in Dendara, one the god of Edfu could in no way contest. In the Late Period, the birth of this son was itself the object of an annual ceremony. Harsomtus was in fact born simultaneously in both Dendara and Edfu, in birth-house temples that Egyptologists, following Champollion, call *mammisis*.[86] As we have seen, one happy consequence of the birth of the divine heir was that it perpetuated terrestrial as well as universal order. The breath of life manifested in the little being in the womb emanated from the creator; the birth of the child seemed to be the expression of a supreme will, which roused the dead god and reincarnated him in his son. "Come in peace, lord of the gods; gladden the abode of life with a pleasant breeze. If you are in the sky, come in haste, the life forces of the gods are behind you. If you are on earth, come to the house of engenderment, while those who reside in the temples are around you. If you are in your form of light air and you are in the hereafter, near Him whose heart is inert (Osiris), enter the house of the bed by opening the leaf of the door, while the secondary deities guard you. . . . Your daughter is pregnant; she has fulfilled the time of her pregnancy; her eyes look to your coming."[87]

As she had conceived her son Harsomtus during the new moon of the month of Epiphi, Hathor brought him into the world in the month of Pharmuthi.[88] The pregnancy had lasted nearly ten months, as was generally the case with infant gods; it was believed that this ensured the increased vigor of their bodies.[89] The milk the newborn infant needed was provided by the primal cow who enabled Re to emerge from the waters and who was very naturally identified with his own mother.[90]

This son of Horus of Edfu and Hathor, who was simultaneously a human being and a falcon, combined the emblems of divine and earthly kingship in his person. He was also the reincarnation of the dead king revitalized by the creator. Thus the three individuals believed to have been responsible for his origin were united in his person. He was both the serpent "Son of the Earth," a latent subterranean force that appeared on earth and an image of the original form of the creator-god. Like the creator, he appeared in a lotus and was identified with the infant form of the sun.[91] The royal heir in whom the dead king and the solar king, whether Horus or Re, were joined, he was, along with Hathor, the theoretical celebrant of the rites for the ancestor gods in the neighboring necropolis. As in Edfu, he performed his ritual activity during the moon festivals, in the context of agrarian fertility rites. "I harvest for you the crop which I place on your path during the feast of the new moon of Pachon. You trample the earth underfoot, you tread upon your foes (and) you reach the mysterious and hidden Duat. You deposit the offerings to the great gods without end and without cease, eternally."[92] One finds here, in connection with the festival of the deceased gods, the same basic elements as in the festival of the sacred marriage in Edfu.[93] The continuity of kingship manifested itself in the cult of the ancestors; it also found expression in the fertility rites, certain aspects of which were assimilated to the struggle against the cosmic enemies.

The triad of father, mother, and son-god gradually came to represent the image of an ideal divine family; eventually, it provided the seemingly obligatory structure of the pantheon of every Egyptian temple. The Osirian triad provides the best known instance. From now on, birth temples were indispensable annexes to the main temples. The date at which they appeared as sanctuaries in their own right makes them late creations of the last centuries in which Egypt was independent. In this period, they integrated the entire nativity story already in evidence in the New Kingdom into the scenes (examined above) recounting the earthly king's miraculous conception.[94] A small New Kingdom sanctuary built within the enclosure of the temple of Mut in Karnak, and today in ruins, seems to bear witness to this shift from the royal to the divine. The oldest scenes depict a royal birth. Much later, through the addition of glosses, they were reinterpreted as an account of the birth of Khonsu, the son of Mut and Amun.[95] Thus, by assigning universal significance, well illustrated by the child Harsomtus, to the ideology of earthly kingship, the mammisi brought about a synthesis between that ideology and the divine ideology of Horus, son of Isis, the model for the living pharaoh. Thanks to the birth temples, every son-god in the Egyptian pantheon could be fitted into this schema, while pharaoh could, even if he was not of Egyptian descent, affirm his divine being on the theological level.

In the mammisi of Philae, the layout of the conception scenes is extremely sober, in both the texts and the iconography. It seems simply to have reproduced its New Kingdom models,[96] except that the queen has been replaced by Isis; the god is still Amun-Re. The god and goddess are called, respectively, "King of the Gods" and "Mother of the Gods." In Egyptian religion, Isis was never considered to be Amun's consort. Involved here, then, is clearly a transposition of the divine birth of the king, as represented on the walls of New Kingdom temples, where Amun-Re appeared before the queen. The birth of Horus the son of Isis had roots in an entirely different tradition, as we have seen. Thus certain problems were created in Isis's temple at Philae by the transposition of the queen's union with the king of the gods, based on material in the sacred archives.

The priests were obviously aware that certain of the scenes portrayed were not adequate renditions of their subject, so much so that the texts accompanying these scenes become quite murky in certain cases.

But let us return to the conception scene. The two gods are seated on a bed whose four corners are decorated with lion heads. Amun-Re holds the sign of life out to Isis. In itself, the scene is not very explicit. Moreover, as the ritual no longer concerns the king of Egypt, but rather his divine prototype, the accompanying text has been stripped of all explicit references to the union between the god and the queen. It confines itself to the theological truth, expressed in conventional terms. Only Amun-Re's order to Khnum to form the young Harpokrates reveals the nature of the act performed here. The potter-god's response underscores the purely mythological character of the scene: "I am acting in accordance with your command, for you are the lord of the gods. I will model him (your son) to resemble your person. Just as your name is perfect as god, so your thought is effective, and everything you say comes into being immediately."[97] Conception here occurs on a purely spiritual level: it is enough for Amun to pronounce words in order to beget a child. The following scene shows Khnum shaping the divine baby on his wheel. Heket, the frog-goddess, holds the sign of life out before his face. From this point on, the baby is alive, but he must still be endowed with his divine nature, and his lifespan must be fixed. The task falls, once again, to Khnum: "After shaping you with my own hands, I create your body as a divine body, I add to your perfection. I make the time of your existence exceed that of the distant sky. For as long as the sky endures, you are king."[98] The gestation process, described in the course of the preceding episodes, is now finished. Thoth can announce to Isis that she will be the mother of a king. The goddess, between Khnum and Heket, who both hold her by the hand, is conducted to the bed where she will give birth. Then the great family of Heliopolis and other gods come in to bestow all the boons in the universe upon the future mother and her child. Amun re-appears, bringing gifts of his own: "I come bringing all life and stability, all health, all joy, all offerings, all nourishment for Isis the venerable, the divine mother of Horus, my son, come forth from my person."[99] The nativity scene is just as allusive. Only the moment immediately following the delivery is portrayed. The scene brings together nearly all the participants in the ritual. The direct influence of the divine birth legend of the human king continues to make itself felt here. Isis is seated on a throne that has been placed on the bed where the delivery took place. But it is the king, doubtless Ptolemy III, who receives the child from the goddess's hands in Amun's stead. Behind the mother-goddess, another, kneeling Isis may be seen.[100] This doubling stems from the royal origins of the ritual in which

Isis, standing behind the queen, played the role of nurse. Meskhenet, protectress of childbirth, presides over the scene: "I have come, I have brought you all life and all stability; all beauty, all joy, all offerings. I have rejuvenated the youth come forth from your body."[101] Then, in conformity with all the other known scenes of the divine union, Hathor presents the baby to his father, who has once again become Amun-Re. We next see the child being suckled by the divine nurses, the cow-goddesses Hesat and Sekhat-Hor.[102] The temple's divine company had long since been informed of the god's intention to give the country an heir. Ever since the announcement had been made, this company had withdrawn from the scene to await the enthronement of the child. It takes place in their presence. Two divinities with shaved heads advance towards the fifteen members of the assembly. The first among them, Heka, holds the baby in his outstretched arms, declaring: "Enthrone the youth in the presence of the great Ennead so that he may be King of Egypt."[103] In Dendara, a fuller formulation recalled the purpose of this ritual: "I uplift your perfection toward the Ennead; this is the seed of an august god who will be monarch; he will govern all the Two Lands."[104]

A subtle, deliberate confusion comes about in the person of the child's father: he is at once the king of the gods and the earthly king. It is the reigning king who receives the child, who is thus both heir to the gods and the king's own earthly heir. In the person of this theoretical child are summed up all the children of all the divine couples; through his cult as well as his identification with pharaoh, he provides the reigning sovereign a guarantee that the royal ideology will function properly.

# CHAPTER TEN

# The Machine of the Universe Tottering on the Brink

During the five epagomenal days, the five days "over and above the year,"[1] the ingenious contract that bound the gods to their earthly heir was seriously threatened by the rupture these days provoked, confronting pharaoh and the gods with the risk of mutual destruction. At the end of the year, both the king's strength and the energy contained in the representations of the gods waned; they had to be restored at all costs. King and gods accordingly underwent rites of regeneration. If these rites differed in form, they nevertheless had a great deal in common as far as the principles underlying them were concerned. The accents varied with the protagonists involved and the dangers they were exposed to, but, in every case, the objective remained the same: to restore the strength of those who actively ensured the cohesion of the universe and to make possible the joyous return of the natural phenomena guaranteeing the stability of creation and the country's prosperity. Once the danger had passed, the gods and the king came together to celebrate the New Year. These rites were the means of renewing the reciprocal exchanges that founded the alliance between the gods and men, as represented by the royal mediator.

## The Gods and the Renewal of the King's Forces

The ceremony that made it possible to renew the king's forces every year took place during the New Year's festivities, which lasted for two weeks.

During this period, which at least in theory immediately preceded the rise of the Nile, the gods had to call upon all their savoir-faire in order to protect their heir on earth. To permit him to overcome all the dangers he faced, they had to enact the rites themselves. We have no real way of knowing whether the first morning ceremonies took place in the palace, as might be supposed, or at the entrance to the temple. The fact that certain gods participated in them, even if only theoretically, inclines one to conclude that all the festivities went on inside the sacred enclosure, where the gods lived. But, as the royal palace usually adjoined the temple, the question remains open. Resolving it would not in any way alter what we know about the gods' attitude or the purpose of their participation in these ceremonies.

As in the daily cult ritual, any and every contact between the human world and that of the gods called for purification; this was the case even where the king was involved. Naturally, it was the god of the inundation who cleansed pharaoh of "the germs of illness which threaten(ed) him,"[2] and it was Horus who washed his face while Seth rubbed his body. Tayet, the goddess of weaving, attired the king in a special garment that warded off any evil that might come near him and protected him against all possible attack.[3] The king then proceeded to the chapel where the jewel amulets were kept. After he had taken his place in a litter, he made his way from the chapel to the pavilion, where he was bedecked with amulets and anointed with various ointments.[4] The first priest to anoint him tied a band of red linen around his neck; thirty white and thirty red crowns had been drawn on it in ink, to either side of a picture of Ptah. This operation took some time, because the ceremony required that as many knots be tied in the laces of the linen band as there were crowns on it—sixty knots in all.

This ritual was assimilated to a rebirth; from the outset, it included allusions to suckling the king. But, as the king was usually an adult, he was, instead of being actually suckled, presented with the amulets of life and domination, which symbolized the blessings conferred upon him by the milk of a goddess.[5] Next, the king was reminded of the divine origins of his person and function. Isis was invoked: "May you nourish Pharaoh, may you suckle him with this (breast) in your closed hand, as you did your (son) Horus!" After the king had received diadems and crowns, he was anointed nine times; the importance of the ceremony is indicated by the fact that the ointments he received were those of the two temples symbolizing Upper and Lower Egypt. The nine ointments served as protection against the dead: "Behold, Protection comes! It repels the dead, so that the dead cannot rise from their restraints."[6] What is more, Isis's magic protection extended to the flesh of the king's body, so that he might celebrate his jubilees without end.[7]

The first ointment lent the king's skin a divine quality that transformed it into a protective covering. The king had to acquire this immunity before the crown and the uraeus attached to it could be placed on his head, because the lion goddess Sakhmet dwelt in the crown, while the uraeus was an equally dangerous fiery being. The ointment rendered the crown harmless for the one who was to receive it; furthermore, it put the destructive powers the crown contained at his beck and call.[8] Sakhmet and the uraeus were actively involved in applying the next two ointments. For these two anointings, the king took his seat on the stepped dais that was normally reserved for his jubilee appearances; apparently he was here identified with the sun-god. The first of these ointments protected him from enemies beyond Egypt's borders; apparently it also guaranteed him the purity of the heavens. "You have crossed the mountains, you have dispelled tornadoes," it was declared.[9] The second enabled the king to manifest himself like the sun emerging at dawn from the Osirian world. It "endowed" him "with that perfect, pure humor that comes from Osiris."[10] Together, these two ointments constituted a magic conjuration effective against the enemies of the universe and thus the enemies of the king; it thwarted their operations for the whole year.

The fourth and fifth anointings extended the preceding logic. They evoked the rising and the setting of the sun in each of his two barks; the two moments meshed in the accompanying texts. The fourth ointment was applied to a headdress worn by the king; this regalia was indispensable for gaining access to the underworld.[11] Atum and Re, who were invoked here, marked the two extremes of the sun's course. The fifth anointing placed the jubilee festival under the sign of rebirth, for here the head of the sun shone brightly, dissipating the darkness. Together, these two anointings ensured the proper functioning of the mechanisms of the universe.

Some of the pure soil of Heliopolis was contained in the sixth ointment, which enabled the king to become a creator-god in his turn, like Re-Atum: "He has created the earth from which he emerged, he has come into being in its initial time, when it came into being! Atum has recognized that Pharaoh is he who sees his place and rules it."[12] With the next ointment, the king became a full-fledged member of the Heliopolitan Ennead. Thus he could come to Atum's aid, helping him carry out his vital tasks and permitting the sun to shine upon the world and give life to all creatures.[13] Next, the pharaoh received an ointment made of red quartzite, olibanum, and pure soil; it allowed him to fulfil his function of ritualist for the Heliopolitan gods. He performed Khepri's and Re-Atum's daily cult and also, it seems, the funerary cult for the city's deceased gods.[14] In accordance with a pattern comparable to the one we saw at Edfu, he made them offerings that permitted them to leave their tomb temporarily.

Every time these "greying creatures" came forth to greet Atum, they became younger.[15]

The last anointing was of the king's loincloth, which was, like the crown, one of the insignia of his office. The accompanying spell again fused the king with the solar creator-god. It evoked the first battles that the god had fought at Heliopolis and the fact that they had made it possible to bring the act of creation to a successful conclusion. By this expedient, the king was endowed with the omniscience of the gods, the sia; it permitted him to see, both intellectually and in the literal sense, the whole of creation.[16] The nine anointings invoked the themes of the creation of the world, the sun's daily journey, and divine regeneration, inscribing them in the universal space whose center was Heliopolis. Immediately afterward, the king was confined within a circle of earth brought from Heliopolis; this placed him under the protection of Atum's entourage.[17] He went on to make an offering expressly intended for all the gods of Egypt. The procession next stopped at the chapel of the House of Life. There the king paid honors to the gods both present and absent; the names of the latter were engraved on a tablet. He then proceeded to the chapel where the royal office was once again to be handed over to him as his inheritance.

There followed acts of performative magic, as was the case at the coronation of the divine falcon of Edfu as well.[18] A first sign, the emblem signifying "(royal) office," was drawn on the sovereign's hand with "resin-gum moistened with saliva."[19] An identical emblem was made out of soft, chewed-up bread. This bread was not to be eaten by any human being besides the king; consuming it guaranteed him the power to rule.[20] A cake with a filling of various plants and minerals was also prepared, and covered with mud that came from the "flooded part of the fields."[21] Its ingredients make one think of the Osirian effigies. That this cake was covered with silt from the most recent Nile inundation may indicate that it symbolized a burial supposed to lead to a rebirth.[22] Seven effigies of the gods of the House of Life, in their animal forms, were also prepared; they were made of clay, "with a flame in their mouths."[23] The ritual text adds: "See to it that divine offerings are presented to them; act as if seven offerings were being presented."[24] There follows a rather obscure passage that suggests that the king spent the night in this chapel. He went to bed after a wooden scepter had been placed in his hands, and the royal inheritance, called "the inheritance of the bull," was placed under his head. The latter consisted of four seals, also made of wood; two of them bore the name of the earth-god, Geb, and the other two, on which images of Neith and Maat had been incised, were used to stamp the cakes that had been prepared earlier. This rite effected the transmission of power from the dead king to his successor and confirmed the sovereign's legitimacy. The fact that the king spent the night in the chapel—we do not know whether he slept or kept a vigil—involves an allusion to the practice of incubation.[25] It may well have been while the king slept that the seals of his predecessor, placed under his head, became active, transmitting the power they contained. It is also quite conceivable that the king stayed awake all through the night he spent in the chapel. In either case, he would have been miming a symbolic death on the last day of the old year, only to be reborn, renewed and regenerated, on the first day of the new year.[26]

Next, two living birds of an unknown species—they may have been passerines—entered into the ritual. They were supposed to be placed near the cake we have just described, while the king's hand rested on it. These birds, messengers of Horus, served as intermediaries between the god and those participating in the ceremony. One of them would, when released, go announce the news that the ritual had been brought to a successful conclusion. Horus's legitimate heir had undergone all the ordeals these difficult days brought with them, and had remained on his throne. The message the bird was to transmit was dictated to him: "You will tell Horus that pharaoh is here, in the process of consolidating his position."[27] The process of consolidation was, moreover, described in terms that made it an exact equivalent of the founding of a temple. The second bird remained by the king's side to play a role much like an oracle's. When his song was transformed into words through interpretation, one could tell whether the bird had or had not declared himself for the king at the end of the ceremonies, that is, whether he had confirmed that the king was worthy of assuming his functions or not.[28]

By means of these rites, the king's power had been renewed; now came the symbolic massacre of the enemy, evoked with the help of two sets of seven plants. The king had first to smell them and cut the tip off each stalk. He was then arrayed in a garment of red linen, the front of which had been decorated with protective amulets. He was given the staff of foreign countries, which was used to strike down his enemies, and white sandals were placed on his feet. Other amulets were placed directly on the king's right hand. To finish exorcising the dangers of the year, the members of the House of Life chanted a hymn. Pharaoh then left the pavilion where he had passed the night, making his way to a place in the temple where he consecrated offerings to the ancestor gods. We have already seen that this ancestor cult constituted the culminating moment of many festivals.

The final ceremony was performed in, once again, the chapel of the House of Life; it will be recalled that this was the place where the earthen effigy of Osiris-Re was fabricated.[29] Here the king was presented with nine living birds of various species. To make sure that the rite about to take place would proceed without a hitch, the king was brought the requisite amulets: a golden falcon, a faience vulture, and a turquoise cat were placed around his neck.[30] At the head of a procession of birds came "the living falcon, he who will be honored by the king on each of the occasions of this year."[31] After turning the bird's head backward, the falconer took a tear from its left eye. On the king's neck, the amulet representing the golden falcon was anointed with the bird's tear, which gave the amulet the power to ward off danger. After the falcon, a vulture was brought in; its head was anointed, and then, like the falcon's, turned backward, after which it was made to spread its wings over the king. This would protect pharaoh against fits of rage in the coming year.[32] A kite was also anointed, and its wings, too, were stretched out over the king's head. The king then proclaimed: "When the bird flies toward the sky, it effaces every baneful threat connected with death (which might materialize in) the vicinity of a god."[33] The same operation was carried out with a Nile goose. Next a *mesyt*,[34] a bird whose name evoked the word for "birth," was ushered in. This bird served as a link between the four birds just described and those to follow. The text suggests that it may have been force-fed. The bird was brought closer and closer to the king, until its wings grazed the back of his neck.[35] When the wings touched him, the king was reborn, coalescing with the Heliopolitan gods.[36] The heads of the birds in the sixth group were also turned backward and anointed, but their wings were not stretched out over the pharaoh's head. The passerine of the House of Life made another appearance here, in the role we mentioned a moment ago.[37] Now it was the swallow's turn. It is described as having gone to see Re, who took the trouble to interrupt his meal and listen to its message. The bird revealed to Re that it was itself a newborn baby and therefore represented the newly reborn king. The crane followed the swallow, asking the sun-god to preserve the king from the threats of the original chaos.[38] The account given of the last bird makes no mention of a message. This curious rite was rounded off with an invocation addressed to all the birds: they were asked to make sure that the king "would be preserved, in good health, safeguarded on this day."[39]

The length and very special nature of these rites is reason enough to ask whether the king actually participated in the ceremonies in person, and, above all, whether he really submitted to all these ritual manipulations. Some of them must have been rather unpleasant, and one may reasonably suppose that the operation that consisted in stretching out the wings of a vulture or any other bird of prey above the king's head was not without its dangers. It is not very likely, despite what the text says,

that real birds were used in enacting this rite, unless they were first somehow rendered harmless. Confirming the power of the king, who was the
guarantor of cosmic equilibrium on behalf of the gods, called for carrying
out a large number of ritual acts; although sometimes quite original, they
often had their source in other liturgies. We noted, in passing, the rites
involving the Osirian resurrection and the exorcising of the cosmic enemies. Plainly, all imaginable procedures were acceptable when it came to
protecting the one and only mediator between the gods and men, at a
point in the year when his divine power was exposed to dangers of all
sorts.

## Union with the Sunlight and the Revitalization of the Divine Images

The ceremonies that took place in this same end-of-the-year period in
southern Egypt in the temple of Horus at Edfu did not involve exorcising
the year's dangers. These ceremonies began on the last day of the last
month of the year and continued through the five epagomenal days, the
first day of the new year, and the four following days.[40] At first glance,
there does not seem to be anything particularly noteworthy about the
rites performed at this time. According to a tradition that seems to have
been well established in all of Egypt's temples, the last day of the last
month and the five epagomenal days provided an occasion for the god of
the temple to renew his wardrobe completely. The Edfu liturgy was no
exception to the rule: it included a six-day long "clothing festival." By the
time the festivities were over, Horus was supposed to have acquired his
new clothes for the whole year. The monotony of this ceremony was only
broken by a wake for Osiris that went on from the last day of the last
month of the year to the first epagomenal day, considered to be the day
of Osiris's birth.[41] On this day, the clothing ritual was devoted to Osiris, in
his aspect of Great Pillar, and to his Ennead. Osiris's statue was accordingly given a place of honor beside Horus and Hathor. We will see that
the presence of a specific aspect of Osiris was by no means insignificant;
it revealed one of the basic purposes of the ceremony. On the other days
of the ceremony, it was Horus, the god of the temple, who benefited from
rites that were the same as those celebrated at regular festivals. In a word,
the epagomenal days, which came in for a great deal of attention elsewhere, were in Edfu nothing more than preliminaries to the New Year's
celebration on the first day of the month of Thoth, considered to be Re's
jubilee festival.[42] The rites enacted then were thus a pendant to the royal
rites we have just witnessed, insofar as these New Year's rites also en-

sured an annual divine regeneration. This regeneration was quite as indispensable as that of the royal mediator; it benefited another form of mediator, the god's statue. The ceremony was doubtless performed in many different Egyptian temples. In Edfu, which will serve as our guiding thread, but elsewhere as well, neither the main cult statue nor the holiest part of the temple, the sanctuary, was involved in these ceremonies.[43] The statue required for this crucial rite was of a special kind. Apparently, it represented the form of the god best fitted to receive the energy imparted to him and transmit it to all the other statues. This was doubtless the god's primordial aspect, represented at Edfu by an ithyphallic falcon with arched claws.[44]

The sequence of the different episodes of the preliminary ceremonies is not always clear in the accounts of them. On each of the six days preceding the new year, the king, accompanied by the celebrants, presented himself at the temple gate in the morning. The offerings were already in place; after the customary purifications, the doors to the ambulatory surrounding the principal sanctuary—called the "mysterious corridor"—were opened. The chapels of all the gods who would participate in the ceremonies opened on to this corridor, as did the treasury and the chapel where clothing was stored. The most beautiful ornaments and the most precious cult objects were brought out from the two last-mentioned rooms. The procession then made its way toward a chapel located on the same axis as the sanctuary, and thus behind the very back of the main cult statue. This axial chapel contained the statue of the crouching falcon, a representation of Hathor that shared the falcon's naos, and two weapons belonging to the fighting god, "the staff of Horus of Edfu" and the "spear which emerged from Nun."[45] The king entered and proceeded to perform the daily cult ritual.[46] Priests acting as porters presented two litters, one for Hathor, the other for Horus. The king then took the falcon in his shrine and placed him on one of the litters. He did the same with Hathor: "The god is placed on the golden statue base which is called the 'base of rest'; the canopy above it is of gold."[47] Hathor's litter is described in almost exactly the same terms. The procession accompanying these gods and their retinue was joined by the Great Ennead of Edfu, made up of all the gods and goddesses who resided in the chapels of the ambulatory. Chanting hymns to Horus and Hathor as it went, the procession left the axial chapel for the "Pure Room."[48] A court open to the sky led to this room, which had a screen wall as its facade. Inside the room, the litters were placed on the floor. The two shrines were turned toward the south, facing the entrance. When they were opened at noon to expose the gods' faces, the gods could see the offerings piled up for them in the court. The purpose of the rites was to dress and adorn Horus and prepare him for his encounter with the solar disk on the first of the year. Afterward, the procession went back down the mysterious corridor to the axial chapel; the gods were once again veiled and put back in their naos.

The ceremonies celebrated on these festival days, anticipations of the New Year's ceremonies, were apparently not characterized by the anguish that certain rituals occurring during the five epagomenal days betrayed.[49] The nature of the Pure Room where these ceremonies took place does not indicate, at first sight, in what way they readied the statue for the final encounter. This chapel does, however, have a special feature: the ceiling is decorated with a representation of Nut. In the open space between her arms and legs are twelve of Re's barks, symbolizing the twelve hours of the day.[50] The accompanying text clearly indicates that, even before the solemn meeting on the roof, an initial face-to-face encounter took place between the statue and the god "so that his ba-soul might unite with his image." It is also spelled out that "the heavenly vault belongs to its master, whose kheperu are on view: Re is there in his bark at noon. The morning bark and the evening bark carry Khepri and Atum (there), eternally."[51] Here, the statue was not united with the solar disk, the sun himself, who is expressly named in connection with the ceremonies enacted on the roof. This encounter was of a different kind: it was an encounter between one image and another, between the statue and the representation of the sun's manifestations carved on the ceiling. This indirect form of exposure is perhaps the one feature that betrays the sinister aspect of the epagomenal days. To expose the statue to the rays of the real sun during these days of rupture would in no way have helped it renew its forces. In contrast, exposing it to the influence of the sun's celestial image, transferred on to a substitute sky, made it possible to conjure away the statue's cosmic weakness even while ignoring it, and, at the same time, to prepare the statue for a direct encounter with the powerful rays of the regenerated sun of the new year. The scenes represented in the Pure Room at Dendara, where identical ceremonies were enacted, would seem to confirm that this cautious practice was the rule.[52]

New Year's Day, the first day of the month of Thoth, was the culminating moment of the festivities; as we have noted, it coincided with Re's jubilee festival. The festivities of the preceding days were repeated, but with greater solemnity. In the Pure Room, the divine statues were dressed, crowned, and adorned. This first stage of the ceremony always took place in the morning. The offerings, which were again placed in the court giving on to the Pure Room, were more lavish. In addition to the ordinary dishes, an oryx was slaughtered and a sheep was sacrificed along with an ibex; birds, who numbered among the god's enemies, met the same fate. All this paved the way for the important ceremony that would take place on the roof of the temple; during this ceremony, the principal rite of the day, the Union with the Disk, would occur.

The procession left the Pure Room. Contrary to usual practice, as the representations on the wall indicate, the offerings, carried on the participants' arms or balanced on their heads, accompanied the procession as it made its way up to the terrace. Those carrying the standards of the gods took the lead. The power of these emblems warded off all possible danger. The priests followed; some wore masks, others carried offerings, still others carried precious objects, rich cloths, semi-precious stones, or incense. The king and the queen, finally, walked ahead of the shrine. One has to picture each divinity, transported in his portable naos and followed by his personal retinue. The parade of gods must have been impressive, as it included at least thirteen aspects of Horus, three of Hathor, and three of Harsomtus.[53] The Ennead of the temple followed—Osiris, Geb, Isis the Great, Nephthys, and others.

The whole procession gradually disappeared into the enclosed eastern staircase, for it was supposed to follow the path of the sun. The ascension of the staircase was itself identified with a sunrise. The texts leave no room for doubt on this score: "There are two staircases, to the right and left, for rising and setting."[54] Given the number of participants and the relative narrowness of the staircase, this small crowd must have made its way up to the roof rather slowly. The text makes a good deal of what might seem to be a mundane situation: "They walk in peace, they proceed joyously on their triumphant march. They all walk slowly, very reverently."[55]

Once everyone had reached the roof, the divine statues were ranged around Horus's statue in a kiosk. The offerings were spread out before them, placed under the direct protection of the gods who assured fertility and abundance. Each divinity sponsored a dish, spice, or ointment, presenting it as if it he had produced it himself. The part of the rite that was then enacted is summed up allusively and very briefly: "He (the god) stops at his kiosk and (there) touches the sun, provided with his offerings, his beautiful face (turned) to the south."[56] After the offerings had been purified, the king began a new ceremonial, following the prescriptions of the texts engraved "in secret writing" on tablets of gold and silver. On these tablets was a formulary "for making one's way to the terrace and (gaining access to the) processional path found there." The king declared: "(I have taken up) the ceremonial of the Union with the Disk, engraved on tablet(s)," then listed the different books he had to read, sing, or perhaps chant. Finally, he intoned "the great secret spells of the terrace."[57] It was at this moment that the face of the god's statue was unveiled. The sun's rays bathed it in their light. Horus of Edfu touched the sun. Via the statue, awash in light, the mystic union of the god and the sun was consummated. Before closing the portable shrines, the priests brought this rooftop ceremony to a close by holding the statue of Horus up before all the participants gathered on the temple's roof. Then, descending by the western staircase, the staircase of the setting sun, the imposing procession ushered the divinities back to their own particular chapels. This jubilee festival of Re's, which was, in fact, the festival of all the gods, had now reached its crowning moment. The celebration would go on, we are told, for another four days, during which the rites of the day we have just seen come to a close would be repeated.

Though it is the Edfu texts that describe the course of these ceremonies in the greatest detail, the ceremonies were also performed in all the other major temples. The minor differences that may have existed between the way they were actually performed in the various sanctuaries depended strictly on the nature of the local god. We have seen that there were similarities between the Pure Room of Edfu and that of Dendara. In the latter city, however, the union of Hathor with the disk enabled the sun to revitalize the image of a goddess who was also an incarnation of the surface and the container from which he had originally emerged. In Heliopolis, it may have been the obelisk, a transposed form of the primeval mound from which the sun first shot forth, that was symbolically erected to meet the life-giving rays.[58] Participation in the rite of the goddess who embodied the hand with which the solar creator-god had, in solitary fashion, brought the first divine couple into the world also evoked the procreative powers that had been restored. In Esna, the insistent recommendations that the statue of the god Khnum not be separated from his potter's wheel indicate that the wheel was an essential part of his image as a primordial god.[59] The sun's rays had to penetrate not only the effigy of the god himself, but, also and above all, the egg of the world that Khnum was always shown shaping on his creative instrument. It was, then, the world itself in its embryonic state that was regenerated through contact with the light.

Overall, these festivities turn out, upon examination, to resemble certain aspects of the royal cult and the jubilee festivals, whose practical objective was to regenerate the individual they were intended to benefit. The god of the temple, thanks to a specific statue, the one that, let us repeat, evoked his primordial image, renewed (like the king) a power that had been used up over the course of the previous year, during which the statue had spent the energies actualized by the cult. This renewal was made possible by the Universal Lord, the sun-god who had fashioned the world in order to make himself a place in it, and then trace a path across it that would ensure him eternal youth. Union with specific, primordial images of the gods directly served the creator's interests. By renewing their power, the creator made possible the perpetuation of the cult men rendered him through the mediation of the royal intercessor.

# Notes

## Abbreviations

JOURNALS

*ASAE*    *Annales du Service des Antiquités de l'Egypte* (Cairo).
*BIE*    *Bulletin de l'Institut d'Egypte* (Cairo).
*BIFAO*    *Bulletin de l'Institut français d'archéologie orientale* (Cairo).
*BJRL*    *Bulletin of the John Rylands University Library of Manchester* (Manchester).
*BSFE*    *Bulletin de la Société française d'égyptologie* (Paris).
*CdE*    *Chronique d'Egypte* (Brussels).
*CRAIBL*    *Comptes rendus de l'Académie des inscriptions et belles-lettres* (Paris).
*CRIPEL*    *Cahiers de recherches de l'Institut de papyrologie et d'égyptologie de Lille* (Lille).
*GM*    *Göttinger Miszellen. Beiträge zur ägyptologischen Diskussion* (Göttingen).
*JARCE*    *Journal of the American Research Center in Egypt* (New York, Baltimore).
*JEA*    *Journal of Egyptian Archaeology* (London).
*JEOL*    *Jaarberichte van het vooraziatisch-egyptisch genootschap* (Leiden).
*JNES*    *Journal of Near Eastern Studies* (Chicago).
*MDIAK*    *Mitteilungen des deutschen archäologischen Instituts. Abteilung Kairo* (Mainz).
*OMRO*    *Oudheidkundige Mededelingen uit het Rijksmuseum van Oudheden te Leiden* (Leiden).
*RdE*    *Revue d'égyptologie* (Paris).
*SAK*    *Studien zur altägyptischen Kultur* (Hamburg).
*ZÄS*    *Zeitschrift für ägyptische Sprache und Altertumskunde* (Berlin).


BOOKS

Alliot, *Culte d'Horus*: Alliot, Maurice, *Le culte d'Horus à Edfou au temps des Ptolémées*, 2 vols. (Cairo, 1949–1954).
Assmann, *Lit. Lieder*: Assmann, Jan, *Liturgische Lieder an den Sonnengott* (Berlin, 1969).
Assmann, *Sonnenhymnen*: Assmann, Jan, *Sonnenhymnen in thebanischen Gräbern* (Mainz, 1983).

Bakir, *Cairo Calendar*: Abdel-Mohsen Bakir, *The Cairo Calendar No. 86637* (Cairo, 1966).

Barguet, *Livre des Morts*: Barguet, Paul, *Le Livre des Morts des anciens Egyptiens* (Paris, 1967).

Barucq-Daumas, *Hymnes et prières*: Barucq, André and Daumas, François, *Hymnes et prières de l'Egypte ancienne* (Paris, 1980).

Borghouts, *Magical Texts*: Borghouts, J. F., *Ancient Egyptian Magical Texts* (Leiden, 1978).

Budge, *BD*: Budge, E. A. Wallis, *The Book of the Dead: The Chapters of Coming Forth by Day: Text* (London, 1898).

Chassinat, *Khoiak*: Chassinat, E., *Les Mystères d'Osiris au mois de Khoiak* (Cairo, 1966–1968).

CT: De Buck, Adriaan, *The Egyptian Coffin Texts*, 7 vols. (Chicago 1935–1961). English translations of the Coffin Texts placed within quotation marks in the present text closely follow the French translations in Paul Barguet, *Textes des Sarcophages égyptiens du Moyen Empire* (Paris, 1986).

Daumas, *Mammisis*: Daumas, François, *Les mammisis des temples égyptiens* (Paris, 1958).

Derchain, *Papyrus Salt*: Derchain, Philippe, *Le Papyrus Salt 825 (B.M. 10051) rituel pour la conservation de la vie en Egypte* (Brussels, 1965).

Goyon, *Confirmation*: Goyon, Jean-Claude, *Confirmation du pouvoir royal au nouvel an* (Cairo, 1972).

Goyon, *Dieux-gardiens*: Goyon, Jean-Claude, *Les Dieux-gardiens et la genèse des temples (d'après les textes égyptiens de l'époque gréco-romaine). Les soixante d'Edfou et les soixante-dix-sept dieux de Pharbaethos* (Cairo, 1985).

Goyon, *Rituels funéraires*: Goyon, Jean-Claude, *Rituels funéraires de l'ancienne Egypte* (Paris, 1972).

Gutbub, *Textes fondamentaux*: Gutbub, Adolphe, *Textes fondamentaux de la théologie de Kom Ombo* (Cairo, 1973).

Hornung, *Conceptions of God*: Hornung, Erik, *Conceptions of God in Ancient Egypt: The One and the Many* (Ithaca, 1983).

Hornung, *Himmelskuh*: Hornung, Erik, *Der ägyptische Mythos von der Himmelskuh. Eine Ätiologie des Unvollkommenen* (Freiburg, 1982).

Jelinkova, *Djed-Her*: Jelinkova-Reymond, E., *Les Inscriptions de la statue guérisseuse de Djed-Her-le-Sauveur* (Cairo, 1956).

Klasens, *Behague*: Klasens, Adolf, *A Magical Statue Base (Socle Behague) in the Museum of Antiquities at Leiden* (Leiden, 1952).

Koenig, *PBoulaq*: Koenig, Yvan, *Le papyrus Boulaq 6* (Cairo, 1981).

Lange, *Mag. Pap. Harris*: Lange, H. O., *Der magische Papyrus Harris herausgegeben und erklärt* (Copenhagen, 1927).

Lefebvre, *Romans et contes*: Lefebvre, Gustave, *Romans et contes égyptiens de l'époque pharaonique* (Paris, 1949).

Massart, *Leiden Mag. Pap*: Massart, Adhémar, *The Leiden Magical Papyrus I 343 + I 345* (Leiden, 1954).

Neugebauer-Parker, *EAT*: Neugebauer, Otto, and Richard A. Parker, *Egyptian Astronomical Texts*, 3 vols. (Providence, 1960–1969).

P. Bremner-Rhind: Faulkner, R. O., *The Papyrus Bremner-Rhind (British Museum No. 10188)* (Brussels, 1933).

Piankoff, *Livre du Jour et de la Nuit*: Piankoff, Alexandre, *Le Livre du Jour et de la Nuit* (Cairo, 1942).

Piankoff, *Quererets*: Piankoff, Alexandre, *Le Livre des Quérerts. Bulletin de l'Institut français d'archéologie orientale*, 41 (1942), 42 (1944), 43 (1945), 45 (1947) (Published separately, Cairo, 1946).

*Pyr.*: Sethe, Kurt, *Die altägyptischen Pyramidentexte*, 2 vols. (Leipzig 1908–1910).

Sander-Hansen, *Anchnesneferibre*: Sander-Hansen, C. E., *Die religiösen Texte auf dem Sarg der Anchnesneferibre* (Copenhagen, 1937).

*Urk.*, vol. 6: Schott, Siegfried, *Urkunden mythologischen Inhalts* (Leipzig, 1939).

Vandier, *Jumilhac*: Vandier, Jacques, *Le papyrus Jumilhac* (Paris, 1962).

## Introduction

1. J. Hani, *La Religion égyptienne dans la pensée de Plutarque* (Paris, 1976), p. 473.

2. Vivant Denon, *Voyage dans la Basse et la Haute Egypte* [repr. of the 1802 ed.] (Cairo, 1989), p. 114.

3. See J. Yoyotte, "Champollion et le panthéon égyptien," *BSFE* 95 (1982): 76–108.

4. J.-F. Champollion, *Lettres écrites d'Egypte et de Nubie en 1828 et 1829* (Paris, 1868), p. 127.

5. J.-J. Champollion-Figeac, *L'Egypte ancienne* (Paris, 1858), p. 245.

6. A. Erman, *La Religion des Egyptiens* (Paris, 1952), p. 17, adapted from the 1934 German edition. The first German edition was published in 1905.

7. For an excellent brief historical survey of the various attitudes Egyptologists have taken toward Egyptian religion, see Hornung, *Conceptions of God*, pp. 15–32.

8. Ibid., p. 17.

9. On the last point, ibid., pp. 237–43.

10. See the following essays from among the rich *œuvre* of P. Derchain: "Anthropologie. Egypte pharaonique"; "Cosmogonie"; "Divinité"; "Rituels égyptiens," in *Dictionnaire des mythologies* (Paris, 1981).

11. Hornung, *Conceptions of God*.

12. P. Derchain, *RdE* 41 (1990): 9–30.

13. P. Derchain, *CdE* 43 (1988): 85.

14. H. G. Fischer, *L'Écriture et l'art de l'Egypte ancienne* (Paris, 1986), p. 25.

15. R. A. Caminos, *JEA* 58 (1972): 219.

16. See G. Posener, *Le Papyrus Vandier* (Cairo, 1985). See also below, pp. 175–76.

17. M. Smith, *Enchoria* 15 (1987): 69 (11–12).

18. CT, vol. 6, 193n.

19. S. Sauneron, *Villes et légendes d'Egypte* (Cairo, 1983), pp. 84–85. For a general account of writings by the gods, see below, pp. 103–5.

20. A version of the adventures of Horus and Seth had already been composed in the Middle Kingdom. See below, p. 68. On magical-literary texts, see A. Roccati, *Mélanges Adolphe Gutbub* (Montpellier, 1984), pp. 201–10.

21. See K. A. Kitchen, *Hommages à François Daumas*, vol. 2 (Montpellier, 1986), pp. 35–39.

## Chapter 1. Origins, Destinies, History

1. H. Grapow, *ZÄS* 67 (1931): 34–38.

2. CT, vol. 2, 33–34.

3. CT, vol. 6, 280u.

4. According to CT, vol. 1, 332c–334c.

5. CT, vol. 1, 354b ff.; vol. 2, 4ab, 29g–30h.

6. CT, vol. 6, 344bd.

7. R. O. Faulkner, *JEA* 23 (1937): 172 ( = P. Bremner-Rhind XXVI, 21–23).

8. R. Parker and L. Lesko, in *Pyramid Studies and Other Essays Presented to I. E. S. Edwards* (London, 1988), pp. 169–70.

9. Alliot, *Culte d'Horus*, p. 515.

10. Ibid., p. 517. See below, pp. 180–81.

11. Vandier, *Jumilhac*, p. 243, n. 992.

12. In this connection, see A. H. Gardiner, *The Admonitions of an Egyptian Sage* (Leipzig, 1909), p. 44 (5, 14-6, 1), where a philosopher, noting the political chaos into which Egypt has fallen, evokes the end of the world and exclaims: "Would that there might be an end of men. . . . O that the earth would cease from noise, and tumult be no more?"

13. E. Hornung, *ZÄS* 81 (1956): 28–32.

14. See below, pp. 21, 115.

15. Klasens, *Behague*, p. 57 (f25).

16. G. Posener, *Annuaire de l'Institut de philologie et d'histoire orientales et slaves* 13 (1953): 472.

17. Lange, *Mag. Pap. Harris*, p. 20 (15).

18. *Pyr.*, § 278–79.

19. Barguet, *Livre des Morts*, p. 260 (chap. 175).

20. B. van de Walle, *JNES* 31 (1972): 80, n. k and l.

21. E. Chassinat, *Le Temple d'Edfu*, vol. 4 (Cairo, 1929): 240 (10–11). Osiris himself is destined to live "for millions of years": Assmann, *Sonnenhymnen*, p. 299, n. b.

22. On the identity of the creator serpent and the serpent in the Nile cave, see B. Stricker, *OMRO* 31 (1950): 57 (II, 16–17) and L. Kákosy, *MDIAK* 37 (1981): 255–60. On a distinction between serpent of chaos and creator serpent, see Goyon, *Dieux-gardiens*, p. 37, n. 9.

23. P. Derchain, *ZÄS* 81 (1956): 4–6; Claudian, *On Stilicho's Consultship*, trans. Maurice Platnauer (Cambridge, Mass., 1972), 2:33.

24. A. Niwinski, *GM* 48 (1981): 41–53; Claudian, *On Stilicho's Consultship*.

25. Already clearly expressed in L. Habachi, *The Sanctuary of Heqaib*, vol. 1 (Mainz, 1985): 36, fig. 3 (l. 8–9).

26. F. Daumas, *Le Temple de Dendara*, vol. 9 (Cairo, 1987), p. 152 (14–15).

27. P. Tresson, *Mélanges Maspero*, vol. 1, pt. 2 (Cairo, 1935–1938), pp. 821, 826, n. 5. See also K. A. Kitchen, *Ramesside Inscriptions: Historical and Biographical*, vol. 2 (Oxford, 1979), 633 (12), where the temple in Luxor restored by Ramses II is considered to exist "after or beyond cyclical time."

28. Barucq-Daumas, *Hymnes et prières*, p. 274 (XII, 4–5). Compare S. Sauneron, *Esna*, vol. 5 (Cairo, 1962), p. 257 (No. 206, 3).

29. Goyon, *Dieux-gardiens*, p. 123.

30. What follows is based on CT, chap. 154 = Book of the Dead, chap. 115; *Urk.*, vol. 6, pp. 63, 16 ff. See J. Yoyotte, *RdE* 30 (1978): 147–50; J.-C. Grenier, *Tôd*, vol. 1 (Cairo, 1980), p. 170; E. Drioton, *Médamoud. Les inscriptions* (Cairo, 1926), pp. 46–47, No. 105.

31. Borghouts, *Magical Texts*, p. 95 (§ 145).

32. The same individual plays a role in Hornung, *Himmelskuh*, p. 39 (verse 70).

33. K. Sethe, *ZÄS* 63 (1928): 50–53.

34. S. Sauneron, *Esna*, vol. 5 (Cairo, 1962), p. 265.

35. See below, p. 115.

36. Jelinkova, *Djed-Her*, p. 43 and n. 3; *Urk.*, vol. 6, pp. 115, 17.

37. Following Massart, *Leiden Mag. Pap.*, p. 59.

38. Mentioned in A. Erman, *Zaubersprüche für Mutter und Kind* (Berlin, 1901), pp. 50–51.

39. Lange, *Mag. Pap. Harris*, p. 59 (9).

40. Borghouts, *Magical Texts*, p. 80 (§ 115).

41. Ibid., p. 73 (§ 99).

42. Jelinkova, *Djed-Her*, p. 40, p. 45, n. 3.

43. Borghouts, *Magical Texts*, p. 78 (§ 111). Horus: p. 72 (§ 96), p. 75 (§ 102), p. 81 (§ 119); the wife of the elder Horus: p. 80 (§ 115).

44. Ibid., p. 79 (§ 112).

45. Ibid., p. 80 (§ 117).

46. CT, vol. 7, 463f–464ab.

47. Assmann, *Sonnenhymnen*, p. 204 (51).

48. What follows is based on Gutbub, *Textes fondamentaux*, pp. 70, n. c, 424, 429 ff., 107, 110, n. l, 67–68. See also S. Sauneron, *Esna*, vol. 5 (Cairo, 1962): 324–25.

49. Compare J.-C. Goyon, *BIFAO* 65 (1967): 98 (34); S. Sauneron, *JNES* 19 (1960): 275 and n. 66.

50. H. W. Fairman, *JEA* 21 (1935): 26–36; A. Blackman and H. W. Fairman, *JEA* 28 (1942): 32–38; 29 (1943): 2–36.

51. Gutbub, *Textes fondamentaux*, p. 509, 521 ff. S. Sauneron, *Esna*, vol. 5 (Cairo, 1962), p. 26 (77, 15–16) mentions the revolt of the "children" of Re; see pp. 374–75.

52. According to H. Junker, *Der sehende und blinde Gott* (Munich, 1942), pp. 77–78; S. Schott, "Die Reinigung Pharaos in einem memphitischen Tempel," *Göttinger Nachrichten*, 1957/3, p. 61. Compare Goyon, *Dieux-gardiens*, p. 373 and n. 2; CT, vol. 7, 20e, with the commentary by P. Kaplony, *Mitteilungen des Instituts für Orientforschung* 11 (1966): 149, n. 56; 157 ff., n. 83.

53. J. F. Borghouts, *OMRO* 51 (1970): 199 ff.

54. Bakir, *Cairo Calendar*, p. 44 (verso IV, 11).

55. Borghouts, *Magical Texts*, p. 37 (§ 58).

56. CT, vol. 6, 144d.

57. D. Meeks, *Archéo-Nil* 1 (1991): 5–15; J. F. Borghouts, *OMRO* 51 (1970): 22–23.

58. Goyon, *Dieux-gardiens*, pp. 371–73.

59. Ibid., pp. 342–43.

60. Bakir, *Cairo Calendar*, p. 16 (recto VI, 4–7).

61. Compare Bakir, *Cairo Calendar*, p. 24 (Recto XIV, 1).

62. What follows is based on Hornung, *Himmelskuh*, pp. 38 ff.

63. Bakir, *Cairo Calendar*, p. 45 (Verso V, 11).

64. F. de Cénival, *Le Mythe de l'œil du soleil* (Sommerhausen, 1988), pp. 31–33.

65. Bakir, *Cairo Calendar*, p. 46 (verso VI, 6).

66. This scene is already painted in Lange, *Mag. Pap. Harris*, p. 17 (I, 9 ff.).

67. Bakir, *Cairo Calendar*, p. 45 (verso V, 1). See L. Troy, *Acta Universitatis Upsaliensis Boreas* 20 (1989): 131–32. The demotic legend was already known in the New Kingdom: G. Posener, *Catalogue des ostraca hiératiques littéraires de Deir el-Médineh*, vol. 3 (Cairo, 1980), no. 1598.

68. CT, vol. 6, 261gh.

69. This moment of separation is already mentioned in CT, vol. 5, 150c–151a. In *Pyr.*, § 1566cd, men are separated from the "efficient" gods.

70. F. Herbin, *BIFAO* 88 (1988): 103.

71. H. S. Smith and W. J. Tait, *Saqqâra Demotic Papyri*, vol. 1 (London, 1983): 104–5, 107.

72. Goyon, *Confirmation*, p. 86, n. 27.

73. Book of the Dead, chap. 82 = Budge, *BD*, p. 180 (8–10).

74. R. Anthes, *Studia Ægyptiaca* 9 (1983): 120–21.

75. A summary of the sources for this story is found in Massart, *Leiden Mag. Pap.*, pp. 95–96.

76. *Pyr.*, § 19, § 831.

77. CT, vol. 2, 107b.

78. Borghouts, *Magical Texts*, p. 45 (§ 72).

79. Ibid., p. 48 (§ 80); Vandier, *Jumilhac*, p. 126 (XIV, 17).

80. Borghouts, *Magical Texts*, p. 30 (§ 43).

81. J. F. Borghouts, *OMRO* 51 (1970): 16–17 and n. 354.

82. *Urk.*, vol. 6, p. 91 (18–19).

83. A list of these misfortunes is to be found in *Urk.*, vol. 6, pp. 19–23, 135 ff.

84. *Urk.*, vol. 6, p. 56.

85. Bakir, *Cairo Calendar*, p. 27 (recto XVII, 10–11); L. Kákosy, *ZÄS* 117 (1990): 151, n. t.

86. A. H. Gardiner, *The Royal Canon of Turin* (Oxford, 1959), col. 1.

87. U. Luft, *Studia Ægyptiaca* 4 (1978): 78–130; W. Barta, *Untersuchungen zum Götterkreis der Neunheit* (Munich, 1973), pp. 41–48.

88. S. Sauneron, *Villes et légendes d'Egypte* (Cairo, 1983), pp. 171–74.

89. Goyon, *Rituels funéraires*, p. 255; D. B. Redford, *Pharaonic King-Lists, Annals and Day-Books* (Mississauga, 1986), pp. 65–82.

90. G. Goyon, *Kêmi* 6 (1936): 7 ff. See U. Verhoeven, in *Religion und Philosophie im alten Ägypten. Festgabe für P. Derchain* (Louvain, 1991), pp. 319–20, for a bibliography of studies of this text.

91. G. Goyon, op. cit., p. 7.

92. S. Sauneron, *Esna*, vol. 5 (Cairo, 1962): 228. Compare below, p. 32.

93. G. Goyon, op. cit., pp. 7, 18.

94. Borghouts, *Magical Texts*, p. 51 (§ 84); Hornung, *Himmelskuh*, p. 37 (verses 2–3).

95. Klasens, *Behague*, p. 61.

96. U. Luft, *Studia Ægyptiaca* 4 (1978): 70.

97. E. Drioton, *ASAE* 44 (1944): 114; Barucq-Daumas, *Hymnes et prières*, p. 267 (V, 2).

98. G. Goyon, op. cit., p. 19.

99. G. Goyon, op. cit., p. 18.

100. U. Verhoeven, *Religion und Philosophie*, pp. 319–30, denies that Geb raped his mother. This version of events is, however, confirmed by the Delta papyrus (XII, 7 and 9).

101. G. Goyon, *Kêmi* 6 (1936): 14–15.

102. Derchain, *Papyrus Salt*, pp. 31–34; there is a possible allusion in Bakir, *Cairo Calendar*, p. 46 (verso VI, 13). The papyrus Salt makes Shu, not Geb, Osiris's father.

103. Some information is to be found in S. Sauneron, *Kêmi* 20 (1970): 12–13.

104. Derchain, *Papyrus Salt*, p. 167, n. 72.

105. R. O. Faulkner, *JEA* 22 (1936): 127 ( = P. Bremner-Rhind IX, 25). For help in understanding this passage, see T. G. H. James, *The Hekanakhte Papers* (New York, 1962), p. 29, n. 74.

106. Derchain, *Papyrus Salt*, p. 138 (IV, 2).

107. E. Drioton, *ASAE* 39 (1939): 75 (10); 76, n. f; K. Sethe, *Dramatische Texte zu altaegyptischen Mysterienspielen* (Leipzig, 1928), p. 23.

108. Derchain, *Papyrus Salt*, p. 138 (IV, 7).

109. J.-C. Goyon, *BIFAO* 75 (1975): 378, n. 2.

110. CT, vol. 6, 306 f.

111. W. Spiegelberg, *ZÄS* 53 (1917): 101 ff. On the surveying of the world, see S. Sauneron, *Villes et légendes d'Egypte* (Cairo, 1983), pp. 68 ff.; Barucq-Daumas, *Hymnes et prières*, p. 218 and p. 228, n. cq (all of "chap. 700") on the title deed.

112. W. Helck, *Die Prophezeiung des Nfr.tj* (Wiesbaden, 1970), pp. 42–43; Helck, *Urkunden der 18. Dynastie* (Berlin, 1958), p. 2027, 11–12; K. Sethe, *Hieroglyphische Urkunden der Griechisch-römischen Zeit* (Leipzig, 1904), pp. 3, 15.

113. J. Assmann, "Königsdogma und Heilserwartung," in *Apocalypticism in the Mediterranean and the Near East*, ed. D. Hellholm (Tübingen, 1983), pp. 345–77.

## Chapter 2. Hierarchies, Prerogatives, Groups

1. A. O. Abdallah, *JEA* 70 (1984): 71, n. k.

2. Assmann, *Sonnenhymnen*, p. 60, n. h; p. 63, n. a; p. 173, n. b; pp. 189–90.

3. Barguet, *Livre des Morts*, p. 105 (chap. 65).

4. Barucq-Daumas, *Hymnes et prières*, p. 336. The translation should be corrected in the light of N. de G. Davies, *The Temple of Hibis*, vol. 3 (New York, 1953), pl. 33, col. 25. Compare E. Chassinat, *Le Temple d'Edfou*, vol. 3 (Cairo, 1928): 323, 8, which should be considered in conjuction with his vol. 4 (Cairo, 1929): 241, 14; vol. 7 (Cairo, 1932): 280, 7.

5. H. Goedicke and E. F. Wente, *Ostraka Michaelides* (Wiesbaden, 1962), pl. XV, col. 2.

6. D. Meeks, *Revue de l'histoire des religions* 205 (1988): 425–46.

7. CT, vol. 2, 42–43. See J. Baines, *GM* 67 (1983): 13–28.

8. *Pyr.*, § 404ac; CT, vol. 2, 157ef; Lefebvre, *Romans et contes*, p. 112; D. Kurth and H.-J. Thissen, *Kölner ägyptische Papyri*, vol. 1 (Cologne, 1980), p. 34 (49). On the "great gods," see also L. Troy, *Acta Universitatis Upsaliensis Boreas* 20 (1989): 130.

9. Barucq-Daumas, *Hymnes et prières*, p. 352 and n. a.

10. Book of the Dead, chap. 123 = Budge, *BD*, 243, 5–6.

11. Hornung, *Himmelskuh*, pp. 23, 45. It is generally assumed that Thoth sends gods who are "greater than he is"; but see the remark by H. G. Fischer, *Egyptian Studies I: Varia* (New York, 1976), p. 86, n. 31.

12. For Thoth's special status here, see G. Posener, *Annuaire du Collège de France 1961–62*, p. 290.

13. W. Helck, *Urkunden der 18. Dynastie* (Berlin, 1958), p. 2081, 13.

14. Bakir, *Cairo Calendar*, p. 25 (recto XV, 1). Compare P. Germond, *Sakhmet et la protection du monde* (Geneva, 1981), p. 69.

15. Koenig, *PBoulaq*, p. 82; J. Yoyotte, *BSFE* 87–88 (1980): 56 ff.

16. CT, vol. 4, 60jk; I. E. S. Edwards, *Hieratic Papyri in the British Museum. Fourth Series* (London, 1960), p. xxii.

17. Assmann, *Sonnenhymnen*, p. 210 (15); p. 213, n. e; p. 255, n. b.

18. On these epithets, see Assmann, *Sonnenhymnen*, p. 83 (13); p. 173, n. a; p. 175, n. a.

19. Lefebvre, *Romans et contes*, pp. 200–201.

20. J.-C. Goyon, *JARCE* 20 (1983): 56 (10).

21. L. Troy, in *The Religion of the Ancient Egyptians: Cognitive Structures and Popular Expressions* (Uppsala, 1989), pp. 59–69; E. Graefe, in *Hommages à François Daumas* (Montpellier, 1986), pp. 345–49.

22. *Urk.*, vol. 6, p. 101, 3–4.

23. H. Te Velde, *JEA* 57 (1971): 80–86, notes that the triad may be analyzed as a way of reducing polytheism to tritheism or "differentiated monotheism."

24. Vandier, *Jumilhac*, p. 125 (XIV, 9 ff.).

25. Ibid., p. 115, § 5.

26. See Barucq-Daumas, *Hymnes et prières*, p. 335: "For who is god as you are?"

27. See D. Meeks, *Revue de l'histoire des religions* 205 (1988): 425–46.

28. Book of the Dead, chap. 151 = Budge, *BD*, p. 382, 14.

29. *Urk.*, vol. 6, p. 27.

30. B. Stricker, *OMRO* 29 (1948): 64. On Seth's "violating the rules," See *Urk.*, vol. 6, pp. 7, 11.

31. CT, vol. 1, 20c ff. For the most recent consideration of Thoth as vizier, see M.-T. Derchain-Urtel, *Thot à travers ses épithètes dans les scènes d'offrandes des temples d' époque gréco-romaine* (Brussels, 1981), pp. 95–106.

32. Bakir, *Cairo Calendar*, p. 33 (recto XXIII, 1). In question here is the *sedjefatery* oath; K. Baer, *JEA* 50 (1964): 179, says that it is a promise made by new office holders not to abuse the prerogatives of office. For the most recent consideration, see S. N. Morschauser, *JARCE* 25 (1988): 93–103, whose explanation does not, however, seem appropriate in the present case.

33. CT, vol. 4, 93g; Sander-Hansen, *Anchnesneferibre*, p. 66; see also p. 68; S. Sauneron, *Kêmi* 20 (1970): 11; Bakir, *Cairo Calendar*, p. 26 (recto XVI, 7–8), p. 33 (recto XXIII, 2); H. Junker, *Das Götterdekret über das Abaton* (Vienna, 1913), pp. 7–8. For a general consideration of the gods' decrees, see U. Luft, *Beiträge zur Historisierung der Götterwelt und der Mythenschreibung* (Budapest, 1978), pp. 32–49.

34. Book of the Dead, chap. 183 = Budge, *BD*, 485, 9; Vandier, *Jumilhac*, p. 126 (XIV, 19). For the relationship between the original document and the stele it was published on, see J.-M. Kruchten, *Le décret d'Horemheb* (Brussels, 1981), pp. 214–23.

35. See another proclamation by Thoth in W. Golénischeff, *Catalogue général des antiquités égyptiennes du musée du Caire. Papyrus hiératiques*, vol. 1 (Cairo, 1927), pp. 106, 15 ff.

36. Barucq-Daumas, *Hymnes et prières*, p. 355 and n. h; Sander-Hansen, *Anchnesneferibre*, p. 137.

37. *Urk.*, vol. 6, pp. 25, 22–23.

38. Sander-Hansen, *Anchnesneferibre*, p. 69.

39. J. Quagebeur, in *Funerary Symbols and Religion: Essays Dedicated to Prof. Heerma van Voss* (Kampen, 1988), pp. 105–26; H. De Meulenaere, *CdE* 63 (1988): 234–41.

40. Borghouts, *Magical Texts*, p. 4 (§ 9).

41. J. Osing, *Aspects de la culture pharaonique. Quatre leçons au Collège de France* (Paris, 1992), pp. 49 ff.

42. E. Suys, *Orientalia* 3 (1934): 71 (II, 8); 74.

43. Hornung, *Himmelskuh*, p. 37 (verse 10 ff., 19 ff.).

44. Sander-Hansen, *Anchnesneferibre*, p. 94.

45. A. H. Gardiner, *Hieratic Papyri in the British Museum: Third Series* (London, 1935), pl. 69 (XIV A, 2).

46. Bakir, *Cairo Calendar*, p. 42 (verso II, 2–3).

47. Ibid., p. 44 (verso IV, 7).

48. The gods, too, can be judged: Barucq-Daumas, *Hymnes et prières*, p. 405, n. bx. The reproach addressed to Osiris is mentioned in Bakir, *Cairo Calendar*, p. 46 (verso VI, 13); the reproach involving Maât is found in ibid. (verso VI, 5). On Osiris, see also above, p. 31.

49. What follows is based on the tale of Horus and Seth: Lefebvre, *Romans et contes*, pp. 184 ff.; Vandier, *Jumilhac*, p. 129 (XVI, 23 ff.), supplemented by other

sources mentioned along the way. Osiris himself is sometimes party to the complaint in question: W. C. Hayes, *Ostraka and Name Stones from the Tomb of Sen-Mut (No. 71) at Thebes* (New York, 1942), No. 149.

50. CT, vol. 7, 371 ff. Already in *Pyr.*, § 958.
51. Lefebvre, *Romans et contes*, p. 184.
52. Ibid., p. 181.
53. Vandier, *Jumilhac*, p. 131; already in Lange, *Mag. Pap. Harris*, p. 14 (I, 6–7); *Urk.*, vol. 6: 8 ff.; K. Sethe, *Dramatische Texte zu altaegyptischen Mysterienspielen* (Leipzig, 1928), pp. 278–79.
54. Bakir, *Cairo Calendar*, p. 16 (recto VI, 1).
55. On what follows, see Vandier, *Jumilhac*, p. 128 (XVI, 10 ff.). Other allusions to this affair are noted by P. Derchain, *RdE* 9 (1952): 31; Koenig, *PBoulaq*, p. 36, n. h.
56. S. Schott, "Thoth, le Dieu qui vole les offrandes et qui trouble le cours du temps," *CRAIBL* (1970): 547–56.
57. CT, vol. 2, 233b ff.
58. CT, vol. 6, 209ef.
59. CT, vol. 2, 234b.
60. CT, vol. 2, 235bc, 249d ff. Compare the myth of Horus in H. W. Fairman, *JEA* 21 (1935): 32.
61. Book of the Dead, chap. 19–20. But see S. Hassan, *Hymnes religieux du Moyen Empire* (Cairo, 1928), p. 98.
62. Lefebvre, *Romans et contes*, p. 189 (5, 5 ff.), p. 199 (14, 2 ff.); Vandier, *Jumilhac*, p. 120 (X, 7 ff.).
63. CT, vol. 1, 166af.
64. E. Drioton, *BIE* 34 (1952): 291–316; already in CT, vol. 1, 4ad; vol. 4, 128 f; Gutbub, *Textes fondamentaux*, p. 247, n. s.
65. Koenig, *PBoulaq*, p. 94, n. a.
66. Vandier, *Jumilhac*, p. 120 (X, 7–8), p. 126 (XV, 1).
67. Ibid., p. 126 (§ XXII).
68. Assmann, *Sonnenhymnen*, p. 109, n. h; CT, vol. 4, 303b.
69. Borghouts, *Magical Texts*, p. 12, bottom of the page.
70. Gutbub, *Textes fondamentaux*, pp. 242–43, 246, n. l; Koenig, *PBoulaq*, p. 28, n. f. For a general consideration, see L. Kákosy, *Oikumene* 3 (1982): 163 ff. Other spirits possess an astral nature: Goyon, *Dieux-gardiens*, pp. 461, 473.
71. Borghouts, *Magical Texts*, p. 12.
72. CT, vol. 1, 278ab.
73. CT, vol. 6, 174i ff.
74. See CT, vol. 6, 271c, where the eye is in the stomach, as magical power is supposed to be. See below, p. 96.
75. Horus's "confederation": CT, vol. 7, 48 ff.
76. K. Sethe, *Thebanische Tempelinschriften aus griechisch-römischer Zeit* (Berlin, 1957), p. 28 (32e).
77. Goyon, *Dieux Gardiens*, pp. 4, 46–110.
78. Assmann, *Sonnenhymnen*, p. 76 (3).
79. Bakir, *Cairo Calendar*, p. 38 (recto XXVIII, 13).
80. A. Massart, *MDIAK* 15 (1957): 178.
81. R. A. Caminos, *JEA* 58 (1972): 211.
82. I. E. S. Edwards, *Hieratic Papyri in the British Museum. Fourth Series* (London, 1960), p. xxii.
83. R. Stadelmann, *Syrisch-palästinensische Gottheiten in Ägypten* (Leiden, 1967), pp. 8–9; G. Matthiae and P. Xella, *Rivista di Studi Fenici* 9 (1981): 147–52.

84. CT, vol. 7, 222i; cf. B. Altenmüller, *Synkretismus in den Sargtexten* (Wiesbaden, 1975), p. 133.

85. For a general discussion, see R. Stadelmann, op. cit.; C. Zivie, *Bulletin de la Société française des fouilles de Tanis* 2/3 (1989): 139–75.

86. Remarks by R. Stadelmann, *Gottheiten in Ägypten*, pp. 124–33.

87. Lefebvre, *Romans et contes*, pp. 106–13. See the detailed analysis by G. Posener, *Annuaire de l'Institut de philologie et d'histoire orientales et slaves* 13 (1953): 461–78, and the remarks by J. van Dijk, *Scripta Signa Vocis: Studies Presented to Prof. J. H. Hospers* (Groningen, 1986), pp. 31–32.

88. For the most up-to-date treatment of the subject, see J. van Dijk, *Scripta Signa Voci*, pp. 31–51.

89. Fragments of the same myth are to found in E. Suys, *Orientalia* 3 (1934): 65; A. de Buck and B. Stricker, *OMRO* 21 (1940): 58 (II, 9–11); Massart, *Leiden Mag. Pap.*, p. 65.

90. L. Kákosy, *ZÄS* 117 (1990): 145 (B, 8); 147 (C,4); 155–56. Further, G. Posener, *Annuaire de l'Institut de philologie et d'histoire orientales et slaves* 13 (1953), pp. 465–66, and J. Leibovitch, *ASAE* 48 (1948): 435–44.

91. Bakir, *Cairo Calendar*, p. 27 (recto XVII, 11).

92. This is the case with Hauron; J. van Dijk, *GM* 107 (1989): 59–68, has shown how his different functions in Egypt can be derived from those he had in his country of origin. See Borghouts, *Magical Texts*, pp. 50–51, where he plays a herdsman's role. On the herdsman of the gods, see chap. 4, p. 84, and note 29 in chap. 4.

93. J.-C. Goyon, *BIFAO* 75 (1975): 386, n. 5. See also P. Lacau and H. Chevrier, *Une Chapelle d'Hatchepsout à Karnak* (Cairo, 1977), p. 149, where the foreign gods acclaim Hatshepsut after she is crowned. The same thing happened to the divine statuette that the Hittite king Tushratta sent to Amenophis III: W. L. Moran, *Les lettres d'El Amarna* (Paris, 1987), pp. 137–38.

94. C. Zivie, *Bulletin de la Société française des fouilles de Tanis* 2/3 (1989): 155.

95. As suggested by P. Derchain in *RdE* 41 (1990): 25–28. On Egyptian gods beyond Egypt's borders, see below, pp. 91–92.

## Chapter 3. Divine Bodies

1. CT, vol. 4, 75e. See also Assmann, *Sonnenhymnen*, p. 204 (156, 26); p. 206, n. p.

2. Gutbub, *Textes fondamentaux*, pp. 335, 353, n. u; Daumas, *Mammisis*, pp. 411 ff.

3. S. Sauneron, *Villes et légendes d'Egypte* (Cairo, 1983), pp. 61–64.

4. R. O. Faulkner, *JEA* 23 (1937): 172 (= P. Bremner-Rhind XXVI, 15).

5. On the difficult problem of the kheperu and iru, see the various comments by J. Assmann, *Lexikon der Ägyptologie*, vol. 2, 759, § c, pp. 764–65; *Lit. Lieder*, pp. 42–43; *Biblische Notizen* 11 (1980): 50. An iru is something a god can put on in the literal sense of the word: Assmann, *Sonnenhymnen*, p. 14 (16, 4), where it is clearly a matter of "putting on an appearance."

6. Lefebvre, *Roman et contes*, p. 183, n. 14; p. 192, n. 61.

7. Vandier, *Jumilhac*, p. 114 (II, 23; III, 13–14).

8. As is indicated by Assmann, *Lit. Lieder*, p. 43, n. 20.

9. Assmann, *Sonnenhymnen*, p. 204 (156, 26); p. 206, n. p.

10. H.-W. Fischer-Elfert, *Literarische Ostraka der Ramessidenzeit in Übersetzung* (Wiesbaden, 1986), p. 29 (3); Assmann, *Sonnenhymnen*, p. 307, n. c.

11. CT, vol. 4, 110g, 112df.

12. CT, vol. 4, 120a.

13. Following the reasoning of J. Baines, *Fecundity Figures* (Warminster, 1985), p. 117.

14. There is another example of this procedure in Vandier, *Jumilhac*, p. 117 (VI, 11 ff.), discussed on p. 77 below. See also below chap. 4, p. 90 and notes 85–87 for chap. 4, where it is shown that a god's appearance and name are not enough to establish his identity; he must also possess a special attribute, a headdress in this case. This schema underlies the game of questions and answers that the deceased who wants to go to the next world must play with the ferryman who is to carry him across the expanse of water separating him from it (CT, chaps. 395–98). The deceased must tell the ferryman the name of his boat and all its parts, connecting them with divine attributes in order to endow them with physical reality. As the parts that are not named do not exist, it is at first impossible to reconstitute the boat; this leads to new questions and answers. By means of this dialogue, the deceased literally creates the ferry that will transport him. In responding to the questions put to him, he is also led to define himself through the statement of his name and attributes. In this way, he acquires his new identity and proves his capacity to recognize *irus* and other beings inhabiting the world of the gods. He thus shows that he is capable of living in the divine community.

15. What follows is based on the tale of Horus and Seth = Lefebvre, *Romans et contes*, pp. 189–90.

16. N. that this situation is quite similar to one evoked earlier (n. 14).

17. For this detail, see W. C. Hayes, *Ostraka and Name Stones from the Tomb of Sen-Mut (No. 71) at Thebes* (New York, 1942), n° 149, verso 4. See also Koenig, *PBoulaq*, p. 77, n. b; J. Baines, *Fecundity Figures*, p. 125. There is an identical scene in Bakir, *Cairo Calendar*, p. 23 (recto XIII, 9–10), but it does not seem to be connected with this trial.

18. See below, p. 75–76.

19. One text, after explicitly naming a series of divinities, uses the expression "all these men" (that is, "all these individuals") when it brings up the list a second time; the term employed, *sa*, is commonly applied to human beings. Sander-Hansen, *Anchnesneferibre*, p. 67.

20. For a general discussion, Ockinga, *Die Gottebenbildlichkeit im Alten Ägypten und im Alten Testament* (Wiesbaden, 1984). But see a mutilated text in Assmann, *Sonnenhymnen*, p. 76 (l. 7), which seems to say that all creatures were made in the image of the creator-god. It would seem that the term used to designate "creatures," *Weneniu*, can be applied only to gods and people.

21. J. Reymond, *The Mythical Origin of the Egyptian Temple* (Manchester, 1969), p. 67.

22. Vandier, *Jumilhac*, p. 124 and n. 370; Lange, *Mag. Pap. Harris*, 38 (3–4); S. Aufrère, *L'Univers minéral dans la pensée égyptienne* (Cairo, 1991), pp. 311 ff.; Koenig, *PBoulaq*, p. 117; S. Sauneron, *Esna*, vol. 5 (Cairo, 1962), p. 143; Book of the Dead, chap. 172 = Budge, *BD*, 445, 16; S. Schott, "Kanais. Der Tempel Sethos I. im Wadi Mia," *Göttinger Nachrichten*, 1961/6, C, 3; C. Kuentz, *ASAE* 25 (1925): 228, note 1. For the bones of gold: Goyon, *Rituels funéraires*, p. 237; Hornung, *Himmelskuh*, p. 52, n. 6; Barucq-Daumas, *Hymnes et prières*, p. 330 and n. b.

23. A. Massy, *Le Papyrus de Leiden I 347* (Ghent, 1885), p. 2; see also the variant in A. de Buck and B. Stricker, *OMRO* 21 (1940): 57 (II, 2), "encircled by an uraeus."

24. Goyon, *Rituels funéraires*, p. 278 and n. 1; Barucq-Daumas, *Hymnes et prières*, p. 331 and n. p.

25. J. von Beckerath, *ZÄS* 119 (1992): 99 (the tale of Khonsemheb and the phantom), and Goyon, *Rituels funéraires*, p. 71: "your corpse shall endure forever, like the rock of the mountains." This should be compared with the texts cited in n. 22.

26. CT, vol. 6, 108fh; G. Burkard, *Grabung im Assassif III. Die Papyrusfunde* (Mainz, 1986), p. 64 (x + 4, 5. 8–9).

27. See also Goyon, *Rituels funéraires*, p. 73: "your complexion will be golden thanks to pure orpiment."

28. On this question, see the remarks by A. H. Gardiner in *The Library of A. Chester Beatty: Description of a Hieratic Papyrus* (Oxford, 1931), p. 31, n. 3; R. O. Faulkner, *JEA* 54 (1968): 42, n. 8; H. Goedicke, *GM* 39 (1980): 28. Compare with S. Aufrère, *L'Univers minéral*, pp. 466–67.

29. S. Cauville, *BIFAO* 90 (1990): 93, n. 8.

30. S. Aufrère, *L'Univers minéral*, p. 336, pp. 473 ff.

31. Explicitly in CT, vol. 5, 376f, 385v. On Re, see CT, vol. 6, 206m.

32. Lefebvre, *Romans et contes*, p. 195.

33. Vandier, *Jumilhac*, p. 125 (XIV, 6); P. Derchain, *RdE* 41 (1990): 18–19.

34. Barucq-Daumas, *Hymnes et prières*, p. 335.

35. E. Chassinat, *Le temple d'Edfou*, vol. 2 (Cairo, 1892), pp. 206, 14. The new moon is also a "black eye": Book of the Dead, chap. 116 = Budge, *BD*, 238, 11.

36. Book of the Dead, chap. 32.

37. Book of the Dead, chap. 166 Pleyte; Goyon, *Rituels funéraires*, p. 110, n. 1; A. Blackman and H. W. Fairman, *JEA* 29 (1943): 14 (B), p. 36, n. 29.

38. Lange, *Mag. Pap. Harris*, p. 59 (6–7); L. Kákosy, *ZÄS* 117 (1990): 149, n. g; J.-C. Goyon, *BIFAO* 75 (1975): 346, n. 1; *Urk.*, vol. 6: 75, 19 ff.; Barucq-Daumas, *Hymnes et prières*, p. 328. On these numbers, see Goyon, *Dieux gardiens*, p. 185, n. 5.

39. Assmann, *Sonnenhymnen*, p. 125 and n. e; Barucq-Daumas, *Hymnes et prières*, p. 221 (IV, 2); p. 227, n. cl.

40. H. S. Smith and W. J. Tait, *Saqqâra Demotic Papyri*, vol. 1 (London, 1983): 90 (1); 91 (18–19); 104–5. The god would later seem to appear on his throne in human form, but there are lacunae in the passage, so that, although the god's "flesh" is alluded to, we do not have a description of it.

41. The forms are not very different from those the gods assume to appear in dreams. See S. Sauneron, in *Les Songes et leur interprétation* (Paris, 1959), pp. 24 ff.

42. Y. Koenig, *Institut français d'archéologie orientale. Livre du centenaire* (Cairo, 1980), p. 137 (verso 1); p. 140, n. q and u; H. S. Smith and W. J. Tait, *Saqqâra*, p. 105b. See also Goyon, *Confirmation*, p. 126, n. 370.

43. Y. Koenig, *Livre du Centenaire*, p. 137.

44. S. Sauneron, *Le papyrus magique illustré de Brooklyn* (Brooklyn, 1970), p. 24.

45. Lefebvre, *Romans et contes*, pp. 86–87.

46. Ibid., p. 27.

47. J. Yoyotte, *BIFAO* 77 (1977): 147 (2°). A cubit equals about 21 inches and is subdivided into 7 palms or 28 fingers (four fingers to a palm).

48. Diodorus, I, 44, 4.

49. Book of the Dead, chap. 149 = Budge, *BD*, 368, 3; 369, 5. Some have buttocks seven cubits wide: Budge, *BD*, 371, 4.

50. A. Blackman and H. W. Fairman, *JEA* 29 (1943): 27, n. 11; 28, n. 12.

51. Assmann, *Sonnenhymnen*, p. 168 (10–11); Book of the Dead, chap. 101 = Budge, *BD*, 212, 13–14. On this question see F. Hoffmann, *GM* 132 (1993): 37–38.

52. See also the Greek text of the dream of Nectanebo, which makes Onuris twenty-one cubits (some three yards) high. S. Sauneron, in *Les Songes et leur interprétation* (Paris, 1959), p. 44.

53. CT, vol. 7, 430ab.

54. Lange, *Mag. Pap. Harris*, p. 73 (15 ff.), p. 80 (9 ff.); L. Kákosy, *ZÄS* 117 (1990): 152, n. n.

55. For a general treatment of this question, see H. Brunner, *Die Geburt des Gottkönigs* (Wiesbaden, 1964), p. 51; Hornung, *Conceptions of God*, pp. 133–34.

56. CT, vol. 7, 511g; K. Sethe, *Urkunden der 18. Dynastie* (Leipzig, 1927), pp. 219, 13; Book of the Dead, chap. 140 = Budge, *BD*, 314, 15; Book of the Dead, chap. 149 (12e).

57. See R. J. Leprohon, *Corpus Antiquitatum Aegyptiacarum. Boston 3* (Mainz, 1991), p. 121 (19). This should be compared with p. 116 (24).

58. Assmann, *Lexikon der Ägyptologie*, vol. 2: 757.

59. Borghouts, *Magical Texts*, p. 1 (§ 1).

60. The tale of Astarte, in Lefebvre, *Romans et contes*, p. 112.

61. Goyon, *Confirmation*, p. 62 (III, 13).

62. F. de Cénival, *Le mythe de l'œil du soleil* (Sommerhausen, 1988), p. 15.

63. K. Sethe, *Dramatische Texte zu altaegyptischen Mysterienspielen* (Leipzig, 1928), p. 32.

64. The frequent nudity of the god Bes (Assmann, *Lexikon der Ägyptologie*, vol. 1, p. 721) may no doubt be partially explained by the god's connections to childhood and premature birth. On these connections, see D. Meeks, in *The Intellectual Heritage of Egypt: Studies Presented to L. Kákosy* (Budapest, 1992), pp. 423–36.

65. Borghouts, *Magical Texts*, p. 36 (§ 53).

66. H. Te Velde, *Studia Aegyptiaca* 3 (1977): 165–66.

67. These ways of depicting Nut are well-known. For Hathor, see Hornung, *Conceptions of God*, p. 122, n. 39. For Kadesh, see E. S. Bogoslovski, *Vestnik Drevnij Istorii* 1972/2, p. 84; R. Stadelmann, *Syrisch-palästinensische Gottheiten in Ägypten* (Leiden, 1967), pp. 115 ff.

68. CT, vol. 2, 219 b = R. H. O'Connell, *JEA* 69 (1983): 74.

69. Vandier, *Jumilhac*, p. 114 (III, 1–2; III, 15, 19).

70. CT, vol. 6, 394d.

71. Herodotus, vol. 2: 42. Something comparable may be found in CT, vol. 6, 353j–m.

72. Assmann, *Sonnenhymnen*, p. 193, n. a; p. 199, n. b.

73. H. Grapow, *ZÄS* 71 (1935): 45–47; Koenig, *PBoulaq*, p. 23, n. o; p. 26, n. b.

74. References in L. Fóti, *Bulletin du musée hongrois des Beaux-Arts* 40 (1973): 5–6.

75. H. Te Velde, "Some Egyptian Deities and Their Piggishness," in *The Intellectual Heritage of Egypt: Studies Presented to L. Kákosy* (Budapest, 1992), pp. 571–78.

76. A. Gasse, *BIFAO* 84 (1984): 203; one finds the same idea in Alliot, *Culte d'Horus*, vol. 1, pp. 414–15.

77. Jelinkova, *Djed-Her*, p. 44.

78. Meeks, *The Intellectual Heritage of Egypt*, pp. 432–33.

79. Borghouts, *Magical Texts*, p. 90 (§ 134); p. 91 (§ 135). Compare Derchain, *Papyrus Salt*, p. 180, n. 154. On this reliquary, see Borghouts, *Magical Texts*, p. 81 (§ 119); Goyon, *Dieux-gardiens*, pp. 200, 334–35; Goyon, *BIFAO* 75 (1975): 384 and n. 2. In the last case, the god in the process of coming into being takes the form of a scarab beetle.

80. Vandier, *Jumilhac*, pp. 125, 121.

81. Ibid., pp. 81–83. See also J. F. Borghouts, *RdE* 32 (1980): 41.

82. S. Sauneron, *Un traité égyptien d'ophiologie* (Cairo, 1989), p. 11, n. 7; p. 12, n. 7.

83. Vandier, *Jumilhac*, p. 128 (XVI, 6).

84. Ibid., pp. 89–90, p. 92, p. 127 (§ XXV, 3).

85. See p. 130 below.

86. CT, vol. 5, 348c.

87. CT, vol. 6, 41f.

88. Borghouts, *Magical Texts*, p. 95 (§ 145); Goyon, *Dieux-gardiens*, p. 186 and n. 4.

89. CT, vol. 7, 150 (48–49).

90. Y. Koenig, *Institut français d'archéologie orientale. Livre du centenaire* (Cairo, 1980), p. 137. The text is very fragmentary. On putting divine animals to death, compare Vandier, *Jumilhac*, p. 90 and n. 2.

91. Lefebvre, *Romans et contes*, pp. 189–90.

92. Ibid., p. 195.

93. Goyon, *Rituels funéraires*, p. 274.

94. G. Posener, *Catalogue des ostraca hiératiques littéraires de Deir el-Médineh*, vol. 3 (Cairo, 1980), no. 1640 (verso x + 4 ff.).

95. One could read the text to mean "slaughtered with a knife." In that case, this would be an animal slaughtered in accordance with the ritual prescriptions.

96. Vandier, *Jumilhac*, p. 133 (XXIII, 8).

97. G. Posener, *Festschrift für Siegfried Schott* (Wiesbaden, 1967), pp. 106–11.

98. Barucq-Daumas, *Hymnes et prières*, p. 474.

99. S. Sauneron, *Esna*, vol. 3 (Cairo, 1968), p. 94, no. 233 (§ 54–55).

100. Borghouts, *Magical Texts*, p. 32 (§ 46).

101. Barucq-Daumas, *Hymnes et prières*, p. 443, n. c; J.-C. Goyon, *Bulletin du cercle d'égyptologie Victor-Loret* 6 (1992): 7–16.

102. H. Gardiner and E. Peet, *The Inscriptions of Sinai* (London, 1955), p. 138 and pl. no. 137.

103. S. Cauville, *BIFAO* 82 (1982): 22.

104. See J.-L. Simonet, *CdE* 62 (1987): 56, 59–72.

105. F. de Cénival, *CRIPEL* 7 (1985): 102 (8–9).

106. Book of the Dead, chap. 153 = Budge, *BD*, 398, 9.

107. Borghouts, *Magical Texts*, p. 25 (§ 35).

108. F. Borghouts, *OMRO* 51 (1970): 72, n. 111.

109. Alliot, *Culte d'Horus*, vol. 1, pp. 233–34; see also D. Dixon, in *Population Biology of the Ancient Egyptians* (London, 1973), p. 440.

110. Klasens, *Behague*, p. 54 (Metternich, l. 171–72).

111. CT, vol. 6, 208–09.

112. CT, vol. 5, 30f.

113. CT, vol. 5, 31bd.

114. Borghouts, *Magical Texts*, p. 47 (§ 75); J. G. Griffiths, *Plutarch, De Iside et Osiride* (Cambridge, 1970), p. 534; B. H. Stricker, *MDIAK* 37 (1981): 465–67.

115. Borghouts, *Magical Texts*, pp. 41–42 (§§ 65–66); Borghouts, *OMRO* 51 (1970): 98 and n. 2; A. Erman, *Zaubersprüche für Mutter und Kind* (Berlin, 1901), p. 12.

116. Borghouts, *Magical Texts*, p. 41 (§ 65, bottom of the page). Concerning snakes, compare S. Sauneron, *Un Traité égyptien d'ophiologie* (Cairo, 1989), pp. 203 ff.

117. *Pyr.*, § 2083; Borghouts, *Magical Texts*, p. 42 (§ 66); on the plant, see S. Aufrère, *BIFAO* 86 (1986): 6–9.

118. CT, vol. 3, 234a ff.

119. Aufrère, *RdE* 34 (1982–1983): 19; CT, vol. 6, 250pq; W. Westendorf, *Festschrift für Jürgen von Beckerath* (Hildesheim, 1990), p. 253; p. 254, n. 3; Lefebvre, *Romans et contes*, p. 199 and n. 90; Book of the Dead, chap. 80 = Budge, *BD*, 177, 5–7. As to what people were not capable of doing, see Barucq-Daumas, *Hymnes et prières*, p. 500.

120. Assmann, *Der König als Sonnenpriester* (Glückstadt, 1970), p. 64; Assmann, *Sonnenhymnen*, p. 249 (12); p. 250, n. d; p. 269 (21).
121. Book of the Dead, chap. 65.
122. CT, vol. 6, 270h.
123. Ibid., 229a.
124. CT, vol. 2, 161a; Assmann, *Sonnenhymnen*, p. 146 and n. a; p. 153 (31); Barucq-Daumas, *Hymnes et prières*, p. 320, n. j.
125. This holds even when the androgynous creator-god is a woman, as in Neith's case (S. Sauneron, *Mélanges Mariette* [Cairo, 1961], pp. 242–44). This goddess is never depicted as being androgynous.
126. Lange, *Mag. Pap. Harris*, p. 32 (8).
127. Sethe, *Dramatische Texte zu altaegyptischen Mysterienspielen* (Leipzig, 1928), p. 57; J. van Dijk, *JEOL* 26 (1980): 13.
128. J. van Dijk, *JEOL*, p. 13, n. 22.
129. Lefebvre, *Romans et contes*, p. 186.
130. B. van de Walle, *JNES* 31 (1972): 82.
131. D. Betz, *The Greek Magical Papyri in Translation, Including the Demotic Spells* (Chicago, 1986), p. 39 (PGM IV, 94–153); J. F. Borghouts, *OMRO* 51 (1970): 38–39; J. G. Griffiths, *Plutarch, De Iside et Osirisde* (Cambridge, 1970), pp. 316–17.
132. Book of the Dead, chap. 183 = Budge, *BD*, 485, 2–4.
133. Goyon, *Kêmi* 6 (1936): 14. See also above, p. 30.
134. Lange, *Mag. Pap. Harris*, p. 62 (8); Borghouts, *Magical Texts*, p. 88 (§ 129) [Kamutef]; Borghouts, *OMRO* 51 (1970): 125, n. 284.
135. Chassinat, *Khoiak*, vol. 2: 672 ff.; Barucq-Daumas, *Hymnes et prières*, p. 373, n. h.
136. H. Gardiner, *Hieratic Papyri in the British Museum. Third Series* (London, 1935), p. 12 (3, 7–8).
137. Lefebvre, *Romans et contes*, pp. 187–88.
138. Drioton, *ASAE* 39 (1939): 72, n. d.
139. Lefebvre, *Romans et contes*, pp. 195–96.
140. L. Griffith, *Hieratic Papyri from Kahun and Gurob* (London, 1898), pl. III; p. 4; W. Barta, *GM* 129 (1992): 36–37.
141. Bakir, *Cairo Calendar*, p. 16 (recto VIII, 9); p. 68, n. 6.
142. Lefebvre, *Romans et contes*, pp. 195–96.
143. See the texts compiled and collected by W. Barta, *GM*, pp. 33–38; add K. Mysliwiec, *ZÄS* 98 (1972): 92, n. 22.
144. This holds for CT, vol. 6, 258g.
145. CT, vol. 6, 333hj. The text states that a person who does not have a son may engage in this act with "the daughter of the phoenix." We do not have a very clear notion as to who is meant.
146. Gutbub, *Textes fondamentaux*, p. 12, n. ao; p. 13, n. ar; p. 79, n. ae (4°); p. 102, n. z; p. 103, n. aa.
147. Sauneron, *Esna*, vol. 5 (Cairo, 1962), pp. 64–66.
148. J. van Dijk, *Scripta Signa Vocis. Studies Presented to Prof. J. H. Hospers* (Groningen, 1986), p. 35, n. i.
149. P. Germond, *Sakhmet et la protection du monde* (Geneva, 1981), p. 61.
150. K. Sethe, *Übersetzung und Kommentar zu den altägyptischen Pyramidentexten*, vol. 3, p. 175 (ad § 632ab); F. Haikal, *Bibliotheca Aegyptiaca*, vol. 15 (Brussels, 1972), p. 51 (I, 9–10); M. Smith, *The Mortuary Texts of Papyrus BM 10507* (London, 1987), p. 62, n. 15(b).

151. M. Smith, *The Mortuary Tents*, p. 36, I, 14. On the premature death of Osiris, see R. O. Faulkner, *JEA* 22 (1936): 125 ( = P. Bremner-Rhind VI, 18).
152. The color of minium: see Vandier, *Jumilhac*, p. 114 (III, 12); see also p. 133 (XXII, 11) and p. 134 (XXIII, 16).
153. Goyon, *Dieux-gardiens*, p. 440.
154. Derchain, *Papyrus Salt*, p. 137. Compare Goyon, *Rituels funéraires*, p. 48.
155. Assmann, *Sonnenhymnen*, p. 217 (4).
156. Vandier, *Jumilhac*, p. 122 (§ 7); R. O. Faulkner, *Mélanges Maspero*, vol. 1 (Cairo, 1938), p. 340 (5,1 ff.).
157. CT, vol. 1, 307de.
158. Vandier, *Jumilhac*, p. 114 (III, 4–5).
159. Ibid., p. 121 (XI, 19).
160. B. Mathieu, *Hommages à François Daumas* (Montpellier, 1986), pp. 499 ff.
161. R. O. Faulkner, *JEA* 23 (1937): 167 ( = P. Bremner-Rhind, 22, 2).
162. Assmann, *Sonnenhymnen*, p. 189, n. c; CT, vol. 6, 270g.
163. Barucq-Daumas, *Hymnes et prières*, 227, n. cl.
164. On Re's nine ka, see CT, vol. 6, 228 f. For Ptah's four ka, see D. Meeks, *RdE* 15 (1963): 35–47; Gutbub, *Textes fondamentaux*, pp. 294 ff.
165. CT, vol. 2, 52i; vol. 6, 392n.
166. CT, vol. 2, 54de, io; vol. 3, 238cd; Assmann, *Sonnenhymnen*, p. 46 (51).
167. CT, vol. 5, 42d, 44c; CT, vol. 6, 207q–208a.
168. Bakir, *Cairo Calendar*, p. 44 (verso IV, 6); p. 45 (verso V, 10); A. H. Gardiner, *Hieratic Papyri in the British Museum. Third Series* (London, 1935), p. 59 (§ 11).
169. G. Goyon, *Kêmi* 6 (1936): 16.
170. R. A. Caminos, *JEA* 58 (1972): 217; Book of the Dead, chap. 175.
171. J. F. Borghouts, *OMRO* 51 (1970), passim.
172. Koenig, *PBoulaq*, p. 53.
173. Gardiner, *Hieratic Papyri in the British Museum*, p. 59 and n. 2.
174. C. E. Sander-Hansen, *Die Texte der Metternichstele* (Copenhagen, 1956), pp. 20 ff. (Spruch III).
175. CT, chap. 157 = Book of the Dead, chap. 112.
176. E. Suys, *Orientalia* 3 (1934): 72, 74.
177. CT, vol. 7, 20b; P. Kaplony, *Mitteilungen des Instituts für Orientforschung* 11 (1966): 149, n. 56. Let us recall that this god's sacred animal was the shrew, which is born blind and has such poor eyesight that it does not always manage to find the entrance to its own burrow. See E. Brunner-Traut, "Spitzmaus und Ichneumon als Tiere des Sonnengottes," *Göttinger Nachrichten*, 1965/7, pp. 128, 150.
178. J. de Morgan, *Kom Ombos* (Vienna, 1902), no. 950; see also a number of remarks by Gutbub, *Textes fondamentaux*, p. 95, n. o.
179. For example, A. H. Gardiner, *The Ramesseum Papyri* (Oxford, 1955), p. 14 and n. 3.
180. CT, vol. 6, 342i; CT, vol. 4, 76b.
181. CT, vol. 5, 323b, 326a.
182. A. M. Blackman and H. W. Fairman, *JEA* 29 (1943): 13(g).
183. C. E. Sander-Hansen, *Die Texte der Metternichstele* (Copenhagen, 1956), p. 61 (l. 170).
184. J. F. Borghouts, *OMRO* 51 (1970): 25–26.
185. Borghouts, *Magical Texts*, p. 43 (§ 69) = J. W. Barns, *Five Ramesseum Papyri* (Oxford, 1956), pl. 13 (B 25).
186. J. F. Borghouts, *OMRO* 51 (1970): 26.

187. Borghouts, *Magical Texts*, p. 43 (§ 69) = J. W. Barns, *Five Ramesseum Papyri*, pl. 13 (B. 26–27).

188. Borghouts, *Magical Texts*, pp. 43 (§ 69); 60.

189. Vandier, *Jumilhac*, pp. 113–14.

190. D. Kurth, in *The Intellectual Heritage of Egypt: Studies Presented to L. Kákosy* (Budapest, 1992), p. 379.

191. J.-C. Goyon, *BIFAO* 75 (1975): 384 [220, 8–11].

192. CT, chap. 158 = Book of the Dead, chap. 113; C. Sturtewagen, *ASAE* 69 (1983): 244–45.

193. Lefebvre, *Romans et contes*, p. 196. One even finds references to the "four hands of Horus." S. Schott, "Die Reinigung Pharaos in einem memphitischen Tempel," *Göttinger Nachrichten*, 1957/3, p. 62.

194. Vandier, *Jumilhac*, p. 125; P. Derchain, *RdE* 41 (1990): 17–23.

195. As early as the Pyramid Texts, the restitution of the eyes is associated with the restoration of the king's forces; see R. Anthes, *Studia aegyptiaca* 9 (1983): 121, and G. Rudnitzky, *Die Aussage über das "Auge des Horus"* (Copenhagen, 1956), pp. 50–51.

196. J. F. Borghouts, *Studien zu Sprache und Religion Aegyptens*, vol. 2 (Göttingen, 1984), p. 711 (13) = CT, vol. 6, 220h.

197. Lefebvre, *Romans et contes*, p. 192. On this legend, see also Aufrère, *L'Univers minéral*, pp. 384–87.

198. Vandier, *Jumilhac*, p. 124 (XII, 23 ff.) and n. 369.

199. Lefebvre, *Romans et contes*, pp. 194–95.

200. See the references in J. Berlandini, *BIFAO* 83 (1983): 43.

201. J. F. Borghouts, *OMRO* 51 (1970): 18 and n. 102; L. Kákosy, *Acta Antiqua Academiae Scientiarum Hungaricae* 19 (1971): 162 (IV, 5).

202. Book of the Dead, chap. 96.

203. Hornung, *Himmelskuh*, p. 37 (verse 11).

204. Vandier, *Jumilhac*, p. 125 (XIII, 19).

205. For example, S. Cauville, *BIFAO* 90 (1990): 87, 93–94 (n. 9 and 10).

206. J. F. Borghouts, *OMRO* 51 (1970): 31.

207. Goyon, *Rituels funéraires*, p. 285 and n. 2.

208. CT, vol. 2, 215b–217b = R. H. O'Connell, *JEA* 69 (1983): 73.

209. T. Bardinet, *Dents et mâchoires dans les représentations religieuses et la pratique médicale de l'Egypte ancienne* (Rome, 1990), pp. 134–35; S. Sauneron, *Un traité égyptien d'ophiologie* (Cairo, 1989), p. 58, n. 6.

210. C. de Wit, *ZÄS* 99 (1973): 41–48.

211. Klasens, *Behague*, p. 10 (Metternich, l. 50).

212. Vandier, *Jumilhac*, p. 117 (VI, 11 ff.). On this procedure, see above, p. 55.

213. Griffiths, *Plutarch, De Iside et Osiride*, pp. 134–35 (§ 12); pp. 292–93.

214. See J. F. Borghouts, *OMRO* 51 (1970): 139, n. 1. Compare R. O. Faulkner, *JEA* 22 (1936): 125 (P. Bremner-Rhind VI, 16); S. Cauville, *BIFAO* 90 (1990): 93, n. 9.

215. F. Haikal, *Bibliotheca aegyptiaca* XV (Brussels, 1972): 54 (II, 24–25).

216. Posener, *Catalogue des ostraca hiératiques littéraires*, vol. 2, no. 1227 (recto 2–3).

217. *Pyr.*, § 1961c ( = R. O. Faulkner, *The Ancient Egyptian Pyramid Texts* [Oxford, 1969], p. 48) = CT, vol. 7, 197b.

218. S. Cauville, *BIFAO* 90 (1990): 91, 114.

219. A. H. Gardiner, *The Library of A. Chester Beatty. Description of a Hieratic Papyrus* (London, 1931), p. 23, n. 1.

220. S. Sauneron, *Esna*, vol. 5 (Cairo, 1962), p. 266.

221. *Urk.*, vol. 6: 105, 21.

222. F. Herbin, *BIFAO* 88 (1988): 103.

223. S. Sauneron, *Un traité égyptien d'ophiologie* (Cairo, 1989), p. 58, n. 6.

224. R. O. Faulkner, *JEA* 22 (1936): 123 ( = P. Bremner-Rhind I, 10 ff.) Compare Faulkner, *Mélanges Maspero*, vol. 1 (Cairo, 1938): 339.

225. Lefebvre, *Romans et contes*, p. 186.

226. Barucq-Daumas, *Hymnes et prières*, p. 188.

227. Ibid., p. 342 and n. b.

228. B. van de Walle, *JNES* 31 (1972): 80, n. k (Thoth); *Urk.*, vol. 6: 39, 4 (Seth).

229. J. Bergman, *Mélanges Gutbub* (Montpellier, 1984), p. 7. On the word "old" applied to women, see J. Baines, *Fecundity Figures* (Warminster, 1985), p. 125.

230. CT, vol. 1, 259e; J.-C. Goyon, in *La magia in Egitto ai tempi dei Faraoni* (Turin, 1987), p. 61.

231. J. Baines, *Fecundity Figures* (Warminster, 1985), pp. 122 ff.; Baines, *JEA* 58 (1972): 304–5; Hornung, *Conceptions of God*, pp. 152–55.

232. Vandier, *Jumilhac*, p. 126 (XV, 5 ff.).

233. Ibid., p. 139 (§ XLVII).

234. Lange, *Mag. Pap. Harris*, p. 29 (3–5).

235. Koenig, *PBoulaq*, p. 113; p. 114, n. g.

236. Assmann, *Lit. Lieder*, pp. 87 ff.; Assmann, *Sonnenhymnen*, p. 140, n. c; p. 360, n. b.

237. CT, vol. 6, 414j; M. Gilula, *JEA* 60 (1974): 249.

238. Hornung, *Himmelskuh*, passim.

239. Gardiner, *Hieratic Papyri in the British Museum*, p. 88.

240. On the tomb of Re, see CT, vol. 7, 19hi; Assmann, *Sonnenhymnen*, p. 214, n. n, p. 242, n. i; for the tombs of Horus or Seth, see CT, vol. 6, 355 l; for Geb's tomb, see U. Kaplony-Heckel, *Aegyptische Handschriften*, vol. 3 (Stuttgart, 1986), 64 (156); 70 (179); Sander-Hansen, *Anchnesneferibre*, pp. 9–10.

241. See above, p. 31.

242. Vandier, *Jumilhac*, pp. 121, 136 (§ XLI); P. Derchain, *RdE* 41 (1990): 13–17.

243. F. Daumas, *BIFAO* 56 (1957): 44–45.

244. J. F. Borghouts, *OMRO* 51 (1970): 79, n. 1; U. Rössler-Köhler, *Kapitel 17 des Egyptischen Totenbuches* (Wiesbaden, 1979), p. 214 (Z.9); p. 240.

245. Borghouts, *Magical Texts*, p. 70 (§ 94).

246. Barucq-Daumas, *Hymnes et prières*, p. 106; compare *Pyr.*, § 581ac. On earthquakes as divine manifestations, see C. Traunecker, *Coptos* (Louvain, 1992), pp. 344 ff.

## Chapter 4. Spaces and Places

1. Assmann, *Sonnenhymnen*, p. 194 (7), p. 197, n. q; compare below, chap. 6, n. 5 below, where it is noted that the creator-god's head was already in the heavens before the disk found a place there.

2. Borghouts, *Magical Texts*, p. 81 (§ 118).

3. Bakir, *Cairo Calendar*, p. 32 (recto XXII, 1–3).

4. E. Suys, *Orientalia* 3 (1934): 75.

5. A. H. Gardiner, *Hieratic Papyri in the British Museum. Third Series* (London, 1935), pl. 61 (verso B 17, 5–6), p. 113.

6. Bakir, *Cairo Calendar*, p. 35 (recto XXV, 2–3).

7. J. F. Borghouts, *OMRO* 51 (1970): 174, n. 425.

8. C. E. Sander-Hansen, *Die Texte der Metternichstele* (Copenhagen, 1956), p. 64 (lines 206–7, 236); J.-C. Goyon, *BIFAO* 75 (1975): 392 [228, 12–15].

9. Koenig, *PBoulaq*, p. 34.

10. Barucq-Daumas, *Hymnes et prières*, pp. 176, 188.

11. See below, p. 56.

12. Bakir, *Cairo Calendar*, p. 23 (recto XIII, 10–11). This episode seems to be different from that of the trial.

13. Koenig, *PBoulaq*, p. 20, n. j and p; p. 77. Compare the chapters about the ferry in P. Barguet, *Textes des Sarcophages égyptiens du Moyen Empire* (Paris, 1986), pp. 340 ff.

14. J. Ray, *The Archive of Hor* (London, 1976), p. 11 (12).

15. R. A. Caminos, *JEA* 58 (1972): 218–19; above all, the Myth of Horus: H. W. Fairman, *JEA* 21 (1935): 28 ff.

16. Borghouts, *Magical Texts*, p. 85, bottom of the page.

17. Ibid., p. 56, top of the page.

18. Vandier, *Jumilhac*, p. 113 (I, x + 10).

19. See the remarks by J. Leclant, *Syria* 37 (1960): 15–18; A. P. Zivie, *Mélanges Mokhtar*, vol. 2 (Cairo, 1985), 387 and n. 26. The Egyptian gods properly so-called were not depicted on horseback until the Late Period; even then, apparently, they were never so depicted in official places of worship.

20. J. Berlandini, *Cahiers de Karnak*, vol. 6 (Cairo, 1980), p. 238, n. 2.

21. G. Goyon, *Kêmi* 6 (1936): 19–20.

22. Ibid., p. 19, top of the page.

23. Ibid., p. 20.

24. On Pe, see R. A. Caminos, *JEA* 58 (1972): 218. On Thebes, Heliopolis, and Memphis, see E. Suys, *Orientalia* 3 (1934): 75. Examples could be multiplied.

25. W. Helck, *Hommages à François Daumas* (Montpellier, 1986), pp. 421 ff.

26. Alliot, *Culte d'Horus*, vol. 2, pp. 467, 812.

27. *Urk.*, vol. 6: 127, 15–16.

28. Borghouts, *Magical Texts*, p. 50 (§ 83).

29. Ibid., p. 51 (§ 83); p. 55 (§ 86); p. 77 (§ 108). Compare CT, vol. 1, 278i–279c. See further Lefebvre, *Romans et contes*, p. 190 ( = Horus-Seth, 5, 10).

30. R. A. Caminos, *JEA* 58 (1972): 219.

31. F. de Cénival, *Le Mythe de l'œil du soleil* (Sommerhausen, 1988), p. 13.

32. E. Suys, *Orientalia* 3 (1934): 65: "Seth had left his house."

33. Jelinkova, *Djed-Her*, p. 28 (lines 55–56).

34. Book of the Dead, chaps. 145 and 146 = Budge, *BD*, 338, 5 ff.; 352, 4 ff.

35. G. Goyon, *Kêmi* 6 (1936): 8 ff.

36. CT, vol. 5, 257c, where mention is made of a room with columns in which there are butcher shops.

37. Alliot, *Culte d'Horus*, vol. 2, p. 745. The deceased could not build his house without Osiris's consent: Book of the Dead, chap. 152; Budge, *BD*, 388, 13 ff.

38. Lange, *Mag. Pap. Harris*, p. 14 (I, 7); Hornung, *Himmelskuh*, p. 37 (verse 19).

39. Jelinkova, *Djed-Her*, p. 74 and n. 6.

40. See above, chap. III, p. 62 and n. 79.

41. CT, vol. 6, 139k; vol. 7, 216c; *Pyr.*, § 1184–85. Compare futher J. F. Borghouts, in *La magia in Egitto ai tempi dei Faraoni* (Turin, 1987), p. 264, where Nemty defines himself as a jar full of arrows.

42. CT, vol. 2, 217ce; R. H. O'Connell, *JEA* 69 (1983): 73–74; Sander-Hansen, *Die Texte der Metternichstele*, p. 62 (lines 185–86). For general considerations on the thicket, see the comments by J. F. Borghouts, *OMRO* 51 (1970): 79, n. 118.

43. R. O. Faulkner, *JEA* 22 (1936): 126; P. Bremner-Rhind VII, 10.

44. Borghouts, *Magical Texts*, p. 59 (§ 90), p. 62 (§ 91); Sander-Hansen, *Die Texte der Mettermichstele*, p. 36 (line 50) = Klasens, *Behague*, p. 10.

45. E. Chassinat, *Le temple d'Edfou*, vol. 6 (Cairo, 1931), 214, 10; 220, 3 = D. Kurth, in *The Intellectual Heritage of Egypt: Studies Presented to L. Kákosy* (Budapest, 1992), pp. 374, 379.

46. Sander-Hansen, *Die Texte der Mettermichstele*, p. 60 (line 169).

47. Borghouts, *Magical Texts*, p. 60.

48. Ibid., p. 65; S. Sauneron, *Un Traité égyptien d'ophiologie* (Cairo, 1989), p. 106.

49. Klasens, *Behague*, 64; Borghouts, *Magical Texts*, pp. 60 ff. For the "bad woman," one should perhaps see R. O. Faulkner, *JEA* 22 (1936): 126 ( = P. Bremner-Rhind VII, 19).

50. Borghouts, *Magical Texts*, p. 63 (Metternich, lines 176 ff.).

51. Ibid., p. 68.

52. Hornung, *Himmelskuh*, p. 37 (verses 17–18).

53. Assmann, *Lit. Lieder*, pp. 86–87.

54. CT, vol. 3, 335j.

55. Barucq-Daumas, *Hymnes et prières*, p. 319 and n. d; Piankoff, *Quererets*, p. 18, bottom of the page; pl. XIV, 3.

56. Assmann, *Sonnenhymnen*, p. 194 (2).

57. Ibid., p. 203 (8–9), p. 205, notes d–e.

58. On this point, see also Barucq-Daumas, *Hymnes et prières*, p. 192 (I, 2).

59. Assmann, *Sonnenhymnen*, p. 250, n. i; CT, vol. 1, 12c.

60. Borghouts, *Magical Texts*, p. 66.

61. R. O. Faulkner, *JEA* 22 (1936): 123 ( – P. Bremner-Rhind II, 2–3).

62. CT, vol. 7, 220f.

63. CT, vol. 2, 110c.

64. Sander-Hansen, *Anchnesneferibre*, pp. 115–16.

65. J. F. Borghouts, *OMRO* 51 (1970): 25, 123, n. 273.

66. Bakir, *Cairo Calendar*, p. 47 (Verso VII, 12–VIII, 1).

67. As in the tale of Khensemhab; see J. v. Beckerath, *ZÄS* 119 (1992): 90–107.

68. CT, vol. 2, 112a.

69. M. Smith, *Enchoria* 16 (1988): 60 (13–14). See also the last paragraph of the Book of the Dead, chap. 100; Budge, *BD*, 211, 12–13; and Goyon, *Rituels funéraires*, pp. 61, 220, 254. H. De Meulenaere, *CdE* 63 (1988): 240–41.

70. CT, vol. 4, 88f ff.

71. Borghouts, *Magical Texts*, p. 70, bottom of the page.

72. Assmann, *Sonnenhymnen*, p. 143, bottom of the page.

73. G. Posener, *Le Papyrus Vandier* (Cairo, 1985), pp. 62, 64.

74. Ibid., pp. 69–70.

75. Bakir, *Cairo Calendar*, p. 43 (verso III, 4–5).

76. Posener, *Papyrus Vandier*, pp. 65 ff.

77. M. Smith, *The Mortuary Texts of Papyrus BM 10507* (London, 1987), p. 36 (line 16). See also p. 63.

78. F. Haikal, *Bibliotheca Ægyptiaca*, vol. 15 (Brussels, 1972), 20 (III, 1 ff.).

79. See above, chap. 3, n. 131.

80. CT, vol. 1, 242 bc.

81. Lefebvre, *Romans et contes*, pp. 200–201.

82. J. F. Borghouts, *OMRO* 51, no. 20 (1970): 25.
83. Alluded to in Lange, *Mag. Pap. Harris*, p. 29 (III, 12).
84. CT, vol. 4, 68b, 70c ff., and Book of the Dead, chap. 78.
85. CT, vol. 4, 76i ff.
86. CT, vol. 4, 86b, j–m.
87. If one is to believe CT, vol. 7, 371bc. See above, p. 55, on the necessity of the attribute.
88. Barucq-Daumas, *Hymnes et prières*, p. 355; K. A. Kitchen, *Ramesside Inscriptions*, vol. 2: 483, 3; K. Sethe, *Thebanische Tempelinschriften aus Griechisch-römischer Zeit* (Berlin, 1957), p. 104b. See also J. E. Reymond, *The Mythical Origins of the Egyptian Temple* (Manchester, 1969), p. 66.
89. H. Te Velde, Seth, *God of Confusion* (Leiden, 1967), pp. 109 ff. On Seth's exile, see *Urk.*, vol. 6: 12, § 9.
90. Koenig, *PBoulaq*, p. 60.
91. J. F. Borghouts, *OMRO* 51 (1970): 155, n. 374; Koenig, *PBoulaq*, pp. 60, 65.
92. E. Chassinat, *Le Temple d'Edfou*, vol. 6 (Cairo, 1931): 21, 3–4; Lefebvre, *Romans et contes*, p. 194.
93. E. Chassinat, *Le Temple d'Edfou*, pp. 20–25.
94. Koenig, *PBoulaq*, p. 88; see also Koenig, *RdE* 38 (1987): 106–07.
95. H. D. Betz, *The Greek Magical Papyri in Translation, Including the Demotic Spells* (Chicago, 1986), p. 247.
96. G. Goyon, *Kêmi* 6 (1936): 11; *Urk.*, vol. 6: 16 ff.
97. Bakir, *Cairo Calendar*, p. 19 (recto IX, 6–7; verso I, 3); Goyon, *Confirmation*, p. 90, n. 58bis; H. W. Fairman, *JEA* 21 (1935): 28 (Horus in Nubia).
98. For the connection between Punt and the sun, as well as the region's being in the southeast, see below, pp. 113–14. On Khons's (the moon's) lying down to sleep there, see CT, vol. 3, 90ef, 114de.
99. Alliot, *Culte d'Horus*, vol. 2: 641, n. 1.
100. On this change, see below, pp. 50–51. On Egyptian temples in Canaan and the Sinai, see S. Wimmer, *Studies in Egyptology Presented to Miriam Lichtheim*, vol. 2 (Jerusalem, 1990), pp. 1065–1106.
101. Lefebvre, *Romans et contes*, pp. 225–32. A foreign king could send a divine statuette to Egypt to similar ends; see above, pp. 50–51 and editorial n. 93.
102. J. Ray, *The Archive of Hor* (London, 1976), p. 11 (lines 12–13); p. 13, n. u, p. 155 (a, 2).
103. M. Lichtheim, *Ancient Egyptian Literature*, vol. 3 (Berkeley, 1980), pp. 152 ff.
104. Sander-Hansen, *Anchnesneferibre*, p. 136.
105. Hornung, *Conceptions of God*, p. 169.
106. D. Meeks, *Bulletin du cercle lyonnais d'égyptologie Victor-Loret* 4 (1990): 40–41.
107. On the topography of the Nun, see J.-F. Pépin, *Akten des vierten internationalen Ägyptologen-Kongresses, München 1985*, vol. 3 (Hamburg, 1988), pp. 342–43.
108. Bakir, *Cairo Calendar*, p. 26 (recto XVI, 6–11). Cf. L. Troy, *The Religion of the Ancient Egyptians. Cognitive Structures and Popular Expressions* (Uppsala, 1989), pp. 130–31.
109. Hornung, *Himmelskuh*, p. 37 (verse 16).

## Chapter 5. Intelligence and Knowledge

1. K. Sethe, *Dramatische Texte zu altaegyptischen Mysterienspielen* (Leipzig, 1928), pp. 59–65.

2. P. Derchain, *RdE* 41 (1990): 16; the literal meaning of the expression used in the text is "to create mightily in the heart."

3. Cf. below, p. 96.

4. S. Sauneron, *Villes et légendes d'Egypte* (Cairo, 1983): 84–85; E. Hornung, *ZÄS* 100 (1974): 33–35. For a general consideration of Thoth's writings, see G. Posener, *Annuaire du Collège de France 1963–64*, pp. 304–5; *Annuaire du Collège de France 1964–65*, pp. 339–41.

5. Such documents can be obtained through prayer: Posener, *Annuaire du Collège de France 1964–65*, p. 339. On the knowledge transmitted by the gods, see J. Assmann, *Der König als Sonnenpriester* (Glückstadt, 1970), pp. 56–57.

6. S. Sauneron, *Esna*, vol. 5 (Cairo, 1962), p. 259.

7. See below, chap. 4, p. 82 and n. 8 in chap. 4.

8. F. Herbin, *BIFAO* 88 (1988): 103.

9. Vandier, *Jumilhac*, p. 114 (III, 17).

10. Hornung, *Himmelskuh*, p. 37 (verse 8); H. Beinlich, *Das Buch vom Fayum* (Wiesbaden, 1991), p. 149 [113].

11. D. Kurth, *Religion und Philosophie im alten Ägypten. Festgabe für Philippe Derchain* (Louvain, 1991), pp. 195–96.

12. CT, vol. 7, 222a.

13. R. A. Caminos, *A Tale of Woe* (Oxford, 1977), p. 50 and n. 3–4, makes the pertinent remark that the hieratic script used in certain manuscripts tends to make the hieroglyphic "sia," which somewhat resembles a scarf, look like a hand.

14. Koenig, *PBoulaq*, p. 57 n. c; Book of the Dead, chap. 80 = Budge, *BD*, 176, 11; R. O. Faulkner, *JEA* 24 (1938): 43; P. Bremner-Rhind XXIX, 27; XXX, 13. Cf. J.-C. Goyon, *BIFAO* 65 (1967): 99 (l. 38); Assmann, *Lit. Lieder*, p. 196 and n. 22–23; F. Daumas, *Mélanges Adolphe Gutbub* (Montpellier, 1984), p. 47.

15. M.-T. Derchain-Urtel, *Thot* (Brussels, 1981), p. 188, n. 9; J. Osing, *MDIAK* 47 (1991): 271, 272, n. b.

16. R. O. Faulkner, *JEA* 23 (1937): 167; P. Bremner-Rhind XXII, 13.

17. Koenig, *PBoulaq*, p. 68, 74; Borghouts, *Magical Texts*, p. 32 (§ 48).

18. Borghouts, *Magical Texts*, p. 2 (§ 3); p. 16 (§ 19).

19. B. van de Walle, *JNES* 31 (1972): 75, n. d.

20. Lefebvre, *Romans et contes*, p. 198; H. Goedicke, *JEA* 47 (1961): 154; D. van der Plas, *L'Hymne à la Crue du Nil* (Leiden, 1986): 99–100. Let us recall that the donkey is one of Seth's emblematic animals. According to the Demotic dream book, seeing oneself about to give birth to a donkey in a dream meant that one would give birth to a stupid child. See S. Sauneron, in *Les Songes et leur interprétation* (Paris, 1959), p. 37.

21. S. Schott, *ZÄS* 99 (1973): 20–25.

22. Koenig, *PBoulaq*, p. 94; G. Posener, *Catalogue des ostraca hiératiques littéraires de Deir el-Médineh*, vol. 2 (Cairo, 1972), no. 1227 (recto, 3). But see the remark in D. Kurth, H.-J. Thissen, and M. Weber, *Kölner ägyptische Papyri* (Opladen, 1980), p. 25, n. 13, to the effect that the sleep of the gods often closely resembled death and was a sign of disorder.

23. CT, vol. 3, 194j and frequently elsewhere.

24. Borghouts, *Magical Texts*, p. 3 (§ 7); Sauneron, *Les Songes et leur interprétation*, p. 21.

25. C. Cannuyer, *GM* 73 (1984): 13 and n. 2; Assmann, *Sonnenhymnen*, p. 196, n. l–m; R. K. Ritner, *JARCE* 27 (1990): 25–41.

26. L. Kákosy, *ZÄS* 117 (1990): 145 (B, 6); 150, n. l, for a bibliography of works on the subject.

27. *Lexikon der Ägyptologie* II, 763–64; J. Assmann, *Biblische Notizen* 11 (1980): 50, 55; Assmann, *Sonnenhymnen*, p. 124, n. k.

28. CT, vol. 1, 322b. Compare Barucq-Daumas, *Hymnes et prières*, p. 224 (IV, 20).

29. Koenig, *PBoulaq*, p. 91, n. b.

30. A. H. Gardiner, *Hieratic Papyri in the British Museum. Third Series* (London, 1935), p. 58 (VII: recto 4, 3); interpretation by E. Drioton, *ASAE* 39 (1939): 69; translations by Borghouts, *Magical Texts*, p. 81 (§ 119).

31. Koenig, *PBoulaq*, p. 120, n. d.

32. Lange, *Mag. Pap. Harris*, p. 57 (4–5).

33. What follows is based on Borghouts, *Magical Texts*, pp. 51–52 (§ 84). For a commentary, see Borghouts, in *La magia in Egitto ai tempi dei Faraoni* (Turin, 1987), pp. 271–99.

34. Klasens, *Behague*, p. 58 (spell V); Posener, *Catalogue des ostraca hiératiques littéraires de Deir el-Médineh*, vol. 3, no. 1603, 5–6.

35. Klasens, *Behague*, p. 15 ( = Metternich l. 57). For the two traditions taken together, see Borghouts, *Magical Texts*, p. 84 (Texte A).

36. Posener, *Catalogue des ostraca hiératiques littéraires de Deir el-Médineh*, vol. 1, no. 1066, 3.

37. Borghouts, *Magical Texts*, p. 53 (§ 84).

38. See also Gardiner, *Hieratic Papyri*, p. 118. For vestiges of the theme, see A. J. Festugière, *Hermétisme et mystique païenne* (Paris, 1967), pp. 89, 145.

39. Posener, *Catalogue des ostraca hiératiques littéraires de Deir el-Médineh*, vol. 2, no. 1212; compare Posener, *RdE* 16 (1974): 214.

40. J. F. Borghouts, *OMRO* 51 (1970): 148, n. 354; Jelinkova, *Djed-Her*, p. 19, n. 8.

41. B. van de Walle, *CdE* 42 (1967): 26.

42. Borghouts, *Magical Texts*, p. 74 (§ 102); Borghouts, in *La magia in Egitto ai tempi dei Faraoni*, p. 264.

43. Borghouts, *Magical Texts*, p. 46, bottom of the page.

44. Borghouts, *Magical Texts*, p. 55 (§ 86).

45. Lefebvre, *Romans et contes*, pp. 193–94.

46. See above, pp. 38–39.

47. G. Posener, *Annuaire du Collège de France 1963–64*, pp. 301–2.

48. J.-C. Goyon, *BIFAO* 75 (1975): 376.

49. Borghouts, *Magical Texts*, p. 84.

50. Assmann, *Sonnenhymnen*, p. 160, n. n.

51. H.-W. Fischer-Elfert, *Literarische Ostraka der Ramessidenzeit in Übersetzung* (Wiesbaden, 1986), p. 23.

52. W. Helck, *Urkunden der 18. Dynastie* (Berlin, 1958), 2091, 14; 2092, 2. Thoth also records Isis's magic formulas: see S. Sauneron, in *Le Monde du sorcier* (Paris, 1966), pp. 38 ff.

53. Book of the Dead, chap. 182 = Budge, *BD*, 481, 16.

54. Goyon, *Rituels funéraires*, p. 175.

55. On Thoth/sia, see Posener, *Annuaire du Collège de France 1963–64*, p. 302. For Thoth "who knows all" (*rekh tem*), see K. Sethe, *ZÄS* 57 (1922): 36, 13* (IVa, 18); for "he who knows" (*rekh sou*), see M.-T. Derchain-Urtel, *Thot* (Brussels, 1981), pp. 64–68.

56. M.-T. Derchain-Urtel, *Thoth*, pp. 51–63.

57. Borghouts, *Magical Texts*, p. 45 (§ 71).

58. P. Marestaing, *Les Ecritures égyptiennes et l'antiquité classique* (Paris, 1913), pp. 35–37; C. Froidefond, *Le Mirage égyptien* (Aix-en-Provence, 1971), pp. 285, 338–39.

59. Borghouts, *Magical Texts*, p. 65.

60. Derchain, *Papyrus Salt*, p. 140 (VII, 4).
61. CT, vol. 7, 193lm. Cf. S. Sauneron, *Esna*, vol. 5 (Cairo, 1962), pp. 39–40.
62. See above, p. 45; see also Koenig, *PBoulaq*, p. 29, n. g.
63. H. S. Smith and W. J. Tait, *Saqqâra Demotic Papyri*, vol. 1 (London, 1983), pp. 90 ff. In oracles, see C. Traunecker, *Coptos* (Louvain, 1992), pp. 380–82.
64. H. Altenmüller, *SAK* 16 (1989): 9.
65. Lefebvre, *Romans et contes*, p. 111 ( = Astarté 2x + 14); Goyon, *Confirmation*, p. 80 (XX, 19). See pp. 280 ff, below.
66. M. Lichtheim, *Ancient Egyptian Litterature*, vol. 3 (Berkeley, 1980), pp. 128 ff.
67. H. D. Betz, *The Greek Magical Papyri in Translation, Including the Demotic Spells* (Chicago, 1986), p. 174 (81); p. 176 (147).
68. U. Verhoeven and P. Derchain, *Le Voyage de la Déesse Libyque* (Brussels, 1985), p. 17 (G 1–2).
69. H. Te Velde, "Some Remarks On the Mysterious Language of the Baboons," in *Funerary Symbols and Religion: Essays Dedicated to Prof. M. Heerma van Voss* (Kampen, 1988), pp. 129–36.
70. Assmann, *Sonnenhymnen*, p. 49 (12).
71. CT, vol. 7, 473m.
72. Barucq-Daumas, *Hymnes et prières*, p. 355 and n. f.
73. S. Sauneron, *BIFAO* 60 (1960): 31–41; J. Černý, *JEA* 34 (1948): 121–22; Barucq-Daumas, *Hymnes et prières*, p. 352, n. b.
74. D. Meeks, *Revue de l'histoire des religions* 205 (1988): 444 and n. 78–79.
75. See above, p. 91.
76. Iamblichus, *Mysteries of Egypt*, VII, 5 (258).
77. According to P. Derchain, *Revue de l'histoire des religions* 161 (1962): 178–79.
78. Assmann, *Sonnenhymnen*, p. 71, n. e.
79. Zandee, *Verbum: Essays . . . Dedicated to Dr. H. W. Obbink* (Utrecht, 1964), pp. 47 ff.
80. Barucq-Daumas, *Hymnes et prières*, p. 293 and n. s.
81. Compare CT, vol. 4, 147no.
82. Koenig, *PBoulaq*, p. 105, n. b; S. Sauneron, *Esna*, vol. 5 (Cairo, 1962), pp. 268 ff.
83. A. Erman, *Zaubersprüche für Mutter und Kind* (Berlin, 1901), verso 4, 8.
84. CT, vol. 7, 214bc.
85. *Urk.*, vol. 6: 127, 3–4.
86. S. Morenz, *Religion und Geschichte des alten Ägypten. Gesammelte Aufsätze* (Weimar, 1975), pp. 328 ff.; Derchain, *Papyrus Salt*, pp. 9, 29; M.-T. Derchain-Urtel, *Mélanges Adolphe Gutbub* (Montpellier, 1984), pp. 55 ff.; Goyon, *Dieux-gardiens*, pp. 434 ff.; M. Malaise, in *Le mythe, son langage et son message*, ed. H. Limet (Louvain, 1983), pp. 97 ff.
87. Assmann, *Sonnenhymnen*, pp. 188–89, 190, n. d.
88. Borghouts, *Magical Texts*, p. 35 (§ 53).
89. W. Fairman, *JEA* 21 (1935): 28 ff.
90. Vandier, *Jumilhac*, p. 125 (XIV, 4).
91. Koenig, *PBoulaq*, pp. 108, n. l; 110, n. a.
92. G. Posener, *Annuaire du Collège de France 1963–64*, pp. 303–4.
93. CT, vol. 2, 380c ff.
94. G. Posener, *Annuaire de l'Institut de philologie et d'histoire orientales et slaves* 13 (1953): 470–71.
95. Book of the Dead, chap. 157; Budge, *BD*, 404, 8, if the translation is correct.
96. Assmann, *Lit. Lieder*, p. 222 and note.

97. According to CT, vol. 7, 204b, the meaning of which is uncertain.
98. Book of the Dead, chap. 182 and 183 = Budge, *BD*, 481, 1; 488, 14; Borghouts, *Magical Texts*, p. 45 (§ 71).
99. Lefebvre, *Romans et contes*, p. 186.
100. CT, vol. 4, 31a.
101. Lefebvre, *Romans et contes*, pp. 199–201.
102. Goyon, *Rituels funéraires*, p. 216; M. Smith, *The Mortuary Texts of Papyrus BM 10507* (London, 1987), p. 35 (I, 1).
103. Book of the Dead, chap. 130 = Budge, *BD*, 285, 7 ff.
104. Lefebvre, *Romans et contes*, pp. 192–93.
105. Derchain, *Papyrus Salt*, p. 139 (V, 9).
106. Ibid.; compare G. Vittmann, *ZÄS* 111 (1984): 167, n. e–f.
107. See above, p. 80.
108. H. Gardiner, *Hieratic Papyri in the British Museum. Third Series* (London, 1935), pl. 61 (IX: verso B 17, 8), p. 113.
109. CT, vol. 6, 74de; J. F. Borghouts, *RdE* 32 (1980): 33–46.
110. B. van de Walle, *CdE* 42 (1967): 24. But see also Jelinkova, *Djed-Her*, p. 19, n. 8.
111. Jelinkova, ibid., p. 61 and n. 8.
112. CT, vol. VI 284b.
113. Barucq-Daumas, *Hymnes et prières*, p. 472.
114. Borghouts, *Magical Texts*, p. 42 (§ 66).
115. See above, p. 97 and n. 20; A. M. Blackman and H. W. Fairman, *JEA* 29 (1943), 13(h).
116. J. F. Borghouts, *OMRO* 51 (1970): 117, n. 250; *Urk.*, vol. 6: 135, 6.
117. Borghouts, *Magical Texts*, p. 58 (end of § 87).
118. Ibid., p. 25 (§ 34).
119. Ibid., p. 59 (§ 90).
120. Ibid., p. 49 (§ 80).

## Chapter 6. The Machine of the Universe and the Universal God

1. Barucq-Daumas, *Hymnes et prières*, p. 175. This is a version of the hymn in chap. 15 of the Book of the Dead.
2. See, for a general discussion, S. Sauneron and J. Yoyotte, *La Naissance du monde* [Sources Orientales 1] (Paris, 1959), pp. 19–91.
3. Neugebauer-Parker, *EAT*, vol. 1, p. 52.
4. See above, p. 18.
5. Barucq-Daumas, *Hymnes et prières*, p. 295; compare chap. 4, p. 81 and n. 1 above.
6. Barucq-Daumas, *Hymnes et prières*, pp. 261, 298.
7. E. Otto, "Das 'Goldene Zeitalter,'" in *Religions en Egypte hellénistique et romaine* (Paris, 1969), pp. 93–108. The first allusions to this golden age are perhaps those in P. Barguet, *Textes des Sarcophages égyptiens du Moyen Empire* (Paris, 1987), p. 269 (chap. 162).
8. S. Sauneron and J. Yoyotte, *Naissance du Monde*, p. 54, doc. 13–14.
9. Barguet, *Textes des Sarcophages*, p. 204 (chap. 640).
10. P. Derchain, *RdE* 27 (1975): 110–16.
11. See above, p. 78.
12. See below, pp. 117–19.
13. Neugebauer-Parker, *EAT*, vol. 3, p. 5; *EAT*, vol. 1, pp. 43–44.

14. Various depictions of Nut appear in a number of royal tombs in the region of Thebes, especially the tombs of Ramses IV, Ramses VI, and Ramses IX. See F. Daumas, *ASAE* 51 (1951): 351, n. 2.

15. Piankoff, *Livre du Jour et de la Nuit*, pp. xi–xii, fig. 2.

16. A. Piankoff, *La Création du disque solaire* (Cairo, 1953), p. 32.

17. Neugebauer-Parker, *EAT*, vol. 3, p. 5; vol. 1, pp. 119–20.

18. Gods of this sort have been described as "special" gods; see Hornung, *Conceptions of God*, p. 69 and note 14. Compare the scene of the beginning of the bark's journey with the description given of it in the *Book of Caverns*, p. 162 below.

19. Piankoff, *Livre du Jour et de la Nuit*, p. 3.

20. Hornung, *Conceptions of God*, p. 277; see H. Te Velde, *JEOL* 21 (1970): 175–86. On these three individuals and the capacities they embody, see also above, p. 162.

21. This idea is more fully developed in the *Book of Caverns*, which we analyze below, pp. 151 ff.

22. Piankoff, *Livre du Jour et de la Nuit*, p. 10, top of the page.

23. Ibid., pp. 10–11.

24. For a general treatment of this place, see R. Weill, *Le Champ des roseaux et le champ des offrandes dans la religion funéraire et la religion générale* (Paris, 1936). This region has its earthly location in the Eastern Delta. In the sky, however, the geography of the heavens and the majority of existing traditions situate it toward the west. Piankoff, *Livre du Jour et de la Nuit*, p. 12.

25. Piankoff, *Livre du Jour et de la Nuit*, p. 20; CT, vol. 2, 369b ff.; Book of the Dead, chap. 109. See also Book of the Dead, chap. 149.

26. Piankoff, *Livre du Jour et de la Nuit*, p. 13.

27. See below, pp. 142 ff.

28. Neugebauer-Parker, *EAT*, vol. 1, p. 82.

29. The oldest versions conflate the first and second hours; see E. Hornung, *Das Buch von den Pforten des Jenseits*, vol. 2 (Geneva, 1980), pp. 29–32.

30. H. Frankfort, *The Cenotaph of Sethi I at Abydos*, vol. 2 (London, 1933), pl. 81 (left).

31. Piankoff, *Livre du jour et de la nuit*, p. 32.

32. A similar stop, which perhaps also takes place at the middle of the night, is mentioned in the *Book of Caverns*; see below, p. 156.

33. See below, pp. 151 ff.

34. Neugebauer-Parker, *EAT* vol. 1, pp. 67–68.

35. B. Altenmüller, *Synkretismus in den Sargtexten* (Wiesbaden), pp. 192–93.

36. Barguet, *Textes des Sarcophages*, p. 202.

37. Neugebauer-Parker, *EAT*, vol. 3, p. 180.

38. Ibid., p. 140.

39. Ibid., p. 139.

40. See above, p. 39.

41. P. Derchain, *La Lune. Mythes et rites* [Sources Orientales 5] (Paris, 1962), p. 23 (§ 2).

42. P. Boylan, *Thoth, The Hermes of Egypt* (London, 1922), pp. 83–84; M.-T. Derchain-Urtel, *Thot* (Brussels, 1981), pp. 27–36.

43. P. Derchain, *La Lune*, p. 39, n. 106.

## Chapter 7. The Gods on Earth

1. What follows is based on Lefebvre, *Romans et contes*, pp. 84 ff.

2. About 21 inches.

3. Lefebvre, *Romans et contes*, pp. 87 ff.

4. On what follows, see H. Brunner, *Die Geburt des Gottkönigs* (Wiesbaden, 1964).

5. Ibid., p. 45.

6. See below, p. 184 ff.

7. In fact, the king ritually plays the role of a god: E. Hornung, *Eranos Jahrbuch* 51 (1982): 479–516. The king is in turn "played" by the priest: Goyon, *Confirmation*, pp. 14, n. 2, 18, n. 1.

8. Gutbub, *Textes fondamentaux*, pp. 32–33.

9. W. Helck, *Die Lehre für König Merikare* (Wiesbaden, 1977), p. 86.

10. Vandier, *Jumilhac*, p. 120 ( X, 8 ff.); Bakir, *Cairo Calendar*, p. 40 (recto XXX, 4).

11. J. Frandsen, "Trade and Cult," in *The Religion of the Ancient Egyptians: Cognitive Structures and Popular Expressions* (Uppsala, 1989), pp. 95–108.

12. On the obelisk as a primordial manifestation of the sun, see below, p. 197.

13. See below, pp. 168 ff.

14. See below, pp. 179 ff.

15. The construction of a temple takes place in accordance with a divine order addressed to the king: J. v. Beckerath, *MDIAK* 37 (1981): 47–48.

16. P. Montet, *Kêmi* 17 (1964): 78 (scene 3).

17. Ibid., p. 79.

18. E. Chassinat, *Le Temple d'Edfou*, vol. 2 (Cairo, 1898): 60, 13, for example.

19. A. M. Blackman and H. W. Fairman, *JEA* 32 (1946): 75–91.

20. H.-W. Fischer-Elfert, *Literarische Ostraka der Ramessidenzeit in Übersetzung* (Wiesbaden, 1986), p. 13 (1–2).

21. K. Sethe, *Dramatische Texte zu altaegyptischen Mysterienspielen* (Leipzig, 1928), p. 68 (lines 59–61).

22. G. Nagel, *Un papyrus funéraire de la fin du Nouvel Empire* (Cairo, 1929), p. 90 (line 11).

23. Assmann, *Sonnenhymnen*, p. 155, n. f; see also Helck, *Die Lehre für König Merikare*, p. 78, which seems to suggest that, beyond his statue, the god is as hard to grasp as the wind.

24. See J. Lipinska, *The Intellectual Heritage of Egypt: Studies Presented to L. Kákosy* (Budapest, 1992), pp. 387–88.

25. K. Sethe, *Urkunden der 18. Dynastie*, pp. 99, 15–17.

26. See above, pp. 17, 92–93.

27. Alliot, *Culte d'Horus*, p. 39.

28. Ibid., p. 42.

29. Ibid., p. 51.

30. In reality, the priest represented the king.

31. H. Nelson and W. Murnane, *The Great Hypostyle Hall at Karnak*, vol. 1/1 (Chicago, 1981), pl. 227; A. Calverley, *The Temple of King Sethos I at Abydos*, vol. 2 (London, 1935), pl. 13.

32. A. Moret, *Le Rituel du culte divin journalier* (Paris, 1902), p. 37.

33. Alliot, *Culte d'Horus*, p. 54.

34. S. Schott, *Bücher und Bibliotheken im alten Ägypten* (Wiesbaden, 1990), p. 147 (386) = A. Calverley, *The Temple of King Sethos I at Abydos*, vol. 1 (London, 1933), pl. 17, 25; vol. 2 (London, 1935), pl. 3, 13. See also R. David, *Religious Ritual at Abydos* (Warminster, 1973), p. 94, n. 1.

35. Alliot, *Culte d'Horus*, p. 78.

36. Alliot, *Culte d'Horus*, pp. 54–55.

37. For a general discussion, see D. Kurth, *Den Himmel stützen* (Brussels, 1975).

38. H. Nelson and W. Murnane, *The Great Hypostyle Hall at Karnak*, vol. 1/1 (Chicago, 1981), pl. 72.

39. Ibid., pl. 9–11, 39, 77, 101, 107–65, 207, 226.

40. Alliot, *Culte d'Horus*, p. 91.
41. Nelson and Murnane, *Great Hypostyle Hall*, pl. 210.
42. A. Moret, *Le Rituel du culte divin*, p. 105.
43. Nelson and Murnane, *Great Hypostyle Hall*, pl. 51.
44. This may have been Montu or else Khonsu.
45. Nelson and Murnane, *Great Hypostyle Hall*, pl. 50, 78.
46. The Egyptian text uses the term "Ennead." Because there were fifteen gods involved in this case, "Ennead" is translated "corporation."
47. Nelson and Murnane, *Great Hypostyle Hall*, pl. 36.
48. Hornung, *Conceptions of God*, p. 136.
49. For a general treatment, see D. Kessler, *Die heiligen Tiere und der König*, vol. 1 (Wiesbaden, 1989).
50. Alliot, *Culte d'Horus*, p. 675.
51. D. Meeks, *Le Temps de la réflexion* 7 (1986): 189.
52. What follows is based on Alliot, *Culte d'Horus*, pp. 565 ff.
53. It is not always easy to determine where the ceremonies were celebrated (whether in the god's main temple or in the temple of the living falcon). The account given here is based on H. W. Fairman, "Worship and Festivals in an Egyptian Temple," *BJRL* 37 (1954): 189–92.
54. P. Germond, *Les Invocations à la bonne année au temple d'Edfou* (Geneva, 1986), p. 21.
55. P. Germond studies these supplications in *Sakhmet et la protection du monde* (Geneva, 1981).
56. Ibid., pp. 34–35.
57. Ibid., p. 41.
58. That is, who launch the sun on his course, and thus inaugurate the new year.
59. Alliot, *Culte d'Horus*, p. 620.
60. Ibid., p. 609.
61. Ibid., p. 622.
62. Ibid.
63. Ibid., pp. 625–26.
64. Ibid., p. 627.
65. Ibid., pp. 628–29.
66. Ibid., p. 630.
67. Ibid.
68. Ibid., pp. 637–38.
69. Ibid., pp. 639–40.
70. Ibid., pp. 639, 641.
71. Ibid., p. 642.
72. Ibid., pp. 646–47.
73. Ibid., p. 652.
74. Ibid., pp. 656–57.
75. K.-T. Zauzich, *Papyri von der Insel Elephantine*, vol. 1 (Berlin, 1978), no. 13547 (6).
76. E. Winter, *Der Apiskult im Alten Ägypten* (Mainz, 1978), p. 16.
77. Ibid., pp. 16, 19.
78. Ibid., p. 19.
79. Ibid.
80. R. Myers and O. H. Myers, *The Bucheum* 1 (London, 1934), pp. 11, 17.
81. W. K. Simpson, "A Running of the Apis in the Reign of Aha," *Orientalia* 26 (1957): 139–42.

82. Vandier, "Memphis et le taureau Apis," *Mélanges Mariette* (Cairo, 1961), pp. 119 ff.

83. This was not entirely the case at Buchis; see D. Valbelle, "Les métamorphoses d'une hyspostase divine en Egypte," *Revue d'histoire des religions* 209 (1992): 15. One needs to bear in mind that the oracular message is expressed in words when this god manifests himself.

84. G. Foucart, in *Encyclopedia of Religion and Ethics*, vol. 4 (Edinburgh, 1911), pp. 792–93; L. Kákosy, *Studia Ægyptiaca* 7 (1981): 144, n. 34.

85. H. S. Smith, "The Death and Life of the Mother of Apis," in *Studies in Pharaonic Religion and Society in Honour of J. G. Griffiths* (London, 1992), pp. 201–25.

86. Myers and Myers, *The Bucheum* 1, pp. 3–9.

87. D. Meeks, *Archéo-Nil* 1 (1991): 9.

88. J. Vercoutter, in *Lexikon der Ägyptologie*, vol. 1, p. 339, n. 11.

89. J. Vercoutter, *Textes biographiques du Sérapeum de Memphis* (Paris, 1962), p. 129.

90. Ibid., pp. 38–39.

91. This description is based on the representations to be found on two limestone relief fragments discovered during the excavations in the city of Memphis (M. el Amir, *JEA* 34 [1948], pl. XVII, 4).

92. J. Berlandini, *BIFAO* 85 (1985): 46–48, n. i. The hypothesis is based on a text, studied by the author, which states that the dances performed for the deceased took place in front of his tomb.

93. D. Meeks, *The Intellectual Heritage of Egypt: Studies Presented to L. Kákosy* (Budapest, 1992): 423–36.

## Chapter 8. The Gods of the Hereafter, the Gods in the Hereafter

1. "Seth has thrown him to the ground," *Pyr.*, § 972, § 1256ab, § 1500ab.

2. P. Barguet, *Textes des Sarcophages égyptiens du Moyen Empire* (Paris, 1987), p. 119 (chap. 74).

3. On the creation of the netherworld, see above, p. 87.

4. Alliot, *Culte d'Horus*, p. 515.

5. P. Barguet, *Textes des Sarcophages égyptiens du Moyen Empire* (Paris, 1987), p. 121.

6. See, among other sources, J. Assmann, *Maât, l'Egypte pharaonique et l'idée de justice sociale* (Paris, 1989), p. 73.

7. Barguet, *Textes des Sarcophages égyptiens*, p. 759.

8. Ibid., p. 625 (chap. 1035).

9. Zandee, *Death as an Enemy* (Leiden, 1960), p. 27.

10. Barguet, *Textes des Sarcophages égyptiens*, p. 632 (chap. 1053).

11. Ibid. p. 634 (chaps. 1062, 1064).

12. Ibid., pp. 585, 595, 612, 759 (chaps. 336, 433).

13. Barguet, *Livre des Morts*, p. 266 (title of chap. 181).

14. Barguet, *Textes des Sarcophages égyptiens*, pp. 585 ff. (chap. 336).

15. Ibid., p. 586.

16. Ibid., p. 587.

17. Barguet, *Livre des Morts*, pp. 203 ff. (chap. 147).

18. Ibid., p. 157 (chap. 125). What follows is drawn from the same chapter.

19. See J. Assmann, *Mâat*, p. 76.

20. Barguet, *Textes des Sarcophages égyptiens*, p. 188.

21. Ibid., p. 168.

22. Ibid., p. 188.

23. J. Zandee, *Death as an Enemy*, p. 160.

24. Barguet, *Textes des Sarcophages égyptiens*, pp. 203–04.
25. J. Zandee, *Death as an Enemy*, p. 201.
26. Barguet, *Livre des Morts*, pp. 160–61 (chap. 125).
27. J. Zandee, *Death as an Enemy*, p. 200.
28. Ibid., p. 201 (B 14 h).
29. Adopting the distinction made by J. Assmann, *Mâat*, p. 71, between those who attain to a life after death and those who are immortal.
30. P. Barguet, *Textes des Sarcophages égyptiens*, p. 242 (chap. 491).
31. Ibid., p. 246 (chap. 500).
32. Ibid., pp. 596, 662, 676.
33. Barguet, *Livre des Morts*, p. 145 (chap. 110).
34. P. Barguet, *Textes des Sarcophages égyptiens*, p. 629 (chap. 1048).
35. Ibid., p. 48.
36. Barguet, *Livre des Morts*, p. 42 (chap. 6).
37. Barguet, *Textes des Sarcophages égyptiens*, p. 163.
38. Ibid., p. 140.
39. Ibid., p. 186.
40. J. Zandee, *Death as an Enemy*, p. 26.
41. Barguet, *Textes des Sarcophages égyptiens*, p. 285.
42. Barguet, *Livre des Morts*, p. 131 (chap. 98).
43. Barguet, *Textes des Sarcophages égyptiens*, p. 583 (129).
44. Ibid., p. 590 (chap. 651).
45. Ibid., p. 664 (chap. 1130).
46. Barguet, *Livre des Morts*, p. 261 (chap. 175).
47. J. Osing, *BSFE* 123 (1992): 20–21.
48. Borghouts, *Magical Texts*, p. 7.
49. J. v. Beckerath, *ZÄS* 119 (1992): 96.
50. The following analysis is based on Piankoff's edition of this text, *Quérerts*, as well as on E. Hornung's translation, *Ägyptische Unterweltsbücher* (Zurich, 1972), pp. 311–424.
51. Piankoff, *Quérerts*, p. 7 and pl. I–II.
52. Ibid., p. 8.
53. Ibid., p. 8, bottom of the page.
54. Ibid., p. 9.
55. Ibid., p. 10, bottom of the page.
56. Ibid., p. 17.
57. Ibid., pp. 17–18.
58. Ibid., p. 19.
59. See above, chap. 3, n. 177.
60. See above, pp. 24–25.
61. Piankoff, *Quérerts*, p. 20.
62. Ibid., pp. 27 ff.
63. Ibid., p. 31.
64. Ibid., pl. XXXV (IV) = E. Hornung, *Ägyptische Unterweltsbücher* (Zurich, 1972), pp. 352–53.
65. Piankoff, *Quérerts*, pp. 37–38.
66. Ibid., pp. 42 ff.
67. Ibid., pp. 56 ff.
68. Ibid., p. 57; see also above, pp. 113–14.
69. Piankoff, *Quérerts*, p. 64.

70. Ibid.
71. Ibid., p. 66.
72. Ibid., p. 67.
73. Ibid.
74. Ibid., p. 72.
75. Ibid., p. 71.
76. Ibid., pp. 99 ff.
77. Ibid., p. 101.
78. Ibid., p. 105.
79. Ibid., p. 106.
80. That is, "He who is in the earth."
81. Piankoff, *Quérerts*, p. 107.
82. See above, p. 175.
83. A. Nibbi, *The Mariner's Mirror* 79 (1993): 5–26, with a review of the discussions bearing on these objects and a bibliography.
84. Piankoff, *Quérerts*, p. 121.
85. Ibid., p. 122.

## Chapter 9. From the Dead to the Newborn God

1. P. Barguet, *Textes des Sarcophages égyptiens du Moyen Empire* (Paris, 1987), p. 250 (chap. 486).
2. V. A. Donohue, *Antiquity* 66 (1992): 871–85.
3. She is mentioned only three times in the Pyramid Texts.
4. See above, p. 118; see also J. G. Griffiths, *Plutarch, De Iside et Osiride* (Cambridge, 1970), p. 34.
5. See below, pp. 178 ff.
6. *Pyr.*, § 1256.
7. *Pyr.*, § 1255–56, § 2144.
8. *Pyr.*, § 1280–81.
9. Griffiths, *Plutarch*, pp. 34–35.
10. *Pyr.*, § 1789.
11. *Pyr.*, § 835.
12. Other myths assert that it was Nut who revived him, as Thoth and Anubis are generally associated with mummification.
13. W. K. Simpson, *The Terrace of the Great God at Abydos* (New Haven, 1972), p. 12 (BM 575).
14. B. Kemp, *Lexikon der Ägyptologie*, vol. 1, col. 28–41.
15. A. Leahy, *JEA* 75 (1989): 55–59.
16. H. Schäfer, *Die Mysterien des Osiris in Abydos unter König Sesostris*, vol. 3 (Leipzig, 1904), pp. 9–42.
17. Ibid., pp. 10, 12.
18. Ibid., pp. 16–18.
19. See above, editorial note 6, and Schäfer, *Die Mysterien des Osiris*, p. 26.
20. Schäfer, *Die Mysterien des Osiris*, p. 30.
21. On Dendara, see S. Cauville, *BSFE* 112 (1988): 31, n. 11.
22. D. Arnold and M. Hopf, *Studien zur altägyptischen Keramik* (Mainz, 1981), pp. 85–87. Cf. A. Leahy, *Orientalia* 46 (1977): 424–34.
23. See M. J. Raven, *OMRO* 63 (1982): 7–34; D. Kessler, *Historische Topographie der Region zwischen Mallawi und Samalut* (Wiesbaden, 1981), pp. 263 ff.

24. History, 2, 171.
25. Chassinat, *Khoiak*, vol. 1: 69 ff.
26. For greater clarity, Egyptian measures have been replaced by their Anglo-American equivalents. A *hin* contains about half a quart, and a *deben* is the equivalent of about 3.25 ounces.
27. Chassinat, *Khoiak*, vol. 2: 766, col. 102–03, p. 767.
28. Ibid., p. 766, col. 106–7, p. 768.
29. Ibid., p. 766, col. 112–13, p. 768.
30. Chassinat, *Khoiak*, vol. 1: 64, 71; vol. 2: 614.
31. Chassinat, *Khoiak*, vol. 1: 57–58.
32. Ibid., p. 69.
33. Chassinat, *Khoiak*, vol. 2: 780.
34. S. Aufrère, *L'Univers minéral dans la pensée égyptienne*, vol. 1 (Cairo, 1991), pp. 339–40.
35. Chassinat, *Khoiak*, vol. 2: 780–81.
36. Ibid., p. 777. These precious receptacles are made of silver, gold, or bronze.
37. Ibid., p. 612; S. Aufrère, *L'Univers minéral*, pp. 337–38.
38. Chassinat, *Khoiak*, vol. 2: 774.
39. Ibid., p. 607.
40. Ibid., p. 606, col. 70. We have already encountered them on a number of occasions; see above, pp. 95, 115.
41. Chassinat, *Khoiak*, vol. 1: 205, col. 21–22.
42. S. Cauville, *BSFE* 112 (1988): 31.
43. Chassinat, *Khoiak*, vol. 2: 629 ff.
44. One must, of course, read "month" here and assume that the birth was premature.
45. Chassinat, *Khoiak*, vol. 2: 757, col. 97–98.
46. Ibid., p. 775.
47. Ibid., p. 756.
48. Derchain, *Papyrus Salt*, p. 38 (IV, 2–3).
49. Ibid., p. 95.
50. Ibid., p. 139 (VII, 1).
51. Ibid., p. 140 (VII, 10).
52. Ibid., p. 140 (VIII, I).
53. Ibid., p. 140 (VIII, 2–3).
54. Ibid., p. 140 (VII, 3–4).
55. As to the exact moment when this figurine was made, see ibid., pp. 62–65, and F. Herbin, *BIFAO* 88 (1988): 102–3.
56. Derchain, *Papyrus Salt*, p. 139 (VI, 1–3).
57. Ibid., p. 144 (XVII, 8–13).
58. Ibid., p. 90; compare the texts of the *Book of Caverns*, above, pp. 151 ff.
59. Derchain, *Papyrus Salt*, p. 144 (XVIII, 2).
60. P. Derchain, *CdE* 65 (1990): 222–23.
61. G. Posener, *Le Papyrus Vandier* (Cairo, 1985), pp. 31–33, pp. 73 ff.
62. S. Aufrère, *L'Univers minéral dans la pensée égyptienne* (Cairo, 1991), p. 342.
63. S. Ratié, *Annecy, Chambéry, Aix-les-Bains. Collections égyptiennes* (Paris, 1984), pp. 84–85.
64. J. Hani, *La Religion égyptienne dans la pensée de Plutarque* (Paris, 1976), p. 282, n. 2.
65. C. Favard-Meeks, *Le Temple de Behbeit el-Hagar* (Hamburg, 1991), p. 414.
66. S. Cauville, *La Théologie d'Osiris à Edfou* (Cairo, 1983), p. 12 (doc. 9).
67. Extending the conclusions of L. Pantalacci, *GM* 52 (1981): 57–66 and A. Egberts, *GM* 111 (1989): 33–45.

68. H. Junker, *Das Götterdekret über das Abaton* (Vienna, 1913), p. 19; Favard-Meeks, *Temple de Behbeit el-Hagar*, p. 428 and n. 1116.

69. Daumas, *Mammisis*, p. 310.

70. H. Junker, *Der Grosse Pylon des Tempels der Isis in Philä* (Vienna, 1958), p. 50

71. Favard-Meeks, *Temple de Beheit el-Hagar*, p. 429 and n. 1112.

72. Alliot, *Culte d' Horus*, vol. 2, p. 508.

73. Ibid., p. 460.

74. Ibid., p. 492.

75. Ibid., p. 499.

76. Ibid., pp. 498–99. Compare above, pp. 25–26.

77. Ibid., p. 501.

78. Chassinat, *Le temple d'Edfou*, vol. 2 (Cairo, 1898): 51, 9–15.

79. Cauville, *La Théologie d'Osiris à Edfou*, p. 55, doc. 36; Alliot, *Culte d'Horus*, vol. 2, p. 514.

80. Alliot, *Culte d'Horus*, vol. 2, pp. 518–19.

81. Or else a goat, as the text spells out; Alliot, *Culte d'Horus*, vol. 2: 520.

82. Ibid., pp. 521, 524–25; P. Derchain and J. Hubaux, *L'Antiquité classique* 27 (1958): 100–104.

83. Alliot, *Culte d'Horus*, vol. 2, pp. 543–44.

84. Ibid., p. 550.

85. Ibid., pp. 554–55.

86. This term is the phonetic transcription of an expression used in Coptic, the final stage of the Egyptian language; it means "place of birth." It is not quite the same expression as is used in the hieroglyphic texts, which refer to the temples as "houses of birth." See Daumas, *Mammisis*, pp. 15–20.

87. Ibid., pp. 431–32.

88. Ibid., pp. 261, 282.

89. D. Meeks, *The Intellectual Heritage of Egypt: Studies Presented to L. Kákosy* (Budapest, 1992), p. 431, n. 84.

90. Daumas, *Mammisis*, p. 200.

91. M.-L. Ryhiner, *L'Offrande du lotus* (Brussels, 1986), p. 183.

92. Favard-Meeks, *Temple de Beheit el-Hagar*, pp. 421–22.

93. See above, pp. 180–81.

94. See above, p. 121.

95. See the texts published by Daumas, *Mammisis*, pp. 43–54.

96. See above, pp. 181–82.

97. Daumas, *Mammisis*, pp. 403–4.

98. Ibid., p. 409.

99. Ibid., p. 437.

100. This is in line with the classical depictions of the ritual of divine birth, in which Isis, in her capacity as nurse, often figures in this position.

101. Daumas, *Mammisis*, p. 446.

102. H. Junker and E. Winter, *Das Geburtshaus des Tempels der Isis in Philä* (Vienna, 1965), p. 108.

103. Daumas, *Mammisis*, pp. 463–64 (as in the mammisi of Dendara).

104. Ibid., p. 464.

## Chapter 10. The Machine of the Universe Tottering on the Brink

1. See above, pp. 78, 113.

2. Goyon, *Confirmation*, p. 53 (I, 3).

3. Ibid., p. 53 (I, 5–6).
4. Ibid., p. 34.
5. Ibid., p. 87, n. 30.
6. Ibid., pp. 55–56.
7. Ibid., p. 56 (II, 1).
8. Ibid., p. 56 (II, 2 ff.)
9. Ibid., p. 57 (II, 9–10).
10. Ibid., p. 58 (II, 11–12).
11. See above, pp. 89–90.
12. Goyon, *Confirmation*, p. 59 (II, 19).
13. Ibid., p. 60 (III, 2–3).
14. In other words, the weary gods, as is explained in Goyon, *Confirmation*, p. 61 and n. 94.
15. Ibid., p. 61 (III, 7–8).
16. Ibid., p. 62 (III, 11–13).
17. Ibid., p. 63 (III, 18–20).
18. Ibid., p. 24.
19. Ibid., p. 72 (XVI, 6).
20. Ibid., p. 72 (XVI, 7).
21. Ibid., p. 72 (XVI, 9).
22. Ibid., p. 25.
23. Ibid., p. 72 (XVI, 10).
24. Ibid., p. 73 (XVI, 11).
25. Ibid., p. 115, n. 281.
26. Ibid., p. 27.
27. Ibid., p. 73 (XVI, 16).
28. Ibid., p. 74 (XVI, 16–19).
29. See above, pp. 173 ff.
30. Goyon, *Confirmation*, p. 78.
31. Ibid., pp. 30–31, 78. For the coronation of the living falcon at Edfu, see above, pp. 130 ff.
32. Goyon, *Confirmation*, pp. 78–79 (XX, 8–10).
33. Ibid., p. 79 (XX, 10–11).
34. Ibid., p. 125, n. 359.
35. Ibid., p. 125, n. 362.
36. Ibid., p. 80 (XX, 15–16).
37. See above, p. 191.
38. Goyon, *Confirmation*, p. 81 (XX, 22).
39. Ibid., p. 81 (XX, 25).
40. Alliot, *Culte d'Horus*, pp. 303 ff.; H. W. Fairman, *BJRL* 37 (1954): 83–89.
41. Alliot, *Culte d'Horus*, pp. 273–74.
42. S. Cauville, *Essai sur la théologie du temple d'Horus à Edfou* (Cairo, 1987), p. 90.
43. H. W. Fairman, *BJRL* 37 (1954): 184–85.
44. See the remarks by Cauville, *Essai sur la théologie*, p. 52.
45. Alliot, *Culte d'Horus*, p. 325.
46. See above, pp. 126 ff.
47. Alliot, *Culte d'Horus*, pp. 327–28.
48. Ibid., p. 337.
49. See above, pp. 187–88.
50. S. Cauville, *Essai sur la théologie*, p. 47.

51. Alliot, *Culte d'Horus*, pp. 349–50.
52. F. Daumas, *ASAE* 51 (1900): 373–400.
53. Alliot, *Culte d'Horus*, pp. 385–88; Cauville, *Essai sur la théologie*, p. 52.
54. Alliot, *Culte d'Horus*, p. 378.
55. Ibid., p. 410.
56. Ibid., p. 418.
57. Ibid., p. 412.
58. Cf. C. Zivie, *Hommages à Serge Sauneron*, vol. 1 (Cairo, 1979), pp. 477–87.
59. Sauneron, *Esna*, vol. 5 (Cairo, 1962), pp. 123, 127 (284, 3).

# Glossary of Major Gods

AKER: a Janus-faced genie who personified the earth in its physical reality and also ensured its cohesion. He was originally represented as a strip of earth with a human head at each end, but subsequently took on the form of a double sphinx. He was charged with guarding the exits of the netherworld and could be hostile to the deceased who attempted to gain entrance to it. Because of this function, he was considered a protector of Osiris.

AMUN: Principal god of the city of Thebes. His name means "the hidden one." He had obscure, humble origins: it is generally assumed that he was merely one member of the company of primordial gods of Hermopolis. From the Middle Kingdom onward, and above all in the New Kingdom, the dynasties of Theban pharaohs took him as their dynastic god. It was then that his cult acquired its full significance. His enormous temple in Karnak testifies to both the high favor in which he was held and the affluence of his priests. As a result of this favorable political climate, he became the chief god of the country: he absorbed the features of the creator sun-god in his person and accordingly bore the name "Amun-Re." (See also Atum.)

ANUBIS: Dog-god, or god with a dog's head, particularly responsible for embalming. In this capacity, he was charged with embalming Osiris, as well as with protecting his body both during and after it was embalmed. He was also the official guardian of cemeteries.

APIS: Bull worshiped since the Archaic Period in the city of Memphis. Initially he was associated with the king, taking part with him every year in a ritual race intended to guarantee the fertility of the country. Later, Apis was associated with the god Ptah, becoming his "spokesman." The oracles he delivered in this capacity were famous in the Late Period.

APOPHIS: Giant serpent who attacks the sun-god every day at different points of his journey across the sky. Each time, the sun-god defeats him with the help of various divinities who accompany him in his bark.

235

ATUM: Creator-god worshiped at Heliopolis. He represents the primordial aspect of the creator-god, finding his ideal solar counterpart in Re. Whereas Re represents the sun at the height of his daytime force, Atum is his senescent form; but he is ready to be reborn in Khepri, the sun coming into being. Under the name of Re-Atum, he becomes a model for all the gods who wish to display their creative nature. (See also Amun, and Creator-God.)

BASTET: Cat goddess of Bubastis who incarnates the peaceful aspects of dangerous goddesses such as Tefnut or Sakhmet. As Atum's eye, she is associated with the moon and protects pregnancies and births.

CREATOR-GOD: The creator of the world who awoke to life in the depths of the Primeval Ocean, Nun. With thought and the spoken word, he created the first elements of the structured universe and precipitated the emergence of the mound of solid land from which the sun, who was nothing other than an aspect of his person, could go forth to shine on the world. At Heliopolis, the primordial aspect of the creator-god was incarnated by Atum, and his solar aspect was incarnated by Re.

ENNEAD: Term that originally designated the nine gods of the Heliopolitan family, which included the members of the first three divine generations to appear after the creator-god. The creator-god, though part of the Ennead, is counted as extra; he is the tenth member of the Ennead and its leader. Based on this model, each temple could have its own Ennead, which would encompass the gods of the local family. In such cases, the number nine was not necessarily respected; Enneads formed in this manner could include a greater number of gods.

GEB: God of the earth, brother of Nut, the goddess of the sky. Aker is under his authority. As god of the spaces of the netherworld, he offers a kind reception to the dead, whom he protects. Within the Heliopolitan family, he represents a model of hereditary kingship.

HAPY: Personification of the Nile inundation. He is the genie par excellence of fertility and plenty.

HARPOKRATES: See Horus.

HARSIESE: See Horus.

HATHOR: Her name, usually translated "mansion of Horus," in fact designates the closed space through which Horus travels as sun-god. Hathor is above all a sky goddess who is often represented as a cow. She plays, vis-à-vis the sun, the role of protective, regenerative container, much like the role that Shentayit plays vis-à-vis Osiris. Also represented from ancient periods onward as a female countenance seen face-on, she symbolizes the face-to-face encounter between the sun and the element in which he appears at the moment of the creation. Thus Hathor can represent the solar eye, incarnating it more precisely in its appeased aspect. Daughter of Re, she usually is the wife of Horus.

HEKA: Inaptly described by specialists as an incarnation of magic, Heka personifies, above all, the life force, or ka, in action. As such, it is the expression of a kind of knowledge that is proper to each divinity and enables him or her to act on the basis of sia, intuitive, omniscient knowledge of all that exists. Human beings also dispose of this life force, which makes it possible for them to exist; thus they, too, can have recourse to heka. This heka enables them to communicate with the divine world, which bathes in the same energy. Heka even permits them, it was believed, to influence the world of the gods. In a religious or ritual framework different from that found in the temples, the use of heka thus made it an approximate equivalent of magic. (See also Hu and Sia.)

HEKET: Frog-goddess, consort of Khnum; at his side, she breathes life into the beings he creates.

HORUS: Name designating various divinities. The best known is Horus, son of Isis, conceived after the death of his father Osiris and summoned to succeed him on the throne of the gods after defeating his uncle Seth. Under the name of Harsiese, "son of Isis" precisely, he incarnates triumphant youth. The little, helpless child exposed to all sorts of dangers bore the name of Harpokrates, or "Horus the child," from the end of the New Kingdom onward. This child represents both the divine or royal heir who ensures the continuity of the royal function and the sun who is reborn every morning. Horus of Edfu (or Horus of Behdet) also is a sun-god and a god of kingship. These two aspects manifest themselves in him in fully mature form. The Elder Horus, god of Letopolis, is a solar divinity whose two eyes represent the sun and the moon. When these two heavenly bodies are invisible, the god goes blind and takes the name Mekhenty-en-irty, "He who has no eyes." When he recovers his eyesight, he becomes Khenty-irty, "He who has eyes." A warrior-god armed with a sword, he is especially dangerous during his periods of blindness. This Horus is the brother of Osiris and Isis but, under the influence of other gods of the same name, he can also be considered the son of Isis. The great sun-gods who bear the name of Horus are often represented as falcons or falcon-headed gods and are generally married to Hathor. In an absolute sense, Horus is the prototype of the earthly king.

HU: Personifies the emission of the creative voice by means of which the creator-god confers existence on all that he names. (See also Heka and Sia.)

ISIS: Sister and wife of Osiris. As a weeping widow, she carries out a long search to recover the scattered members of her husband in order to reconstitute his body. This operation makes possible the posthumous conception of their heir Horus. While bringing up her son in difficult conditions, she ensures the protection of Osiris's tomb and of the body that rests in it. As a result of these various activities, she gradually comes to be considered to play an important role in Osiris's rebirth. She is then assimilated to a number of different divinities whose role is to receive or regenerate the dead god, like, for example, Shentayit.

KHENTY-IMENTIU: Ancient god of the dead of the city of Abydos; his name means "He who is at the head of the Westerners," the Westerners in question being the dead. He is gradually absorbed by Osiris, until his name becomes little more than one of Osiris's epithets.

KHEPRI: Incarnation of the newborn sun coming into being, Khepri is represented in the form of a scarab beetle or a man with a scarab beetle in place of his face.

KHNUM: Ram-headed god whose task was to fashion living beings on his potter's wheel. In certain temples, such as that of Esna, in which he was an object of special veneration, he was also believed to have fashioned the primordial egg from which the sun sprang when the world began.

MAAT: Goddess personifying the integrity and equilibrium of the cosmos desired by the creator-god when he created the universe. It is by means of Maat that the unity of the created world is maintained. The gods nourish themselves on Maat, and men have to respect what she incarnates to ensure the regular return of the natural phenomena that guarantee life.

MIN : Ancient fertility god. He is represented in ithyphallic form, squeezed into a tight-fitting garment that gives him a mummiform appearance. The festivals during which his image was carried in procession heralded the harvest season. Lettuce was grown for his use; its whitish milk sap was thought to be an aphrodisiac. Worshiped in Koptos and Akhmim, he was also the protector of the trails that ran from the Nile Valley to the Red Sea coast.

MONTU: Falcon-god especially venerated in the region of Thebes. The conquering pharaohs of the New Kingdom liked to compare themselves to him. It was said that, in the thick of battle, they incarnated his irresistible warlike force.

MUT: Consort of Amun at Thebes. Her origins are as obscure as her husband's. Her name means "mother" and is written with the hieroglyph for "vulture." She seems to have inherited some of her traits from the vulture-goddess Nekhbet.

NEITH: Goddess of the city of Sais, represented as armed with a bow and arrows. She is one of the rare female figures in the Egyptian pantheon to be considered a creator. In this capacity, she was described as androgynous, two-thirds of her person being male, one-third female.

NEKHBET: Vulture goddess of the city of Elkab. She is the protectress of kingship in the South, as Wadjet is the protectress of Northern kingship. She is often represented in the form of a bird hovering over the king. She was also considered to be a maternal goddess who protected childbirth.

NEKHEB-KAU: Primordial serpent who ensured the cohesion of all the forces of life (the kas) in creation. He was believed to be immortal and to reside in the Primordial Ocean, Nun.

NEMTY: Official ferryman of the gods, responsible for transporting them from one riverbank to the other, he eventually came to demand a fee for his services. He could be influenced by offers of gifts and occasionally succumbed to bribery.

NEPHTHYS: Sister of Isis and wife of Seth. After the death of Osiris, who was assassinated by her own husband, she joined Isis in her misfortune and helped her perform certain tasks.

NUN: The Primordial Ocean that was all that existed before the creation, which drove him back to the periphery of the created world. He offers a refuge to both the negative forces that seek to win back the space occupied by creation and the positive forces that, like the Nile inundation, are essential to the proper functioning of the world. The creator-god, who rested in his waters before the creation, inert, will return to them at the end of the world, after having reabsorbed the whole of creation in himself.

NUT: Goddess of the sky, represented in the form of a woman arching over the earth while bracing herself on her fingers and toes. She was believed to swallow the sun in the evening and give birth to him in the morning. With her brother Geb, she engendered five children: Osiris, the Elder Horus, Seth, Isis, and Nephthys. These "Children of Nut" are also known under the name of "Children of Disorder" because of the disturbances their quarrels caused in the creation.

OPHOIS: Jackal-god whose name means "He who opens the roads." He went ahead of processions to clear the way for them, so that those following him would not encounter any hostile force.

OSIRIS: Dead god and god of the dead, brother and husband of Isis. He did not truly begin to exist until he was assassinated by Seth. Almost nothing is known about him before his death. When it is said that Osiris lives, the reference is always to his resurrection, which takes place in the hereafter, not in this world, definitively closed to him. The rites that make possible his resurrection ensure that the king, and, later, all the dead, will have a fate identical to his after death.

PTAH: Creator-god, patron of craftsmen, worshiped at Memphis. He is represented in human form, wrapped in a tight-fitting garment from which only his hands are seen to emerge. He is associated with Apis, his spokesman, with the funerary god Sokar, and, finally, with the primordial god Tatenen.

RE: The quintessential sun-god, worshiped mainly at Heliopolis. The sun is nothing other than the iris of his eye. Re is imagined traveling through the sky in his bark by day and shining on the residents of the hereafter at night. He is assimilated to Atum, of whom he is the highest solar manifestation. Every god who comes to assume a universal role as a result of political circumstances borrows solar and creative functions from Re.

SAKHMET: Lioness-goddess who incarnates the flaming eye of the sun. Her function is to annihilate the creator's enemies with her flame. A squad of fearsome genies are under her command. The dangerous forces that she incarnates are unleashed during the last five days of the year. During this period, people seek to appease her by reciting litanies, so as to prevent her devastating anger from jeopardizing the equilibrium of the world.

SECHAT: Goddess who patronizes writings and architectural plans. She counsels and assists the king during the construction of temples.

SELKIS: Scorpion-goddess with a fearsome sting. She protects Horus the child when he takes refuge in the papyrus thicket, but fails to prevent one of her sister scorpion goddesses from stinging the young god. Isis is able to cure him thanks to her magic powers. Several scorpion-goddesses who are emanations of Selkis would later be considered wives of Horus.

SETH: Bother of Osiris, whom he kills in order to seize royal power, which, in the normal course of things, should have been assumed by Horus. Many battles and a long court procedure were required before Seth could restore power to the legitimate heir. Seth was aggressive and pugnacious, but nevertheless rendered the sun-god an important service by defeating the monster Apopis. Seth's voice was nothing other than the rumbling thunder. Because he had murdered Osiris, Seth was gradually assigned responsibility for the cosmic troubles and was finally banished from the territory of Egypt in the proper sense. Never defeated, he continued to threaten the gods' peace from time to time.

SHENTAYIT: Originally a cow-goddess. Her name means "the widow," with reference to the dead Osiris. She incarnates the protective container in which Osiris is regenerated. Thanks to her special role, she is assimilated to Isis under the name of Isis-Shentayit. (See also Hathor.)

SHU: God of the air in the Heliopolitan family, he represents more precisely the space that permits the sun's light to be diffused. The creator-god charged him with separating heaven and earth by lifting his daughter Nut, goddess of the sky, into the heavens. He and his sister Tefnut were the first couple created by the creator-god, through a process of solitary procreation.

SIA: Incarnation of the gods' intuitive omniscience, which only the creator-god possessed in full. Along with Hu and Heka, Sia enabled the creator-god to imagine, enounce, and organize creation.

SOBEK: Crocodile-god, lord of the waters, fearfully voracious. Sobek's particular mission was to eliminate the enemies who lived in aquatic environments.

SOKARIS: Like Ptah, Sokaris was depicted with his body squeezed into a tight-fitting vest. He was the funerary god of Memphis. He was usually depicted as having a falcon head. Like Ptah, he was a patron of craftsmen. It seems, however, that the two gods divided their labors. Ptah seems to have been more closely associated with stone-working, Sokaris with metal-working.

TATENEN: His name means "the earth that rises." He incarnates the first solid land to have emerged at the beginning of the world. From the New Kingdom onward, he is associated with Ptah the creator under the name of Ptah-Tatenen.

TEFNUT: Sister and wife of Shu, with whom she makes up the first couple brought into being by the creator-god. A lioness-goddess, she also incarnates, as does Sakhmet, the solar eye. More specifically, she represents the goddess who goes into self-exile in Nubia. It is Shu who is dispatched to look for her, and Thoth is the one who, with his beautiful speeches, induces her to return to Egypt.

THOTH: Ibis-headed moon god. His connections with the moon make him the reckoner par excellence: he is the one who establishes the various divisions of time and thus the calendar. Good at making calculations, he is also the master of writing. It is Thoth who introduces the practice of writing, records events in the annals, and transmits knowledge. He assists the creator in governing the world and functions as a messenger or intermediary for the gods. He plays a leading role in the divine tribunal; it is Thoth who settles the conflict between Horus and Seth.

WADJET: Serpent-goddess of Buto. She is the protectress of kingship in the North as Nekhbet is the protectress of that of the South. She is often represented in the form of a cobra coiled around a papyrus stalk.

# Chronology

| | |
|---|---|
| Archaic Period | circa 3100–2700 B.C.E. |
| Old Kingdom | circa 2700–2200 B.C.E. |
| First Intermediate Period | circa 2200–2000 B.C.E. |
| Middle Kingdom | circa 2000–1750 B.C.E. |
| Second Intermediate Period | circa 1750–1550 B.C.E. |
| New Kingdom | circa 1550–1070 B.C.E. |
|   XVIIIth Dynasty | circa 1550–1295 |
|   XIXth–XXth Dynasties (Rameside period) | circa 1295–1070 |
| Third Intermediate Period | circa 1070–745 B.C.E. |
| Late Period | circa 745–332 B.C.E. |
|   XXVIth (Saitic) Dynasty | circa 672–525 |
| Ptolemaic Period | 332–330 B.C.E. |

# Index

Abydos, 165–68, 171, 174
acolytes, 46–48
Aker. *See* Double Sphinx
amulets, 134, figures 1, 16
Amun, 2, 184, figure 10; animal form of, 61; and sacred animal, 129, 132; and speech, 103; travel outside Egypt, 91
Amun of Xois, 29
Amun-Re, 2, 9, 184–86; ithyphallic form of, 128, figure 27; and king, 121–22, 129
Anat, 21, 50, 69
ancestors, 179–81, 183–84
animals: ape, 129, figures 2, 3, 16; as aspects of gods, 60–63; bull, 129, figures 3, 17; cattle, 84; crocodile, 129, 147, 159, 181, figures 3, 22; and the dead, 145; dog, 62; donkey, 21, 136; as enemies, 25, 74, 135, 195; falcon, 61, 129, 130–36, 140, 183, 192; hippopotamus, 24, 145, 181; ibis, 129; and king, 191–92; in lands of the gods, 84; language of, 102–3; *mesyt*, 192; passerine, 191, 192; pelican, 17–18; phoenix, 91, 161, 162; presence to gods of, 62–63; sacred, 129–40; sacrifice of, 195; scarab beetle, 61, 156, 162, figures 20, 22, 23; selection of, 130; size of, 63; transformation of, 61–62
*ankh*, 129, figures 3, 7, 12, 25, 26
Anubis, 54, 75, 95, 125, 178, figures 4, 16, 21; and the dead, 145, 146; and hereafter, 88, 155, 158, 161, figures 16, 21, 23; as Seth's son, 89; statuette of, 170
Apis bull, 129, 136–40
Apophis, 20, 48, 54, 115, 159, figures 3, 22

Astarte, 49–50, 67
Atum, 54, 159, 195, figure 21; and Apophis, 20, 21; body of, 57; and the dead, 143; eye of, 73; family line of, 29; and Horus the child, 85; and king, 129, 189; reign of, 30; and sacred animal, 132. *See also* Khepri; Re

*ba* (soul), 81, 158, 161, 195, figures 16, 17, 20, 23
Baal, 50
Baalat, 49
Babi, 42, 44–45, 48
Balamun, 128
Bastet, 35
Bastet-Sakhmet, 65
birth, 77, 78, 183, 184; and rebirth, 133, 134, 157, 159–63, figures 21, 22
Black Head, 153, figure 19
bodies of the gods: and aging, 79; and creative energy, 69–71; divine scent, 59; faces, 53–54, 55; facets of, 54; and illness, 71–74; influences on, 53; and nudity, 60, figure 3; recognition, 55; redoubling of, 79–80; restoration of, 72; secondary, 76–77; secretions of, 69–71; stature of, 58–59
Book of Caverns, 151–63, figures 18–23
Book of the Dead, 5, 7, figures 2, 16
Book of the Opening of the Mouth, 7
Buchis bull, 137
Busiris, 164, 166, 171, 172, 173
Byblos, 49

cannibalism, 138, 148
caverns, 151, 152
cenotaphs, 167

Chamber of the Bed, 171–72
Champollion, 1, 2, 183
Champollion-Figeac, 2
chaos, 72; and darkness, 21–22; as serpent, 17, 20
children of disorder. *See* Children of Nut
Children of Horus, 170, 177
Children of Nut (Children of Re), 24, 78, 113, 142, 178; as heavenly bodies, 117–18
Claudian, 19
Coffin Texts, 5, 14, 49, 59, 143
coronation, 74, 133–34
creation: and bodily secretions, 69–71; created space, 16–18; creative voice (*hu*), 103–4; creative words, 47, 103–4, 159, 185; and end of the world, 17–19; essential elements of, 14; first beings, 22; and *ka*, 71; primeval beings, 71; and Re, 111–12; three stages of, 14–15; and uncreated, 22, 90, 92–93
creator-god, 14, 18, 77, 159; acts of, 39; aging of, 112; body of, 58; and divine birth, 183; and equilibrium, 120; frailty of, 22–23; and Horus-Seth conflict, 41; and jubilees, 197–98; king as, 189; and physical identities of gods, 53–54; separation from humanity of, 26–27, 79, 113, 120–21; and Seth, 28; sexuality of, 66; and *sia*, 95; as sun-god, 54, figures 6, 11, 27; will of, 22, 33, 104. *See also* Re
cult, 80; funerary, 123, 136, 138, 189–90; of Horus, 104; and life, 37; of Osiris, 105; principal statuette of, 126

dead: *ba*-souls of, 148–49, 154, figures 16, 17; blessed, 18, 148, 149, 154, 157; damned, 144, 152, 155, 156, 160, figures 18–23; and enemies, 143–44; first, 16; as gods, 148–49; gods as, 79–80; and the hereafter, 87; hope of, 141; impersonation of gods by, 145; journey of, 141–46, 150; and knowledge, 150; and labor, 149; life span of, 18; and Re, 151–52; and reading, 145–46; and Re's bark, 149–50; spells for, 143; torture of, 153, 157; tribunal, 146–47, 154; weighing of, 146; written guides for, 142–43
Deir el-Bahari, 164
Demotic literature, 7–8
Dendara, 2, 171; festival of, 183–86; temple of, 169
Denon, Viviant, 2
Derchain, Phillipe, 4
Diodorus, 137
Djed, 173

Djer, 167
Double Lion, 90
Double Sphinx, 156, 157, 163, figure 20
dwarfs, 140
dynasties: Eighteenth Dynasty, 167; Eleventh, 169; Fifth Dynasty, 121; Fourth Dynasty, 121; Twenty-Sixth, 138

eating, 64–66
Edfu, 84, 128; clothing festival, 193–98; falcon, 130; festival of, 178–82; great Ennead of, 194–95
Egypt, 84–85; as eye of Horus, 14; and foreign countries, 90–93; and language, 103; as Two Lands, 28, 101, 131; and writing, 5
Egyptology, 4; anthropological approach, 4; classical authors, 1; contradictions in, 3; cultural bias in, 3; Greek view of, 1; material records of, 4–5; monotheism theory, 3–4; and multivalued logic, 4; polytheism theory, 1, 3; and Supreme Being, 1–2
Elder Horus, 18, 22, 23, 27–29, 78, 154, figure 19; blind aspect of, 24–25, 72, 157–58; eye of, 27–28; greatness of, 35; titles of, 40. *See also* Horus; Osiris
enemies, 19–22, 30; animals as, 25, 74, 181, 195; birds as, 92–93; and the dead, 143–44; punishment of, 20; and Re's journey, 159; and ritual, 134; and sacred animal, 135, 136; and sun's journey, 158
Ennead, 17, 26, 36, 112; as divine tribunal, 45–46; Great, 44, 129; of Heliopolis, 29; and judgment, 41; and king, 129; of Osiris, 193; Small, 44; and temple building, 124; of temple god, 132
equilibrium, 15–17, 30, 135, 159; and authority, 38; battles for, 19–22; and divine heir, 183; and Horus's eyes, 24; internal, 18; and prayer, 37
Erman, Adolf, 2–3
Esna, 197
Eudoxus, 137
eye: Hathor as Re's, 179; and knowledge, 95; solar (*udjat*-eye), 47, 48, 58–59, 76, figures 1, 2, 3, 22; as sun and moon (*udjat*-eyes), 72, 73, figures 3, 11; *udjat*, 134, figures 1, 2, 3, 11; vulnerability of, 72–73

Fields of Reeds, 115

Geb, 30, 50, 76, 98, 112, 196, figures 6, 11, 20, 22, 25; crowning of, 71; dwelling

Geb (*continued*)
place of, 81; and hereafter, 156, 159; and homosexuality, 69; and illness, 71–72; and king, 129, 190; and nudity, 60, figures 6, 11; and Osirian mysteries, 174; and procreation, 113; quarrels of, 27; reign of, 30–31; sexuality of, 66, 67, 78
genies, 48, 153; and the dead, 147–48; dwelling places of, 85; travel modes of, 83
Germanicus, 137
goddesses, 178–79; dangerous, 47, 99, 128, 131, 158; scorpion-goddesses, 86; Seed (Venom), 50; snake-goddess, 71–72. *See also* Bastet; Bastet-Sakhmet; Hathor; Isis; Sakhmet
gods: animal forms of, 60–63, 152; bodily secretions of, 65, 66; categories of, 33; clothing of, 59; community organization of, 39–40; dead, 18, 79–80, 154–55, 180, 184, 189–90; decapitation of, 24–25; diminished power of, 26; of divine tribune, 155; dwelling places of, 81, 85; and eating, 63–66; family groups (triads), 2, 36–37, 184; first battle of, 22–25; first generation, 14; foreign, 48–52, 83; functions of, 9, 50–51; Heliopolitan family, 123; hybridization of, 51; identity of, 209n.14; ithyphallic, 67, 128, 156, 159, 194, figures 3, 6, 20, 22, 27; king-gods, 122–26; lack of objectivity, 44; materiality of, 57–58; minerals of, 57; as mummies, 180–81; number of, 33; personalities of, 105–7; pragmatism of, 94; prayer and worship among, 37; ram-headed, 159, figures 6, 18–23; rank of, 23; regalia of, 59–60; regeneration of, 152; representation of, 125–26; second battle of, 25–26; sexuality of, 66–69; sleeping habits of, 97; subaltern, 35; travel outside Egypt, 90–93
Golden Age, 7, 16, 20
Great Bear, 115, 118, 124
Greco-Roman period, 51
guards, 47–48, 143–45, 158

Ha, 124
Hani, J., 1
Hapy, 55, 66
Harendotes, 104, 158, 178, figure 21. *See also* Horus
Harpokrates, 78, 185
Harsomtus, 183–84, 196
Hathor, 26, 165, 181–82, figures 24, 27; aspects of, 196; birth of, 78; body of,

60; as cow, 164; of Dendara, 178–80; and eating, 64; of Edfu, 193, 194; and foreign gods, 51–52; as Happy Year, 131; and hereafter, 88; and Horus-Seth conflict, 42; and king, 129, 131; as Lady of Inebriety, 179, 182; as Lady of the Boat, 115; and Re's eye, 179; and sacred animal, 132–33; and Southern Egypt, 131
Hatshepsut, 164
heavens, 117–19
Heka, 115, 186
*heka*, 96, 98, 100, 115
Heket, 121, 185
Heliopolis, 20, 89, 119, 189; Ennead of, 29; family of, 9, 44; and king, 192
hereafter, 82, 87–90, 142–50; basement register of, 152, 158, 160; and communication, 88–90; demons in, 152, 155; Duat, 161, 184; executioners in, 147, 157; Field of Felicities, 149; gates of, 146, 147; gates to, 143–45; guards of, 143–44, 158; Lake of Fire, 143; roads to, 142–43; Squatters, 147; sun's voyage through, 151–63, figures 18–23; western cliffs of, 164
Hermes. *See* Thoth
Hermopolis, 21
Herodotus, 61, 169
hierarchy: assemblies, 46; of beings, 33–34; and biological rank, 34; and etiquette, 34–35, 36; familial organization, 36; and judgment, 40–41; and lineage, 36; of places, 82; and power relations, 34; and rank, 45
hieroglyphs, 1, 100, 114. *See also* writing
Hornung, Erik, 3, 4
Horus, 27–29, 165, figures 3, 5, 9, 16, 23, 26, 27; aspects of, 196; battle with Seth, 22, 27–29, 42; the Behdetite, 178–82, figure 27; birth of, 77; blind aspect of, 154–55, figure 19; body of, 57, 58; communication with Osiris, 89–90; and the dead, 147; decapitation of Isis, 55; as doctor, 99, 106; of Edfu, 193; eye of (*udjat*-eye), 14, 72, 75; and falcon, 129, 130; Followers of Horus, 16; four Sons of, 172, figure 16; fragmented personality of, 77–78; funerary cult of, 123; and heavenly bodies, 118; and hereafter, 160, figure 21; of Hierakonopolis, 178–80; and king, 120, 129, 188, 191; and labor, 106; lifespan of, 78–79; litigation with Seth, 63, 83; mutilation of, 74–75; myth of, 23–24, 104; and names of gods, 99; and Osirian mysteries, 171,

Horus (*continued*)
174; and Osiris's tomb, 176–77; quarrels of, 27; regalia of, 59–60; reign of, 31–32; and sacred animal, 129; servants of, 47; and sexuality, 67, 68; as the Slaughterer, 174; and sleep, 97; statuette of, 170; and sun's voyage, 115; and temple building, 124–25; travel outside Egypt, 91; as warrior, 64. *See also* Elder Horus; Horus the child
Horus of Edfu, 132, 133, 179–80, 183, figure 27
Horus-Re, 132
Horus-Seth conflict, 22, 27, 41, 42, 57, 63, 73, 76, 78–79, 100, 105, 144. *See also* Horus; Seth
Horus the child, 77, figures 3, 9; animal form of, 61, 62; birth of, 184; conception of, 142, figure 8; and eating, 65; and foolishness, 97; and illness, 73–74; illnesses of, 82, 88; and kingship, 32; and papyrus thicket, 85–87; as Savior, 106
Hotep, 149
House of Life, 105, 173–74, 190, 191
Hu, 115, 171
*hu*, 103–4, 115
humankind, 107; bestial humans, 20–21, 33–34; destiny of, 16; and foreign gods, 52; as gods, 34; knowledge of, 94–95; and language, 102; and papyrus thicket, 86; rebellion of, 20–22, 32, 86, 87; and second battle of the gods, 25–26
hymns (worship), 111

Iamblichus, 103
ichneumon, 157–58, figure 21
Ikhernofret, 167–68
Imhotep, 58
incubation, 191
Inert Ones, 15
*iru*, 54–55, 62, 74, 79
Isis, 18, 77, 78, 95, 196, figures 7, 8, 9, 21; animal form of, 61; body of, 57; cult of, 2; disguises of, 76, 96; and eating, 65; as headless, 55; and hidden identity, 55–56; and Horus the child, 82, figure 9; and king, 120, 121, 129, 188; and labor, 106; medical knowledge of, 106; and murder of Osiris, 142; mutilation of, 76; and Osirian mysteries, 171–74; and Osiris's regeneration, 31; and Osiris's tomb, 176–78; personality of, 107; quarrels of, 27; and Re's journey,

157, figure 21; and Re's name, 98–99; and ritual for Osiris, 38; search for Osiris, 165–66; and sexuality, 69; as Shentayit, 169; statuette of, 170; temple of, 177–78, 184–86; travel outside Egypt, 83, 92; and trial of Seth, 41; and writing, 105
Isis-Sirius, 118

jubilee, 137, 188, 189, 195–98

*ka*, 71, 181
Karnak, 128, 129
Khay-tau, 49
Khemmis, 135
Khenty-imentiu, 165, 167, 169–70, 172. *See also* Osiris
*kheperu*, 54–55, 195
Khepri, 54, 59, 159, 179, 189, 195, figure 21. *See also* Atum; Re
Khnum, 7, 85, 106, 185, 197; and creation of gods, 54; of Esna, 69; and king, 121, 129
Khoiak, mysteries of, 169, 170–72, 176
Khonsu, 61, 92, 184
king, 32; as creator-god, 189; dead, 183; divine model for, 120–22, 184–86; and equilibrium, 120; as heir to Re, 122; and hereafter, 155; and Horus, 120, 191; inheritance of the bull, 190–91; as intercessor, 120–22, 193, 194, 198; and king-gods, 122–26; as member of Ennead, 189; and Osirian mysteries, 167–68; and physical resemblance, 56; renewal of, 187–93, 194; and ritual, 8–9, 122–24, 127–29, 190, 196, figures 13–15, 26; and royal succession, 28–29; and sacred animal, 136, 140; and temple, 122–26
knowledge: and the dead, 145, 150; as divine creation, 94; and eye of creator-god, 95; and foolishness, 96–97; of a god's name, 97–100; and *heka*, 96; human, 94–95; and imagination, 97; and intestines, 96; and learning, 95, 96; and literacy, 145–46; and memory, 101; and omniscience, 95–96, 190; *rekh*, 96
Kom Ombo legends, 69, 72
Kothar, 50

Lamentations of Isis and Nephthys, 176
Late Period, 129, 138
Lord of the Universe. *See* creator-god; Re

Maat, 14, figures 13, 16; and the dead, 143, 146; and eating, 65, 66; and equi-

Maat (*continued*)
librium, 15, 40, 123; and sun's night journey, 116; and writing, 100
Manetho, 29
Mehen, 116
Memphis, 136, 137
Meskhenet, 121, 186
Middle Kingdom, 5, 143, 166, 167, 169
Min, 67
Montu, 35, 64, 129
mummies, 16, 37, 70, 115, 142; canopic jars, 139; gods as, 180–81, figures 3, 7, 16, 18–22; and sacred animal, 138–39
Museum of Turin, 29
Mut, 178, 184
Myth of Horus, 23–24, 104, figures 3, 8, 9

names, 97–100, 103–4
naos, 126, 127, 195
Naref, 117
Nebyt, 129
necropolis, 138, 139, 166–67
Nedyt, 165, 168
Neith, 42, 105, 107, 190
Nehebkau, 71, 155, figure 20
Nekhen, 75
Nemty, 56, 75–76, 96, 99, 107
Nepay, 159, figure 22
Nephthys, 18, 50, 78, 79, 89, 142, 196, figures 7, 8, 21; and heavenly bodies, 118; and Horus the child, 73; and king, 121, 129; and labor, 106; and Osirian mysteries, 172–73; and Re's journey, 157; sexuality of, 67; statuette of, 170
netherworld. *See* hereafter
netjer, 37–38
New Kingdom, 5, 138, 144, 184
Nile, 17, 19, 26, 53, 70, 92, 129, 144, 179, 188, 190
Nilopolis, 137
norm. *See* equilibrium
Nubia, 91, 167
Nun, and creation, 30; dwelling place of, 92–93; as nonbeing, 15; and sacred animal, 132, 133. *See also* Primeval Ocean
Nut, 26, 50, 114, 195, figures 11, 22; animal form of, 61; and hereafter, 159, 163, figure 22; and Horus the child, 73; and king, 129; and nudity, 60, figure 11; and Osirian mysteries, 171, 172, 174; and procreation, 113; quarrels of, 27; sexuality of, 66, 78; as sky, 112–13; space occupied by, 113–14, 116; and stars, 117; and sun's journey, 116–17, 151

obelisk, 123
Odoacer, 19
offerings, 37, 125, 126–27, 183–84, figures 7, 11, 24; and the dead, 147
Old Kingdom, 165
Onnophris, 89, 146, 168, figure 15
*On Stilicho's Consulship* (Claudian), 19
Onuris, 26. *See also* Shu
Onuris-Shu, 128
Opening of the Mouth, 7, 125–26, 139, 174
oracles, 137–38
Orion, 118, 149, 162, figure 23
Osiris, 18, 27–28, 39, 77, 89, 196, figures 7, 16, 18–22, 24; acolytes of, 48; animal form of, 62; Apis-Osiris, 139; *ba*-soul of, 158; and bodily secretions, 70; bodyguards of, 47; body of, 58; as Bull of the West, 157; and clothing festival, 193–98; and creative acts, 104; crowning of, 72; cult of, 105, 167, 176–77; and the dead, 144, 146; and death as life, 31; death of, 80; and enemies of death, 43; Ennead of, 193; and flow of time, 45; greatness of, 35; as great Pillar, 193; and heavenly bodies, 118; history of, 164–65; and Horus-Seth conflict, 43; illnesses of, 144–45; isolation of, 88–89; ithyphallic form of, 156; and king, 120, 123, 129; kingdom of, 142–50; and labor, 106; lifespan of, 78; as mummy, 142, 155, 160, 166, figure 7; murder of, 40–41, 142, 165; as Orion, 162, figure 23; Osirian Mysteries, 167, 168–69, 171–74; Osiris Khenty-imentiu, 169–70; Osiris-Re, 191; as passive, 164; personality of, 107, 148, 164–65; and Re, 36; rebellion of, 31; rebirth of, 157, 159–63; reconstituted body of, 166, 168, figure 7; reconstitution of, 171, 175; reign of, 31; relics of, 171; and ritual, 37–38, figure 15; second coronation of, 88; servants of, 88; sexuality of, 67; and Sobek, 64; statuettes of, 168–76, 190; and sun's journey, 115, 153, figures 18–22; tomb of, 176–78; transformation of, 155–56; triad of, 2, 184; and trial of Seth, 40–41; twelve aspects of, 155; as vegetal, 169; and writing, 105. *See also* Elder Horus
Ouroboros, 19, 116

pharaoh. *See* king
Pharbaithos, 84
Philae, temple of, 177–78, 184–86

places: classification of, 82; papyrus thicket, 82, 85–87
Plato, 101
Pliny, 137
Plutarch, 1, 27, 31
Primeval Ocean, 14–17, 79, 101; and bodies of the gods, 60; and temple building, 124
Psamtik III, 139
Ptah, 41–43, 49, 106, 139; and king, 188; and sacred animal, 132, 136; and temple building, 125; temple of, 137
Ptah-Tatanen, 9
Ptolemy, 131–32
Ptolemy III, 185
Punt, 91
Pure Room, 194–96
Pyramid Texts, 5, 27, 165

Qadesh, 60
quarreling, 16, 18, 25, 105–6

Ram of Mendes, 41–43, 106
Ramses II, 92, 128
Ramses VI, 114, 115
Re, 54, 66, figures 2, 18–23; aging of, 79; and Apophis, 20, 21; *ba*-soul of, 154; and blindness, 72; body of, 59; and caverns, 152–63; city of, 115; and the damned, 155–56; and the dead, 149–52; distance from humanity, 113; divine birth of, 183; dwelling place of, 81; and equilibrium, 24; as healer, 30; heart of, 175; and heavenly bodies, 118; and hierarchy, 36; and Horus's mutilation, 74–75; illness of, 89; as judge, 40; as Khepri, 59; and king, 120–22, 189; manifestations of, 127–28; name of, 98–99; omniscience of, 95; and Osiris, 36; personality of, 107; as ram-headed god, 152, 155, figures 6, 18–22; Re-Atum, 55, 189; rebirth of, 155, 157, 159–63; Re-Harakhti, 54, figure 2; and sacred animal, 132, 136; and sexuality, 69; and sleep, 97; as solar bird, 22; solar character of, 111–12; and Thoth, 100–101; travel of, 83, 91; and writing, 105, 175. *See also* Atum; creator-god; Khepri; sun
Red Mountain, 21
*rekh*, 96, 101
Renenutet, 49
Reshep, 49
*rimay*, 70
rituals: and clothing of the gods, 128, figure 15; and coronation, 133–34; end-of-

year, 187–93; fertility rites, 183–84; and floral bouquet, 132–33; and king, 122–24, 190, figures 13–15; and meal, 135–36; New Year's festival, 187–93; offerings, 126–27; Opening of the Mouth, 7, 125–26, 139, 174; purification ceremony, 134, 188, figure 26; and rebirth, 133, 134, 140; religion, structure of, 9; Tent of Purification, 139; Union with the Disk, 196–97, figure 27
*romay*, 70
Royal Canon, 29

Sakhmet, 35, 47, 48, 54, 189; and the dead, 144; as eye of Re, 25–26; and king, 131–32; and Northern Egypt, 131; and sexuality, 69
Sakhmet-Uraeus, 132
Saqqara, 136, 138
Sekhat-Hor, 186
Seperteres, 98
Serapeum, 138, 139
serpents, 159, 183, figures 3, 18–23; of chaos, 17, 20; and creation, 15–16, 71; in hereafter, 152; Nehebkau, 71, 155; Nik, 161; as uncreated creator-god, 18–19
servants, 46–48
Seshat, 85, 119, 124, 132
Sesostris III, 167
Seth, 18, 27–29, 77, 78, 85, figure 3; animal form of, 61, 72; banishment of, 29, 43; defeat of, 181; and donkey, 136, 149; and eating, 64; and equilibrium, 38; as evil, 28–29; and foolishness, 97; and foreign gods, 51–52; and heavenly bodies, 118; homosexual tendencies of, 50, 68–69; and king, 188; and labor, 106–7; and language, 104; lifespan of, 78–79; murder of Osiris, 27, 165, 166; mutilation of, 74; as Nephthys's spouse, 89; and Osiris's body, 45, 95; personality of, 107; and physical transformation, 54; reign of, 31; servants of, 47; sexuality of, 67; travel outside Egypt, 91; trial of, 40–41; as troublemaker, 23; as warrior, 50
Seti I, 128
Shed, 83
Shentayit, 169, 170. *See also* Isis
Shu, 14, 26, 71, 76, 112–13, 162, figure 11; and cities, 84; and the dead, 144; and eating, 65; and king, 129; and Osirian mysteries, 173, 174; reign of, 30; and sacred animal, 135; sexuality of, 69; travel outside Egypt, 91

Sia, 114–15, 124, 171
*sia*, 95–96, 101, 103, 105
Sirius, 139
Sobek, 42, 64, 74, 129
Sobek-Re, 129
Sokar, 168–76
solar bark, 82, 95, 162, 189, figures 2, 11, 23; crew of, 48; and dead, 141
solar disk, 112, 152, 154, 155–56, 159, 195, figures 2, 3, 6, 9, 10, 11, 18–23, 24, 27; in the hereafter, 161, figures 18–23
solar eye (*udjat*-eye), 47, 48, 58–59, 76, 179, figures 1, 2, 3
space, organization of, 82, 83–84
speech, 96, 103–4; of animals, 102–3; and creation, 14, 15; wordplay, 104. *See also* writing
Spirits of the North, 116
statuettes, 168–76; casting process, 169–70, figures 4, 5, 9
stele, 45, 139, 167, figure 3
sun: animal form of, 61–62; aspects of, 54; daily combat of, 20, 21; diurnal voyage of, 113–16, figures 2, 11; as egg, 15, 22; night voyage of, 116–17, figures 18, 23; phases of, 74; rituals of, 193–98. *See also* Re

Ta-Bitjet, 99
Tanenet, 129
Tatenen, 159, 179, figure 21
Tayet, 160, 188, figure 21
Tefnut, 30, 112, 129, 144; and Osirian mysteries, 173, 174
temple, 37, 122–26, 166–67; birth, 184; building, 124–26; as dwelling places, 85; Ennead of, 132; and king, 124–26; main, 184
Thamos. *See* Atum
Theos, 140
Thoth, 26, 55, 107, 124, 185, figures 2, 3, 11, 26; birth of, 78; and children of Nut, 18; conflict with Babi, 44–45; and convocations, 40; and cure of Horus, 82, 86–88, 102; and the dead, 144, 147;

as god of moon, 68, figure 11; as god of wisdom, 38; and heaven, 118–19; and hereafter, 88, figure 16; home of, 21; and Horus-Seth conflict, 43; as intermediary and messenger, 39–40; and knowledge, 94, 100–102; and Osirian mysteries, 174; personality of, 107; place of in hierarchy, 35; reign of, 29; as Re's assistant, 23, 35, 38–39, 45, 106; and sacred animal, 129, 132, 134; and shape of world, 90; and speech, 103; statuettes of, 170; and stolen offerings, 102; and temple building, 124; and time, 102; and writing, 7, 105
time: cyclical, 26–27, 87; disturbance of, 102, 118; linear, 19; and Osiris, 45
triads, 36–37; Isis-Osiris-Horus, 2, 184
Two Lands, 101

uncreated, realm of, 22, 90, 92–93
Universal Master. *See* creator-god
uraeus, 30, 72, 128, 135, 147, 170, 179, 188, figures 3, 4, 9, 11, 16, 18, 21, 22, 26, 27
*uryts*, 48

votive shrines, 166

Wennefer (Onnophris), 89, figure 15
Wepwawet, 166, figure 25
West. *See* hereafter
writing, 96, 101–5, 174–75; day of exchange, 105; function of, 104–5; guides for the dead, 142–43; mythological texts, 5, 7–8; practice of, 105; sacred texts, 5–6, 94–95, 173; special status of, 8; and Thoth, 100–101. *See also* hieroglyphs; speech

Yamm, 49–50
year, 118; calendar, 67, 118–19; end-of-year rituals, 187–93; epact, 118; epagomenal days, 187, 193; months of, 183, 184, 195; and sacred animal, 131; and sun's journey, 114